REALITY AND THE MIND

Epistemology

REALITY AND THE MIND

EPISTEMOLOGY

CELESTINE N. BITTLE, O.M.Cap.

THE BRUCE PUBLISHING COMPANY

NEW YORK   MILWAUKEE   CHICAGO

PREFACE

The validity, or truth-value, of human knowledge is the crucial problem in modern philosophy. It has agitated the minds of philosophers for three centuries, and the effects of their discussions are felt in every department of science. Naturally so. Since it lies in the very nature of epistemology to question the capability of man's mind to contact reality and to know what things are in themselves, the validity of all knowledge, and consequently also of science, is at stake. The foundations of human knowledge are challenged, examined, and frequently attacked. An acquaintance with this problem and its possible solution will be, therefore, a matter of prime importance for every seeker of truth and for every student of philosophy.

The present book is intended for those who have no previous acquaintance with the subject. In accordance with this purpose, the author has endeavored to place the problem in its proper historical setting, showing its origin and development, without confusing the issue with a large amount of historical detail. For the same reason, the subject is treated in a constructive manner, seeking a positive solution of the epistemological problem rather than giving an extensive criticism and refutation of the individual opposing systems of thought. The language, so far as consistent with the matter under discussion, is plain and simple, avoiding what Hugh S. Elliot styles "sesquipedalian verbiage." Much of our modern philosophical jargon is so well-nigh incomprehensible as to make the underlying ideas opaque: unintelligibility is not necessarily depth. Obscurities, of course, remain, because the nature of knowledge itself is obscure; no amount of words will ever be able to clarify completely the mystery of the mind.

As for the plan of the book, the first part treats of the possibility of valid knowledge in general. The second part then takes the sources of knowledge (experience and intellection) and examines them in their individual manifestations — consciousness, sense-perception, ideas, judgments, reasoning. The investigation arrives at the conclusion that our sources of knowledge are essentially valid and trustworthy.

It is the hope of the author that this book, like his *Science of Correct Thinking,* will be of value as general reading, as supplementary to classwork, and as a textbook for students. The problem is vital and deserves concentrated study.

June 7, 1936.   C. B.

ACKNOWLEDGMENTS

We hereby express our gratitude to the following publishers for permission to quote from their works: the Macmillan Company; Longmans, Green and Company; the D. Van Nostrand Company, Inc.; Charles Scribner's Sons; the Abingdon Press; Henry Holt and Company; and the Yale University Press.

CONTENTS

PART II

THE VALIDITY OF HUMAN KNOWLEDGE

SECTION I

EXPERIENCE:

CONSCIOUSNESS, SENSE-PERCEPTION

SECTION II

INTELLECTION:

IDEAS, JUDGMENTS, REASONING

Efficient Causality - that which flows positively into a being.

PART I

THE POSSIBILITY OF VALID KNOWLEDGE

Chapter I

STATEMENT OF THE PROBLEM

Knowledge is at once the simplest and the profoundest of human experiences.

Nothing seems more plain to the ordinary man, and more beyond the possibility of any doubt, than the everyday facts of his knowledge. He is utterly convinced of the truth and certainty of the happenings in and around him. It never enters his mind to question the validity of his convictions concerning the knowledge of his experience. We may imagine him sitting in his lounging chair before a window and communing with his thoughts:

"It is certainly pleasant to sit here in comfort and watch the world go by. People are hurrying home from their business, chatting noisily with one another as they walk along the street. The sun appears flatter, larger, and redder every minute, as it slowly sinks in the west, and little by little the blue of the sky seems to turn into fire and gold. Soon the darkness will be here, and I shall see the distant stars. I did not think the wind was so very strong, but I see that it broke a branch from the tree in the square opposite. It is much colder than it was yesterday; I believe that will cause a frost tonight. The air is very raw outside. I ought not have gone without a topcoat this morning. I believe I have caught a cold; I felt miserable all afternoon, I had a headache, the old pipe didn't taste, and my mind was so foggy that I couldn't control my thoughts properly, and I made a number of errors. I am not myself now. I must see my physician tomorrow; he knows my body almost as well as I know my soul."

All this seems so simple and matter-of-fact, and the knowledge contained in these statements seems so obvious and transparent, that we should scarcely consider it worthy of second thought. Much less should we think that philosophers could discover any deep and mysterious problems hidden in the desultory musings of an old gentleman seeking comfort in his easy-chair. Such, however, is precisely the case.

FACTS AND KNOWLEDGE

Many things are directly mentioned as existing, and a spontaneous conviction is expressed regarding 'facts' and 'knowledge,' in the self-communing quoted above. He 'watches the world go by.' So he is sure that there is a real world of substance, an existing universe of tremendous magnitude, consisting of earth and sun and stars. He may have no conception of the exact dimensions of this universe, nor of the distance and volume and nature of the stars; but he is sure that they are really there and that he does not merely imagine them. He speaks of *space* and *space-relations:* for people are walking 'along the street,' there is a 'square opposite,' the sun is 'sinking in the west'; he notices a 'here' and 'there,' an 'outside' and 'inside.' He mentions *time* and *time-relations:* 'yesterday,' 'tonight,' 'tomorrow,' 'soon'; and the elements of succession in time are designated by the phrase 'every minute.' *Mathematical quantities* are affirmed: 'square,' 'larger,' 'flatter.' And also *numerical quantities* appear: 'people,' 'stars,' 'tree.' He notices the relation of part to whole in the 'branch' that is broken off the 'tree.' There are *qualities,* like 'blue,' 'strong,' 'cold'; *actions,* like 'walking,' 'sinking,' 'broke off'; *reactions,* like 'caught a cold,' the branch 'broken' by the wind; *posture,* like 'sitting in comfort'; *habitus,* like 'being clothed with a topcoat.'

Facts of *sense-experience* are enumerated: he 'sees' the things about him on the earth and in the sky; he 'hears' people chatting; he 'tastes' his pipe; he 'feels' sick; he is 'conscious' of his body. And so, too, facts of *intellectual experience* are noted: consciousness of the Ego or 'self,' 'thoughts,' 'knowledge,' 'soul'; states of mind, like 'belief,' 'errors'; states of will, like 'I must,' 'I ought not.'

He is aware of the great distinction between his self and things-other-than-his-self; between mind and matter; between living and inanimate things; between the subjective and objective; between the ideal and the real; between substantial and accidental being; between appearance and reality; between knowledge and opinion; between truth and error; between certainty and probability.

And many other things are contained in the data of his musings by *implication*. He is convinced that his senses, by and large, give him a true picture of the world about him and that he can trust them in their function of bringing the world into contact with his mind by means of the sense-organs of his body. He is also convinced that his intellect, through judgment and thought, can acquire a knowledge of the world and of himself which is true and valid and certain. He realizes that his mind can make 'errors' and that appearances may deceive (as when the sun 'appears' flatter, bigger, and redder, and when the sky 'seems' to turn into fire and gold); but he also realizes that his mind can detect errors and correct deceiving impressions, finally arriving at truth. Furthermore, he knows that truth is objective, that his mind does not fabricate truth but merely discovers it, and that his mind will possess *truth* only when it agrees in its judgments with the things *as they are in themselves.*

SPONTANEOUS CONVICTIONS

Facts of everyday experience, such as those mentioned above, could be multiplied indefinitely. The ordinary man has a *spontaneous and unshakable conviction* that they are genuinely true. No amount of argument could convince him that his knowledge is not valid. He may not be very clear in his own mind about the scientific and philosophic grounds and proofs for this conviction, but of the reality of the world and of the truth of the facts he entertains not the slightest doubt. His common sense tells him that he is right. Every moment of his life, from the cradle to the grave, confirms his convictions that the world outside and around him is as he experiences it to be and that his knowledge of it is a correct insight into its reality. The whole substance of these convictions can be summed up in this: *the world is objectively real and man has a genuine knowledge of it as it is.*

They are not forced convictions, accepted by the mind against its better judgment; rather, they are *spontaneous* for the very reason that they are the *natural* and *obvious* interpretations of the things and happenings in which man lives, and all together they form a system of knowledge which agrees with the demands of his rational nature. Man lives with and by and in these convictions, and these convictions are found by daily experience to be in accord with the facts as he knows them. Hence, he never questions their truth and validity; to him they are self-understood and self-demonstrative, and he feels perfectly safe in their possession.

This, of course, is strong *presumptive evidence* in their favor. If man's whole life can be regulated by them, in a practical as well as in a rational manner, then it is a *prima facie* proof that he is right in his assumptions. It would, then, seem superfluous for the scientist and philosopher to investigate the grounds and reasons of these spontaneous convictions. But such is not the nature of the human mind in its insatiable desire for deeper and more extensive knowledge. Man's mind simply cannot rest satisfied with the obvious and transparent explanation of facts. The urge for knowledge prompts him to investigate the *foundations,* the *ultimate grounds* and *reasons,* the 'how' and 'why,' of these spontaneous convictions.

THE PROBLEM OF KNOWLEDGE

It is this urge for knowledge which accounts for the rise and development of the *sciences.* Not satisfied with the superficial appearance of things, as the ordinary man sees and knows them, chemistry searches for the component elements of bodies, their activities and energies, their nature and qualities, their workings and the laws of their combinations. Gases (e.g., air), fluids (e.g., water), and solids (e.g., stones) are now understood to be, not bodies consisting of homogeneous material, but chemical compounds of very divergent elements united in definite quantities according to definite proportions under definite laws through the expenditure of definite amounts of energy. Not satisfied with the ordinary explanations of physical happenings in nature, physics attempts to discover their underlying causes and to chart their course of action from start to finish. Not satisfied with the common view that life in all its phases and functions is an inexplicable mystery, physiology and biology and kindred sciences have probed deeply into the hidden recesses of living organs and tissues and have wrested from them many secrets hitherto unsuspected. Many things concerning life have advanced into a clearer stage of scientific knowledge: among others, cell organization and function, the origin and growth of organisms, bacterial infection with corresponding medical treatment and international disease control, aseptic surgery, the proper distribution of nutritive values in foods. Similar progress has been made in the other sciences, due to the urge for deeper knowledge inherent in the human mind.

All of this shows that scientific investigation of such problems is not a futile occupation. In many instances age-old spontaneous convictions have been confirmed by science, and in other instances they have been disproved. Many supposedly certain truths have had to be discarded, to give place to more reliable information. Thus, to mention a case in point, the Ptolemaic geocentric system, in which the earth was considered to be at the center of the universe with the sun and moon and stars revolving around it, has been proved by science to be false and has had to make room for the Copernican heliocentric system, in which the earth was relegated to the secondary position of one among many planets revolving around the sun.

This one instance has an important bearing on the problem of spontaneous conviction and knowledge. From the standpoint of human experience, nothing appears more plain than that the sun revolves around the earth. Yet we now know that the moon does, and the sun does not; but to all appearances *both* sun and moon travel through the sky in the same way. Similarly, due to the atmospheric refraction of light, both sun and moon are seen in the east *before* they are above the horizon, and in the west they are seen *after* they are below the horizon. Both are seen as deep-red in color when they rise and set; and both balloon out to a number of times their normal size, with bulging sides and flattened upper and lower poles; they shrink as they ride to the zenith and grow larger as they descend. Actually, however, the sun and the moon do not increase and decrease in bulk, and at no time are they red in color. Again, the sun never actually grows warmer in the course of the day, nor is it any hotter in summer than in winter, nor does it change its position in the sky during the seasons of the year: its position in the firmament and its temperature are always the same. But the testimony of our senses seems perfectly clear regarding these changes, and mankind for thousands of years has had a firm, spontaneous conviction of the truth of this testimony. And even though science has furnished indubitable proof that our spontaneous conviction is wrong, our sense-experience still testifies to the same phenomena as before. Of course, there is an explanation for these phenomena; but the fact remains that *spontaneous convictions can be radically wrong,* even when based on apparently irreproachable evidence of the senses. This, as will be seen later, is borne out by many instances besides the case mentioned above.

From the above it will be clear that the philosopher has a right to question the validity of the spontaneous convictions of man and to investigate their claim to truth and certainty. Just as it is necessary to examine the foundations of the ordinary man's views on nature and physical phenomena, so philosophy needs to lay bare the ultimate grounds and reasons of man's knowledge and spontaneous convictions, in order to see whether they will survive the test of a *critical* examination in the light of reason. If they survive, then they will be so much the firmer, since they will rest upon a *scientific* foundation; if they are disproved, then they must be discarded as obsolete and irrational, the same as many naïve and unscientific ideas of a bygone age regarding physical phenomena and their causes. Man is a part of nature, and his knowledge is also a phenomenon of nature; as such it should be analyzed and examined in its origin, development, and truth-value, to see whether it really gives us a true interpretation of the world around us and can lead us to a well-reasoned certitude. For that is the purpose and function of philosophy: to investigate and demonstrate the ultimate grounds and reasons of things.

To the ordinary man nothing seems simpler than his knowledge; but to the philosopher the problem of knowledge is by no means so simple as it seems. The speculative mind of the philosopher discovers a multitude of knotty questions which puzzle him sorely and for which he would fain find a solution. He is not at all sure that the spontaneous convictions and beliefs of the ordinary man deserve the credence accorded them. Science has disillusioned man regarding many of his century-old notions and convictions; and science itself has gone through many battles of conflicting opinions and hypotheses, reversing its conclusions in more than one instance. It is, therefore, no idle question to ask: What can we know? How far can the mind of man reach? Is valid knowledge really attainable? Is truth objective? Can we be absolutely certain about anything?

The *inductive* sciences, such as physics, chemistry, astronomy, geology, biology, physiology, and anthropology, are all based on ideas, principles, and laws derived from the objects and operations of nature, and the knowledge acquired in and through these sciences is almost entirely the result of sense-experience and experiment. Even the *deductive* sciences, like arithmetic, algebra, geometry, trigonometry, and calculus, are based on the ideas of quantity derived from space and number in material nature. The sciences, therefore, depend upon the

validity of sense-perceptions and intellectual concepts to guarantee the foundations upon which they rest. Science, after all,
is a body of universally applicable truths, formulated by the
intellect as the result and expression of innumerable inductions
and deductions. The value of the sciences will, therefore, necessarily remain in doubt until philosophy has given a satisfactory
account of truth, certainty, and the ultimate validity of human
knowledge in general. Thus it is imperative to vindicate the
validity of knowledge both from the empirical and intellectual
side, because science is the combination of both these phases.

EPISTEMOLOGY, THE SCIENCE OF KNOWLEDGE

Epistemology (from the Greek, ἐπιστήμη, knowledge, and
λόγος, doctrine) is the *science of the validity, or truth-value, of
human knowledge.* It is a *'science';* that is, it is a definite body
of truths, derived from reasoned demonstrations of causes and
reduced to a system. It is the 'science of *human knowledge.*'
Here we have the general subject-matter of epistemology: it is
not the purpose of this department of philosophy to investigate
the nature of the human mind and its faculties, but that phase
of the mind's activity which we designate by the term 'knowledge.' It is the 'science of the *validity, or truth-value,* of human
knowledge.' This is the special or formal subject-matter of epistemology, distinguishing it from the other departments of philosophy and from every other science. The sciences are concerned with knowledge, because they increase our knowledge
of things; but they do not treat of knowledge from the standpoint of its 'validity' or 'truth-value.' It is the purpose of epistemology to submit our knowledge to a critical examination and
investigate the *rational grounds* on which it rests, so as to
discover *whether* and *why* we are justified in having the spontaneous conviction that our knowledge is *valid* and *true* in its
claim to be a faithful interpretation of reality.

The definition shows us in what way epistemology differs
from logic and psychology — two sciences closely related to
epistemology. *Logic* is the science of 'correct' thinking. It gives

us the laws and methods which we must follow, if we desire to avoid error and inconsistency in our mental acts; it is concerned chiefly with the proper arrangement of our ideas, judgments, and argumentations, so that a legitimate conclusion can be drawn from given truths. *Psychology* is the science of the soul in its nature and activities. This embraces everything pertaining to the soul of man, including knowledge. But so far as knowledge is concerned, psychology endeavors to lay bare its origin and nature, rather than its validity or truth-value. *Epistemology,* as a special science, leaves aside the formal correctness, the origin and nature of the act of knowledge, and seeks to establish its 'validity' and 'truth,' in so far as it is supposed to be a knowledge *of things*. For that is a peculiarity of human knowledge: we are convinced that it actually makes us acquainted with reality and gives us a true conception of reality as it is in itself. This conviction, however, cannot simply be assumed; it must be established beyond reasonable doubt, otherwise philosophy and science will be without secure foundation. It is plain that, because of the close relationship existing between logic, psychology, and epistemology, epistemology must at times reach over into the fields of the other two sciences, because an understanding of the laws and nature of thinking is necessary to form a proper judgment about the truth-claim of knowledge. As such, then, epistemology differs from logic and psychology.

The term 'epistemology' is of comparatively recent origin. Formerly it often went under the names of 'applied logic,' 'material logic,' 'critical logic,' or 'noetics.' Now it is customary to separate this part of philosophy from logic and treat it as a special science. The reason for this procedure lies in the fact that the problem of knowledge has become the major philosophical problem of the past three centuries. This does not mean that the validity of human knowledge had received little attention in the preceding ages. It had been discussed since the very beginnings of philosophy in ancient Greece; but it has never held the predominant position in the minds of thinkers that it occupies today. Today it is *the* problem of philosophy. The importance of the problem will become apparent as we advance in our investigation.

Epistemology is sometimes called *criteriology*. But there is a distinction between the two. Criteriology, as the term implies, is the science of the *criteria of truth*. The criterion of truth is the norm or test or standard which enables us to distinguish truth from error. Any theory of knowledge, to be complete, must treat of the criterion of truth; but there are many other questions involved in the validity of knowledge. Criteriology, therefore, is only a *part* of epistemology and as such does not cover the entire field usually assigned to what is known as 'the problem of knowledge.' Epistemology, on the other hand, considers this wider and more fundamental problem in all its phases. Criteriology asks the question: What distinguishes truth from error? Epistemology asks the question: Is our knowledge of things objectively valid and true? Plainly, we can inquire into the existence and nature of the criterion of truth only after we have established the prior fact of the validity, or truth-value, of our knowledge in general.

This, then, is the problem which confronts us: To investigate human knowledge and seek to determine the *rational grounds* upon which the *validity* of our spontaneous convictions are based. If we can establish this validity, these convictions will be critically and philosophically justified; if we cannot, our common and scientific knowledge must be considered to be nothing better than conjectures which may give us more or less probability but never the security of philosophic certitude.

SUMMARY OF CHAPTER I

The act of knowledge seems a very simple thing; it is, how-ever, a rather mysterious and profound experience.

1. *Facts and Knowledge.* To the ordinary man his knowl-edge is without question *valid*. This refers as well to intellectual knowledge as to sense-knowledge.

2. *Spontaneous Convictions.* Man has the spontaneous conviction that the world is objectively real and that his knowledge of it is true. He possesses many convictions of this sort regarding physical, intellectual, and moral matters. The convictions are *natural,* and as such they have a strong presumptive value. The philosopher, however, feels the necessity of inquiring into the *ultimate rational grounds* of these spontaneous convictions.

3. *The Problem of Knowledge.* The natural urge for knowledge accounts for the progress of the sciences. Science has *disproved many spontaneous convictions* of the past, for instance, the conviction that the sun moves around the earth. The truths of science depend on the validity of sense-perception and of intellectual concepts. Hence, it is necessary to establish the *validity* of knowledge.

4. *Epistemology.* It is the *science of the validity, or truth-value, of human knowledge.* Epistemology is also called 'applied logic,' 'material logic,' 'critical logic,' or 'noetics.' *Criteriology* is a part of epistemology.

READINGS

P. Coffey, *Epistemology,* 1917, Vol. I, pp. 1–24; D. Card. Mercier, *A Manual of Modern Scholastic Philosophy,* 1916, Vol. I, pp. 343, 344; J. G. Vance, *Reality and Truth,* Ch. I; J. Barron, *Elements of Epistemology,* 1935, Ch. I; B. P. Bowne, *Personalism,* Ch. I; R. W. Sellars, *Critical Realism,* Ch. I.

Chapter II

IDEAS FUNDAMENTAL TO THE PROBLEM

Before we can undertake the investigation of the problem of knowledge as such, it will be necessary to examine and define the ideas underlying the problem. Altogether too much confusion arises from a loose use of terms, and this obscures the issue and hampers proper thinking. In giving these nominal definitions it should be borne in mind that in no way do we intend to prejudge the fundamental validity of these ideas. Their ultimate value will have to be determined by the outcome of our investigation as a whole. But we must begin somewhere, and the ideas and terms used must have some definite meaning to start with. We, therefore, accept these ideas and terms in their obvious and current meaning. It is in this meaning that the problem has originated, and it is precisely in this meaning that the problem has significance. Ideas such as 'knowledge,' 'truth,' 'error,' 'certitude,' 'doubt,' 'subject' and 'object' have a distinct connotation in the minds of the ordinary man, and it is their ultimate validity which is at stake. Hence, the signification of such ideas must be clear before we can intelligently proceed to the problem itself.

KNOWLEDGE

When we speak of the 'problem of knowledge,' it is not a question whether man possesses 'knowledge.' That is a fact which no one denies. So we must begin with the idea of 'knowledge.'

Knowledge is a primary fact of human life and experience. Everyone understands what it means 'to know,' 'to have knowledge.' But when we attempt to explain and analyze this idea, we immediately encounter difficulties. Just because it is a *primary fact of experience,* the idea of 'knowledge' eludes every effort at an exact definition. We can point out certain *characteristics* of 'knowledge' and adduce definite *instances* of 'knowledge,' but we cannot really define it. 'To know' is on a par with 'to see,' 'to taste,' 'to touch,' 'to imagine,' 'to will.' Man is simply conscious of these states of his being and gives them a name; and thus he arrives at the idea and the term. It is useless to try to explain to a man born blind what 'color' or even 'seeing' is; just as it is useless to explain to a man born deaf what 'sound' or 'hearing' is.

We can place a man in a certain position and say to him: 'Open your eyes and tell me what you see across the park.' 'I see the Court House.' 'You are sure of it?' 'Yes, I am sure of it.' 'Then you *know* that the Court House is there.' Or we can say to him: 'Listen; do you recognize the melody?' 'It is the Funeral March of Chopin.' 'Good; then you *know* the melody.' Again, we may notice that he looks ill and ask: 'What is the matter?' 'I have a headache.' 'Well, then you *know* what pain feels like.' And so on. It is the experience of this sort which constitutes 'knowing' and 'knowledge.'

Now, there are three elements which enter into knowledge: the knowing *subject,* the known *object,* and the *mental act of knowing* (cognition). The 'subject' is the one who knows; the 'object' is the thing that is known; and 'cognition' or 'knowing' is the mental act which makes this object known to the subject.

The *subject,* the knower, is man, as we notice it in the phrase: 'This man knows his business.' Taken individually, it is the Ego, the 'I myself,' who am the knowing subject, for we say: 'I know this house, this game, this boy.' All our activities are referred to the Ego as the subject. We become aware of this, if we reflect upon the following expressions: 'I walked a mile; I saw an accident occur; I feel a pain in my side; I taste garlic in my food; I smell a pleasant odor in the kitchen; I thought about the depression; I know about the plans of my friend;

Plato - an exaggerated realist

I was conscious of the act.' Knowledge, then, as a mental activity, belongs to the *Ego,* the *self,* as the 'subject' who knows. And it is in this sense that the idea of 'subject' must be taken in the epistemological problem of knowledge, because that is the spontaneous conviction involved in our way of thinking.

The *object* of knowledge is anything and everything that is, or becomes, or can be, known by man. According to man's spontaneous conviction the objects of his knowledge comprise his own self, various conscious states of his self, and also realities-other-than-self. That he knows his own self, is clear from expressions like these: 'I myself will go; I am myself and no other.' That he knows his own conscious mental states we have seen in the preceding paragraph. That he knows realities-other-than-self, is a plain fact which he manifests in numberless judgments of everyday life: 'The sun is shining; the wind is blowing; the meal is good; this building is tall; some roses are red.' In all such judgments the ordinary man refers his knowledge to some object, and he is sure that the object is as real as the subject. Whether his common-sense view that such 'realities-other-than-self' belong to an exterior world with an independent existence of their own outside man's mind, is precisely one of the problems to be solved. But that every act of knowledge must be a 'knowledge of *something*' and therefore refer to some 'object,' is perfectly clear and is disputed by nobody.

The 'object' becomes known to the 'subject' by the *act of knowing*. This act, of course, takes place in the subject or knower. It is a *unitive* act, in as much as it brings the object and the subject into contact with each other, thereby rendering the object 'present to' the subject and making the subject 'aware' of this presence of the object. Before being known, the object is merely an 'object-in-itself'; but through and in the act of knowing it now becomes an 'object-to-the-mind.' And it is by becoming an *object-to-the-mind* that a thing becomes 'known.' Somehow or other, then, an external physical object (if there be such) must become united to the mind of the subject by means of the cognitional act and be *presented* to the

Ego as an 'object-to-the-mind,' in order that it can become 'known' by the subject; in other words, the object must become *intra-mental* and *intra-subjective,* before it can be known. A simple example may make this clearer. I see a burning house and 'know' it to be burning. How do I get to know this fact? The house is perhaps a hundred yards from where I stand. Surely my mind does not leave my person, cross the intervening space, and physically contact the flaming building; nor does the burning house leave its foundation, travel over to me, enter my mind, and then actually burn inside my person. Nevertheless, the burning house and my mind must become united in some way, or *I* could not *know* that the *house* is burning. Since the house has no physical presence inside my mind, it must have a *cognitional presence* there by means of sense-perception and thought. An object, then, in order to become 'known' by the subject, must acquire an intra-mental and intra-subjective presence or existence, must become an 'object-to-the-mind,' must have a 'mental objectivity,' must become an 'ideal being.' The very act of knowledge demands this sort of presence of the object in the subject; otherwise no union would take place between subject and object, and 'knowledge' would not be possible. The question, of course, arises: Has this object (for instance, the burning house mentioned above) a real, extra-mental existence of its own outside the self and the mind, independent of the cognitional existence which it has in the mind in the act of knowledge? The ordinary man is convinced that it has an objectively real existence outside the mind; idealists on the contrary, assert that we can know nothing but what takes place subjectively in our mind, and that we therefore have no right to affirm the existence of any thing-other-than-self. And so we again are face to face with the fundamental problem of knowledge. Whatever the solution, this much is clear and recognized by all: an 'object,' in order to be known, must be *cognitionally present* in the 'subject' in the 'act of knowing.'

The 'subject,' the 'object,' and the 'act of knowing' are thus the essential elements necessary for knowledge. Whatever pertains to, or proceeds from, the subject is *subjective;* and whatever pertains to, or proceeds from, the object is *objective.* The state or condition of 'being subjective' or 'being objective' is then styled 'subjectivity' or 'objectivity.' And anything that pertains to, or proceeds from, the act of knowing or cognition is termed *cognitional* or *intentional.* Knowledge will thus be either subjective or objective; viewed from the standpoint of the subject who knows, it is 'subjective'; and considered as referring to the object which is known, it is 'objective.' So much for knowledge as it exists in the knower.

TRUTH AND ERROR

Knowledge has the quality of *truth* and *error.* The absence of knowledge in a being capable of possessing it is termed *ignorance;* thus, a man who does not know whether zinc is an element or a compound is in ignorance as to the nature of zinc. The absence of knowledge in a being incapable of possessing it is termed *nescience;* an animal, like a dog, does not and cannot know whether zinc is an element or a compound, and he is in a state of nescience regarding this fact.

It is only in the act of knowledge that we have truth and error. Truth and error enter into our knowledge, when this knowledge is expressed in *judgments;* that is, when we affirm or deny something of something else. If what we affirm is really so as we affirm it to be, we have truth; but if it is not really so, we have error. And reversely, if what we deny is such that it is correctly denied, we have truth; otherwise we have error. For instance: I take a piece of metal in my hand, examine it, and state mentally, 'This is brass and not gold.' I both affirm and deny something here of the metal in my hand; I affirm it to be 'brass' and I deny it to be 'gold.' If this metal is really brass and not gold, then my double assertion (affirmation and denial) contains truth; but if it be really gold and not brass, then I am mistaken, and my double assertion contains error. As long as I merely look at the metal and form an idea of it, my knowledge is neither true nor false; but as soon as I apply an idea to the metal and mentally assert (affirm or deny) something about this metal in a judgment, then this judgment-knowledge automatically becomes true or false, depending upon whether or not my judgment and assertion corresponds to the reality-in-itself. Truth and error, therefore, are found in the judgment. This is mental or *logical truth,* and it consists in the *conformity of the mind to the thing. Logical error* is defined as a *disconformity of the mind to the thing.* When we speak of truth as the 'conformity' of the mind to the thing, we do not mean that the 'nature' of the mind must conform to the 'nature' of the thing; we mean that the mind must conform to the thing 'cognitionally' in its judgment.

There is, however, also *truth* in the *things.* We have, for example, a very definite notion of the metal called 'silver.' This notion or idea of 'silver' involves a number of subordinate ideas regarding the color, the specific gravity, the malleability, the hardness, the chemical constitution of silver; and this notion is a norm or standard to which a metal must conform in order to be designated 'silver.' If the metal agrees with this standard, it is true silver, otherwise it is false silver. The silver used in jewelry and that used in government coins is true 'silver'; but German silver, being an alloy of copper, zinc, and nickel, is false silver, because the real 'silver,' being a chemical element of its own, contains none of these metals. When a stenographer copies a letter, and the copy does not agree with the original, then the copy is false or erroneous; only if the copy agrees in every respect with the original is it considered a true copy. When, therefore, objects conform to a recognized mental norm or standard, they are said to possess 'truth of being' or 'ontological truth.' *Ontological truth* is thus defined as the *conformity of a thing to the mind.* Reversely, *ontological error* consists in the *disconformity of a thing to the mind.*

From the above explanation it will be clear how *truth in general* must be defined: it is the *conformity between mind and thing. Error in general* is the *disconformity between mind and thing.* Men universally distinguish between truth and error and consider them irreconcilable opposites. In epistemology we must deal with *logical* truth and error, because its problem is concerned with the validity of human knowledge. The fundamental question is this: Can the mind *transcend itself,* reach to reality outside itself, *conform to reality,* and thereby acquire *truth?* There can, of course, be no question whether men *think* they can acquire a true knowledge of reality; all men have a natural, spontaneous, universal, and unshakable conviction that their mind knows many truths which give them a trustworthy insight into the nature and qualities of things. They are certain that their knowledge *does* conform to reality. The *fact* of this conviction concerning the possession of logical truth is acknowledged by all; whether and how far this conviction is *justified,* will have to be determined by the critical examination of all the data and facts in the case. At present we are merely interested in acquiring a clear conception of the ideas and terms involved. For that purpose it was necessary to specify the exact meaning of 'truth' and 'error' in so far as they may be found in human knowledge.

DOUBT, OPINION, CERTITUDE

Regarding many things man is certain that he possesses knowledge. He is equally certain that there are far more things of which he is totally ignorant. Again, he is conscious of the fact that he has made many errors in the past and that much of his present knowledge may be erroneous. He realizes also that he has no exhaustive and fully adequate knowledge of things, not even of himself. The consciousness of all this is reflected in his mental attitude toward the things he knows or thinks he knows. These attitudes are *doubt, opinion,* and *certitude.*

Doubt is that state of the mind in which a *suspended judgment* ensues, due to the mind's inability to decide whether the judgment is true or false. If the mind can discover no reasons, or practically no reasons, which enable it to come to a decision regarding the truth or error of its judgment, then the doubt is *negative*. If it has discovered reasons, but if they are of practically equal weight for and against the truth of the judgment, thereby making a decisive judgment impossible, then the doubt is *positive*. In both cases the result is the same: the fear of error cannot be overcome, and the judgment remains suspended. For example: Dark, heavy clouds are scurrying across the sky, and it looks as if it would rain. But the wind is high, and the clouds are traveling fast. Will it rain? The appearance of the weather indicates rain; but, the high winds may drive the clouds away. It might rain, but I fear it will not, and so I suspend my judgment: I doubt. Another case: Will the Army or the Navy win this year's football game? Both have brilliant players; the one team is noted for its power, the other for its deceptive plays. The situation is such that the mind can come to no real decision: it doubts. And so there are innumerable instances where man cannot overcome his doubts.

Opinion is a state of the mind in which it *decides* for the truth of a judgment, but with *fear of the possibility of error*. The best that the mind can attain with regard to the truth of its judgment is a certain amount of *probability*. The reasons are good on both sides of the question; but the mind realizes that reasons for making the decision are weighty enough to justify adherence to one side of the question rather than to the other. The fear of error, however, hinders the mind from giving an unqualified assent to the judgment; there is still lack of certitude. Here is a case in point: Will the communists continue to rule for any great length of time in Russia? The fact that they have ruled so many years is a good reason to assume that they will. But the fact that their rule is imposed by force and is fundamentally contrary to human nature, is apparently a better reason to suppose that it cannot last. If I decide for the latter side of the question, I have an 'opinion' that the communists will not continue to remain in power for any great length of time. Or, supposing all the evidence in a

criminal case has been presented in court, and it is circum-
stantial and conflicting. I may weigh this evidence and decide
that the defendant is guilty, although I realize that there is
good evidence against such a judgment: I have formed an
opinion on the case.

Both in doubts and opinions there is lack of certitude. In
doubts I can come to no decision, but in opinions I make a
decision. In neither instance, though, can I overcome the fear
of the possibility of error. The mind is in a condition of
hesitancy and uneasiness and remains in this attitude as long
as a *prudent* fear of error lingers on. As soon as this fear of
error is definitely overcome, hesitancy and uneasiness vanish,
and the mind is at rest in a state of certitude.

Certitude is the state of the mind in which it gives a *firm
assent* to a judgment *without fear of the possibility of error,
due to recognized valid reasons.* Three elements, therefore,
enter into the concept of certitude: the firm assent to the judgment, the absence of fear of possible error, and the understanding of the valid reasons which exclude this fear. The absence
of the fear of possible error is the *negative* factor which distinguishes certitude from doubt and opinion, while the consciously
apprehended valid reasons for the firm assent of the mind are
the *positive* factor of conviction or certitude. This, of course,
does not mean that the mind is really infallible in these convictions and that error is impossible in all these judgments. What
it does mean, though, is that the mind is subjectively certain of
its grounds and does not fear the possibility of error; it is
convinced that it is in possession of knowledge which is true
and valid. The educated man and the savage alike are convinced that the sun is an existing reality in the sky. The savage,
furthermore, is convinced that the sun actually travels through
the sky from east to west in the course of the day, while the
educated man is certain that it does not; one of these two
(subjective) certitudes must be wrong, because they are contradictory and mutually exclusive and cannot be true at the same
time. While, then, subjective certitude does not exclude the

possibility of error, it does always exclude the *fear* of error in the mind of him who possesses certitude.

Concerning the *motive of certitude,* which influences the mind in giving a firm assent to a judgment, there exists a difference in value; and this difference in value produces increasing *degrees of certitude.* We are conscious of the fact that we are not equally certain of all truths, even though all these truths are certain to our mind. There is a considerable range of 'more and less' in our certitude. Thus, I am sure beyond doubt that a country like China exists, even though I have never been there; but I am more sure of the existence of the United States than I am of China, for the simple reason that I live in the United States. So, too, I am convinced of the spirituality of my soul, because I can prove it to my mind beyond reasonable doubt; but I am more certain of the reality of my body, because I have an immediate awareness of my body's presence. And so with many other truths.

There is *moral* certitude, *physical* certitude, and *metaphysical* certitude. *Moral* certitude is based upon a moral (not to be confounded with 'ethical') law, upon the customary natural conduct of human beings in a given environment and under given conditions. It has been observed that men under such circumstances act and react uniformly in the same way. We are, for instance, certain that 'Parents love their children.' While we realize that some parents do not conform to this law of human conduct, and that consequently we might be mistaken in individual cases, we feel certain that the law, generally speaking, expresses a truth. 'A nation, whose citizenry lives in reasonable comfort, is not prone to revolution,' is a similar truth which is morally certain. 'Youth is gay and craves excitement,' is another.

Physical certitude is based upon a physical law of nature, and the latter is considered to be uniform, necessary, and universal. Exceptions to such a law are impossible in the natural order of things. Only nature's Creator and Lawgiver could

suspend the effects of a physical law. Such laws are, for
example: 'Gases expand in heat'; 'water will freeze at sea level,
when the temperature drops to $+ 32°$ F.'; 'a body, whose
specific gravity is less than that of water, will float in water';
'two parts of hydrogen, when united to one part of oxygen,
form water'; 'a magnet will attract iron.' In such and similar
cases we are physically certain that our judgments are true.
We have no fear that the opposite will happen, except through
a miracle. Physical certitude is far greater than moral certitude.
Necessity rules in the physical laws; while in matters of customary conduct the human will can bring about individual
exceptions.

Metaphysical certitude is based upon a metaphysical law, an
exception to which is intrinsically impossible, because it would
involve a contradiction in itself. We are utterly convinced that
no power, not even the Omnipotent Himself, can change truths
like the following: '$2 + 2 = 4$'; '$7 + 5 = 20 - 8$'; 'the part
is smaller than the whole'; 'everything must have a sufficient
reason for its existence and being'; 'every change demands an
adequate cause'; 'a circle is no square.' There is an absolute
necessity to these things which nothing can ever alter, and
our certitude is in proportion to this recognized necessity: it is
an irresistible certitude.

A mere glance at the truths contained in the judgments
expressing these three classes of truths will show us that there
are *increasing degrees* in our certitude regarding them. We
have moral certitude concerning many things, but it does not
give us the firmness of assent which we possess with respect
to truths of the physical order; and the firmness of our assent
in metaphysical certitude is far superior to that given to truths
of the moral and physical order. All three classes of truths
produce certitude in our mind; but the *motive* of certitude is
greater in the one than in the other, causing a correspondingly
firmer assent.

Once again, however, it must be remembered that our sole
purpose here is to explain and delimit the idea of *certitude*

as it is found to be present in our consciousness, without intending to presuppose the reasonableness and justifiability of this idea. The fact is that we do possess these different types of certitude and that men in general are convinced of their validity. How far they are justified in this assumption is a question still to be answered in the course of our investigation. We may not prejudge the issue. Clarity in our ideas, however, is an essential requisite for rational discussion. We can hope to arrive at a correct solution of this difficult and important problem only when the fundamental ideas of 'knowledge,' 'truth,' 'error,' 'doubt,' 'opinion,' and 'certitude' are clearly understood in their relation to each other and to the problem at large.

These ideas are basic; they lie at the very root of knowledge; and their proper understanding should assist materially in preparing us to meet the problem of knowledge in an intelligent manner.

SUMMARY OF CHAPTER II

It is necessary to examine and define the ideas underlying the problem of knowledge.

1. *Knowledge,* being a primary fact of experience, like 'seeing,' 'hearing,' etc., is incapable of an exact definition. 'Knowing' is simply a matter of experience and consciousness. Three elements enter into knowledge: subject, object, and the act of knowing.

The *subject* is the one who knows — man, the Ego, the 'I myself.' The *object* is the thing known. Man knows his self, his conscious mental states, and realities-other-than-self. The *act of knowing* makes the object 'present to' the subject and makes the subject 'aware' of this presence of the object. In the act of knowing, an object becomes an 'object-to-the-mind,' an 'ideal being,' by means of its 'cognitional presence.'

2. Knowledge has the quality of *truth* and *error* in its *judgments*. *Logical* truth is the conformity of the mind to the thing; logical error is the disconformity of the mind to the thing. *Ontological* truth is the conformity of the thing to the

mind; ontological error is the disconformity of the thing to the mind. *Truth in general* is the conformity between mind and thing; *error in general* is the disconformity between mind and thing. Men universally distinguish between truth and error and consider them irreconcilable opposites. The fundamental problem is: Can the mind *transcend itself, conform* to outside reality, and thereby acquire *truth?*

3. The attitude of the mind toward knowledge is threefold: doubt, opinion, and certitude.

Doubt is that state of the mind in which a *suspended judgment* ensues, due to the mind's inability to decide whether the judgment is true or false. It is either negative or positive.

Opinion is a state of the mind in which it *decides* for the truth of a judgment, but with fear of the possibility of error.

Certitude is a state of the mind in which it gives a *firm assent* to a judgment *without fear of the possibility of error.* The absence of this fear is the negative factor of certitude; the consciously apprehended reasons for the firm assent are the positive factor. There are *degrees* of certitude. If the *motive* of certitude is based on the law of customary human conduct, we have *moral* certitude; if it is based on a physical law, it is *physical* certitude; if it is based on a metaphysical law, it is *metaphysical* certitude: the firmness of the assent increases in this order.

It is the purpose of epistemology to investigate the validity of these ideas.

READINGS

P. Coffey, *op. cit.,* pp. 25–43; 71–90; D. Card. Mercier, *op. cit.,* pp. 346–350; John Rickaby, *The First Principles of Knowledge,* 1926, Part I, pp. 1–68.

Chapter III

SPECIFICATION OF THE PROBLEM

The first requisite for a rational solution of the problem of knowledge is a clear understanding of the ideas and terms which underlie the problem as a whole. The preceding chapter has made us acquainted with these basic ideas and terms. The next requisite will be an exposition of the general *facts* which are *given* and *granted by all,* which form the common ground upon which all stand, which constitute the undisputed basis of the problem, and which are the universal starting point of all inquiry.

Knowledge we have. No one seriously doubts that we possess what is termed 'knowledge,' considered as a subjective state of the mind. What worries the philosophers is the firm and spontaneous conviction entertained by the generality of men, educated and uneducated alike, that this knowledge is a faithful representation of *reality as it is in itself*. They are not so sure that the ordinary man's claim to 'truth' in this knowledge is justifiable beyond reasonable doubt. They feel that these spontaneous convictions must be critically investigated before their validity can be admitted. These convictions are obvious facts. We have them, and they cannot be argued out of existence. That they produce in us a *subjective certitude,* is also admitted as a fact; but what philosophers desire to establish is, whether this subjective certitude is grounded on *objective reality*. That is the vital question. It will be necessary, therefore, to make a general survey of these spontaneous convictions of mankind, considered solely as facts, in order to obtain a clearer conception of the problem.

CONVICTIONS BASED ON SENSE-PERCEPTION

All epistemologists admit that we have sense-perceptions, viewed as subjective states of our mental life. The knowledge obtained thereby is derived through various bodily senses; and man has the spontaneous conviction that this knowledge acquaints him with the reality of a material world.

There is the sense of *sight*. Nothing is clearer to the ordinary man than that what he sees is actually what and where he sees it to be. His own body, buildings, trees, fields and hills, the sun and the moon and the stars — he is convinced that he sees these things simply because they are parts of the outside world around him. They are present, whether he sees them or not; they have an existence of their own, independent of his perception of them, and they will retain their reality even when he is blind or dead. So, too, color and light are objective realities for him: the sun and the stars really shine, the rose is really red, and the grass is really green. The whole matter is simply too evident to be doubted. He feels so safe in accepting this knowledge conveyed to him by the sense of sight, that he would rather question the sanity of anyone doubting these things than entertain any misgivings concerning this knowledge itself.

Taste and *smell* confirm him in his conviction of the reality of things. Sugar is sweet, acid is sour, quinine is bitter, brine is salty. The ordinary man is certain that these objects possess these *flavors* as objective qualities. He is also convinced that objects emit real *odors*. Odor may be fruity, as in the peach, or spicy, as in cloves, or flowery, as in the rose, or foul, as in carrion, or scorchy, as in burned wood, or resinous, as in pine pitch. But whether agreeable or disagreeable, he always refers these flavors and odors to things which are real and independent of his own person.

Hearing, according to his conviction, perceives sounds which emanate from actual objects. The human voice in its speech, the rapturous melody of the nightingale, the roar of the lion, the crash of the thunder — they actually exist in nature as he hears them. Sound to him is real; and he simply cannot understand that, in the absence of hearing in men and animals, nature would be totally devoid of sound.

The sense of *touch* also reveals various qualities which he considers to be objectively real. What is commonly called 'the sense of touch' consists of a number of distinct senses. The *skin senses* convey the sensations of temperature, pain, and touch proper. The *kinesthetic* or muscle sense is located in the muscles, tendons, and joints, and makes us aware of the movements and position of our bodily limbs and also of resistance and pressure. The *organic* sense has its seat in the internal organs of the body and enables us to perceive hunger, thirst, nausea, and general bodily well-being. How far these senses are fundamentally distinct is a matter for the psychologist to decide. Whatever their nature, the ordinary man is certain that they reveal to him his own body and other bodies, together with definite qualities, which are real in the world of physical objects.[1]

Besides the senses just enumerated, the human organism possesses what may be roughly designated the *internal senses,* because they enable man to apprehend facts of a subjective character in a sensuous manner. We are not concerned here with their ultimate nature and difference, but with certain undeniable facts of internal experience in so far as they have a bearing on the problem of knowledge.

The *common* or *central sense* makes us aware of our sense-acts. It is the seat of sense-consciousness, notifying us of the presence of the perceptive acts mentioned above, of feelings, such as pleasure, grief, anger, desire, and of appetitive striving. The central sense enables us to distinguish in a concrete way between the various organs and perceptions and to locate them

---

[1]In the course of this book there will be occasion to speak of these senses again. For the sake of brevity and in deference to usage, the senses just mentioned will be grouped under the common term 'touch.'

central sense

in the bodily system. That this is not a form of 'intellectual' knowledge, can be seen from the actions of animals. They manifest no intellectual knowledge, but they are conscious of the different kinds of sense-perceptions and of the various parts of their body. The main point here is that man is convinced of the reality of his body and of outside objects as revealed by the co-ordinating action of the central sense.

The *imagination* uses the material supplied by the sense-perceptions to form images of its own fashioning. Dreams are the product of the imagination. But man also uses his imagination creatively, constructing a world of fancy which exists nowhere but in his mind. Man is conscious of the distinction between the figures of his fancy and the people of real life, between the pictured events of his dream and the actual occurrences of external happenings. During a dream he may be unable to recognize events as unreal, but upon awakening he becomes aware of their imaginary character. The essential difference between fancy and reality is perfectly clear to the ordinary man and forms one of his strongest spontaneous convictions.

Sense-memory recalls perceptions and events and recognizes them concretely as having been experienced before. It is able to 'locate' these experiences in their proper sequence of time and place. We not only remember the persons and objects we have seen before, but we also remember the time and place of seeing them. That these memory-images represent a reality distinct from these images, is another spontaneous conviction of man.

The connection of *instinct* with the problem of knowledge is slight. While instinct plays a prominent part in the life history of animals, its function in man is limited, due to the predominant part exercised by man's intellect in the ordering of his actions. It is the cognitive function which apprehends material objects as things either harmful or useful to the organism consequent upon their perception. The influence of instinct is noticed chiefly in actions which are necessary for the preservation of the individual and of the race. Whatever instinct may amount to in man, it is stimulated by external objects and events and always has a reference to external reality: such is man's natural conviction.

All senses convey knowledge of the *reality of the physical world* in some form or other. That, at least, is the view of the average person, and of this he is certain beyond doubt. How far this obvious, spontaneous conviction can be justified before the bar of critical reason, is precisely the duty of the epistemologist to examine and determine.

CONVICTIONS BASED ON INTELLECTION

We now come to *intellectual knowledge.* This is distinctly 'human' knowledge, because animals manifest no signs of it. Intellectual knowledge appears in three phases: *ideas, judgments,* and *inferences.* We are not concerned here with the nature of the intellect as such; we are interested in its knowledge as found in these three products of mental activity. Whatever we may think of their validity and truth, we cannot seriously doubt that we have ideas and judgments and inferences. They are facts, and they lie at the very core of the problem of knowledge.

An *idea* is the intellectual representation of a thing. My idea of a thing is very different from my sense-perception of that thing. For example: As I walk along, I see a man. He is white of skin, six feet two inches in height, with black eyes and black hair, slim but muscular, and a slight limp gives him a somewhat halting gait. He wears a cap, a brown suit, a gray topcoat, blue socks, and black oxfords. This is the picture of an individual human being as he meets the eye and is perceived by the sense of sight. But my 'idea' of this man is that he is a 'bodily, living, sentient, rational substance'; in other words, this man is a 'rational animal.' The sense perceives him in all his concrete individuality, with all the peculiar traits and characteristics which make him to be *this* man and differentiate him from every other human being. My 'idea,' however, apprehends him in those essential attributes which he has *in common* with all other human beings, leaving aside all the individualizing and differentiating marks peculiar to himself. Sense-perception, therefore, represents man in the *concrete;* the idea represents him in the *abstract*.

Passing on to the *judgments* of the intellect, we find that a judgment is an act of the mind affirming or denying one idea of another. Three factors are involved in the making of a judgment: two ideas which are known; the mutual comparison of these two ideas; the mental pronouncement of their agreement or disagreement. The intellect, for instance, consciously apprehends and compares the ideas 'tree' and 'plant'; it finds that they agree; then it pronounces this agreement in the judgment, 'The tree is a plant.' But on comparing the ideas 'tree' and 'animal,' the intellect perceives that they do not agree and then makes the pronouncement, 'The tree is not an animal.' If my assertion (affirmation or denial) in the judgment is correctly made, it is a true judgment; but if incorrectly made, it is false. Judgments, therefore, contain *truth or error*. It is just this characteristic of the judgment, that it contains truth or error, which makes the judgment such an important element in the problem of knowledge. Internal and external sense-perceptions present or represent things concretely, and ideas represent the essence of things abstractly; but judgments claim to express the truth about *reality as it actually is in itself*. When I say, 'This man is an Indian,' I mean to assert that he *really is* an Indian; I certainly do not intend to convey the impression that I am merely combining the two ideas 'this man' and 'Indian' in my mind. In fact, the ordinary man never adverts to the fact that his judgment consists of a 'subject' and a 'predicate' and a 'copula'; for him his judgments simply express reality as he sees and knows it to be, and he is certain that his judgments do actually represent reality.

The same is true of *inferences*. The mind does not always

perceive the agreement or disagreement between two ideas by a direct comparison of the two, so that it can make an immediate judgment about them. That 'Two plus two are four' I know from a mere analysis of these ideas, and that 'The sun is shining' I know by opening my eyes and looking at the sky; but that 'The human soul is a spirit' is something I can neither see with my eyes nor perceive by a direct comparison of these two ideas. If, however, I can bring in a third known idea with which, upon comparison, I find the two ideas to agree, then I am justified in saying that these two ideas agree with each other. This is inference or reasoning; and it is defined as the mental process by which, from certain truths already known, the mind passes to another truth distinct from these but necessarily following from them. That man reasons and makes inferences of this kind, is a fact of everyday experience. And man is convinced that these inferences, since they consist of judgments and lead to a final judgment, are a valid form of knowledge and contain truth regarding *reality as it is.* Whenever people argue among themselves about facts and events, about politics or religion or science or sports or anything else, it is always with the conviction that these arguments can lead them to truth and valid knowledge. The deductive reasonings of mathematics and the inductive processes of the experimental sciences are all based on this assumption.

Man possesses also *intellectual consciousness.* He is aware of the intellectual acts of apprehension (ideas), judgments and reasoning, and also of other states and acts of his being, as love, hatred, sorrow, happiness, volition. Furthermore, man is conscious of *self,* of his own *Ego,* in the acts of thinking, willing, and sense-perceiving, and he recognizes his own self as the *subject* of these acts, the agent who performs them and in whom they occur. He is also aware that these acts in their varying forms differ among themselves, while he, in whom they take place and in whom they inhere as their subject, is *one and indivisible.* These facts are expressed by him in phrases like the following: 'I think,' 'I will,' 'I see,' 'I was angry,' 'I walk,' 'I am aware of myself.' These judgments show that man realizes that he consists of a *body* as well as of a *mind* and that these are different entities belonging to the same Ego. They also show that his Ego persists as an *unchanging, permanent reality* amid all the changing acts and states which come and go within his person. Finally, man perceives that, while his body is a part of his Ego, there are *other bodies* which do not belong to his Ego; there is, therefore, a *world* or universe distinct from his Ego, with an existence and reality of its own.

Such are the undeniable spontaneous convictions of man as manifested by his conscious states and expressed in his judgments.

CLASSES OF TRUTHS

Truth, as we know, lies in the judgment. Not all truths, of course, are of equal value to man. That my shoe squeaks, is a truth of no importance, unless, perhaps, I were a burglar or a detective; so, too, the fact that there is a solitary cloud in the sky this morning, is not a truth which will startle mankind. Such truths are commonplace and mean little. But scientific truths have far greater value. That water, for instance, consists of one part oxygen and two parts hydrogen, is a truth the discovery of which meant a distinct advancement in human knowledge and progress, because it enabled man to acquire great quantities of these two useful elements. Philosophic truths possess even greater importance than scientific truths, because the validity of science depends upon them. Thus, the Principles of Contradiction and of Sufficient Reason underlie all being and knowledge and constitute the very foundation of the sciences. It will, therefore, not be amiss to classify the different kinds of truths as found in the judgments of the intellect, since the value of man's spontaneous convictions is closely connected with his insight into these truths. The valid-

ity of man's knowledge can be established only if the validity
of such truths is established, and so it is well to know these
classes of truth.

First of all, we possess *analytical* judgments, which contain
truths *directly evident to the intellect* through a comparison or
analysis of the ideas of the judgment, without the aid of any
immediate sense-perception or logical reasoning. For instance:
'The whole is greater than any of its parts'; 'a plane square
incloses four right angles'; 'it is impossible that a thing exist
and not exist at the same time'; 'something cannot be true and
false at the same time'; 'everything must have a sufficient
reason.' Such judgments, called 'first principles,' are immediately evident to the intellect by merely analyzing the ideas
contained in them, provided the intellect knows what these
ideas mean. They need no demonstration and no direct sense-
perception to verify them. If I know what a 'plane square' is
and what a 'right angle' is, a mere comparison of these two
ideas will make it clear to the intellect that 'A plane square
incloses four right angles,' one in each corner of the figure.
Again, if I know what 'whole' and 'part' mean, it is evident
to me that 'The whole is greater than any of its parts.' And so
with similar axioms. Such principles are at the bottom of all
knowledge, and they are, as all admit, indubitably present in
our spontaneous convictions. Axioms, like the Principle of
Identity, the Principle of Contradiction, and the Principle of
Sufficient Reason, are used, consciously or unconsciously, in
every act of reasoning and are considered to be universally,
necessarily, and absolutely true.

Secondly, we have *immediate* judgments containing truths
which are derived from *direct experience* through internal and
external *sense-perceptions.* Here are examples: 'That lady
walking along the street has a package under her arm.' 'That
boy is running.' 'I have a pain in my tooth.' 'I am thinking
and writing.' Such judgments refer to individual concrete facts,
events, persons, and objects. We do not arrive at the truth of

these judgments through a mere analysis of the ideas contained in them. Take the judgment, 'That boy is running.'
On comparing the ideas 'boy' and 'running' alone by themselves, independent of experience, I cannot know whether I
should unite them into a judgment, because there is no necessary connection between the ideas 'boy' and 'running'; the
boy might just as well be 'standing' or 'sitting' or 'walking.'
That I actually judge, 'That boy is running,' is due to my
actual experience of seeing him run. Such judgments, then,
are not analytical but *synthetic;* they contain *empirical* truths,
based on direct experience. As such, therefore, they are not
considered to be universal, necessary, and absolute truths; they
are contingent and experiential truths which may change with
changing circumstances. A comparison between this and the
foregoing group of judgments will reveal at a glance that the
synthetic judgments have by no means the general truth-value
of the analytical judgments, so far as knowledge is concerned.

The third class of truths are those contained in *mediate*
judgments *deduced by inference* (reasoning) from *'first principles.'* These mediate judgments are based on self-evident
'first principles' or 'axioms,' but they themselves are not self-
evident; it takes a process of reasoning to show that they
follow necessarily from these axioms. Mathematical deductions are examples of this class of judgments. That 38,400 is
divisible by 2,560 fifteen times is not in itself directly clear;
but if we perform the division, or multiply 2,560 by 15, we can
prove the truth of the judgment. Similarly, that the square
of the hypotenuse of a right-angled triangle is equal to the
sum of the squares constructed on the other two sides, is clear
enough when the proof is furnished by a process of reasoning;
but it is not a self-evident truth like the statement that a plane
square incloses four right angles. A mere explanation or comparison of ideas will not suffice in these cases to perceive the
truth of such judgments by means of immediate intuition;
mediate inference is required to establish the logically neces-

sary connection between such truths and the axioms upon which they are based. However, once this connection is demonstrated, these *deductive* judgments are as true as their 'first principles,' unless it can be proved that man's reasoning powers are essentially invalid in their operations. Man's conviction is, of course, that he can reason in a valid manner. Provided, then, that man's reasoning powers are essentially valid, these mediate judgments derived from 'first principles' possess universal, necessary, absolute truth.

The fourth class of truths is contained in *mediate* judgments which are the result of an *inductive process* generalizing the individual, concrete data of direct sense-perception into *laws* of a universal character. The generalizations and laws of experimental science are of this type. After careful investigation and extensive experimentation the intellect perceives the *essential* elements in a series of repeated phenomena and occurrences and then expresses the true cause in a definite judgment or law. It is not necessary for science to investigate every single case of the past and present; that, in fact, would be impossible. Since it has arrived at a knowledge of the essential elements of the phenomenon in question, the law which the intellect has formulated has a universal and necessary value and applies with equal force to each and every phenomenon of that class. An instance will make this clear. It was noticed that the boiling point of water is always $+ 212°$ F. at sea level. Taking this as a starting point, scientists made a great number of experiments of boiling water at sea level, and the result was in each case the same: water boiled at $+ 212°$ F. Thus the law was formulated by means of a generalization: 'The boiling point of water is $+ 212°$ F. at sea level.' This being an essential characteristic of water, it was not necessary to take every drop of water on the globe to sea level and boil it; scientists know that it will boil, because such is the *nature* of water. Every such law is a mediate judgment which expresses a *necessary* and *universal* truth, based upon the Principle of Sufficient Reason and the Principle of Causality.

The above brief account furnishes us with a survey of the *sources* and main *facts* of knowledge as revealed in the *spontaneous convictions* of men. Sense-perception, intellection, and self-consciousness, all contribute their share toward the sum total of man's knowledge. There is one trait characteristic of all these spontaneous convictions: *man's knowledge is a faithful and genuine representation of reality as it is in itself.* And this reality is twofold: Ego and non-Ego; the ideal world of thought and the material world of physical objects; man himself and a universe distinct from man. And *man's mind can transcend itself,* reach out and contact this outside world, assimilate it cognitionally, and thereby acquire a *valid knowledge* of things. This is the sum and substance of the facts as given in man's convictions.

THE EPISTEMOLOGICAL PROBLEM

No one questions the fact that the ordinary man, whether educated or uneducated, has these spontaneous convictions. Philosophers all admit that man has these experiences, considered as 'subjective states' of his being, and that he is 'subjectively convinced' that these experiences reveal to him an objectively existing world-other-than-his-self. There is a vast difference, though, philosophers contend, between these experiences as such and the *interpretations* man makes of them. The facts they admit; but whether the physical world as *real* (if there is a real world) actually corresponds to the world *as perceived,* that is a different question entirely. Of course, the ordinary man judges and is convinced that the two correspond; however, the truth of this judgment and conviction, philosophers assert, *cannot be assumed* to be valid, but must be vindicated on solid rational grounds, before it can be admitted as a philosophic certainty. After all, these experiences, and the spontaneous convictions based on them, are only the data, the facts, the raw materials, of the problem of knowledge; it is the duty of the epistemologist to investigate whether the ordinary man's interpretation of these facts is the one and only legitimate explanation possible.

And the philosophers are right. The matter is not as obvious as the ordinary man thinks it is. For one thing, many of man's spontaneous convictions have been *proved to be wrong*. The first chapter pointed out a few instances; and there are many others which are clearly wrong or at least of very doubtful validity. That being the case, it is but natural to ask: Are these spontaneous convictions really trustworthy? Might it not be found, on closer examination, that the whole structure of these convictions is without a solid foundation in reason? If some are false, might not the majority of them be false? Since many judgments, to which man gave the firm assent of certitude, were afterwards discovered to contain error and not truth, what test have we to enable us to distinguish between truth and error in our judgments and convictions? Apparently too much importance has been attached to spontaneous convictions.

Here is another consideration: Are these convictions justified when we consider the *nature of knowledge*? Knowledge, after all, is subjectively present in the knower. The cognitive acts are *subjective, intra-mental states* of the knowing subject or Ego. All perceptions, ideas, judgments, inferences, and self-consciousness take place *within* man as the result of his own cognitive activities. Is not all knowledge, then, purely subjective and intra-mental? And if so, how can we feel so certain that it represents an objective, extra-mental reality at all?

Even if we assume that there exists an objective, extra-mental world which somehow contacts our mind, it would still be a fact that the *mind* of man *actively co-operates in producing knowledge*. The different sense-organs and the intellect, each with its own proper mode of action, clearly show this. How much of our knowledge, then, is due to the influence of exterior reality and how much to our internal faculties? Might not this influence of our internal perceptive powers be so subjectively different from the influence of the exterior reality as to completely transform our knowledge? We would have knowledge of reality, of course, but it might not correspond to reality-as-it-is-in-itself. It might thereby become an *idealized* representation of reality, with more of the 'idea' in it and less of the 'reality.' How are we to know?

Many philosophers find a practically insurmountable difficulty in the very notion of the mind knowing the physical world. Ever since René Descartes (1596–1650) injected the idea into philosophy that the essence of the mind is 'thought' and the essence of matter is 'extension' and that there exists an irreconcilable antithesis between the two, the problem of how the mind can possibly contact matter and come to a knowledge of it has been acute. It is certainly not easy to understand how an *unextended mind* can conform itself to *extended matter,* or how the latter can make a cognitional impression on the former. And if both are such irreconcilable opposites, as Descartes claimed, then each should be a closed entity in itself, incapable of contact with the other. The logical tendency on the part of thinkers will then be to reduce all human knowledge either to a mere perception of the material world (*materialism*) or to a mere system of intellectual thought (*idealism*). And that is what has happened. Others, realizing the inadequate nature of both these extreme theories of knowledge and desiring to give the spontaneous convictions of man their due, have endeavored seriously to discover a *bridge* between mind and matter, so as to safeguard the fundamental validity of human knowledge acquired through sense-perception and intellection (*realism*). The problem is admittedly difficult and deserves deep study.

The *general problem* of knowledge, then, is this: *Have our spontaneous convictions a rational foundation, so that they are based on impressions derived from reality and actually give us knowledge of reality as it is in itself?* Such is the problem of knowledge which we must attempt to solve.

SUMMARY OF CHAPTER III

The facts which form the basis of the problem of knowledge are the *spontaneous convictions* of the ordinary man, in so far as they are considered by him to convey a genuine knowledge of *reality* as it is in itself.

1. *Convictions Based on Sense-Perception.* The senses are: sight, taste, smell, hearing, and touch; central sense, imagination, sense-memory, and instinct. All convey knowledge of the physical world in some form or other, and the ordinary man is convinced that things really are as perceived.

2. *Convictions Based on Intellection.* Intellectual knowledge appears in three phases: ideas, judgments, inferences. By means of them, man is certain, the mind possesses a true knowledge of reality.

3. *Classes of Truths.* These are: *analytical* judgments, containing truths directly evident to the intellect through an analysis of the ideas involved; *synthetic* judgments, containing truths derived from direct experience; *mediate analytical* judgments, deduced by inference from first principles; *inductive laws* and generalizations.

The common characteristic of all spontaneous convictions is: Man's knowledge is a genuine representation of reality as it is in itself.

4. *The Epistemological Problem.* Philosophers admit these convictions as *subjective facts,* but they contend that these convictions, as *interpretations* of reality, must be validated. The main reasons are:

Many such convictions have been proved to be wrong. The nature of knowledge is such that cognitive acts are subjective; may not all knowledge be purely subjective? The active co-operation of the mind in the process of knowledge may produce an 'idealized' representation of reality.

The *general problem* of knowledge, then, is as follows: Have our spontaneous convictions a rational foundation, so that they are based on impressions derived from reality and actually give us knowledge of reality as it is in itself?

READINGS

P. Coffey, *op. cit.*, pp. 43–71; D. Card. Mercier, *op. cit.*, pp. 350-353; J. G. Vance, *op. cit.*, pp. 1–20; J. Barron, *op. cit.*, pp. 14–18; B. P. Bowne, *Personalism*, Ch. II; W. E. Hocking, *Types of Philosophy*, Ch. I; C. A. Strong, *Why the Mind Has a Body*, Ch. VIII; R. W. Sellars, *Critical Realism*, Ch. II.

Chapter IV

SKEPTICISM AND DESCARTES' DOUBT

It is the purpose of epistemology to test the validity of man's spontaneous convictions and see whether they are justifiable before the bar of rational criticism. If they are vindicated after a thorough investigation of their ultimate grounds and causes, they become *reflex* and *philosophic certainties* and will rest upon a firm, scientific basis. If, however, a critical examination should show that these spontaneous convictions are blind assents of the mind or are the result of some compulsory internal mechanism of the human mind, their truth-value will either be disproved or will remain forever in doubt.

In approaching the problem, the *method* employed will be a matter of great importance. A wrong method may produce disastrous results, just as a march from a false starting point, persistently carried on, will take the traveler far away from his goal; not every route will lead to the desired destination. We must never overlook the fact that, while investigating the mind and its faculties, we are using this very mind and its faculties as the instruments of our investigation. On the face of it, this seems an unwarrantable procedure. Since the validity of the mind and its faculties is at stake, how can their use in this investigation be legitimate? The answer is: the truth of our whole domain of knowledge being under examination, the only legitimate procedure available is to analyze our knowledge *reflectively* and watch the operations of our mind in the formation of its spontaneous convictions, so as to see whether they are based upon truly rational grounds; there is no other way possible. The only alternative would be to approach the problem in the *attitude of complete doubt*. The *initial state of mind* would then be to doubt *absolutely everything,* including the capability of the mind and its faculties to attain to any and all true knowledge. This, of course, would mean to approach the problem of human knowledge with the method of *universal skepticism*. At first blush, this would seem to be the logical thing to do — doubt everything from the start and then work our way upward toward certitude and truth. But this method would be fatal in its very inception.

HISTORY OF SKEPTICISM

A number of ancients and moderns have defended speculative skepticism. Among the ancients we find *Protagoras* (fifth century B.C.), *Gorgias* the Sophist (contemporary of Protagoras), *Pyrrho* (360–270 B.C.), the real founder of speculative skepticism, *Arcesilaus* (316–241 B.C.), *Carneades* (219–129 B.C.), *Aenesidemus* (first century B.C.), *Agrippa* (contemporary of Aenesidemus), and *Sextus Empiricus* (about second century A.D.). Agrippa and Sextus Empiricus formulated the reasons for universal skepticism under five heads: the differences of opinions and theories among men; the necessity of an infinite regress for every demonstration; the subjective and relative character of all perception; the gratuitous assumption of all axioms and principles; the vicious circle, or begging of the question, involved in every syllogism.

Among Christian philosophers universal skepticism never made headway. But the Renaissance, with its blind adoration of everything Grecian, again brought skepticism to the fore. *Michael de Montaigne* (1533–1592) in his *Essais*[1] defended it. Others who followed Montaigne in this trend of thought were *Charron* (1541–1603), *Sanchez* (1562–1632), *Huet* (1632–1721), *Pascal* (1623–1662), *Bayle* (1647–1706), and *Jouffroy* (1796–1841). Some of these were not really skeptics in principle. They attempted to show the constitutional inability of the human mind in its natural powers to arrive at truth, in order to

---

[1]*Essays*, tr. by Charles Cotton, ed. by W. C. Hazlitt (London, 1923), 5 vols., Bk. II, Ch. XII, especially pp. 276, 277.

vindicate the necessity of faith in divine revelation. It was a case of faulty apologetics.

Modern skepticism has its most noteworthy representative in *David Hume* (1711-1776). According to Hume, knowledge consists of mere perceptions, and these are twofold in character: impressions, which are the more lively perceptions; and ideas, which are but faint images of impressions. Thought is thus reduced to sense-knowledge. All axioms and principles of science are the result of mere associations of impressions, made by the mind through force of habit; they are, therefore, purely subjective in nature and have no objective value. He considered the arguments of the skeptics to be unassailable. In an indirect way, Hume's skepticism has exerted a powerful influence on modern thought.

It is obvious that a universal skeptic, who really and seriously doubts or denies the validity of *all* knowledge, cannot be convinced by any argument which may be advanced against his position: he would be forced to doubt the fact that such an argument has been advanced. He is as isolated in his skepticism as a fly buzzing in a vacuum; if, indeed, a fly can buzz in a vacuum, when both the fly and the vacuum probably are nonexistent. When we argue against skepticism, it is not our purpose to convert the skeptic himself; we intend to show non-skeptics that universal skepticism is folly. In doing so, we achieve a double result: we show directly that universal doubt is an *improper approach* to the problem of knowledge, and we demonstrate indirectly that any system which logically leads to skepticism must be *intrinsically wrong*.

Our contention is that universal skepticism cannot be the proper initial state of mind with which to approach the problem of knowledge, because it is a practical impossibility and a philosophic absurdity.

FALLACY OF UNIVERSAL SKEPTICISM

Skepticism is a *practical impossibility*.
No sane human being can live without certitude of a practical

kind. Even the most confirmed skeptic, no matter how many reasons of a theoretical and speculative nature he may have for doubting the possibility of genuine certitude, cannot lead a human life without denying his skeptical theory all day long in his *conduct*. His life shows that he is certain of very many things: the physical world, with its seasons and changes of weather, with its periods of day and night, with its differences of time and space relations; his own body, in all its concrete reality, in its conditions of health and sickness, in its physical needs of food, drink, and sleep; the existence and knowability of other people and other minds, some of whom agree with him while others disagree, with whom he communicates by means of conversation and writing, and whom he tries to convince of the truth of universal doubt. The story is told of Pyrrho the Skeptic that, when chased one day by a rabid dog, he ran for safety without allowing his skepticism to exercise its doubt about the existence and viciousness of the brute. When the bystanders laughed at him and ridiculed him for the inconsistency of his action, he is said to have made the sage remark (completely out of keeping with his theory): "It is difficult to get away entirely from human nature." After all, he could not doubt, in an untheoretical moment, that his body and the dog were real objects.

This *discrepancy between fact and theory,* between life and philosophic system, between practical certitude and speculative doubt, is an incontrovertible proof that universal doubt is an impossibility except as a mere formulation of the mind. When facts and theories clash and contradict each other in such transparent fashion, the sane man will not deny the facts and cling to his theories, but will realize that something is radically wrong with his views. Facts cannot be denied. To persist in universal skepticism in the face of a million contradicting facts of life bespeaks either insanity or stubbornness of mind. When the inconsistency between life and theory cannot be harmonized, it will not do to deny life, because that would be ridiculous; the theory must be abandoned as essentially faulty. Universal skepticism, therefore, must be rejected as a practical impossibility.

Universal skepticism is also a *theoretical absurdity*.

One simply cannot doubt all things and principles, not even in a speculative way. The skeptics prove this by their own intellectual *inconsistencies*; and inconsistencies are the stigma of every false theory. Any normal person will realize the inherent contradiction of universal skepticism, if it is real and genuine, upon considering the following points.

Skeptics contend that real certitude in knowledge is impossible, so that we must always suspend our judgment because of a real doubt as to the truth of our judgment. This, in their view, is the only logical and rational thing to do. But then, they have at least arrived at *this truth* that we *cannot be certain;* and there is at least no doubt that we must doubt. Therefore, even skeptics possess certitude about something, and their fundamental tenet of universal doubt is involved in a contradiction.

Skeptics claim we must suspend our judgment regarding any question, because we might fall into *error*. But error is the opposite of truth. Consequently, they acknowledge that there is a difference between 'truth' and 'error,' and the two are not the same. Similarly, they must admit that 'certitude' and 'doubt' are not the same; otherwise, why should we doubt rather than be certain? Their very insistence on this difference shows plainly that they recognize the fact that something cannot be true and erroneous, certain and doubtful, at the same time. But thereby they surreptitiously admit the certainty of the truth of the Principle of Contradiction.

Skeptics either have valid reasons for their universal doubting, or they have no valid reasons for it. If they have valid reasons, they surely know something that is valid, and they no longer are real skeptics. If they have no valid reasons, they have

no reason to doubt. In the first case their position is inconsistent, and in the second case their position is irrational.
Whichever way they turn, their position is untenable.

Skeptics, in defending the necessity of universal doubt, must
naturally be *conscious* of their doubt and its necessity; for, if
they were not conscious of this, they could neither be aware
of their doubt nor speak of it. Consequently, they rely upon
the *testimony of their consciousness* as a source of valid knowledge. But that involves certitude regarding their own existence
and person and regarding the trustworthiness of consciousness.
They cannot, in consistency, cast a doubt upon the testimony
of consciousness, because the argument of St. Augustine, in
speaking to the skeptics, would apply to them: "If I err, I exist.
For one, who does not exist, cannot err; and by the very fact
that I err, I exist. Since, therefore, I exist, if I err, how can I err
about my existence, when it is certain that I exist if I err?"[2]
That the skeptic must admit and acknowledge the certain
existence of various states of his own consciousness, has been
pointed out by St. Augustine in another passage, marked by
a keen appreciation of the facts in the case: "If he doubts, he
lives; if he doubts, he remembers why he doubts; if he doubts,
he understands that he doubts; if he doubts, he wants to be
certain; if he doubts, he thinks; if he doubts, he knows that he
does not know; if he doubts, he judges that he must not give
a hasty consent."[3] Notwithstanding their claim to universal
doubt, therefore, the skeptics by their doubting actually, though
inconsistently, express certitude concerning a great number of
facts and principles. Universal skepticism collapses under the
weight of its own folly.

And thus we see that universal skepticism is a *philosophic
absurdity*.

---

[2]*De Civ. Dei, lib.* II, c. 26.
[3]*Loc. cit.*

REFUTATION OF SKEPTIC ARGUMENTS

But what about the arguments of the skeptics? Do they not show that valid knowledge is impossible of attainment for the human mind? A close examination will reveal the fact that *the arguments of the skeptics are fallacious.* Some of their contentions have been answered in the preceding paragraphs, and so we will restrict ourselves to those of a more formal and logical character, since they are more pertinent to the present problem.

Conflicting and *erroneous opinions, they contend,* have been held by men on every question that has ever engaged the attention of the human mind. This complete lack of uniformity in their views and the presence of errors in these views proves conclusively that the human mind is constitutionally incapable of knowing truth with certitude. The answer to this is simple. That many errors exist, due to careless thinking, hasty conclusions, faulty education, and lack of observation, is true enough. But this would militate against the possibility of certitude only if the mind were *congenitally* unable to detect and correct its errors of judgment. This is not the case; otherwise we could never change our views with the *consciousness that we have been in error.* The very fact that we recognize error as error (even the skeptics are constantly pointing out errors), is a sure indication that the human mind possesses a criterion or test whereby to distinguish truth from error. All that is required, then, is to be careful in our investigation and apply this test with greater accuracy. That we cannot eliminate all errors, is simply due to the limitations of our intellectual powers, but not to the essential inability of our mind to discover and recognize truth. Error is thus *accidental,* but not essential, to the human mind.

Sextus Empiricus formulated an argument somewhat along the following lines. Whoever thinks he has acquired a knowledge about something with certitude, can have acquired it only in one of three ways: either he proves his judgment by a proof which needs another proof, and this second needs a third proof, and this third needs another, and so on, without ever arriving at a final proof; or he stops at a certain proof, which he does not prove in turn, but simply assumes to be true without proof of any kind; or he proves his statement by some principle, and then later on proves this last principle by his original statement. In the first instance he is guilty of an *infinite regress,* which cannot prove anything, because one can never come down to the final proof; in the second instance he is guilty of a *gratuitous assumption* which leaves the final proof open to the question of truth or error, thereby settling nothing; and in the third instance he is guilty of a *vicious circle,* and a vicious circle proves nothing at all. This seems a rather formidable argument in favor of universal skepticism. Unfortunately, one other alternative was omitted and that a vital one. Some proofs do not need a subsequent proof to establish their truth and certainty. There are truths which are so self-evident to the mind, that their validity is perceived by an act of *immediate intuition* and demands no further demonstration. That 'I am writing at this moment' is a truth so obvious to me that I need not look for any deep philosophic or scientific proof to give this judgment validity: I simply experience the fact, and that is all there is to the matter; no argument of the skeptics can invalidate this fact for me, because it is self-evident. I am guilty neither of an infinite regress, nor of a gratuitous assumption, nor of a vicious circle, in making this true statement of fact. Incidentally, if the above argument of the skeptics were true, then their argument itself would be invalid for the very reasons which they adduce; and since it is a false argument (according to their own principles), it cannot prove anything in favor of skepticism. The fact, however, that skeptics consider it a true and valid argument, proves that they do consider some knowledge true and valid; and that is just one more example of their inconsistency.

The main argument of *Montaigne* was that an infinite regress would be necessary for every demonstration. He, too, overlooked the fact that first principles are *self-evident* and need no demonstration. That $2 + 2 = 4$, is clear by a simple analysis of the ideas involved.

DESCARTES' METHODIC DOUBT

René Descartes (1596–1650) is responsible for the predominance of the problem of human knowledge in modern philosophy. Many of the systems of philosophy and theories of knowledge which have arisen in the last three centuries can trace their lineage directly to the influence of the questions Descartes raised and the method he employed in answering them. He promulgated the principle of 'science without presuppositions' and thereby introduced a new epoch in science and philosophy. It will, therefore, not be amiss to analyze his fundamental ideas and evaluate his method.

As his starting point Descartes begins with the contention that we rely entirely too much on traditional doctrines and spontaneous convictions, so that our supposed knowledge of truth rests mostly on *unproved presuppositions.* This makes it difficult for us to distinguish between truth and error, since we do not know what is true knowledge and what is unwarranted belief. Hence, he would tear down the whole edifice of knowledge and rebuild it from the foundation, and he would not begin to build until he had reached the one and ultimate truth which was the bedrock of human knowledge. Being a mathematician, he felt convinced that he could deduce all truth from a single fundamental principle. As the instrument of his search for truth he used a *universal methodic doubt.* His own words will best reveal his line of thought.

"I. In order to seek truth, it is necessary once in the course of our life, to doubt, as far as possible, of all things.

"As we were at one time children, and as we formed various judgments regarding the objects presented to our senses, when as yet we had not the entire use of our reason, numerous prejudices stand in the way of our arriving at the knowledge of truth; and of these it seems impossible for us to rid ourselves, unless we undertake, once in our lifetime, to doubt of all those things in which we may discover even the smallest suspicion of uncertainty.

"II. We ought also to consider as false all that is doubtful.

"Moreover, it will be useful likewise to esteem as false the things of which we shall be able to doubt, that we may with greater clearness discover what possesses most certainty and is easiest to know.

"III. We ought not meanwhile to make use of doubt in the conduct of life. . . .

"IV. Why we may doubt of sensible things.

"Accordingly, since we now only design to apply ourselves to the investigation of truth, we will doubt, first, whether of all the things that have ever fallen under our senses, or which we have ever imagined, any one really exists; in the first place, because we know by experience that the senses sometimes err, and it would be imprudent to trust too much to what has even once deceived us; secondly, because in dreams we perpetually seem to perceive or imagine innumerable objects which have no existence. And to one who has thus resolved upon a general doubt, there appear no marks by which he can with certainty distinguish sleep from the waking state.

"V. Why we may also doubt of mathematical demonstrations.

"We will also doubt of the other things we have before held as most certain, even of the demonstrations of mathematics, and of their principles which we have hitherto deemed self-evident; in the first place, because we have sometimes seen men fall into error in such matters, and admit as absolutely certain and self-evident what to us appeared false, but chiefly because we have learned that God who created us is all-powerful; for we do not yet know whether perhaps it was His will to create us so that we are always deceived, even in the things we know best: since this does not appear more impossible than our being occasionally deceived, which, however, as observation teaches us, is the case. And if we suppose that an all-powerful God is not the author of our being, and that we exist of ourselves or by some other means, still, the less powerful we suppose our author to be, the greater reason will we have for believing that we are not so perfect as that we may not be continually deceived. . . .

"VII. We cannot doubt of our existence while we doubt, and this is the first knowledge we acquire when we philosophize in order.

"While we thus reject all of which we can entertain the smallest doubt, and even imagine that it is false, we easily indeed suppose that there is neither God, nor sky, nor bodies, and that we ourselves have neither hands nor feet, nor, finally, a body; but we cannot in the same way suppose that we are not while we doubt of the truth of these things; for there is a repugnance in conceiving that what thinks does not exist at the very moment when it thinks. Accordingly, the knowledge, *I think, therefore I am,'* is the first and most certain that occurs to one who philosophizes orderly."[4]

This is indeed a most radical procedure, a veritable revolution of method. Descartes applies the method of universal doubt to 'all things,' attempting to empty the mind completely of all traditional views, preconceived ideas, and spontaneous convictions without exception. Nothing is allowed to remain, no matter how seemingly clear and evident. Even the simplest arithmetical and geometrical problem is not permitted to stand, like '2 + 3 = 5' and 'A square has but four sides.' As he expresses himself: "How do I know that I am not also deceived each time I add together two and three, or number the sides of a square, or form some judgment still more simple, if more simple indeed can be imagined?"[5] Not only the whole physical

---

[4]*Principia Phil.*, Pars I. Translated by John Veich, LL.D., 13 ed. (Will. Blackwood and Sons, Edinburgh and London, 1902). Also *Méditations, passim;* also *Discours,* Part IV.

[5]*Méditations,* I.

world, our own body, sense-perception, and the internal states of our consciousness, are thus drawn into universal doubt,[6] but also the *trustworthiness of our cognitive faculties* and the fundamental *laws of thinking,* like the Principle of Sufficient Reason and the Principle of Contradiction. This is a most important feature of his method that must not be overlooked.

Descartes' universal methodic doubt is not merely simulated for the sake of an unprejudiced search after truth; it is a *real, genuine doubt.* "As I desired to give my attention solely to the search after truth, I thought . . . that I ought to reject as absolutely false all in regard to which I could suppose the least ground for doubt, in order to ascertain whether after that there remained aught in my belief that was wholly indubitable."[7] Mark the words: "to reject as *absolutely false.*" He does not intend to hold his mind in a state of suspended judgment, or merely to leave his spontaneous convictions aside for the time being, in order to investigate their possible validity, which would be *methodic doubt* as generally understood; he is convinced that he ought 'to reject them as absolutely false,' and he actually carries out his plan, so that he really rejects everything down to the one indubitable fact: *'Cogito, ergo sum —* I think, therefore I exist.'* This is more than mere doubt, because a doubt presupposes a suspended judgment due to the absence of all reasons for and against a proposition (negative doubt) or reasons of more or less equal value for and against it (positive doubt). Descartes "supposes, for a time, that all these opinions are entirely false and imaginary,"[8] and he "will continue always in this track until he shall find something that is certain, or at least, if he can do nothing more, until he shall know with certainty that there is nothing certain."[9] He assumes the attitude that all spontaneous convictions and laws of thought are *errors.*

---

[6] *Loc. cit.*
[7] *Discours,* IV. ". . . je pensai que . . . je rejetasse comme absolument faux tout ce en quoi je pourrois imaginer la moindre doute."
[8] *Méditations,* I, toward the close.
[9] *Loc. cit.,* II, beginning.

It makes little difference whether Descartes could and did, actually and really, doubt everything without exception; or whether he merely thought he could and did. The fact is, he did thus doubt everything *in principle*. He was, of course, not a skeptic, since his purpose was to arrive at the ultimate base of certainty and truth and to rebuild on this indubitable foundation the edifice of knowledge. He compared himself to Archimedes. "Archimedes, that he might transport the entire globe from the place it occupied to another, demanded only a point that was firm and immovable; so also, I shall be entitled to entertain the highest expectations, if I am fortunate enough to discover only one thing that is certain and indubitable."[10] Descartes was fortunate enough to discover his firm and immovable fulcrum: *his own existence* — 'I think, therefore I am.' He had now his fulcrum; what would be his lever?

It would have to be the *trustworthiness of his reasoning powers*. But how could he establish this, seeing that this also was involved in universal doubt and destroyed with all other spontaneous convictions? Descartes hit upon an ingenious idea. He would demonstrate the existence of an infinitely perfect Being, who must have given man faculties which are trustworthy and capable of discovering truth. The only thing absolutely certain so far for Descartes was his own existence; and from this fact alone he would be obliged to deduce God's existence.

Here is his line of thought. We have in our mind the idea of God as an infinitely perfect Being. But an infinitely perfect Being must have existence, otherwise it would not be infinitely perfect. Ergo, God exists.[11] This is an *a priori* or *ontological* argument. Descartes attempts to prove God's existence *a posteriori*, by means of an argument from *causality*. We have the idea of God in our mind. Since this idea represents an infinitely perfect Being, we, as finite beings, cannot have originated such

[10]*Loc. cit.* II, beginning.
[11]*Princ. Phil.*, Pars I, XVIII.

an idea in virtue of our own powers. This idea being beyond our mental capacity, it could have originated only from a Being who possesses such infinite perfection. Ergo, God exists.[12]

Having proved to his own satisfaction that God exists, Descartes proceeds to show that He is the creator of man.[13] But the infinitely perfect God cannot be a deceiver; consequently, He cannot have given man deceptive powers of knowledge, and man's faculties are thus shown to be *trustworthy,* "provided we separate what there is of clear and distinct in the knowledge from what is obscure and confused."[14] In the light of this criterion of 'clear and distinct' knowledge all previous doubts about the world, sense-perception, and intellection must vanish. Skepticism is defeated, and valid knowledge is possible.

FAILURE OF DESCARTES' METHOD

Descartes' fundamental purpose was laudable; he desired to defend human knowledge against the attacks of skeptics. Generally speaking, he was justified in demanding that the investigation into the nature and limits of knowledge exclude preconceived ideas, traditional doctrines, and unwarranted presuppositions as evidence and proof, since the validity of all spontaneous convictions was at stake. But when he proposed to approach the problem in an attitude of *universal real doubt,* discarding even the capability of the human mind to know truth and refusing to accept such essential principles as the Principle of Contradiction and the Principle of Sufficient Reason, he made the solution of the problem impossible for himself. Here are a few considerations which compel us to reject his system.

Descartes began his inquiry by doubting *all* knowledge without exception; he was even willing to accept it as 'entirely *false.*' This being the case, what about the *idea of God* as an all-perfect Being, since he admits that he discovered this idea

---

[12]*Princ. Phil.,* Pars I, XVIII.

[13]*Ibid.,* Pars I, XX.

[14]*Ibid.,* Pars I, XXIX, and XXX.

in his own mind? According to his own principle of universal doubt, he simply *cannot know* whether this idea of God is correct or incorrect; as a matter of fact, according to this principle, he should consider it as 'entirely false,' until proved otherwise. But if his idea of God as an all-perfect Being may be incorrect, he cannot logically deduce from this idea God's existence and veracity. Since the very idea of God is doubtful, these other things must remain doubtful, and the trustworthiness of man's faculties must also remain doubtful. Descartes cannot escape his own real doubt.

Irrespective of the intrinsic value of the proofs with which Descartes attempts to demonstrate God's existence, we must not overlook the fact that he uses a *process of reasoning* to make this demonstration. Since his very reason and the process of reasoning is as yet of doubtful validity, how can he validly demonstrate God's existence and veracity? The trustworthiness of Descartes' reasoning powers is supposed to flow as a necessary *consequence* from the infinite perfection of God; and God's infinite perfection is made certain to him by means of a proof developed by these very reasoning powers, *before* he has proved that these reasoning powers are valid and trustworthy: he thereby gratuitously *assumes* the very thing *beforehand* which he intends to prove *afterwards*. He unconsciously accepts the trustworthiness of his faculties in attempting to demonstrate the existence and infinite perfection of God, and that is an illegitimate procedure; because a doubtfully valid faculty can produce only a doubtfully valid argument, and a doubtfully valid argument can only lead to a doubtfully valid conclusion. The whole argument for God's existence and veracity is thus nullified by his doubtful reason and reasoning process; and, since he proves the reliability of his reason and reasoning process by means of God's veracity, which (according to his supposition) must be doubtful, the proof for the trustworthiness of his own powers is nullified and can never be established beyond doubt. His attempt, therefore, to vindicate the validity of human knowledge failed essentially, because, by rejecting the reliability of his

own powers to discover and know truth, he made it impossible
for himself to extricate himself from the net of his own
universal doubt.

Moreover, there are *glaring inconsistencies* in his procedure.
He claims to reject everything, even the Principle of Contradiction and the Principle of Sufficient Reason. But he does not.
He surreptitiously *assumes the truth* of these principles and
uses them continually. As obvious a fact as the *'Cogito, ergo
sum'* is really based on the validity and truth of the Principle
of Contradiction. This principle asserts that it is impossible for
something to be and not to be at the same time. Descartes
becomes certain of his own existence by the very fact of his
'thinking' or 'doubting.' True. But why? Because he perceives
clearly that it is impossible to 'think and not think,' to 'exist
and not exist' at the same time. If Descartes were consistent
and really doubted the Principle of Contradiction, he would
have to affirm that it *could be possible* for a being to 'think
and not think,' to 'exist and not exist' at the same time. But
then, according to his own supposition, he could not be sure
after all that the ultimate fact of his existence is certain, and
his famous *'Cogito, ergo sum'* has no real objective value. Only
by granting the validity and truth of the Principle of Contradiction beforehand, can his existence be established as an
objective fact; and that is exactly, though inconsistently, what
Descartes does.

The same line of reasoning applies to his *proofs for God's
existence* and infinite perfection. Notwithstanding his proofs,
his rejection of the Principle of Contradiction will forever invalidate his arguments, because, as long as this principle is not
established and accepted, he could never be sure whether it
would not be possible for God to 'exist and not exist,' to 'be
infinitely perfect and not infinitely perfect' at the same time.
Similarly, he would always be compelled to remain in doubt
whether God could not be 'veracious and not veracious,' 'deceiving and not deceiving,' unless the Principle of Contradiction

were taken as granted *before he begins to prove* God's existence. Unwittingly Descartes *does* accept this Principle of Contradiction throughout his demonstrations, but that is an inexcusable inconsistency.

So, too, Descartes conducts his inquiry under the supposition that he has doubted the Principle of Sufficient Reason and the Principle of Causality. But he does not hesitate to use these principles *before he has established their validity.* Consider his *a posteriori* argument for the existence and infinite perfection of God. He contends that the idea of God as an all-perfect Being could not have originated in our mind, because such an idea would exceed the causality of the human mind, the latter being less perfect than the contents of the idea itself; consequently, this idea had to be produced in us by God Himself (and this proves that God exists as an infinitely perfect Being), otherwise there would be no sufficient reason for the presence of such an idea in our mind. This line of reasoning shows plainly that Descartes uses the Principles of Sufficient Reason and Causality in demonstrating God's existence, although he *doubts their validity.* Now, if he lets these principles stand as doubtful, his entire demonstration is vitiated and nullified by doubt; and if he accepts them as valid prior to establishing their validity, he acts contrary to his fundamental doubt and is inconsistent: in either case he makes the demonstration of God's existence impossible. His actual procedure in all the arguments he makes is such, however, that he *presupposes* the validity of these laws of thought; and that is for him a glaring inconsistency, since his *universal* methodic doubt will not permit him to accept their validity before he has proved the existence and veracity of God.

Finally, Descartes' universal methodic doubt *leads logically to universal skepticism.* No certitude can ever be attained in a system where the very foundations of human reason are completely destroyed. When he rejects as doubtful and even as 'absolutely false' all in regard to which he could imagine the least ground for doubt (*absolument faux tout ce en quoi je pourrois imaginer la moindre doute*), he saws off the very limb upon which he is seated. If the nature of his mind and the laws of thought are called into real doubt (not to speak of considering them to be 'absolutely false'), then all acts and facts of consciousness, all ideas, judgments, and inferences, can no longer be trusted. But how can the mind attempt to validate its own trustworthiness except by means of these things? If Descartes mistrusts the simple judgments '2 + 3 = 5' and 'A square has four sides,' how can he trust his faculties in making the far more complicated arguments with which he tries to prove God's existence and infinite perfections?

The effort of Descartes to find his way back to certitude by means of the roundabout detour of the existence and veracity of God, shows the desperate plight in which he had placed himself by his universal doubt. The steps he takes in retracing his way are these: his own existence; the existence and infinite perfection of God; God's absolute veracity; his creation by God; the trustworthiness of his faculties, due to the veracity of God who created him; the truth and validity of all those spontaneous convictions of his mind which are 'clear and distinct.' But we have seen that Descartes could not consistently prove God's existence, since he could only do so by means of a reasoning process which, according to his own principles, was essentially doubtful in its validity, and even 'absolutely false.' The only thing of which he could ever be certain was his own existence; and this, too, strictly speaking, Descartes should have doubted, because he had doubted the Principle of Contradiction and the testimony of his own consciousness. Our modern Archimedes had indeed found his fulcrum, namely his own existence; but now he could not move the world, because he had thrown away his lever.

Descartes, if he had been consistent, should have embraced universal skepticism, because his universal doubt left him no other choice: he had no way of retracing his course. He was like a mariner who scuttles his boat and swims to a rock in mid-ocean. The rock is the solitary fact of his own existence. True, he had found a solid point. But it is a lonely and desolate spot; and he is marooned on it forever, doomed to die of mental starvation, surrounded by an unbridgeable ocean of doubt.

The Cartesian universal methodic doubt, therefore, is not a proper approach to the problem of human knowledge. It is in reality only a variation of universal skepticism, and as such it is absurd. We will have to make our approach in a different fashion.

The necessary conclusion to be drawn from the above critical examination of universal skepticism is obvious: *Complete doubt cannot be the proper approach to the problem of human knowledge.* It would be fatal. Starting with complete doubt, we can no more reach a solution of the problem of human knowledge than a bird can fly with amputated wings.

Another important conclusion is this: *Any theory of knowledge which leads logically to universal skepticism is intrinsically false.* Nothing could be plainer. There must be an essential flaw in a theory which, if consistently carried out to its logical conclusions, ends in the absurdity of skepticism. This principle will enable us to pass a condemnatory verdict on many systems of thought, even though we may not always be capable of discovering the exact fallacy underlying the systems.

SUMMARY OF CHAPTER IV

In making a critical examination of the spontaneous convictions of man, *improper methods of approach* must be avoided. Such are universal skepticism and Descartes' universal methodic doubt.

1. *Skepticism a False Method.* It is a practical impossibility. No sane man can live without many practical certainties, denying his theoretical skepticism in his daily conduct. It is also a *theoretical* absurdity, because it is full of inconsistencies. Skeptics are 'certain' that we must doubt. They distinguish between

'truth' and 'error,' 'certitude' and 'doubt,' realizing that these opposites cannot be identical; thereby they admit the validity of the Principle of Contradiction. They give reasons for skepticism which they consider cogent and valid, contrary to their skeptic principles. They are conscious of their doubts; they thus accept consciousness as a valid source of knowledge.

2. *Refutation of Skeptic Arguments.* Erroneous opinions do not prove that certitude is impossible; errors are accidental, because we can detect and correct them. It is not true that every argument involves either an infinite regress or a gratuitous assumption or a vicious circle; self-evident truths avoid all these logical difficulties and form the ultimate basis of knowledge.

3. *Descartes' Methodic Doubt.* In his endeavor to place knowledge upon a firm basis, Descartes sought for an indubitable truth as his starting point, doubting everything in the meantime. He found this truth in the fact of his own existence. He then deduced God's existence from his idea of God. God, being infinitely perfect, cannot deceive; consequently, He must have given man trustworthy faculties. Man's faculties having been proved to be trustworthy, man can now acquire true and valid knowledge.

4. *Failure of Descartes' Method.* Since he doubts everything, he cannot be certain that his idea of God is correct. He uses a reasoning process to demonstrate God's existence; but his reason is of doubtful value, until he proves its trustworthiness from the veracity of God. He is guilty of inconsistency, in as much as he presupposes the validity of the Principles of Contradiction, Sufficient Reason, and Causality, although their validity has not been established by him. His procedure, if consistently carried through, would lead logically to universal skepticism.

Conclusions to be drawn: complete doubt cannot be the proper approach to the problem of human knowledge; any theory of knowledge which leads logically to universal skepticism is intrinsically false.

READINGS

P. Coffey, *op. cit.*, Chs. III and IV; D. Card. Mercier, *op. cit.*, pp. 353–357; J. Rickaby, *op. cit.*, Part I, Chs. VIII and IX; J. G. Vance, *op. cit.*, Chs. II and IV; T. Pesch, *Institutiones Logicales*, Pars II, Vol. I, pp. 55–75; J. Barron, *op. cit.*, Chs. II and III; A. J. Balfour, *A Defense of Philosophic Doubt;* G. T. Ladd, *Knowledge, Life, and Reality*, Ch. VII; W. P. Montague, *The Ways of Knowing*, Ch. VI; W. E. Hocking, *Types of Philosophy*, Ch. VIII.

Chapter V

THE PRIMARY TRUTHS

The proper approach to the problem of human knowledge is an important matter. Since universal skepticism would produce a paralysis of our reasoning powers, any initial attitude of mind which would involve skepticism must be excluded as wrong from the beginning. For this reason Descartes' methodic doubt, because it was intended by him as a real and genuine doubt about everything without exception prior to all investigation, was doomed to failure: it could lead only to skepticism, if consistently carried out. Such attempts, however, have done this much good, that they show us certain pitfalls which must be avoided. We are now better able to understand the *proper attitude* which is required in our approach to the problem.

The proper approach must be determined by the *purpose* of the whole investigation, and the purpose of epistemology is neither more nor less than this: to inquire into the rational grounds and ultimate reasons of our spontaneous convictions by means of a critical examination, in order to see whether these spontaneous convictions are *justifiable before reason* and can thus become philosophic certainties. This entails a number of things.

INITIAL STATE OF MIND

For one thing, we must accept the *data of the problem,* at least in so far as they are subjective facts in our mental life. This includes the entire body of spontaneous convictions as outlined in previous chapters. Whatever may be the outcome of our investigation, we cannot deny that we actually have these convictions. These convictions, then, must be accepted as the raw materials upon which our reason must work in attempting to solve the problem in question.

Again, it must be borne in mind from the start that the purpose of epistemology is not to discredit and disprove our spontaneous convictions. If anything, its purpose is rather the opposite — to prove and *vindicate* them. This does not mean that the philosopher should not investigate their claims in all critical severity; that is both his right and his duty. But the fact is, as we pointed out in the first chapter, that these convictions have a strong *prima facie evidence* in their favor, since they are *spontaneous* and *natural* and are in agreement with the facts of our whole *ordinary life*. In the research work of any of the sciences this would be considered sufficient proof for a well-grounded *hypothesis,* and we should also, therefore, accept the validity of these spontaneous convictions as *hypothetically true*. As a consequence of this, only proofs and reasons of the most serious nature should compel us to recede from this position.

Furthermore, it must be obvious that we cannot take up the single spontaneous convictions present in our mind and investigate them individually. This would be a hopeless task. They are far too numerous and detailed, comprising the whole field of knowledge contained in the various sciences and in our ordinary life. It will be more advantageous to group them into *broad classes* and submit these classes to a critical examination; the individual convictions will then stand or fall with their respective class as a whole. If, for instance, we can prove that our senses are valid sources of knowledge, then our convictions based on sense-perception will be valid *as a class;* and that would be sufficient to show that these have a rational foundation.

Finally, we cannot begin our critical inquiry by really doubting everything, since that would be universal skepticism, and skepticism, as we have seen, is irrational; consequently, *we must begin by accepting something as certain.* On the other hand, we cannot begin with *unwarranted presuppositions,* be cause, by the very fact that they are unwarranted, they would be of doubtful validity, and thus our entire investigation would rest upon a doubtful foundation. How can this initial difficulty be overcome?

Big paragraph

X There is only one way in which this can be done: We must begin with some truths which will be so transparently clear and *irresistibly evident* to our reason that a little reflection will give us *reflex* and *philosophic certitude.* In this way we will be guilty neither of skepticism nor of unwarranted presuppositions; the fact that they are certain excludes skepticism, and the fact that they are irresistibly evident to our reason saves them from being *unwarranted* presuppositions. Certitude, as we know, is the state of the mind in which it gives a firm assent to a judgment without fear of the possibility of error, due to recognized valid reasons. If we were to give such an assent to a judgment without recognizing any valid reason for this assent, then indeed we would have an unwarranted presupposition; we would simply presuppose it to be true without knowing why, and that would be unwarranted. But if we understand the ground or reasons which exclude all reasonable fear of error, then our assent to such a judgment would be warranted and *rationally justified.* Hence, if we could find some such *basic truths,* we would have a solid footing for our inquiry and proceed from there in the investigation of our spontaneous convictions. Are there any such truths?

There are; many of them. At present, however, we are only concerned with those which are *essential to all valid knowledge* without exception. There must be some truths which form the bedrock of all knowledge, which lie at the bottom of all thinking, and which constitute the indispensable foundation of all reasoning. These truths, which must be present in every act of knowledge, we must establish and vindicate first, before we can safely investigate the various classes of spontaneous convictions. With a little thoughtful reflection we will perceive

that there are *three primary truths* which are most fundamental to the human mind and absolutely necessary in all its
operations: I experience my own existence but I don't know it.

The *First Fact:* my own existence — 'I exist.' The *First
Principle:* the Principle of Contradiction — 'It is impossible for
something to be and not to be at the same time.' The *First
Condition:* the essential trustworthiness of my reason — 'My
reason is capable of knowing truth.'

These three primary truths are, of course, spontaneous convictions of our mind, and as such they are accepted without
question and never doubted by the ordinary man. That he is
convinced of his own existence, goes without saying. That he is
convinced of the truth and validity of the Principle of Contradiction, is equally certain. He may not be able to formulate
the principle in words; but that the *meaning* of this principle
is well known to him and accepted in all its rigor, cannot be
doubted. He shows it in all his thinking and reasoning. It is
contained *implicitly* in all his statements. When he says 'I am
not feeling well,' he is conscious of the fact that it is impossible
to 'feel well' and 'feel ill' at the same time. And when he says
'You are wrong,' he realizes that one cannot be 'right' and
'wrong' in the same way at the same moment. And so with
other judgments; they all involve the Principle of Contradiction. The same is true of the essential reliability of his reason.
He is conscious, of course, that he can and does make many
errors of judgment; but he is also conscious of the fact that
these errors are only incidental and do not invalidate the
essential capability of his reason to know truth and to distinguish it from error. The ordinary man, whether educated or
uneducated, once he is aware of the full grounds underlying
the subject in question and can say 'I understand this,' never
doubts that his knowledge is true and valid. Man's daily life
in all its phases is regulated by his spontaneous conviction of
the validity of these primary truths.

PROOF OF THREE PRIMARY TRUTHS

This brings us face to face with the vital question: Must we then accept these primary truths without demonstration or proof? Without demonstration, yes; without proof, no. We must be clear in our own mind what we understand by 'demonstration' and 'proof.' A 'demonstration' is a *mediate inference,* a process of reasoning, by means of which, from something that is better known, we conclude to the truth of something that is less well known. A 'proof' is anything that makes the truth of a thing *indubitably clear* to our mind, whether this be by means of a demonstration proper or by means of an immediate insight into the truth due to the *irresistible clearness of the truth itself*. In the latter case (immediate insight based on self-evidence) a 'demonstration' will be superfluous, because the truth is clear in itself and does not need a clearer truth to demonstrate it; it is only when something is not clear in itself that a 'demonstration' becomes necessary to prove its truth. Bearing this distinction in mind, the answer to the question is as follows:

The three primary truths cannot be demonstrated; nor do they need a demonstration, because they are self-evident.

They cannot be demonstrated. The only way I could possibly demonstrate my own *existence* would be by deducing it from some other idea more clear to me than my existence itself. But what can be clearer to me than my own existence? The only imaginable way would be to deduce it from my thinking, my willing, or some other operation of mine. But these operations presuppose and *include* my existence. Such a demonstration could not be formulated except in the following manner: 'Everyone who thinks, exists; I think; ergo, I exist.' The major premise is a general truth; well and good. The minor premise, however, expresses a fact, 'I think.' This minor premise is really nothing else than 'I am one who thinks,' and 'I am' is the same as 'I exist.' Consequently, my existence is already contained in my premise directly, and that is a begging of the question. The demonstration is invalid, because the minor premise, since it already involves my existence, is not really clearer to me than my existence, which I intend to demonstrate. Hence, I cannot demonstrate my own existence.

Nor can I demonstrate the *Principle of Contradiction.* Any demonstration which I might use to prove it, would have to consist of premises which are true and not erroneous, in order to be a valid demonstration. But to be 'true and not erroneous' presupposes that I know that 'truth' and 'error' are not, and cannot, be the same. That, however, again presupposes and involves the truth of the Principle of Contradiction, namely that 'it is impossible for a thing to be and not to be at the same time.' Again, such a demonstration would have to possess consistency, in order to be valid. But that implies that 'consistency' and 'inconsistency' are opposed and cannot be the same; and that is due to the Principle of Contradiction. Hence, the truth of the Principle of Contradiction cannot be demonstrated, but must be presupposed for the validity of every demonstration.

Similarly, I cannot demonstrate the *reliability* of my own reason. I could only attempt such a demonstration by formulating an argument *with my own reason.* But this very attempt at a demonstration by means of my own reason *presupposes* that my reason is really reliable and capable of making a valid demonstration. The trustworthiness of my reason would thus already be presupposed and involved in the demonstration itself, and that would make the demonstration invalid.

Any attempt, therefore, to prove the three primary truths by means of a real demonstration can amount to nothing more than a begging of the question. Does that mean that they are *gratuitous* assumptions, *unwarranted* presuppositions? If that were the case, then our knowledge would indeed be grounded on an irrational foundation. We must remember, however, that only those truths demand a demonstration which are so obscure in themselves or so doubtful to our mind that we need another and clearer idea to manifest them to us. If they are perfectly clear and self-evident, we do not need a demonstration to make them clear, because the very purpose of a demonstration is already fulfilled. Under such circumstances, therefore, a truth would *not* be a gratuitous assumption nor an *unwarranted* presupposition. And that, precisely, is the case with the three primary truths: they need no demonstration, because *they are self-evident*.

Consider the First Fact — 'I exist.' The truth of my own existence is so evident to me that I am compelled by irresistible necessity to accept it, because I have a *direct insight* and an *immediate intuition* of myself as existing. I could not doubt this fact, even if I tried. The very doubt or denial of my existence would prove my existence, since I could not 'doubt' or 'deny,' if I did not exist. Why, then, should I demand or need a demonstration of this perfectly obvious fact? It would be unreasonable to demonstrate something which is clearer to me than any demonstration.

The same applies to the First Principle; it requires no demonstration, because it is *intuitively clear* to the mind and certain beyond doubt and denial. No one can doubt or deny the validity of the Principle of Contradiction without asserting its validity by his very doubt or denial. If he actually denied or doubted it, he would by this fact alone affirm that 'truth' and 'error,' 'doubt' and 'certitude' are not, and cannot be, the same. And why are they not the same? Because of the validity of the very Principle of Contradiction which he doubts or denies. Since it is the Principle of Contradiction alone which guarantees the validity of every demonstration, and no demonstration can be valid without it, it is evident that no demonstration can give validity to the First Principle itself; the First Principle is so obvious and clear to the thinking mind, that the mind needs no demonstration to make it clear.

And so it is with the *First Condition*. It needs no demonstration to manifest its truth, since not only every argument in its favor presupposes the reliability of our reason, but every doubt or denial does the same. By the very fact that I would doubt or deny the trustworthiness of my reason, I would take it for granted that my *reason is reliable and trustworthy in its doubt or denial,* since I thereby affirm that I understand clearly the difference between truth and error and also the objective value of the reasons or grounds which should govern my assent. Even the skeptic thinks that he is right in doubting everything, because of the many proofs he has discovered against certainty; but thereby he asserts indirectly that his own reason is reliable in its investigation. When, therefore, a thing is so clear and evident that I cannot doubt or deny it without affirming it by my very doubt or denial, I need no demonstration to prove its truth and validity.

After all, clearness of insight due to the *evidence of truth itself* is the basis of knowledge for our mind. When the analysis of a judgment does not make its truth clear to us, then we must have recourse to a demonstration, in order to obtain the necessary clearness of insight into its truth; if the demonstration gives our mind this insight and convinces it, it is simply because it has made *truth evident* to the mind. When, however, our mind obtains this insight into truth by a mere analysis and contemplation of the judgment, due to the irresistible evidence of the truth itself without the aid of a demonstration, then we have truth and certainty in its purest, simplest, and *most rational* form. Such is the truth and certainty of the three primary truths as just shown.

We see, then, that the three primary truths are not unwarranted assumptions and presuppositions. They are eminently rational and philosophically well grounded. Our assent to their truth is based on undeniable and unshakable evidence of the most convincing nature and not upon some blind and unaccountable compulsion of our mental constitution. This being the case, the First Fact, the First Principle, and the First Condition are no longer only the spontaneous convictions which we share with the ordinary man, but *reflex* and *philosophic certainties* which have stood the test of our critical examination. They form the foundation of all knowledge, science, and philosophy. With these three primary truths critically established and philosophically certain, our investigation of the problem of human knowledge has been placed upon a solid basis, and we can now proceed with confidence and definite hope of success.

not in any texts

CRITICAL DOGMATISM

The primary truths being *rational presuppositions,* which must be accepted without positive demonstration (which, of course, they do not need, as we have shown), and which are considered prerequisites for every process of thinking and reasoning, are styled *dogmas of epistemology.* The system of epistemology which, after a critical examination of their validity, accepts these three primary truths as essentially necessary for every process of thinking and reasoning prior to the investigation of the various classes of spontaneous convictions themselves, is called *critical dogmatism.* We are, therefore, critical dogmatists. That these 'dogmas' are not to be confounded with the dogmas of theology, is evident. The term is derived from the Greek word δόγμα and means any accepted doctrine or tenet. Here, of course, it is taken in a philosophical sense.

Critical dogmatism, then, is the only logical and rational approach to the problem of human knowledge. We must accept it, if we do not wish to be caught in the inescapable net of universal doubt. Universal doubt, as an initial state of mind in approaching the problem, would mean the paralysis of all thought, the bankruptcy of science, the suicide of reason; it would condemn us to failure before ever we started. The only alternative is critical dogmatism.

D. Card. Mercier, together with other neo-scholastics of the Louvain School, objects strongly to the acceptance of these three primary truths or 'dogmas.' He considers this an 'exaggerated dogmatism.' Here is his attitude in the question:

"These supposed primary truths, if we except the principle of contradiction, are not so self-evident as to call for no proof. If they do not demand demonstration in the strict sense of the word, yet certainly an attentive examination is necessary to bring out their evidence. Especially does the capability of the mind to know the truth need consideration, if not actual demonstration, for is it not the very subject of this treatise? To affirm it *a priori* is to ignore the problem of certitude instead of solving it.

"We can, then, assert *a priori* neither the essential *incapability* of the human reason (universal doubt) nor its general *capability* to know the truth (exaggerated dogmatism). Between these two extreme theories there is room for an intermediate one which we adopt as our own, one which we shall call mitigated or rational dogmatism. It may be stated thus:

"1. As regards the capability of our *faculties* or powers of acquiring knowledge, mitigated dogmatism *deliberately abstains* from making a judgment, holding that at the beginning of the study of the problem of certitude it is impossible either to affirm or to deny our mental capability of knowing truth. Before a judgment can be pronounced we must first study the value of the mind's acts. The first and immediate subject for our reflection is not the power as such but the acts, from which alone we come to a knowledge of the nature of the faculty that elicits them. If by dint of reflection we can discover that our mental acts, our assents, are objective, that is, conformable to things as they are in reality, then and then only shall we be able legitimately to infer that our mind is capable of attaining true knowledge. After all, this manner of procedure is a truly scientific method based upon observation: to use a homely comparison, a good digestion is the only proof of the stomach's ability to digest properly.

"2. As regards our judgments or *the acts* of the mind by which truth is attained, the initial state of the intelligence at the outset of the study of epistemology differs according as these judgments are *mediately* or *immediately* evident. In the case of the former, *doubt* cannot be avoided, whilst in that of the latter, which stand firm against any doubt, a state of certitude is always present."

He then goes on to show that these mediate judgments must be demonstrated, until they finally rest upon evident, indemonstrable propositions. And he concludes his exposition with the words:

"Sooner or later, then, the demonstration of mediate propositions leads us back to indemonstrable premises which we call *immediate propositions:* such are all propositions in which the identity or the nonidentity of the predicate with the subject is seen by the simple comparison of the terms. These immediate propositions, although indemonstrable, are by no means doubtful: their very evidence makes them indemonstrable, that is to say, incapable of being referred to propositions which are more evident. And when they are reflected upon by the mind, they necessarily draw its assent, *they force their truth upon the mind.*

"In setting out to solve the problem of certitude we therefore suppose only *two facts,* which skeptics themselves are willing to admit, namely, the existence of necessary spontaneous assents and the power to examine these by reflection. To disallow these data would make the problem of certitude impossible, inasmuch as to suppress *'id de quo* quaeritur' necessarily involves the suppression of *'id quod* quaeritur.' There is, however, all the difference in the world between taking these data for granted and the *a priori* assertion that we are sure to find skepticism wrong, that the result of our investigation must be the dogmatic thesis that the mind is capable of knowing truth."[1]

Mercier here states that the initial state of mind in setting out to solve the problem of certitude consists in supposing only

---

[1] D. Mercier, *A Manual of Modern Scholastic Philosophy,* Vol. I, Criteriology, Nos. 19–22 (Kegan Paul, Trench, Trübner and Co., Ltd., London, 1916). See also his *Critériologie Générale* (1906), Nos. 44–59.

two facts, namely, "the existence of necessary spontaneous assents and the power to examine these by reflection." But what is this 'power to examine by reflection'? It is *reason.* Reason is the instrument of reflection. And he intends to *use* this reason as the instrument of his reflection in examining these necessary spontaneous assents or convictions, although, as he himself states, "we can assert *a priori* neither the essential incapability of the human reason nor its general capability to know the truth." But if the *essential* capability of this reason is in doubt, then the whole process of examining these convictions is a doubtful process, and the whole *result* of this examination (being the result of a doubtful examining faculty) must also remain in doubt: a doubtful reasoning faculty can produce only doubtful conclusions.

Again, Mercier says: "If by dint of reflection we can discover that our mental acts, our assents, are objective, that is, conformable to things as they are in reality, then and then only shall we be able legitimately to infer that our mind is capable of attaining true knowledge." How are we "to discover that our mental acts are conformable to things as they are in reality"? He gives the answer when he says "by dint of reflection." And with what are we to make this reflection? With our reason, of course. He, therefore, presupposes that our reason can discover by reflection that our mental acts or assents (spontaneous convictions) actually conform "to things as they are in reality," and from this "then and then only shall we be able legitimately *to infer* that our mind is capable of attaining true knowledge." This means that we must *demonstrate* the reliability of our reason by means of a 'legitimate inference' from its own acts. The capability of human reason will, therefore, be the conclusion drawn by means of this *inference;* and this inference is made by this very reason whose 'essential capability' is in question. The whole process simply *presupposes* the capability of human reason to begin with; and if the 'essential capability' of human reason is doubtful, then the whole inference is doubtful, and the 'essential capability' of this reason is not, and never can be, established. The entire procedure is a begging of the question.

Mercier's method can never solve the problem, if the capability of human reason is supposed to be the final outcome of the investigation. This investigation can be valid only if human reason, the *instrument* of this examination, is known to be valid, and this validity must be established *before* any special investigation is started. And the very fact that Mercier surreptitiously presupposes the capability of human reason in making his investigation and formulating his arguments, although this capability is *still in question,* shows plainly that it cannot really ever be doubted in seriousness without becoming involved in inconsistencies. Mercier, therefore, unwittingly accepts the First Condition, the essential capability of human reason to know truth.

And when he asserts that we must "examine these spontaneous convictions by reflection," he also accepts the dogma of the First Fact, his existence. For how could he 'examine' and 'reflect,' if he were not certain of his own existence *prior* to this examination and reflection? And how can he "by dint of reflection discover that our convictions are conformable to things as they are in reality," if the First Principle, the Principle of Contradiction, did not hold? This 'conformity to things' is, as he states rightly, 'true knowledge.' But how can he know this, unless the Principle of Contradiction be established and accepted *beforehand?*

Without realizing it, then, Mercier accepts the three dogmas or primary truths. His mitigated or rational dogmatism is an illusion, and he has no right to call the acceptance of the three primary truths an *exaggerated* dogmatism. We are justified (as we have shown above) in saying of them what he says of immediate propositions: "their very evidence makes them indemonstrable, that is to say, incapable of being referred to propositions which are more evident; and when they are reflected upon by the mind, they necessarily draw its assent, *they force their truth upon the mind.*"

These three dogmas or primary truths are, therefore, *not a priori assertions,* as he contends. They are proved to be 'immediate propositions,' self-evident in their truth, based upon critical reflection; as such they are no longer merely spontaneous convictions, but *reflex* and *philosophic certainties.*

And thus the basis of human knowledge in its essential foundation is seen to be rational.

Is the problem of knowledge solved by the proof of these primary truths? Not at all. We have merely gained the proper *starting point* for our investigation of the general problem. We have indeed established the fact that we exist, that it is impossible for something to be and not to be at the same time, and that it would be unreasonable to doubt the capability of our reason to know truth. These are merely *preliminary* truths, necessary to conduct our investigation; the general problem still remains. We must now examine the data of consciousness, of sense-perception, of intellectual ideas, of first principles, of rational inference, and see whether the spontaneous convictions derived from these sources of knowledge are based on rational grounds and therefore philosophically certain.

SUMMARY OF CHAPTER V

The proper approach to the problem of knowledge must be determined by the *purpose* of epistemology: namely, to inquire into the rational grounds of our spontaneous convictions, in order to see whether they are justifiable before reason and can thus become philosophic certainties.

1. *Initial State of Mind.* We must accept the *data* of the problem, in so far as they are subjective facts in our mental life. Since our spontaneous convictions have a strong *prima facie* evidence in their favor, we must accept them as *hypothetically true* and try to vindicate them. It will be necessary to investigate these convictions as classes. Since we cannot doubt

everything, we must begin our inquiry by accepting something as certain. These are the three *primary truths:* the First Fact, our existence; the First Principle, the Principle of Contradiction; and the First Condition, the essential capability of the mind to know truth.

2. *Proof of Primary Truths.* These primary truths cannot be proved by a positive demonstration, because they are presupposed and involved in every demonstration. But they need no demonstration, because they are so *evident* that any attempt to doubt or deny them would already mean their affirmation and acceptance. They are, therefore, grounded in reason.

3. *Critical Dogmatism.* These three primary truths are called the 'dogmas of epistemology,' and the system which accepts these doctrines or principles is called *critical dogmatism.*

Mercier advocated a *mitigated dogmatism.* He accepts only two facts: the data of our spontaneous convictions and the power to examine them. Inadvertently, however, he presupposes the validity of these three primary truths. And if the essential capability of reason in its reflection is not admitted, the whole investigation must remain doubtful.

READINGS

P. Coffey, *op. cit.,* pp. 127–135; D. Card. Mercier, *op. cit.,* 357–362; J. G. Vance, *op. cit.,* Ch. III and Ch. V; J. Rickaby, *op. cit.,* Part I, Ch. X; T. Pesch, *op. cit.,* pp. 75–86; J. Balmes, *Fundamental Philosophy,* Bk. I, Ch. II.

PART II

THE VALIDITY OF HUMAN KNOWLEDGE

Section I. EXPERIENCE: Consciousness, Sense-Perception

Section II. INTELLECTION: Ideas, Judgments, Reasoning

CHAPTER VI

THE TRUTH-VALUE OF CONSCIOUSNESS

We are now in a position to make a critical inquiry into the validity of the various classes of spontaneous convictions of man furnished by the different sources of our knowledge. Skepticism with its universal doubt, as we have seen, is a practical impossibility and a philosophic absurdity; certitude, as a consequence, is and must be attainable. The three primary truths — the First Fact, the First Principle, and the First Condition — have also been established as self-evident and undeniable certainties; they form the rational starting point from which our investigation can legitimately proceed.

We will now examine the truth-value of the sources of our knowledge. By the *sources of knowledge* we understand the means or *media through which we arrive at truth and certitude*. These are the cognitive operations and faculties of man, in as much as it is through them that the knowing subject is brought into contact with objects and through them that these objects become known to the subject. Knowledge, as we have pointed out before, essentially involves three factors — the subject which knows, the object which becomes known, and the cognitive process or act which makes the object known to the subject; the object must act upon the subject, the subject must react to the object by means of a mental assimilation, and this mental assimilation takes place in the process or act of knowledge.

There are *two main sources* of knowledge from which our spontaneous convictions flow: *experience* and *intellection*. Experience is the source of our knowledge of concrete, individual, contingent facts. It is twofold: *consciousness,* by which we become aware of our intra-mental states and acts; and *sense-perception,* which enables us to apprehend external, material objects. Consciousness is internal experience, while sense-perception is external experience. Intellection comprises three operations — *ideas, judgments,* and *inferences;* it is the source of our intellectual knowledge of necessary and universal truths. Taken individually and separately, these are the sources of our knowledge which we will have to submit to a critical analysis: consciousness, sense-perception, ideas, judgments, and inferences.

THE PROBLEM OF CONSCIOUSNESS

Since human knowledge begins in the child with external experience or sense-perception, it would seem that sense-perception should be the first source to be examined for its truth-value. We must remember, however, that it is not the validity of the child's knowledge which is at stake, but the validity of *knowledge in general* as we find it in our adult mind. Now, a thing can only become known to us, and knowledge can only become knowledge for us, in so far as we are *conscious of its presence in our mind.* No one denies that our spontaneous convictions are at least subjective facts of our consciousness; they are the acknowledged data of the whole problem. It will be best then, to begin our inquiry by investigating the truth-value of consciousness itself as a primary source of our knowledge.

A number of important terms have become current in the modern philosophy of knowledge, and great confusion has arisen from the fact that the exact meaning of these terms has not always been recognized and kept distinct in the discussion. They are: *Ego* and *non-Ego, self* and *non-self, mental* and *extra-mental.* Whatever may be their ultimate validity, they have a definite signification, and we should be clear before-hand just what their signification implies. When speaking about the universe in connection with human knowledge, it has become common usage to say that the universe consists of the 'Ego' and the 'non-Ego,' the 'self' and 'non-self,' the 'mental' and 'extra-mental.' This division and designation is taken from the standpoint of man's consciousness. *Ego* is Latin, and it is identical with the English terms 'I,' 'myself,' and 'self'; *non-Ego* is identical in meaning with 'non-self.' By 'Ego' or 'self' we understand man in his whole person, con-sisting of body and mind together as a unit; and by 'non-Ego' or 'non-self' we understand the whole world which is distinct from man's body and mind and outside his person, as some-thing 'other-than-self.' By *mental* we mean anything that belongs and pertains to man's mind, and in this discussion 'mind' is taken in the sense of the 'conscious knowing subject' which is the seat and source of all cognitive and affective states in man; and by *extra-mental* we mean everything found out-side, or not pertaining to, the mind. Whether an objective reality corresponds to these terms, is something which will have to be decided later; at present we are concerned only with the *meaning* which is attached to these words, so that we can discuss the problem of knowledge intelligently. The mutual relationship existing between these sets of terms can be seen from the subjoined diagram:

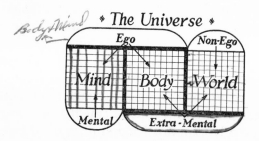

Parts marked by horizontal lines belong to the Ego.
Parts marked by vertical lines belong to the extra-mental.

The most conspicuous thing noticeable in these terms is that 'Ego' and 'extra-mental' are overlapping terms, while 'non-Ego' and 'mental' are mutually exclusive. The 'body' of man (if there be a 'body') is considered as an integral part of his person or Ego, together with the mind; but the 'world' (the material world as distinct from man's body, if there be such a 'world') is outside man's person or Ego entirely. At the same time, this 'body' is distinct from man's mind, and it is, therefore, not mental but 'extra-mental.' The body (provided it exists) is thus seen to be a part of the 'Ego' and also 'extra-mental'; as such it is the connecting link between the 'mind' and the material 'world' at large, occupying a middle position between these two extremes.

With these terms and ideas fixed and clear, we are now ready to turn our attention to the problem of consciousness and its truth-value. The only scientific way to proceed is to examine critically the facts of consciousness and then draw our conclusions concerning the validity of consciousness as a source of true and certain knowledge.

Just what is 'consciousness'? It is the intuitive 'awareness' by which we recognize something as cognitively present in the mind. Now, there is nothing more certain than that we have a 'conscious' mind.

FACTS OF CONSCIOUSNESS

Here are the evident *facts*.

Our mind is aware or conscious of the various acts of *external sense-perception*. I open my eyes and am aware that I see things: my desk, my books, the building outside, an auto turning the corner, the sun shining in the sky. I listen and am aware that I hear sounds: the heavy chugging of the motor of a truck, the conversation of two men passing my window, the scratching of my pen over the paper. I taste the pungent flavor of the piece of candy I am dissolving in my mouth, and I am aware of this sensation. I smell the fragrant odor of the tobacco I have been smoking, and I am aware of this perception. I experience the sensation of touch, and I am aware that I feel things: the hardness and smoothness of the wood of my desk, the pressure exerted by my fingers upon the pen as I write, the coldness of the air as it blows through my open window. All these sensations, as *perceptive acts*, have become *mentally present* to my mind, and I am conscious that they affect me while they are present; if I were not 'conscious' of them, I could not be aware that I am at this moment seeing, hearing, tasting, smelling, and touching.

Again, I am conscious of the presence in my being of certain *internal sense-states*. I am aware that I feel hunger and thirst, that I have a slight headache, that I am rather fatigued just now, that I experience pleasure in leaning back in my chair and relaxing for a while, that I feel depressed in my nerves. I am also aware that my imagination is evoking images within me of the stroll I intend taking to the library, and of the books I contemplate reading, and of the luncheon I expect to have, and of the persons I plan to meet. And I am aware, too, that my memory is recalling the celebration I attended some time ago and the many friends I met on that occasion after years of separation.

All these sense processes and states are not only present in me, but I experience and feel and am *aware of their presence:* I am conscious of them as actual happenings while they last. I possess a direct and immediate awareness of them as *concrete, individual facts.*

But I am also conscious of a higher order of acts and functions in my being — those of *intellection* and *volition*. As I proceed in my work, I am conscious of forming many ideas, of combining them into manifold judgments and propositions. of linking them together into a variety of inferences and arguments, proofs and refutations; I am thus conscious that I think, judge, reason. Furthermore, I am conscious that I desire to finish a certain portion of my task, and that I decide to continue until I have reached the goal which I have previously set out to attain, and that I make a distinct effort to overcome

the obstacles which make the attainment of this goal a difficult procedure; I am conscious of appetition (conation).

Going a step farther in the introspective analysis of my consciousness, I realize that I possess a reflective power which
enables me to obtain *reflex knowledge* of my conscious states
and acts. I not only know, but I know that I know; I not only
have knowledge, but I have a knowledge of my knowledge; I
not only am conscious, but I am conscious of my consciousness. But most important of all: in these various perceptive
acts and states of consciousness *I am conscious of my self, my
Ego,* as the one in whom they take place and who is the
subject affected by their presence. By means of this reflex act
of self-consciousness I become aware that I, the thinking and
conscious subject, *apprehend myself concretely* in these acts
and states; for *self*-consciousness is the knowledge which the
mind has of its acts *as its own.*

When I survey these perceptive acts of my consciousness, I
notice that they possess an *objective reference;* that is to say,
whenever I 'perceive,' I always perceive an 'object' distinct
from the act of perception itself. Thus, when I 'see,' I am not
only aware of the act of 'sight' as such, but I am also aware
that I see, for instance, 'a green house'; when I press my hand
upon my knee, I am not only aware of the act of 'touching'
itself, but I am also aware of my 'hand' and my 'knee' as the
objects which I feel. And it is my spontaneous conviction that
these objects, at least in many instances, are *objectively real,*
distinct from their 'mental presence' as 'objects of the mind'
in cognition; in other words, I am convinced that they are
real things which I perceive.

Is this spontaneous conviction warranted? Have these objects an 'objective existence' aside from their 'mental existence'
in the act of perception? Am I justified in passing from the
'mental order' to the 'objective order'? Does my consciousness
tell me anything at all about *real, extra-mental things?* If so,
what? Is my consciousness a reliable source of true and valid
knowledge? These important questions will now have to be

answered, and the answer will be the first step in the philosophic justification of human knowledge.

We're relying on it for intermal thoughts,

THE TRUTH-VALUE OF CONSCIOUSNESS

Consciousness is a valid source of truth in the domain of knowledge.

No internal lack reported except through Consciousness

Nothing is more intimate and more *fundamental* to me than my consciousness. All knowledge of whatever kind is rooted ultimately in my consciousness, because I cannot 'know' anything unless I am 'aware' of it. Every single act of sense-perception and intellection becomes an act of 'knowledge' for me only in so far as it conveys some information about an object to me, the subject; I thereby become a *knowing* subject. But I will be a 'knowing' subject only when I am *conscious* of the mental presence of the object within my perception and my thinking. If I were unconscious of its presence, I would be totally ignorant of it even as a 'mental object' and I could know absolutely nothing about it. Knowledge must simply be 'conscious' knowledge, in order to be 'knowledge' at all. Consciousness, therefore, is the *indispensable condition of all knowledge,* whether sensory or intellectual, so that, so far as I am concerned, knowledge in any form is utterly impossible without it. Consequently, if any knowledge can be true and certain and if any source of knowledge can be reliable at all, it can only be so under the condition that my consciousness is reliable and *essentially free from error.* If my consciousness is not essentially free from error, I cannot trust any other source of knowledge, because no other source is so intimate and evident to me as my consciousness and because every other source presupposes the trustworthiness of consciousness as the basis of its own.

The matter is quite plain and simple. I see, hear, taste, smell, touch; I form ideas, make judgments, produce inferences of deduction and induction. But all these cognitive acts take place in and through my consciousness. Since these cognitive acts are the means whereby I collect and construct my knowledge, and since without them I can have no knowledge at all, it is obvious that the truth and certainty of these sources of knowledge will depend entirely upon the trustworthiness of my consciousness. The reliability of sense and reason, therefore, *presupposes* the reliability of my consciousness; as sources of knowledge they stand and fall with my consciousness. If my consciousness is not essentially free from error, then every part and parcel of knowledge, whether common or scientific or philosophic, will of necessity always remain doubtful in its validity. But that would mean the bankruptcy of all science and philosophy and the suicide of my reason. There would then be no use in proceeding any further in my inquiry, because my investigation would be doomed beforehand to futility. The inevitable result of such a view would be universal skepticism. But universal skepticism, as was shown above, is a practical impossibility and a philosophic absurdity. If I wish, therefore, to avoid the intellectual death of universal skepticism, I must perforce accept the trustworthiness of my consciousness as capable of giving me true and certain knowledge. This is the only reasonable course for me to pursue, because my consciousness is the *last court of appeal* before the tribunal of reason, and its verdict is final: if there is any truth at all, the testimony of my consciousness must be true. My consciousness, therefore, is essentially free from error in the acts and facts of which it gives me direct and immediate awareness.

Moreover, if I were to doubt the reliability of my own consciousness as a source of true and certain knowledge, I would, *by my very doubt, assert its reliability*. To have a reasonable doubt, I must have reasons to doubt; otherwise I would act in an irrational fashion. But how can these reasons be valid unless I am certain of their validity? And how can I be certain of their validity, except by an act of consciousness vouching for their presence in my mind? And how can my consciousness vouch for their presence and validity, if it were unreliable? Therefore, even a valid doubt presupposes the reliability of my consciousness, and thereby its reliability is established.

There are a number of things, to which my consciousness

testifies as certain facts and truths, which I cannot possibly doubt, if I am in my right mind. I am certain, for instance, beyond the shadow of a doubt that I exist, that I think, that I perceive, that I reason; I am doing these things at this very moment as I write, so how can I doubt them? It would be sheer nonsense on my part to doubt or deny that I see, touch, hear, taste, smell, imagine, remember, think, judge, reason, considering these acts merely as *subjective facts* present in my mind. They are present as modifications of my being, and no amount of theorizing can argue them out of existence. If they were not present in my mind, and if my consciousness were not reliable in testifying to their existence, how could I know about their presence and think about them? I am *directly and immediately* aware of their existence within my Ego; and this evidence is so clear and irresistible, that I can doubt or deny this testimony of my consciousness only under penalty of renouncing my reason. True, I *cannot demonstrate* the trustworthiness of my consciousness by means of a strict inference, since an inference of this kind would really presuppose the trustworthiness of my consciousness, and that would mean a begging of the question; but such a demonstration is not needed, because all that is required is to show by introspection and analysis that I cannot doubt or deny its reliability without falling into the folly of universal skepticism. And that is clear to me from the above.

My consciousness, therefore, is a valid source of truth in its own domain of knowledge, provided its data are *self-evident.*

TRUTHS REVEALED BY CONSCIOUSNESS

We must distinguish clearly between the data of consciousness and the interpretation of these data. The data are the internal, subjective, intra-mental acts of perception and intellection, emotion and volition, which pass before my consciousness and of whose presence I become aware by the fact that they are there. My consciousness does not pass any judgment upon them but merely notices and registers their presence; and in

this 'noticing' and 'registering' it cannot err, because it perceives
these internal states by an act of *immediate experience* due to
the evidence of its own direct intuition. It is my intellect which
passes judgment upon the data of consciousness and interprets
them; and here error is possible, since my intellect may
mis-interpret the data and draw false conclusions from them.
But when my intellect does nothing more than state explicitly
what is implicitly contained in the data of consciousness, then
my consciousness will also be aware that the interpretation is as
true and certain as the data themselves, provided the data are
intuitively evident and not vague and indistinct. What truths,
then, does my consciousness reveal?

By introspection I discover that every act of knowledge involves three factors — *act of perception, object,* and *subject.*
Directly and primarily, it is the 'act of perception' which is
noticed and registered by my consciousness. Since, however,
my consciousness is aware of this act of perception in its
concrete reality, it also notices *in* this act the perceiving subject
and the perceived object as concrete parts of the concrete whole.
Thus, when a sensation of 'hunger' arises in my consciousness,
I am aware of the 'hunger' which is felt and of 'myself' as the
one who 'feels' the 'hunger.' The three factors form a concrete
whole, and I am concomitantly aware at the same time of the
act of perception, the object, and the subject. I express this in
the evident judgment: 'I (subject) feel (perception) hunger
(object).' From this triple standpoint my consciousness reveals
to me a number of important truths.

From the standpoint of the *act of knowledge,* my consciousness gives indubitable evidence that there is a great *difference*
in the character of my acts. 'Hearing' is not the same as 'seeing'
or 'tasting,' nor are these perceptions the same as 'touching'
or 'smelling': they affect my Ego in different ways. Similarly,
the experiences I undergo in the operations of the central sense,
imagination, instinct, and memory are unlike each other and
differ from the perceptions just mentioned. And all these acts

are registered in consciousness as radically different from intellectual ideas, judgments, and inferences. I also perceive within me affective and appetitive states and acts, such as joy, grief, anger, desire, volition; they are nonperceptive states, and the difference between them and the perceptive states is even greater than the differences existing between the perceptive states as such.

Consciousness, of course, does not group these various acts and states into classes; nor does it specify in any way whether they are material or spiritual in nature: it merely 'registers' their existence and their differences in a *concrete* manner. It is the *intellect* which classifies them by interpreting the data revealed by consciousness. If an error is made in this interpretation, this is due to a faulty analysis on the part of the intellect. Consciousness itself can never be mistaken in its clear testimony of the presence of an act or state within the mind.

From the standpoint of the *object of knowledge* my consciousness is concretely aware of the *object* of perception at the same time that it is aware of the *act* of perception. I cannot 'perceive' without perceiving 'something,' an object; and I thus become aware of colors, sounds, flavors, odors, tactile objects of sensation (heat and cold, hardness and softness, muscular and motor feelings), ideas, judgments, and inferences, as the objects of the various operations of my sense and intellect. I can no more deny their presence and existence within my consciousness than I can deny the presence and existence of the perceptive acts themselves, because act and object form one *concrete whole*. At the same time I am aware of their *concrete difference:* sounds are not colors; muscular feelings are not flavors; odors are not heat or cold; and all these sense-objects are not ideas or judgments or inferences.

Then again, I am intuitively conscious of *extendedness* in one or the other of my perceptions. Color-perception always reveals *colored surfaces,* not merely color alone for itself. There is a side-by-sideness of spatial parts in all color-objects, and extendedness in at least two dimensions — length and width. I never see 'green' alone; but I see a 'green lawn,' a 'green sea,' 'green leaves,' a 'green house.' I never see 'blue' alone; but I see a 'blue sky,' 'blue violets.' I never see 'red' alone; but I see 'red sealing-wax,' 'red roses,' 'red sunsets.' And so with the other colors: they are always extended and surfaced. Moreover, these extended surfaces are consciously perceived as having concrete *shapes,* and these shapes are recorded as having a concrete *difference* among themselves. I am intuitively aware of squares, triangles, disks, ellipses, and every kind of irregular figure in these colored surfaces. For instance, what I call an 'orange' is not merely 'yellow,' but a 'round' yellow object; the 'house' I see is a 'square' brown object; the 'moon' I perceive is a 'crescent-shaped' silvery object; the 'rose' I am looking at is an 'irregularly shaped' red object. These various configurations of shape are given directly with the color-object as an 'extended colored surface,' and my consciousness makes me immediately aware of them in the act of color-perception. *In some form,* therefore, *extension must exist,* otherwise it could not be a datum of my consciousness.

Similar to sight, but in a somewhat different manner, *touch reveals extension.* The sensation of side-by-sideness of spatial parts is even more immediately and intimately a datum of my consciousness in touch than it is in the sight of colored surfaces, because there is a *direct contact* in touch which is missing in the act of sight. When I pass my hand over a book, I *feel* the spatial extendedness of the book, and this contact-experience gives to the sensation a value which cannot be denied. Sight reveals a two-dimensional extension, but touch reveals dimension in three directions. When I handle a book, a pen, a bottle, an apple, or when I grasp my left wrist with my right hand, or when I feel my head with both hands, I am concretely conscious of *solidity, voluminousness, triple dimension.* Besides this, my consciousness reveals the difference of a total 'otherness,' when I touch my arm or head or thigh, and when I touch a book or a table or a fruit. The former are perceived to be a *part of my being,* while the latter are foreign to myself and 'outside' my being. This will become clearer, when we analyze the 'subject' of the act of knowledge.

From the standpoint of the *subject of knowledge,* my consciousness reveals a number of most interesting and vital truths. Primarily, I am aware of the acts of sense-perception and intellection which are present within me as concrete states of knowledge; but just as these acts manifest the object perceived, so they also reveal the *perceiving subject,* and this subject is my self, my *Ego.* Nothing is clearer to my consciousness than the fact that *I myself* am the active and passive subject of all internal states and modifications which I recognize as coming and going within me. All perceptive acts and affective states I concretely observe to be *my own;* they belong to *me* and modify *me.* Analyzing the data of my consciousness, I perceive with intuitive evidence that it is *I* who hear, see, touch, taste, and smell; it is *I* who imagine and remember; it is *I* who think, judge, and reason; it is *I* who am hungry and thirsty, sad and glad, peaceful and angry, healthy and sick, in pleasure and in pain; it is *I* who decide and will, strive and reject. It is my *selfsame Ego* which is active throughout, whether in the domain of sense or in the domain of intellect, and my *Ego is one, single individual;* there is no duality or multiplicity here, notwithstanding the radical difference between the acts and states themselves. Even my consciousness is only a modification of my self or Ego, because I am conscious of *myself as conscious* in the same way that I am conscious of myself as seeing, hearing, thinking, and willing; I express both facts in an identical manner, namely, '*I* hear a sound' and '*I* am conscious of myself.'

The Ego is not consciousness; it is the *possessor* of consciousness. The Ego is not experience; it is the *experient.* And so, too, the Ego is not memory; it is the *bearer* of memory. The act of remembering is a present act, but it always has a reference to past persons or events. I perceive with evidence that

I, the Ego, who am conscious at this very moment, am the *self-identical Ego* who have had the 'past' experiences recorded by my memory. I am writing at this instant; but I am also conscious through my memory that I was writing ten minutes ago, that I took a walk half an hour ago, that I consulted a physician this morning. Notwithstanding the fact that I was in a state of complete unconsciousness during my sleep last night, I am aware that 'I' am the self-identical 'Ego' who existed, worked, ate, wrote, perceived, and reasoned yesterday, a week before, a month ago, and through all the years down to my youth and childhood. These events belonged to me before; and my Ego preserved its self-identity, while they came and passed on. How could I remember them as 'mine,' as having happened to 'me,' if my Ego were not a permanently existing reality *in whom* they occurred? My Ego is clearly perceived to be the *abiding subject* of these transitory states. It is the duty of psychology to pass judgment on the nature of the Ego, but the data of my conscious states show plainly that my Ego is distinct from the conscious states themselves; the latter are only modifications of the permanent Ego, existing *in* and *by* and *through* my Ego as their agent-patient subject. So much is evident to me from an analysis of the data of memory.

Of what does my Ego consist, so far as I am informed by my consciousness? Since the Ego is the 'thinking subject,' whatever is 'mental' belongs to it; the *mind,* therefore, is an integral part of the Ego. But some of my perceptions also show that my Ego is an *extended reality*. When I grasp a book or a pen, I am aware that these objects are extended and that they are 'other-than-self'; however, when I grasp my arm or my head or my ankle, I am aware that they are extended and that they differ among themselves, but also that they are 'identical-with-self.' In other words, they are perceived to be *integral parts of my Ego,* they belong to my being and my person; they are 'my head,' 'my eyes,' 'my ears,' 'my hands,' 'my chest,' 'my arms,' 'my legs,' 'my toes.' Hence, if I stub the toes against a stone, I say: *'My* foot hurts,' and *'I* feel a pain in *my* foot.' Since these objects are clearly perceived by touch and sight to be extended, and since my consciousness testifies that they belong to me as integral parts of my Ego, it is obvious that my *Ego is extended with and through them.* These parts, however, taken together, form what we call the 'body,' and this body is clearly perceived to be distinct from the 'thinking subject' or mind; the body is 'extra-mental.' My Ego, therefore, according to the indisputable evidence of my consciousness, consists of something 'mental' and 'extra-mental,' of *mind and body.* It is, then, untrue to say that the Ego consists of purely mental states; it also consists of an extra-mental body which has various extended parts side by side; and both mind and body form a unit, the one and *undivided whole* which is my Ego.

Such are the facts of consciousness regarding the *act, object,* and *subject* of knowledge. And it is from such evident, undeniable facts that my intellect forms such ideas as 'being, existence, sense-perception, intellection, appetition, extension and space, mind and body, mental and extra-mental, Ego and non-Ego.' They are not mere fancies and figments, but *valid ideas,* possessing objective reality, derived by the intellect from the critically observed and analyzed data of my consciousness; and, as we see, they are not the results of a blind instinct, but the conscious products of an intellectual insight based on the *intuitive evidence of immediate experience* which cannot be doubted or denied without falling into complete skepticism. Any 'immediate judgments' then, which my intellect forms as interpretations of these facts by means of such ideas, must be as *true, valid,* and *certain* as these facts themselves, because my consciousness testifies that in such instances my intellect is merely stating explicitly that which is contained implicitly in the data as mentally present. Such immediate judgments are: 'I exist; I am a being; I experience various acts of sense-perception, intellection, and appetition, and there is an objective difference between them; extension is a reality; I possess an extended body; I have a mind; my body is an extra-mental reality as certainly existing as my mind; mind and body are integral parts of my Ego; I, the Ego, am the possessor of this mind-body combination; I have perceptions of objects which I consciously apprehend as being outside my Ego and as belonging, therefore, to the non-Ego.' These immediate judgments are now no longer simply spontaneous convictions but *scientific, reflex, philosophic truths and certainties,* the result of a critical analysis of my conscious mind in its revealed data. It will be obvious that these ideas and truths are basic to the problem of knowledge and must be considered as partly solving the problem. The validity of the 'body' and of the external 'world' as 'objective realities' will be treated later.

Consciousness, then, is a valid source of true and certain knowledge concerning those acts and facts of which it has immediate cognition. This validity is based on the indubitable evidence of *primary experience.* To doubt the essential freedom from error on the part of consciousness is to destroy the validity of any and all other knowledge, because such knowledge has its ultimate foundation in the intuitive character of the knowledge of consciousness.

SUMMARY OF CHAPTER VI

1. The sources of knowledge are the media through which we arrive at truth, and they are twofold: experience and intellection. *Consciousness,* a form of experience, is the intuitive awareness by which we recognize something as 'mentally present.' 'Ego' and 'non-Ego,' 'self' and 'non-self,' 'mental' and 'extra-mental,' are cognate ideas whose meaning should be clearly grasped.

2. We possess a *conscious mind.* We are aware of sense-perception, intellection, and appetition. Consciousness reaches its highest expression in the knowledge of *Ego* or *self;* the Ego observes itself concretely as the subject and bearer of the internal acts and states of consciousness. All perceptive acts have an 'objective reference.'

3. Consciousness is *essentially free from error* in the knowl-

edge it conveys, when the data are perceived with intuitive evidence. Otherwise no other knowledge would be valid, and certitude would be impossible, because all other forms of knowledge presuppose the validity of consciousness. To doubt the validity of consciousness is tantamount to asserting its validity, since the reasonableness of this doubt could not be established except on the supposition that consciousness is a valid source of knowledge. Some facts attested by consciousness are so obviously true, that we cannot doubt them except under penalty of renouncing our reason. If consciousness is not essentially free from error, universal skepticism must follow.

4. The *act* of knowledge reveals the various kinds of internal states and their differences in a concrete manner. The *object* of knowledge reveals the objects of various perceptive and non-perceptive acts and their concrete differences. In particular, sight reveals extension in two dimensions, while touch reveals it in three dimensions. Touch also shows that part of my own being is extended. The *subject* of knowledge reveals the fact that my self or Ego is the active and passive agent of all internal states, that my self or Ego possesses a mind and body as a unit.

READINGS

P. Coffey, *op. cit.,* Vol. II, Ch. XIII; D. Card. Mercier, *op. cit.,* pp. 388–391; J. Rickaby, *op. cit.,* Part II, Ch. V; T. Pesch, *op. cit.,* pp. 151–160; M. Maher, *Psychology,* Chs. III, XVII, XXII.

Conscience Concerned with intellect in regard to right or
wrong of my acts.

CHAPTER VII

DEVELOPMENT TO IDEALISM

The problem of the validity of sense-perception is the crucial problem in modern epistemology. It is the dividing point of the various theories of human knowledge. Depending on their interpretation of the cognitional value of sense-perception, philosophers and scientists have devised the most divergent systems in order to explain the facts so obvious to all. The fundamental facts are admitted. All agree that sensations are real in so far as they are subjective, mental states of the knowing subject: we see colors, hear sounds, taste flavors, smell odors, and feel pressure and resistance, heat and cold, pleasure and pain, muscular and organic conditions. But as to whether the perceived *objects* are *purely intra-mental* and *intra-subjective,* or whether they are *extra-mental* and *extra-subjective,* the interpretations are as far apart as the poles. People in general have the spontaneous conviction that the world which they perceive is *physically real,* with a reality independent of the mind and its perception.

The problem thus arises: Is this spontaneous conviction true and valid? And this proposes further questions: Do our sense-perceptions reveal to the mind an extra-mental and extra-subjective reality? Can the mind transcend itself and contact an external world? Can the physical world (if there be a physical world) become intra-mental through sense-perception, so that the mind can know its existence and nature? How can an extended world make an impression on an unextended mind, and how can an unextended mind conform itself to an extended world?

The problem is by no means so simple as it seems. There are grave difficulties in either view. In order to appreciate the importance of the problem, it will be necessary to review briefly its *origin* and *development* from Descartes up to the present day.

DESCARTES' ULTRA-SPIRITUALISM

Descartes' views on the nature of mind and matter and on the validity of human knowledge have been largely responsible for the widespread confusion in subsequent philosophy and for the rise of numerous theories of knowledge. By means of his methodic doubt he called all accepted truths into question, discarded the validity of all human knowledge, and attempted to place philosophy upon a new foundation. This attempt was futile, but the seed of doubt was sown and produced abundant fruit. It was particularly in the domain of *sense-perception* that the destructive influence of his criticism became apparent. Here is his own line of reasoning concerning the truth-value of sense-perception.

"Merely because I know with certitude that I exist, and because, in the meantime, I do not observe that aught necessarily belongs to my nature or essence beyond my being a thinking being, I rightly conclude that my essence consists only in my being a thinking thing [or a substance whose whole essence or nature is merely thinking]. And although I may, or rather, as I shall shortly say, although I certainly do possess a body with which I am very closely conjoined; nevertheless, because, on the one hand, I have a clear and distinct idea of myself, in as far as I am only a thinking and unextended thing, and as, on the other hand, I possess a distinct idea of body, in as far as it is only an extended and unthinking thing, it is certain that I [that is, my mind, by which I am what I am], is entirely and truly distinct from my body, and may exist without it."[1] "Extension in length, breadth, and depth, constitutes the nature of corporeal substance; and thought the nature of thinking substance. For every other

[1] *Méditations*, VI, *loc. cit.*, p. 157.

thing that can be attributed to body presupposes extension and is only some mode of an extended thing; as all the properties we discover in the mind are only diverse modes of thinking. Thus, for example, we cannot conceive figure unless in something extended, nor motion unless in extended space, nor imagination, sensation, or will, unless in a thinking thing."[2]

Let us pause and digest these principles. The essence of the mind is 'thought,' and thought is 'thinking.' Descartes included in this 'thinking' all intellection, willing, and sense-perception; in short, the essence of 'the mind, by which I am what I am,' consists in the *conscious states*. The Ego, therefore, consists solely in consciousness; the body is outside the Ego. There is, of course, a human body, to which the mind is 'closely conjoined'; but the two do *not* form an *organism* in any way, so that the mind would be a vitalizing principle or agency or soul, making the body-soul compound a living subject capable of sense-perception. All sense-perception takes place in the mind only. The mind is united to the body only in the brain (in the pineal gland, according to Descartes), and all nerve-tremors concentrate in the brain; since, however, the essence of matter is 'extension' and the essence of mind is 'thought,' there can be *no cognitional communication between mind and body*, because the disparity between them is too great. What really happens is that certain 'corporeal movements' of the body reach the brain, and at the *occasion of their presence* the mind produces the ideas or representations of external and extended things entirely in itself and by itself. Ideas are thus potentially *innate*.

That Descartes really meant this is clear beyond a doubt. "I suppose that the body is merely a statue or earthen machine made by God on purpose to resemble us as much as possible. . . . I want you to consider that all the functions which I have attributed to this machine [the human body], such as the digestion of meat, the pulsation of the heart and of the arteries, the nourishment and growth of the limbs, breathing, waking and sleep, seeing, hearing, smell, taste, feeling hot, and any other properties of the external senses; the impression of their ideas upon the organ of the common sense and of the imagination, and the retention or imprinting of these ideas upon the memory; the internal movements of the appetites and passions; and lastly, the external movements of all the members which follow so opportunely the many operations of the things that are presented to the senses as well as the passions and impressions that are to be found in the memory, that they imitate so closely those of a real man — I want you, I say, to consider that *these functions quite naturally follow in this machine from the mere arrangement of the organs, neither more nor less than the movements of a clock or other automaton, from its weights and works,* so that so far as they are concerned we need *not think of any vegetative or sensitive soul in it, or of any other principle of life or motion* than the blood and the spirits continually stirred up by the fire constantly burning in the heart, a fire which does not differ by nature from any other fires to be found in other inanimate bodies."[3]

It is in this manner that Descartes reduced the mind to thought and its activities to states of consciousness, while he reduced all matter (including the human body) to extension and its activities to mechanical motion. This absolute opposition and disparity between mind and matter gives to his philosophy a double characteristic: an *ultra-spiritualistic* interpretation of the mind, and an *ultra-mechanistic* interpretation of the body and of the extra-mental and external world.

The fundamental mistake of Descartes consisted in his arbitrary assumption that the essence of the mind consists in 'thinking' and in 'thinking' *only.* He had no right to restrict

---

[3] *Oeuvres de Descartes,* ed. Cousin, IV, pp. 336, 347–349, *apud* Mercier, *The Origins of Contemporary Psychology* (Kenedy and Sons, New York, 1918, pp. 22–25), (Italics mine. — Author).

the essence of the mind to 'thought.' If the activities of man demand that the Ego possess a living soul united to the body with the triple functions of *vegetation, sentiency,* and *'thinking,'* so that body and soul form a joint living organism together, and if sense-perception cannot be explained except by means of an organic union between mind and body, then Descartes committed an unpardonable error in arbitrarily limiting the essence of the mind to 'thought' alone. When he stated 'I think, therefore I exist,' he expressed a fact which was indubitably true: 'thinking' is a primary experience of the Ego, an evident datum of intuition. But he overlooked the fact that 'thinking' was *not the only primary experience* revealed by consciousness. I am equally conscious that I walk and eat and drink, taste and smell and hear, see and touch; I am conscious that my body has a part in these activities, and that these activities are as real and actual as 'thinking'; and I am also conscious that these activities reveal objects-other-than-self. These are *vital* activities which are also *bodily* and *extended.* What right, then, had Descartes to assume that the body is a mere machine and exclude it from the Ego and its vital functions? This is an arbitrary and one-sided restriction which does violence to the facts recorded by consciousness.

Descartes, of course, defended the dualism of mind and matter, of the world of the Ego and of the world of the non-Ego; but this was an *excessive dualism,* making any interaction between them unintelligible. The theory that soul and body form a unitary organism is the *aristotelian-scholastic* view. This theory had been the traditional doctrine for centuries. In discarding it for his own ultra-dualistic theory, Descartes rendered a doubtful service to philosophy, because the problem of finding an *epistemological bridge* between mind and body now became the crucial problem of modern philosophy. Chaos followed the Cartesian riddle. Since his endeavor to found a philosophy 'without presuppositions,' it became a philosophic dogma that the only certain thing man can know is his own mind and its conscious states.

OCCASIONALISM, ONTOLOGISM

Arnold Geulincx (1625–1669) and *Nicholas Malebranche* (1638–1715) developed the teachings of Descartes. Since there can be no causal interaction between mind and body, the evident co-ordination existing between them can only be the result of God's causality. On the occasion of bodily stimuli, God produces corresponding ideas in the mind; and on the occasion of ideas and volitions in the mind, God produces corresponding motions in the body: creatures are mere instruments of God's action. This is *occasionalism*. Malebranche went a step farther. Instead of Descartes' theory that man acquires his knowledge from innate ideas, he maintained the view that man's mind envisions all things by means of a direct intuition of God's ideas. This theognostic theory is called *ontologism*.

SPINOZISM, MONADISM

Baruch Spinoza (1632–1677) chose a different solution for the problem cast up by Descartes in his arbitrary definition of mind and matter. The latter's definition set up an irreconcilable opposition between the world and the mind. Spinoza attempted to bring them into a higher unity, thereby dissolving all differences between them. He defined 'substance' as that which exists in itself and is conceived by itself, so that it does not need the concept of another in order to be understood. Now, there can be only *one such substance,* as expressed in this definition, and that is the infinite substance, God. This infinite substance has as its *attributes* 'extension' and 'thought.' Considered under the determination of 'extension,' God is nature or matter; considered under the determination of 'thought,' God is the human mind. And thus Descartes' antithesis between mind and matter is resolved in the higher unity of the infinite substance: God and all beings are one in substance. This is *pantheistic monism*. This absolute, metaphysical monism is, of course, the very opposite of Descartes' dualism.

Gottfried W. Leibnitz (1646–1716) sought to equalize the

difference between mind and matter in the opposite direction. The ultimate beings are individual *monads*. Monads are absolutely indivisible; no two are alike; and all possess the 'power of representation.' Each monad in its representation mirrors within itself whatever takes place in all other monads throughout the universe; some do it consciously, like the mind-monads, others unconsciously, like ordinary body-monads. Each monad is thus a little universe, endowed with the attributes of 'extension' and 'thought.' All knowledge is *innate:* the monads are 'windowless.' The knowledge of each monad corresponds with the facts of external reality by means of a *pre-established harmony* which God placed in them. Mind and body, therefore, do not interact, but they are like two clocks running in perfect co-ordination. By thus postulating that all bodies have minds and all minds have bodies (*pan-psychism*), Leibnitz was convinced that he had overcome Descartes' ultra-dualism.[4]

EMPIRICISM, PSYCHOLOGICAL IDEALISM

John Locke (1632–1704) strenuously opposed Descartes' doctrine of innate ideas. All knowledge has its origin in *experience*, in sense-perception. The elements of knowledge are the *ideas*, and Locke explains the idea in the following manner: "It being that term which, I think, serves best to stand for whatever is the *object* of the understanding when a man thinks, I have used it to express whatever is meant by *phantasm, notion, species, or whatever it is which the mind can be employed about in thinking*."[5] Descartes placed all sense-perception in the spiritual mind, thus identifying sense-perception with spiritual activity; Locke here does the reverse, by reducing ideas, at least in part, down to the level of sense-perception (phantasm, species). By thus arbitrarily blurring the nature of the 'idea' so as to include sense-perception, he laid the foundation for *sensism*, where all 'thinking' is nothing but a form of

---

[4] *The Monadology*, tr. by Robert Latta (Oxford University Press, 1925).

[5] *An Essay Concerning Human Understanding*, Introduction; edited by A. C. Fraser (Oxford, 1894), p. 32.

'sensation.' Another important feature of this definition of 'idea' is, that the 'idea' is the *object* of our understanding, instead of the reality of things being the object of our knowledge.

Ideas, according to Locke, are derived from two sources — sense-perception and reflection; and all knowledge is restricted to ideas. "Since the mind, in all its thoughts and reasonings, hath no other immediate object but its own ideas, which it alone does or can contemplate, it is evident that our knowledge is only conversant about them. *Knowledge, then, seems to me to be nothing but the perception of the connection of and agreement, or disagreement and repugnancy of any of our ideas.* In this alone it consists."[6] This means, of course, that we do not really *know objects* or things-in-themselves, but ideas or *conscious states* of the mind; and this is the standpoint of Descartes and idealism. Locke, however, did not deny the existence of material substances, such as bodies, nor of spiritual substances, such as the soul and God; but 'substance' is unknowable to us, whether material or immaterial. "Our idea of substance is equally obscure, or none at all, in both: it is but a supposed I-know-not-what, to support those ideas we call accidents. . . . By the complex idea of extended, figured, colored, and all other *sensible qualities, which is all that we know of it,* we are as far from the idea of the substance of the body, *as if we* knew nothing at all."[7] While Locke, therefore, admits the existence of material and spiritual 'substances,' he asserts that they are unknowable; 'accidents' or 'phenomena' alone are knowable: he is in last instance an *empirical phenomenalist.*

George Berkeley (1685–1753) took issue with Locke. He pointed out the inconsistency of Locke in maintaining that our knowledge is limited to ideas only and then asserting that we have a sense-knowledge of the qualities of extra-mental objects. Berkeley accepted the initial standpoint of Descartes

---

[6]*Essay,* Vol. 2, Bk. IV, Ch. I, p. 167.
[7]*Essay,* Vol. I, Bk. II, Ch. 23, pp. 406–407.

and Locke that 'the mind can know nothing but its own ideas or conscious states'; but from this he drew the conclusion that *all things are ideas* and *a physical world does not exist*. Ideas are the sole 'objects of cognition' for the mind; things, therefore, have 'being' only in so far as they are 'perceived' (*esse est percipi*). Physical things, being outside the mind, cannot be perceived at all; consequently, they are nonexistent.

We observe Berkeley's trend of thought in the following quotations. "It is evident to any one who takes a survey of the *objects of human knowledge,* that they are either *ideas* actually imprinted on the senses; or else such as are perceived by attending to the passions and operations of the mind; or lastly, *ideas* formed by help of memory and imagination. . . . That neither our thoughts, nor passions, nor ideas formed by the imagination, exist without the mind is what everybody will allow. And to me it seems no less evident that the various sensations or ideas imprinted on the Sense, however blended or combined together (that is, whatever objects they compose), cannot exist otherwise than in a mind perceiving them. I think an intuitive knowledge may be obtained of this, by any one that shall attend to what is meant by the term *exist* when applied to sensible things. The table I write on I say exists; that is, I see and feel it: and if I were out of my study I should say it existed; meaning thereby that if I was in my study I might perceive it, or that some other spirit actually does perceive it. There was an odor, that is, it was smelt; there was a sound, that is, it was heard; a color or figure, and it was perceived by sight or touch. This is all that I can understand by these and the like expressions. For as to what is said of the *absolute* existence of unthinking things, without any relation to their being perceived, that is to me perfectly unintelligible. Their *esse* [being] is *percipi* [being perceived]; nor is it possible they should have any existence out of the minds or thinking things which perceive them.

"It is indeed an opinion strangely prevailing amongst men, that houses, mountains, rivers, and in a word all sensible objects, have an existence, natural or real, distinct from their being perceived by the understanding. But, with how great an assurance and acquiescence soever this Principle may be entertained in the world, yet whoever shall find in his heart to call it in question may, if I mistake not, perceive it to involve a manifest contradiction. For, what are the forementioned objects but the things we perceive by sense? and what do we perceive besides our own ideas or sensations? and is it not plainly repugnant that any of these, or any combination of them, should exist unperceived? . . .

"From what has been said it is evident there is not any other Substance than *Spirit,* or that which perceives. But, for the fuller proof of this point, let it be considered the sensible qualities are color, figure, motion, smell, taste, and such like, that is, the ideas perceived by sense. Now, for an idea to exist in an unperceiving thing is a manifest contradiction; for to have an idea is all one has to perceive: that therefore wherein color, figure, and the like qualities exist must perceive them. Hence it is clear there can be no unthinking substance or *substratum* of these ideas."[8]

According to Berkeley, then, physical, external objects have no existence of their own: their *esse* is *percipi*. Locke considered the 'secondary' qualities (color, taste, sound, heat, etc.) to be subjective, but the 'primary' qualities (extension, figure, motion, etc.) were real and objective. Berkeley reduces primary and secondary qualities and *all material things* to 'ideas' whose sole existence consists in 'being perceived': there are no material objects as such. This is *idealistic immaterialism.* The only realities which exist are God and human minds. How then account for our ideas of extra-mental and external objects, like the human body and the physical world? They are not the product of the human mind, they are objectively produced by God in the mind, *as if* there were a real world outside us. Berkeley is a psychological and acosmistic *idealist.*

[8] *Principles of Human Knowledge,* Part I, sections 1–8, ed. by A. C. Fraser (Oxford, 1901), pp. 257–261.

no real objects, independent of our perception of them

PAN-PHENOMENALISM

David Hume (1711–1776) went a step farther. He denied the existence of *all* substances. "I would fain ask those philosophers, who found so much of their reasonings on the distinction of substance and accident, and imagine we have clear ideas of each, whether the idea of *substance* be derived from the impressions of sensations or reflection? If it be conveyed to us by our senses, I ask, which of them; and after what manner? If it be perceived by the eyes, it must be a color; if by the ears, a sound; if by the palate, a taste; and so of the other senses. But I believe none will assert, that substance is either a color, sound, or taste. The idea of substance must therefore be derived from an impression of reflection, if it really exist. But the impressions of reflection resolve themselves into our passions and emotions; none of which can possibly represent a substance. We have therefore no idea of substance, distinct from that of a collection of particular qualities, nor have we any other meaning when we talk or reason concerning it."[9] And thus all substances — physical bodies, soul, God — are argued out of existence. The only things which we know to exist are *phenomena,* and the mind consists of nothing but a heap or collection of different perceptions united by certain relations. This is *pan-phenomenalism* and extreme *subjectivism.* Hume ended as a skeptic.

TRANSCENDENTAL IDEALISM

Emmanuel Kant (1724–1804), alarmed at the trend of thought manifested by the English philosophers, especially Hume, felt the urge to revindicate human knowledge. Like them, however, he took as his starting point the principle of Descartes that the mind of man can know only its own internal states and cannot go outside and beyond the limits of consciousness. He considered it to be the essential error of all

---

[9]*Treatise on Human Nature,* Part I, 6.

previous philosophic systems that they endeavored to make the mind conform to the objects; he would reverse the principle and make the *objects conform to the mind*. "Hitherto it has been supposed that all our knowledge must conform to the objects; but, under that supposition, all attempts to establish anything about them *a priori,* by means of concepts, and thus to enlarge our knowledge, have come to nothing. The experiment therefore ought to be made, whether we should not succeed better with the problems of metaphysic, by assuming that the objects must conform to our mode of cognition, for this would better agree with the demanded possibility of an *a priori* knowledge of them, which is to settle something about objects, before they are given us."[10]

Before entering upon Kant's views on the nature of sense-perception, it will be necessary to understand what he means by *a priori* and *a posteriori knowledge;* this distinction is the basis of his theory.

"It is therefore a question which deserves at least closer investigation, and cannot be disposed of at first sight, whether there exists a *knowledge independent of experience,* and even of all impressions of the senses? Such *knowledge* is called *a priori,* and distinguished from *empirical* knowledge, which has its sources *a posteriori,* that is, in experience. . . ."[11]

There is, then, according to Kant, a double knowledge (and consequently also a double source of knowledge) in the human mind: knowledge *a priori,* independent of all experience; and knowledge *a posteriori,* derived through experience. How can we tell which knowledge is the one and which is the other? Experience can reveal nothing to us except what is *individual* and *contingent;* it never reveals to us anything that is strictly universal and necessary. "Experience teaches us, no doubt, that something is so or so, but not that it cannot be different. . . . Experience never imparts to its judgments true

[10]*Critique of Pure Reason,* tr. by Max Müller (Macmillan Co., 1927), Preface to Second Edition, Suppl. II, p. 693.

[11]*Loc. cit.,* p. 715.

or strict, but only assumed or relative, universality (by means of induction), so that we ought always to say, so far as we have observed hitherto, there is no exception to this or that rule. If, therefore, a judgment is thought with strict universality, so that no exception is admitted as possible, it is not derived from experience, but valid absolutely *a priori*. . . . Necessity, therefore, and strict universality are safe criteria of knowledge *a priori,* and are inseparable one from the other."[12] Whenever, therefore, knowledge is *strictly necessary and universal,* it is *a priori* and cannot have been acquired through experience. Such *a priori* knowledge must proceed directly *from the mind itself.*

There are various *elements* which enter into the making of our empirical knowledge or sense-perception, and Kant is explicit in explaining the process through which our knowledge must be acquired in experience. Here is the process in his own words:

"The effect produced by an object upon the faculty of representation (*Vorstellungsfähigkeit*), so far as we are affected by it, is called sensation (*Empfindung*). An intuition (*Anschauung*) of an object, by means of sensation, is called empirical. The undefined object of such an empirical intuition is called phenomenon (*Erscheinung*).

"In a phenomenon I call that which corresponds to the sensation its *matter;* but that which causes the manifold matter of the phenomenon to be perceived as arranged in a certain order, I call its *form.*

"Now it is clear that it cannot be sensation again through which sensations are arranged and placed in certain forms. The matter only for all phenomena is given us *a posteriori;* but their form must be ready for them in the mind (*Gemüth*) *a priori,* and must therefore be capable of being considered as separate from all sensations. . . . In the course of this investigation it will appear that there are, as principles of *a priori*

[12] *Loc. cit.,* pp. 716, 717.

knowledge, two pure forms of sensuous intuition (*Anschau-ung*), namely, *Space* and *Time*."[13]

Bearing in mind Kant's axiom that nothing necessary and universal can be derived from experience, but must proceed exclusively and *a priori* from the mind itself, Kant finds that sense-perception contains a double element: the 'manifold' of sense impressions, which is derived from experience, and 'space' and 'time,' which are pure forms of the mind. External to the mind there exists a world of things-in-themselves (*Dinge-an-sich*) or noumena; they are real, physical beings. These make impressions on the sense-faculty, and the faculty responds with an 'intuition' or perception. These impressions are un-arranged, chaotic. This chaotic 'manifold' must be arranged in a certain order, and this is done by means of the two sense-forms 'space' and 'time.' Space and time are *in no way attri-butes of the things-in-themselves,*[14] but merely "cause the mani-fold matter of the phenomenon *to be perceived* as arranged in a certain order," i.e., as arranged in the order of 'space' or in the order of 'time.' Since all intuitions or perceptions appear as arranged in a spatial and temporal order, 'space' and 'time' are universal and necessary conditions of sense-perception and as such must exist *a priori* in the mind. They are like mental molds into which the unarranged raw materials of sense are poured, so that, after the molding process of cognition is com-pleted, all phenomena *appear* arranged and molded in 'space' and 'time.' The objects themselves are, so far as we know, spaceless and timeless.

Do we really perceive external objects, so that the objects of sense actually exist, *as we perceive them,* outside our person? We do not. The real objects of the physical world can never be perceived; we know absolutely nothing about the noumena or things-in-themselves: "All our intuition is nothing but the representation of phenomena. . . . Nothing which is seen in space is a thing-in-itself, nor space a form of things supposed

[13]*Loc. cit.,* pp. 16, 17.
[14]*Loc. cit.,* pp. 18–20, 24–28.

to belong to them by themselves, but objects by themselves are not known by us at all, and that what we call external objects are nothing but representations of our senses [phenomena]."[15] All we can know, then, are the *phenomena* or appearances, and these are always subjective in character, without any resemblance to the things-in-themselves. Even man's perception of his own body is thus seen to be only 'phenomenal'; whether any extra-mental reality corresponds to what he perceives to be his 'body,' man can never know. Kant admits the existence of things-in-themselves as the *exciting cause* of sense-perception on the grounds of inference; but they remain an unknown and unknowable X. Kant is thus a *hypothetical realist* and *dualist;* since, however, all our knowledge in sense-perception is limited to intra-subjective phenomena, he is a *transcendental idealist.* He failed to overcome the Cartesian antithesis between mind and matter; the mind remains imprisoned in its conscious states and can know nothing of the external world and non-Ego objects.

ABSOLUTISM

Kant's philosophy left the antithesis between mind and matter, noumenon and phenomenon, the thing-in-itself and the Ego, unsolved; the unity between these opposing elements, so evident in our knowledge, was still unexplained. His followers in idealism attempted to develop his ideas to their logical conclusions.

Johann Fichte (1762–1814) took up Kant's principle that the 'things must conform to the mind' and dissolved the antithesis between the Ego and the 'thing-in-itself' by *identifying all reality with the Ego.* It was his contention that thought cannot be deduced from being, but being must be deduced from thought; *thought,* therefore, *is the ultimate and only reality,* and the laws of thought are the laws of being. And since all thought is contained in consciousness, there is no other

---

[15]*Loc. cit.*, pp. 34, 24.

reality but the *Ego;* hence, all reality is unified in the Ego. The Ego, of course, does not mean merely human consciousness, but the universal consciousness of the Absolute or God. Such is Fichte's system of *Pan-Egoism.*

Friedrich Schelling (1775–1854) propounded a number of theories at variance with each other. His third system is most characteristic of his thought. Like Fichte, he sought a common formula or principle in which mind and matter, spirit and nature, could be harmonized. He also identified the real and the ideal in the *Absolute;* but while Fichte derived them from the 'self-activity' (*Tathandlungen,* deed acts) of the Absolute (Universal Ego), Schelling derived the ideal and the real (subject and object, spirit and nature, mind and thing-in-itself) from the *indeterminateness* of the Absolute. Because the Absolute is 'indeterminate' in its being, it gives rise to the ideal and the real in its development, so that they are but two phases of the ultimate reality which is the Absolute.

Georg Hegel (1770–1831) also identified all things in the Absolute. But with him the Absolute is pure *Thought* or *Idea,* dynamic with immanent activity, not static like Schelling's 'indeterminateness.' Since the Absolute is pure Idea, it evolves by means of a purely *logical and rational process of thought* into the ideal and real, into subject and object, into spirit and nature, into mind and matter. The Absolute is continually in a dialectic evolution, so that all being is thought realized. His system is idealism driven to its highest peak.

It is difficult to compress the vastness of Hegel's system into a brief survey. According to him, all reality is idea, and the laws which govern the development of idea are the identical laws which govern the development of reality. Nature and spirit do not proceed from the Absolute, as Schelling stated, but the Absolute gradually *becomes* nature and spirit in a process of self-actualization. It is the law of development for thought and being (for both are the same) to realize itself by passing from a state of *in-itself* (*an-sich*) through the state of *out-of-*

self (*für-sich,* otherness) into the state of *for-itself* (*an-und-für-sich*). The dialectic or logical movement of evolution thus comprises three stages: the position or *thesis,* the contraposition or *antithesis,* and the identity of position and contraposition or *synthesis;* or, to express it in a different way — affirmation, negation, and the negation of negation.

This self-evolution of the Absolute begins with Being. Being is abstract, indeterminate, empty of all content, and as such it is indistinguishable from Nothing. Here is Hegel's view: "The distinction between Being and Nought is, in the first place, only implicit, and not yet actually made: they only *ought* to be distinguished. A distinction, of course, implies two things, and that one of them possesses an attribute which is not found in the other. Being, however, is an absolute absence of attributes, and so is Nought. Hence, the distinction between the two is only meant to be; it is quite a nominal distinction, which is at the same time no distinction. . . . Nothing, if it is thus immediate and equal to itself, is also conversely the same as Being is. . . . In Being we have Nothing, and in Nothing Being. . . . In Becoming the Being which is one with Nothing, and the Nothing which is one with Being, are only vanishing factors; they are and they are not."[16]

It is *Becoming* that constitutes the all-important process of evolution for Being. "Becoming is the first concrete thought, and therefore the first notion: whereas Being and Nothing are empty abstractions."[17] Through this process of Becoming indeterminate Being becomes 'determinate Being.' Hegel gives the following account of Becoming. "Even our ordinary conception of Becoming implies that somewhat (something) comes out of it, and that Becoming therefore has a result. . . . Becoming always contains Being and Nothing in such a way that these two are always changing into each other, and reciprocally cancel each other. Thus Becoming stands before us in

---

[16] *Logic,* tr. by W. Wallace (Clarendon Press, 1892), §§ 87, 88, 89, pp. 162, 163, 167, 169.

[17] *Ibid.,* § 88, p. 167.

utter restlessnesss — unable, however, to maintain itself in this abstract restlessness: for since Being and Nothing vanish in Becoming (and that is the very notion of Becoming), the latter must vanish. . . . The result of this process, however, is not empty Nothing, but Being identical with the negation — what we call Being Determinate (being then and there): the primary import of which evidently is that it *has become.*"[18]

Since Being is Idea and Idea Being, it is by means of the logical process of Becoming that the Being-Idea gradually and successively passes from a state of indeterminateness to the determinateness of all beings, evolving progressively into nature (the world) and spirit (consciousness), until it finally harmonizes all differences of being in the Absolute Spirit. In this manner Hegel attempts to reduce all unity and plurality, all identity and change, to the supreme self-differentiating unity of the Absolute Idea-Being. Unity essentially involves diversity and self-negation, and it is this 'power of negativity' (*Macht der Negativität*) which is the eternal driving urge of self-evolution in the Absolute.

As the final result of this self-actualization of Being-Idea, all beings and all selves are but modes and manifestations of the Absolute. There is, of course, no creation. All finite things are but the 'expression,' the 'appearance' of the Absolute; the Absolute becomes all things in a process of logical necessity. There is *no thing-in-itself* distinct from the all-inclusive reality of the Absolute. All dualism between thought and thing is obliterated, and man and the world possess no 'otherness' of their own: all is 'thought realized.'

Most philosophers, Descartes and Kant included, maintained the essential dualism of thought and thing, subject and object, mind and matter, spirit and nature, God and world, real and ideal; even though they confused some of these opposites, they upheld the distinction in others. But Fichte, Schelling, Hegel, and their followers, eliminated this dualism and asserted the *one-ness* of all things in the Absolute: they defended the

---

[18]*Ibid.,* § 89, p. 170.

doctrine of *idealistic, pantheistic monism*. In the field of knowledge this involved an *epistemological monism* — the doctrine
of the identity of thought with the object of thought.

The ultra-spiritualistic tendency of Descartes' principles here
reached its ultimate peak of development. Kant and Hegel,
particularly the latter, exerted a tremendous influence on subsequent philosophy. For decades Hegel's idealism held complete
sway. Not to be a Hegelian was, for a long time, a sign of
obscurantism. Eventually, however, some philosophers refused
to follow these thinkers into the speculative clouds of Absolutism and preferred to remain closer to the homely soil of the
earth. A reaction set in toward the more human philosophy
of *realism*.

SUMMARY OF CHAPTER VII

A number of modern theories have arisen in an attempt to
solve the problem of sense-knowledge.

1. *Descartes' Ultra-Spiritualism*. *Descartes* defined the mind
as 'thought' and matter (body) as 'extension.' There is no real
cognitional interaction between mind and body in man, because their disparity is too great; the body is a mere automaton,
and all knowledge is potentially innate in the mind. The mind
can know nothing but its own conscious states.

2. *Occasionalism, Ontologism*. *Geulincx* and *Malebranche*
maintained that God produced all knowledge in the mind on
the occasion of stimuli in the body. Malebranche also defended
the ontologistic view that man's mind has an intuition of God's
ideas and thus comes to know the world outside.

3. *Spinozism, Monadism*. *Spinoza* asserted the one-ness of
mind and matter in the infinite substance of God; this infinite
substance has 'extension' and 'thought,' so that the world and
the mind are but two determinations of God. According to
Leibnitz, the ultimate beings are monads. There is no interaction between monads. All knowledge in monads is innate;
it corresponds with reality, due to a pre-established harmony.

4. *Empiricism, Psychological Idealism*. *Locke* maintained

that all knowledge comes from experience, and it is restricted to conscious states. We can know nothing of material substances. *Berkeley* denied the existence of a physical world; its 'being' is 'being perceived.' He is a psychological and acosmistic idealist.

5. *Pan-Phenomenalism. Hume* denied the existence of all substance. All we can know are phenomena. He was a subjectivist and skeptic.

6. *Transcendental Idealism. Kant* claimed that some elements of our sense-knowledge are *a posteriori,* derived from experience, while others are *a priori,* derived from the mind anterior to all experience. Sense-perception is the result of the empirical element of sensations and the mental element of subjective, innate 'forms.' The noumena or things-in-themselves excite sensations, producing the 'intuition' of an object; the object of this intuition is the *phenomenon.* 'Space' and 'time' are not qualities of bodies; they are *a priori forms* making perception possible by arranging the manifold of sense in the order of extension and succession (space and time). Noumena actually exist, but we can have no knowledge of them; our knowledge is limited to phenomena and as such has only subjective value.

7. *Absolutism. Fichte* endeavored to dissolve the antithesis between mind and matter by identifying all reality with the Ego: thought is the ultimate and only reality. By 'Ego' he means the universal consciousness of the Absolute. *Schelling* also identified the real and the ideal with the Absolute; mind and matter proceed from the indeterminateness of the Absolute, constituting its two phases. *Hegel* substituted 'immanent activity' for the 'indeterminateness' of the Absolute and made the Absolute or Being-Idea evolve by means of a purely logical and rational process of thought into the real (world) and the ideal (mind), synthesizing everything in the Absolute Spirit. Absolutism is pantheistic idealism.

The ultra-spiritualistic principles of Descartes were thus developed into Absolutism.

READINGS

D. C. Macintosh, *The Problem of Knowledge;* D. Card. Mercier, *The Origins of Contemporary Psychology;* D. S. Robinson, *An Anthology of Modern Philosophy;* L. J. Walker, *Theories of Knowledge;* O. Willmann, *Geschichte des Idealismus;* R. W. Sellars, *The Principles and Problems of Philosophy;* W. Turner, *History of Philosophy;* M. F. McDonald, *The Progress of Philosophy;* M. W. Calkins, *The Persistent Problems of Philosophy;* R. F. A. Hoernlé, *Idealism as a Philosophy;* W. E. Hocking, *Types of Philosophy,* Chs. XIX–XXVI.

CHAPTER VIII

RETURN TO REALISM

It was but natural that a reaction would set in against the exaggerated spiritualism of some of Descartes' principles. Locke and Hume insisted strongly on the role of the *senses* in the acquisition of knowledge. After all, it is hard for men, even if they be philosophers, to rid themselves of the conviction that the external world is real and that, somehow, we can and do perceive the world as it is. Later on, the extreme idealism of the transcendentalists also brought about a reaction toward realism.

Locke had opposed the innateness of sense-perception as defended by Descartes, whereby the latter identified it with 'thinking'; but Locke went to the other extreme by debasing 'ideas' more or less to sense-impressions. Hume finished by reducing all ideas to a sense-knowledge of phenomena. Herein lay the seeds of sensism, positivism, and materialism.

Sense-knowledge is the only true & scientific knowledge

SENSISM, POSITIVISM, MATERIALISM

Thomas Hobbes (1588–1679) was a confirmed materialist and sensist. The *Abbé Condillac* (1715–1780) made sensation the sole source of all knowledge, so that all operations of the soul — judgment, reflection, and emotion — are nothing but 'transformations of sensation.' He did not deny the immateriality of the soul, but he considered consciousness itself to be but a form of sensation. Other representatives of the movement were *John S. Mill, Alexander Bain,* and *James Sully.*

Positivism owes its origin to *Auguste Comte* (1798–1857). Positivism identifies knowledge with empirical, *physical science.* We can know nothing but facts and the relations of facts. Only natural phenomena of matter and force, and the

limits our knowledge to things which are known to senses

laws governing them, form the subject matter of positive science, and these alone are the objects of man's knowledge. Sensation is the only source of this knowledge; all else is futility and illusion. Positivism is the philosophic doctrine of many scientists. Modern defenders are: Spencer, Huxley, Tyndall, Congreve, Beesly, Allen, Bridges, Ribot, Ardigo, Laas, and Riehl.

Sensism was bound to end in *materialism*. Its main protagonists were *Karl Vogt* (1817–1895), *Jakob Moleschott* (1822–1893), *Ludwig Büchner* (1824–1899), and *Ernst Haeckel* (1834–1919). The only reality which exists is matter and mechanical motion; the mind is but a form of matter, and knowledge but a form of motion. Descartes' mechanistic interpretation of the human body and its relation to the mind hereby reached its lowest level; it is the extreme opposite of the idealistic pantheism attained in Hegel's philosophy. *Idealistic monism* and *materialistic monism* are the two epistemological poles of modern philosophy, the logical result of Descartes' illfated antithesis between mind and body.

NATURAL REALISM, TRANSFIGURED REALISM

In opposition both to Humian skepticism and Kantian transcendentalism, the Scottish School reverted to *natural realism*. *Thomas Reid* (1710–1796) defended the immediate perception of external things; yet, oddly enough, he asserts that we are not conscious of this perception. James McCosh and T. Case were defenders of a realism very similar to that of Reid.

Sir William Hamilton (1788–1856), though a follower of Reid, was strongly influenced by Kantian ideas and maintained that we can know nothing but the *relative* and *phenomenal*. He accepts "the great axiom that all human knowledge, consequently that all human philosophy, is only of the relative and phenomenal. In this proposition, the term *relative* is opposed to the term *absolute;* and, therefore, in saying that we know only the relative, I virtually assert that we know nothing absolute, — nothing existing absolutely; that is, in itself and for itself, and without relation to us and our faculties. . . . Thus, mind and matter, as known and knowable, are only two different series of phenomena or qualities; mind and matter, as unknown and unknowable, are the two substances in which these two series of phenomena or qualities are supposed to inhere. The existence of an unknown substance is only an inference we are compelled to make, from the existence of known phenomena. . . . Our whole knowledge of mind and matter is thus, as we have said, only relative; of existence, absolutely and in itself, we know nothing."[1] He is, therefore, a reasoned realist, but a relativist and phenomenalist.

Herbert Spencer (1820–1903) was a naturalistic evolutionist. There exists an objective reality which is extra-mental, otherwise we cannot account for the 'persistence' and the 'definite character' of our sense-perceptions. This reality is the cause of our sensations. We cannot, however, go beyond the phenomena of things and know what the ultimate reality is like: the *ultimate reality* in nature is forever *unknown and unknowable*. We know 'that' it is, but we do not know 'what' it is. We think of reality in the terms of God, soul, mind, space, time, matter, motion, force, and similar ideas, but these are only *symbols* of the underlying reality, totally unlike the objects they represent. Spencer is, therefore, a *hypothetical realist* and *dualist,* but also a *phenomenalist.* *restricts all knowledge to a phenomena*

"The reality underlying appearances is totally and forever inconceivable to us."[2] "Ultimate religious ideas and ultimate scientific ideas, alike turn out to be merely symbols of the actual, not cognitions of it. . . . The reality existing behind all appearances is, and must ever be, unknown."[3] "Admitting, or rather asserting, that knowledge is limited to the phenomenal, we have, by implication, asserted that the sphere of knowable is co-extensive with the phenomenal — co-extensive

[1]*Lectures on Metaphysics,* ed. by H. Mansel and J. Veitch, 1859, Lec. VIII, pp. 96, 97.
[2]*First Principles* (New York: Appleton and Co., 1883), Part I, Ch. V, p. 98. The entire first Part of this book treats of the Unknowable.
[3]*Op. cit.,* Part I, Ch. IV, pp. 68, 69.

with all modes of the Unknowable that can affect consciousness."[4]

"Though Space, Time, Matter, and Motion are apparently
all necessary data of intelligence, yet a psychological analysis
. . . shows us that these are either built up of, or abstracted
from, experiences of Force. . . . Force, as we know it, can be
regarded only as a certain conditioned effect of the Unconditioned Cause — as the *relative reality* indicating to us an Absolute Reality by which it is immediately produced. And here,
indeed, we see even more clearly than before, how inevitable
is that *transfigured realism* to which skeptical criticism finally
brings us around."[5] And thus, the ultimate data of our knowledge are effects (phenomena) produced in our consciousness
by some unknown cause (noumenon); the phenomena are the
'symbols' of this unknown ultimate reality, but the 'symbols'
give us no likeness whatever of the things-in-themselves. This
is an *agnostic idealism,* similar to Kant's, but without Kant's
'mental forms.'

POST-KANTIAN REALISTIC TRENDS

Kant was not able to overcome Hume's agnosticism. Since
the outcome of his philosophy was that we can know only
phenomena but never the noumena (things-in-themselves), his
agnosticism was as pronounced as Hume's. He indeed admitted the existence of things-in-themselves, but that was a
mere postulate, an assumption. Some of his followers, dissatis-
fied with this conclusion, attempted to bridge the gap between
phenomena and noumena. They desired to show that we
could acquire *some* knowledge of *what* the thing-in-itself
really is. Prominent among these are *F. H. Jacobi* (1743–1819),
J. F. Fries (1773–1843), *J. F. Herbart* (1776–1841), *E. Husserl,* and *A. Meinong.*

Jacobi claimed that we can attain to a knowledge of supra-

---

[4] *Op. cit.,* Part II, Ch. XII, p. 278.
[5] *Op. cit.,* Part II, Ch. III, pp. 169, 170. (Italics mine. — Author.)

sensible reality, such as God and the soul, by means of a rational intuition of faith (*Gefühlsglaube*). Fries maintained that we have a 'presentment' (*Ahnung*) of the suprasensible in the sensible. Herbart looked for a speculative knowledge of the thing-in-itself in a rational criticism of the phenomena. If we analyze the Ego and the thing-in-itself we arrive at a multiplicity of 'reals' (*Realen*). Ultimately, therefore, nature consists of 'reals'; they are somewhat similar to the Leibnitzian monads, but they possess no power of representation and they have no activity except the power of self-preservation. While we have no experience of these 'reals,' the presence of phenomena prove their existence. Herbart's realism represents an approach to modern realistic philosophy. Husserl's and Meinong's 'objects' are not existential, but rather logical realities. These thinkers could not break through the phenomenalism of Kant; their doctrines form a system of logical realism which is at bottom a disguised logical idealism. However, their views greatly influenced contemporary realists.

NEO-ABSOLUTISM

Kant, while an idealist, maintained the essential difference between phenomena (appearances) and noumena (things-in-themselves), as distinct parts in our universe; he was a hypothetical dualist. Fichte, Schelling, and Hegel removed this essential difference between the 'subject' and 'object' in knowledge and made both *immanent* within knowledge, thereby identifying both 'subject' and 'object,' mind and universe, in a common and single ground, the Absolute. The Absolute is an Organic Whole, a Unity-in-Difference, absorbing and harmonizing all reality. Such is the idea underlying Hegelian Absolutism.

A. Schopenhauer (1788–1860) and *E. von Hartmann* (1842–1906) conceived the Absolute in a different manner. Schopenhauer was a voluntarist. Instead of the Idea being the ultimate root of all reality, it is the Will. It is as much the Absolute as Fichte's Ego and Hegel's Being-Idea. The universe is but an objectification of the Will, and the essence of the world consists in a blind impulse, an unconscious, irrational striving of the Absolute Will in an eternal struggle for existence.[6] Von Hartmann attempted a reconciliation of Hegel's idealism and Schopenhauer's voluntarism. The Absolute is the Will, but it is guided by ideas; since, however, it is not aware of this, it is unconscious. The Absolute, therefore, is the Unconscious.[7]

Neo-Hegelians subscribe to the general principles of Hegel; they differ, however, in their methods of approach and in minor points of doctrine. It is characteristic of these philosophers that they approach their problem through *experience* rather than by means of aprioristic speculations.

F. H. Bradley, for instance, begins with the obvious data of the qualities of bodies and attempts to show that they are unreal. He then takes substance and accident, relation and quality, space and time, motion and change, causation and activity, things and self, and comes to the general conclusion that our ideas of their nature are 'unintelligible,' self-contradictory, and full of inconsistencies. As far as we know the universe, it is a mass of contradictions and appearances. But these appearances must be a qualification of reality in some way, and the contradictions must be overcome in a higher unity. This is done in the Absolute. "Everything phenomenal is somehow real; and the absolute must at least be as rich as the relative. And, further, the Absolute is not many; there are no independent reals. The universe is one in this sense that its differences exist harmoniously within one whole, beyond which there is nothing. Hence the Absolute is, so far, an individual and a system. . . . The Absolute is one system, and *its contents are nothing but sentient experience.* It will hence be a single and all-inclusive experience, which embraces every partial diversity in concord. For it cannot be less than appearance, and hence no feeling or thought, of any kind, can fall outside its

---

[6]*The World as Will and Idea,* tr. by R. B. Haldane and J. Kemp (Kegan Paul, Trench, Trübner and Co.).

[7]*Philosophy of the Unconscious,* tr. by W. C. Coupland (Macmillan, 1884).

limits."[8] "The Absolute is not personal, nor is it moral, nor is it beautiful or true. . . . The Absolute stands above, and not below, its internal distinctions. It does not eject them, but it includes them as elements in its fulness. To speak in other language, it is not the indifference but the concrete identity of all extremes. But it is better in this connection to call it super-personal."[9]

According to *T. H. Green,* "the terms 'real' and 'objective' have no meaning except for a consciousness which presents its experiences to itself as determined by relations, and at the same time conceives a single and unalterable order of relations determining them. . . . When we analyze our ideas of matter of fact, can we express it except as an idea of a relation which is always the same between the same objects; or our idea of an object except as that which is always the same in the same relation? And does not each expression imply the idea of a world as a single and eternal system of related elements, which may be related with endless diversity but must *be* related still? If we may properly call the consciousness which yields this idea 'understanding,' are we not entitled to say that understanding is the source of there being for us an objective world, that it is the principle of objectivity?"[10] "The concrete whole, which may be described indifferently as an eternal intelligence realized in the related facts of the world, or as a system of related facts rendered possible by such an intelligence, *partially and gradually reproduces itself in us,* communicating piece-meal, but in inseparable correlation, understanding and the facts understood, experience and the experienced world."[11] And thus the knowing subject and the known object, the ideal and the real, the self and the world, are but the distinct realizations of the 'eternal intelligence,' or Absolute, reproducing itself in finite forms.

---

[8]*Appearance and Reality* (Macmillan Co., 1893), Ch. XIV, pp. 144, 146. (Italics mine. — Author.)

[9]*Op. cit.,* Ch. XXVII, p. 533.

[10]*Prolegomena to Ethics,* §§ 13, 14 (Clarendon Press, Oxford: 1884).

[11]*Ibid.,* § 36. (Italics mine. — Author.)

Other philosophers, who belong more or less to this class, are W. Wallace, J. H. Stirling, J. Caird, E. Caird, J. Watson, J. Royce, B. Bosanquet, A. E. Taylor, W. E. Hocking, W. T. Harris, B. Croce, G. Gentile, J. A. Leighton, M. W. Calkins, A. S. Pringle-Pattison, R. F. A. Hoernlé, F. Paulsen, W. Windelband, H. Rickert, H. Münsterberg, F. Münch, H. Cohen, P. Natorp, E. Cassirer.

NEO-PSYCHOLOGISM

Neo-Psychologism is the outcome of a closer union between empirical science and psychology. Psychological idealism maintains in general that things depend for their existence on being perceived by the mind or in consciousness; their 'being' is 'being perceived,' and they are, therefore, non-existent except as 'ideas.' Berkeley and Hume were exponents of this doctrine. The neo-psychologists, however, are influenced by other systems of thought, which modify the general theory. Neo-psychologism attempts to bridge the gap between mind and matter by applying the principles of empirical science to consciousness; it thus represents a step away from idealism and *an approach toward realism.*

According to *J. H. Poincaré,* all external objects are but sensation-complexes united together by relations. Since we can only think of thoughts, thought is all that exists, and all that is not thought is pure nothingness. Later on his tendency was more toward realism. To *E. Mach* the Ego is a mass of sensations in coherence; bodies are groups of sensations; there are no material realities corresponding to our ideas of objects like atoms and molecules; everything is at the same time physical and psychical, so that there is no fundamental difference between the 'real' and the 'experience.' *R. Avenarius,* in his 'empirio-criticism,' also assumes as his starting point the principle that nothing exists save experience. All our perceptions are subjective; they do not reveal to us the external objects themselves. Logically his principles lead to subjectivism and materialism.

W. Wundt, in his 'ideal-realism,' takes a stand midway between idealism and realism; as a scientist he leaned toward realism, and as a Kantian he could not free himself from idealism. His 'theory of actuality' denies the existence of all substance: "The contents of psychological experience should be regarded as an *interconnection of processes*. This concept of *process* excludes the attribution of an objective and more or less permanent character to the content of psychical experience. Psychical facts are *occurrences,* not objects."[12] The concept of 'mind-substance' has no value except to satisfy "a mythological and metaphysical need."[13] There is nothing but a manifold of interrelated occurrences, an inner (psychical) and outer (physical) experience. This is the system of a *psycho-physical parallelism.*

There is no completely uniform body of doctrine among any set of idealists. However, the general trend of their ideas warrants the placing of the following thinkers in this group: W. K. Clifford, Karl Pearson, H. R. Marshall, G. S. Fullerton, S. H. Hodgson, J. H. Muirhead, D. G. Ritchie, J. Petzoldt, T. Lipps, H. Vaihinger, A. Fouillée, H. Bergson, C. Renouvier.

PERSONALISM

A new philosophic movement is coming to the front in our day. It is closely allied to classic idealism, yet seeks to avoid the absolutistic implications of the latter. In general, it is more voluntaristic than intellectualistic, and it is more in accord with the traditional idea of God than with the pantheistic notion of the Absolute. There are in it, however, many odd and conflicting elements, which time will have to sift and eliminate, before it can reach a final stage of clarification.

Some forms of personalism are *non-typical* and hardly deserve the name. The personalism of J. M. E. McTaggart (1866–1925) is atheistic; that of Wilhelm Stern is pantheistic; that of C. Renouvier (1815–1903) is relativistic; that of E. Caird, J. Royce, and Sir Henry Jones is absolutistic; and that of G.

---

[12]*Outlines of Psychology,* tr. by C. H. Judd (1897), Introd., § 2, n. 9, p. 14.
[13]*Loc. cit.,* § 22, n. 4, p. 312.

W. Howison, W. Vatke, and H. W. Carr is teleological (i.e., God is not the First Cause or creator of the universe, but its Final Cause or goal).

Typical personalism is theistic; it accepts a *personal God* and seeks the ultimate explanation of all things in Him. From this standpoint it differs radically from the non-typical forms of personalism just mentioned. God is the creator of the universe, and this point distinguishes personalism from the systems of Spinozism and Hegelianism. In epistemology it favors dualism rather than monism; there is a real distinction between thought and thing. Personalism, on the other hand, contends that whatever is ontologically real can be found only in personality. Personalism is also more voluntaristic than traditional theism. The will counts more than the intellect. A cogent rational demonstration of God's existence is impossible; our acceptance of His existence rests ultimately on faith, not on reason. And faith, not reason, is the foundation of all philosophy. The reality of the soul or self as a 'person' is of the very essence of personalism; but the soul is, as a rule, considered to be rather a 'power of action' than a real substance. Most personalists lean toward occasionalism.

Albert C. Knudson gives the following definition of personalism: "We may define personalism as that form of idealism which gives equal recognition to both the pluralistic and monistic aspects of experience and which finds in the conscious unity, identity, and free activity of personality the key to the nature of reality and the solution of the ultimate problems of philosophy."[14] Among the main representatives of the philosophy of personalism Knudson mentions *H. Lotze* (1815–1881), A. C. Fraser (1819–1914), J. Ward (1843–1925), A. J. Balfour, A. S. Pringle-Pattison, J. C. Wilson (1849–1915), H. Rashdall (1858–1924), W. R. Sorley, C. C. Webb, R. Eucken (1846–1926), G. T. Ladd (1842–1921), and *Borden P. Bowne*

---

[14]*The Philosophy of Personalism* (New York: Abington Press, 1927), p. 87.

(1847–1910). Of these, Bowne is undoubtedly the most out-standing proponent of the new philosophy.

From the above it will be clear that personalism is far from being a definitely finished and cohesive system. Bowne has this to say of himself: "It is hard to classify me with accuracy. I am a theistic idealist, a Personalist, a transcendental empiricist, and idealistic realist, and a realistic idealist; but all these phrases need to be interpreted. They cannot well be made out from the dictionary. Neither can I well be called a disciple of any-one. I largely agree with Lotze, but I transcend him. I hold half of Kant's system, but sharply dissent from the rest. There is a strong smack of Berkeley's philosophy, with a complete rejection of his theory of knowledge. I am a *Personalist,* the first of the clan in any thoroughgoing sense."[15] Bowne was the systematizer of personalism. He improved on Lotze by intro-ducing "as an essential and controlling factor the thought of *free* self-activity. . . . Bowne made freedom the touchstone of reality."[16] Personalism, it seems, may be destined to help some devotees of idealism find their way back to theism.

---

[15]From a letter dated May 31, 1909, and printed in *The Personalist,* 1921, p. 10; quoted by Knudson, *loc. cit.,* p. 16.

[16]Knudson, *loc. cit.,* p. 433. Other pertinent literature: Renouvier, *Le Personal-lisme,* 1903; Stern, *Person und Sache,* 1906; Bowne, *Philosophy of Theism,* 1887, *Theism,* 1902, *The Immanence of God,* 1905, *Personalism,* 1908; Rashdall, *Per-sonality, Human and Divine,* Oxford Essays, 1902; McTaggart, *The Value and Destiny of the Individual,* 1913; E. Caird, *Evolution of Religion,* 1892; Royce, *The Conception of God,* 1897; *The World and the Individual,* 1901; Jones, *A Faith that Enquires,* 1922; Hocking, *The Meaning of God in Human Experience,* 1912; Fraser, *Philosophy of Theism,* Gifford Lectures, 1894–95, 1895–96; Ward, *Naturalism and Agnosticism,* 1899, *The Realm of Ends,* 1912; Balfour, *Theism and Humanism,* 1915, *Theism and Thought,* 1923; Pringle-Pattison, *Hegelianism and Personality,* 1887, *The Idea of God,* 1917, *The Idea of Immortality,* 1922; J. Wilson, *Statement and Inference,* 1926; Rashdall, *Philosophy and Religion,* 1910; Sorley, *Moral Values and the Idea of God,* 1910; Webb, *God and Personality,* 1918, *Divine Personality and Human Life,* 1920; Eucken, *Life's Basis and Life's Ideal,* etc.; Ladd, *Philosophy of Knowledge,* 1897; *Theory of Reality,* 1899; H. Lotze, *Microcosmus,* 1885.

PRAGMATISM, HUMANISM

Pragmatism and humanism are a strong repudiation of Kantian rationalism and Hegelian absolutism. They propose to take man down from the clouds of intellectual abstraction, from the "supercelestial heavens of Pure Reason," and it is their "avowed aim of *humanizing* Truth and bringing it back to earth from such altitudes."[17] Pragmatism originated as a modern theory of knowledge with *Charles S. Peirce* in 1878, and its chief exponents are *William James, F. C. S. Schiller,* and *John Dewey.* Pragmatism and humanism are so closely akin that they can be considered one, the latter being an extension and an expansion of the former. Schiller explains the relation between the two: "Pragmatism will seem a special application of humanism to the theory of knowledge. But humanism will seem more universal. It will seem to be possessed of a method which is applicable universally, to ethics, to aesthetics, to metaphysics, to theology, to every concern of man, as well as to the theory of knowledge."[18] Both are therefore identical in principle and are more or less interchangeable terms.

Pragmatism is a return *to empiricism* and a protest *against apriorism.* As James puts it: "Pragmatism represents a perfectly familiar attitude in philosophy, the empiricist attitude, but it represents it, as it seems to me, both in a more radical and in a less objectionable form than it has ever yet assumed. A pragmatist turns his back resolutely and once for all upon a lot of inveterate habits dear to professional philosophers. He turns away from abstraction and insufficiency, from verbal solutions, from bad *a priori* reasons, from fixed principles, closed systems, and pretended absolutes and origins. He turns towards concreteness and adequacy, towards facts, towards action and towards power. That means the empiricist temper regnant and the rationalist temper sincerely given up. It means the open air and possibilities of nature as against dogma, artificiality, and

---

[17] F. C. S. Schiller, *Studies in Humanism* (Macmillan Co., 1907), Preface.
[18] *Loc. cit.,* p. 16.

Pragmatism — works for the benefit of mankind

the pretence of finality in truth. At the same time it does not stand for any special results. It is a method only. . . . Being nothing essentially new, it harmonizes with many ancient philosophic tendencies. It agrees with nominalism for instance, in always appealing to particulars; with utilitarianism in emphasizing practical aspects; with positivism in its disdain for verbal solutions, useless questions and metaphysical abstractions. . . . No particular results then, so far, but only an attitude of orientation, is what the pragmatic method means. *The attitude of looking away from first things, principles, 'categories,' supposed necessities; and of looking towards last things, fruits, consequences, facts."*[19]

The truth is 'made' by means of postulate and experiment, so that something is 'true' if it satisfies some human need of ours and 'false' if it does not. "Pragmatism," says Schiller, "essays to trace the actual 'making of truth,' the actual ways in which discriminations between the true and the false are effected, and derives from these its generalizations about the method of determining the nature of truth. It is from such empirical observations that it derives its doctrine that when an assertion claims truth, *its consequences are always used to test its claim.* In other words, what follows from its truth for any human interest, and more particularly in the first place, for the interest with which it is directly concerned, is what establishes its *real* truth and validity. . . . Human interest, then, is vital to the existence of truth: to say that a truth has consequences and that what has none is meaningless, means that it has a bearing upon some human interest. Its 'consequences' must be consequences to some one for some purpose."[20]

Truth is nothing permanent, necessary, universal, objective, absolute; it is relative, transient, particular, subjective, *personal.* If an idea, judgment, assumption, axiom, postulate, theory, or system of thought 'works' and satisfies our mental or emotional

---

[19] *Pragmatism* (Longmans, Green and Co., 1907), pp. 51 ff.
[20] *Studies in Humanism*, pp. 4–6.

or social needs, *it is so far and so long as it does this,* valuable and 'true.'

"*True ideas are those that we can assimilate, validate, corroborate and verify. False ideas are those that we cannot.* That is the practical difference it makes to us to have true ideas; that, therefore, is the meaning of truth, for it is all that truth is known as.

"This thesis is what I have to defend. The truth of an idea is not a stagnant property inherent in it. Truth *happens* to an idea. It *becomes* true, is *made* true by events. Its verity *is* in fact an event, a process: the process namely of its verifying itself, its veri-*fication.* Its validity is the process of its valid-*ation.*"[21]

John Dewey stressed the *instrumentalism* of knowledge. Thinking is a biological function; consequently ideas are only instruments for interpreting and arranging experience, and the mind is only an instrument for controlling the environment. The theory is an application of the principle of evolution to the function of thought.[22]

Henri Bergson, though actually a vitalistic idealist in his general doctrine, must be placed among the pragmatists so far as his *intuitionism* is concerned. Evolution has developed consciousness in two opposing directions: intellect and intuition. "Intelligence, by means of science, which is its work, will deliver up to us more and more completely the secret of physical operation. . . . But it is to the very inwardness of life that *intuition* leads us — by intuition I mean instinct that has become disinterested, self-conscious, capable of reflecting upon its object and of enlarging it indefinitely."[23] The intellect can give us only static pictures, 'snapshots,' 'cinematographical views,' of reality. Reality is in a process of perpetual change;

---

[21] James, *Pragmatism* (Longmans, Green, 1907), pp. 200–202.

[22] See his *Studies in Logical Theory* (Univ. of Chicago Press, 1903); *How We Think* (Heath Co., Boston, 1910); *Essays in Experimental Logic* (Univ. of Chicago Press, 1916); *Certainty* (Minton, Balch Co., 1929).

[23] *Creative Evolution*, tr. by A. Mitchell (New York: 1923), p. 176. By permission of Henry Holt and Co., publisher.

knowledge, therefore, is forever in the making, and it is intuition which reveals to us the inner nature of reality. "On our personality, on our liberty, on the place we occupy in the whole of nature, on our origin and perhaps also on our destiny, it throws a light feeble and vacillating, but which none the less pierces the darkness of the night in which the intellect leaves us."[24] Intuition is better than intellect.

Hans Vaihinger defends a theory of *fictionalism*. All concepts are fictions of the mind; they have a certain amount of fictional value as mental constructions of reality, but though they 'work' in this respect they need not be true in themselves. Concepts are only means toward the end of adapting ourselves to our environment; as such they possess only a provisional character.[25]

Another offshoot of pragmatic thought is the *imaginism* of *Douglas Fawcett* and a few others. Along lines similar to the universal consciousness of idealists, Fawcett considers 'imagination' to be the creative force of all reality. This cosmic imagining is a conscious infinite activity. Human thought is purely instrumental, necessary for adjustment to environmental conditions.[26]

J. M. Baldwin advocates an esthetic pragmatism, which he calls *pancalism. Maurice Blondel,* one of the founders of modernism, propounds a form of religious pragmatism. *E. LeRoy* combines religious pragmatism with Bergsonian philosophy; scientific laws are mere instruments of practical life, not true expressions of reality.

A number of pragmatists have expressed their views conjointly in a volume, applying the doctrine to various departments of knowledge. The authors are: J. Dewey, A. W. Moore, H. C. Brown, G. H. Mead, H. W. Stuart, J. H. Tufts, H. M. Kallen, B. H. Bode. The book is entitled *Creative Intelligence.*[27]

---

[24]*Loc. cit.,* p. 268.
[25]*Philosophy of As If* ('*Als Ob'*), tr. by C. K. Ogden (Harcourt, Brace, 1924).
[26]See *Imaginism,* in *Contemporary British Philosophy* (Macmillan), 2nd Series, p. 93.
[27]*Creative Intelligence* (Holt and Co., 1917).

NEO-REALISM

In 1910 there appeared the 'Program and First Platform of Six Realists,' and in 1912 these six collaborators published their views in a joint volume, *The New Realism*.[28] The authors were *Edwin B. Holt, Walter T. Marvin, Will. P. Montague, Ralph B. Perry, Walter B. Pitkin,* and *Edward G. Spaulding.* Though they disagree in details, their fundamental tenets are the same.

The essential issue of this new realism is outlined as follows: "The escape from subjectivism and the formulation of an alternative that shall be both remedial and positively fruitful, constitutes the central preëminent issue of any realistic protagonist. . . . The new realists' relational theory is in essentials very old. To understand its meaning it is necessary to go back beyond Kant, beyond Berkeley, beyond even Locke and Descartes — far back to that primordial common-sense which believes in *a world that exists independently of the knowing of it,* but believes also that that same independent world can be *directly presented* in consciousness and not merely represented or copied by 'ideas.' In short, the new realism is, broadly speaking, a return to naïve or natural realism."[29]

In their endeavor, though, to avoid subjectivism and exaggerated dualism, the neo-realists have gone to the opposite extreme. Instead of identifying external, material objects with the conscious states of the knowing mind, they practically identify mind, consciousness, and Ego with these objects. There are no substances. "I believe," says Holt, "that no knower, or Ego, such as metaphysics means, exists."[30] The world is a four-dimensional (spatio-temporal) manifold of 'quality-groups.'[31] This is, of course, very much like Hume's phenomenalism. Perry is in accord with this view: "Modern realism is closer to the monistic realism of 'ideas,' suggested by Hume, than to the

---

[28]*The New Realism* (Macmillan, 1912).
[29]*Loc. cit.,* p. 10. (Italics mine. — Author.)
[30]*Loc. cit.,* p. 366.
[31]*Loc. cit.,* p. 263.

dualistic realism of mind and matter, propounded by the Scottish School; and this in spite of the fact that the Scottish philosophy was primarily a polemic, in the name of 'realism,' against Hume, as the last and most outrageous of the idealists. The new realism, while it insists, as all realism must, that things are *independent,* asserts that when things are known, they *are* ideas in the mind. They may enter *directly into* the mind; and when they do, they become what are called 'ideas.' So that ideas are only things in a certain relation; or, things, in respect of being known, are ideas."[32] " 'Epistemological monism' means that when perceived, things are directly and identically present in consciousness."[33]

How can things be directly and identically present in consciousness? Because consciousness is really identical with the things themselves in nature. As Perry expresses himself: "The difference between knowledge and things, like that between mind and body, is a relational and functional difference, and not a difference of content."[34] Or, as Holt puts it: "We have become wedded or indeed welded to the phrase — my thought is of an object, when we ought to say and mean — my thought is a portion of the object — or better still, — a portion of the object is my thought: — exactly as a portion of the sky is the zenith."[35] The 'mind' is identical with the nervous system, and 'thinking' is a function of it. The mind is thus eliminated as a distinct entity and with it the 'knower'; all that remains is the 'object' and the process of 'knowing.' Knowing, therefore, and consequently also 'consciousness,' must be a relation or modification of the objects themselves.[36] Montague calls this doctrine *hylopsychism* and explains: "By hylopsychism I wish to denote the theory that all matter is instinct with something of the cognitive function."[37] Since all matter is thus 'instinct

---

[32]*Present Philosophical Tendencies* (Longmans, Green and Co., 1912), p. 307.
[33]*The New Realism,* p. 143.
[34]*Present Philosophical Tendencies,* p. 312.
[35]*The Concept of Consciousness* (Macmillan, 1914), p. 149.
[36]*The New Realism,* pp. 353–355.
[37]*Loc. cit.,* p. 283.

with something of the cognitive function,' it is obvious that the psychical and physical, mind and matter, are ultimately the same reality. And since the neo-realists always insist that the material objects are real, it follows that mind is reduced to matter. This is plain phenomenalistic materialism. The 'epistemological monism' of neo-realism thus ends in *materialistic monism*.

Not all neo-realists subscribe to all the views outlined above. The English neo-realists, like *G. E. Moore, B. Russell, S. Alexander, T. Nunn,* and others, are somewhat more conservative. Within the general framework of this epistemological monism they differ very much among themselves. Since, however, all seem to agree that consciousness is merely a modification of the objects themselves, neo-realism is *pan-objectivism*.

skip CRITICAL REALISM

As in the case of neo-realism, a group of 'programmists' launched critical realism in 1916 — *D. Drake, A. O. Lovejoy, J. B. Pratt, A. Rogers, G. Santayana, R. W. Sellars,* and *C. A. Strong.* In opposition to idealism and subjectivism they all maintain the existential independence of physical objects from consciousness and the mind. They all agree, however, that the secondary qualities of colors, sounds, and the like, are not present in the objects as they appear in perception; they are subjective, though causally produced by external objects in the organism. Their treatment of the primary qualities of extension, motion, and so on, is not so clear and uniform.

Since the fundamental trend of critical realism is *materialistic* and *evolutionary,* mind and consciousness are ultimately reducible to 'brain-events' and to a 'functional variant' of the nervous system.[38] Drake believes in *pan-psychism:* "The term 'pan-psychism' may properly be applied to our theory; but we must understand that it is only mind-*stuff* that is universal, not

---

[38]R. W. Sellars, *Critical Realism* (Rand, McNally and Co., 1916), pp. 247, 252, 253.

mind itself. The attribution of quasi-human forms of conscious-ness to the inorganic world is poetic and fanciful, not at all an implication of our view. The whole world is indeed, in a sense, alive. But it does not know itself to be alive. . . . We are therefore free to believe that the *stuff* that is deployed in this or that order throughout the universe is the same sort of stuff that composes *us,* sentient beings that we are. . . . Our theory puts an end to the need of introducing such magical entities as 'souls' or 'entelechies,' and (as we shall see) explains conscious-ness in natural terms."[39]

In describing the process of sense-perception, critical realists use a terminology of their own. The elements involved are thus described by Strong: "By 'object' I mean the real thing, existing in one continuous space and one continuous time. An 'essence' is anything that can be given, whether to sense-percep-tion or to thought, considered not as given but simply in itself. A 'datum' is an essence considered as given. 'Consciousness' is the function by which things are given — i.e., the same as 'awareness' or 'givenness.' The 'Ego,' or 'self,' is the being (located in or the substance of the organism) to which things are given. By 'psychic state,' finally, I mean the concrete state of the self which makes it possible for things to be given, or a similar state. . . . Of these the two most important are (1) that what is given in sense-perception is not the object as an existence, but only the object as an essence, (2) that in addition to the essence no givenness is given. So that, on both grounds, the datum of sense-perception is a bare essence."[40]

To understand what Strong means by the term 'essence,' we must go to Santayana, who introduced it into epistemology as a factor in sense-perception. It is "a universal, of any degree of complexity and definition, which may be given immediately, whether to sense or to thought. Only universals have logical or aesthetic individuality, or can be given directly, clearly, and

[39]*Mind and Its Place in Nature* (Macmillan, 1925), pp. 99, 100.
[40]*The Origin of Consciousness* (Macmillan, 1918), pp. 35, 36.

all at once."[41] "That which appears, when all gratuitous implications of a world beyond or of a self here are discarded, will be an *essence*."[42] "The inalienable individuality of each essence renders it universal; for being perfectly self-contained and real only by virtue of its intrinsic character, it contains no reference to any setting in space or time, and stands in no adventitious relations to anything. . . . After things lose their existence, or before they attain it, although it is true of them that they have existed or will exist, they have no internal being except their essences, quite as if they had never broached Existence at all: yet the identity of each essence with itself and difference from every other essence suffices to distinguish and define them all in eternity, where they form the Realm of Essence."[43] "The realm of essence, like the empyrean, is a clear and tranquil region when you once reach it."[44]

From all these characterizations of Santayana it is clear that "essence" is very much like the Universal Idea of Plato — a logical, ideal entity, which may or may not be embodied in physical things. This idea has been taken over into epistemology by the critical realists, though not always in this pure form. Strong, for instance, calls the 'datum' of sense-perception "the logical essence of the real thing. By 'essence' I mean its *what* divorced from its *that* — its entire concrete nature, including its sensible character, but not its existence."[45] But Lovejoy is opposed to these essences as 'universals,' when applied to physical 'reals' (objects), at least in the meaning that the senses can perceive these essences themselves.[46] Drake explains the matter this way: "Anything that *could* be imagined, or that might exist, any describable somewhat, is an 'essence.' . . . Every particular existent is the existential embodiment of some particular essence. . . . These ideas, essences, characters, logical

[41]*Essays in Critical Realism* (Macmillan, 1920), p. 168, footnote.

[42]*The Realm of Essence* (Scribners, 1927), p. 2.

[43]*Loc. cit.*, pp. 18–25.

[44]*Loc. cit.*, p. 26.

[45]*Essays in Critical Realism*, p. 223.

[46]*The Revolt Against Dualism* (Norton and Co., 1930), p. 114.

entities, are merely possibilities of existence, and possibilities of discourse."[47]

Though the critical realists differ in their interpretation of the term 'essence,' they all agree that the 'datum,' or 'essence,' or 'content,' or 'thing-experience,' or 'character' (the terms mean the same thing), is the only thing which is *intuited* in perception. The *physical object itself is never perceived directly*. After all, then, the 'datum' is only a *symbol* of reality, and no one can be certain that the symbol adequately reveals the reality symbolized. Critical realism at best is a disguised form of *representative realism*.

EMERGENT EVOLUTION

Modern theories of realism are conjoined, as a rule, with the theory of evolution. From this combination there has arisen a new doctrine of realism, called evolutionary naturalism or *emergent evolution*. The basic idea is that nature is the product of evolution in such a manner that *entirely new* and *unpredictable properties* originate through synthesis and thereby form new and *higher levels of reality*. These new properties are not mere 'resultants' obtained by addition or subtraction from among previously existing properties; rather, these new properties have no counterpart in the lower levels and simply 'emerge' with specific characters not discoverable in the former (lower) levels.[48] W. McDougall characterizes emergence as follows: "It is claimed that each instance of emergence is creative of real novelty, of some new quality or property of a type that did not exist before the emergence; that it is unpredictable before the event on the basis of any knowledge, no matter how complete, of the things or events that enter into the synthetic event; that, because it is unpredictable, it is to be regarded as non-mechanistic; further, the new kind of

---

[47] *Mind and Its Place in Nature*, pp. 196, 198. — See also D. Drake, "That Elusive Doctrine of Essence," *The Philosophical Review*, 1928, and R. W. Sellars, "A Re-Examination of Critical Realism," in *The Philosophical Review*, 1929.

[48] C. Lloyd Morgan, *Emergent Evolution* (William and Norgate, London, 1923), p. 3. See also his *Life, Mind, and Spirit* (1926).

relatedness, or the new quality or property, has causal efficacy, makes a difference to the further course of events."[49]

According to *S. Alexander* the root of all things in evolution is Space-Time. "The world actually or historically develops from its first or elementary condition of Space-Time, which possesses no quality except what we agreed to call the spatio-temporal quality of motion. But as in the course of Time new complexity of motions comes into existence, a new quality emerges, that is, a new complexity possesses as a matter of observed empirical fact a new or emergent quality."[50] In this manner all new levels of reality 'emerge': "Material things have certain motions of their own which carry the quality of materials. In the presence of light they are endowed with the secondary quality of color. Physical and chemical processes of a certain complexity have the quality of life. The new quality life emerges with this constellation of such processes, and therefore life is at once a physico-chemical complex and is not merely physical and chemical, for these terms do not sufficiently characterize the new complex which in the course and order of time has been generated out of them."[51] *Mind* is also such an emergent: "Mind is a new quality distinct from life, with its own peculiar methods of behavior."[52]

Emergent evolution thus travels upward along the following lines: matter, life, mind, and (according to some) deity. *Morgan* represents the whole trend by means of a diagrammatic pyramid, whose base is space-time, and all emergents are built up from this base — "atom-pyramids near the base, molecules a little higher up, yet higher, things (e.g., crystals), higher still, plants (in which mind is not yet emergent), then animals (with consciousness), and near the top, our human selves."[53]

---

[49]*Modern Materialism and Emergent Evolution* (D. Van Nostrand Co., New York, 1929), p. 92.

[50]*Space, Time, and Deity* (Macmillan, 1927), Vol. II, p. 45.

[51]*Loc. cit.*, p. 46.

[52]*Loc. cit.*, p. 45.

[53]*Emergent Evolution*, p. 11.

Other emergentists are: *L. T. Hobhouse* (who seems to have relinquished his views later), *C. A. Strong, D. Drake, E. Noble, R. Sellars*,[54] but they disagree on certain vital points.[55] It will be noted that these philosophers attempt to bridge the gap between mind and matter by means of 'emergence.' The relation of this theory to the problem of knowledge is indirect; all emergentists are realists in explaining the process of cognition. Among biologists who favor the theory of emergent evolution one might mention H. F. Osborn, C. J. Herrick, H. S. Jennings, G. H. Parker, S. R. Lillie, W. M. Wheeler, W. E. Ritter, and others.

skip

OBJECTIVE RELATIVISM

Objective relativism (or, as William P. Montague[56] calls it, *relativistic objectivism*) attempts to harmonize two theories of knowledge which seem mutually exclusive: objectivism and relativism. *Objectivism* contends that things are, when not experienced by us, just what they seem when experienced by us. *Relativism,* on the other hand, maintains that every known object is relative (in relation) to the knowing subject and as such is dependent in its being upon the knowing subject and incapable of existing apart from consciousness. 'Objective relativism,' then, is the doctrine which holds that all perceivable objects are *relative* to the perceiver, so that they owe their nature and existence to the relations in which they stand to the perceiver; and this relativity is of such a character that the perceived objects (phenomena) are *physically objective* precisely as they appear in the act of perception, according to the standpoint of the individual perceiver.

This seems very obscure and complicated, but it is really

---

[54]Hobhouse, *Development and Purpose* (Macmillan, 1913); Strong, *Why the Mind Has a Body* (Macmillan, 1903), *Origin of Consciousness* (Macmillan, 1918); Drake, *Mind and Its Place in Nature* (Macmillan, 1925); Noble, *Purposive Evolution* (Holt, 1926); Sellars, *Evolutionary Naturalism* (Open Court Publ. Co., 1922).

[55]McDougall, *loc. cit.*, pp. 195-223.

[56]*The Ways of Knowing* (Macmillan, 1925), p. 242. Montague himself, however, is not a relativistic objectivist.

quite simple. Three persons look at a penny from three different angles. The first sees it as a circle; the second sees it as an ellipse; the third, looking at it edgewise, sees it as a straight thin line. Which of these three 'appearances' is the objectively true one? All three are; the penny is objectively and actually circular and elliptical and straight-lined, depending on the 'context' or 'experience-set' of the individual observer. Two persons look at a table top; one sees it as a square and the other as a rhombus. The table is really both a square and a rhombus at the same time. If a patient suffering form *delirium tremens* sees pink elephants and green monkeys, these animals are as real and genuine for him as those he sees in a zoological garden. What you perceive, that *is*. And as objects appear in perspective, that is what they *objectively are*. There is no objective difference between 'real' and 'unreal' appearances.

What, then, are the *objects?* Nothing but the 'aspects' of things seen in perspective. As *Bertrand Russell* says: "Instead of supposing that there is some unknown cause, the 'real' table, behind the different sensations of those who are said to be looking at the table, we may take the whole set of these sensations (together possibly with certain other particulars) as actually *being* the table. That is to say, the table which is neutral as between different observers (actual and possible) is the set of all those particulars which would naturally be called 'aspects' of the table from different points of view. . . . We have only, therefore, to notice how they [the particulars which are its aspects] are collected together, and we can keep the collection without assuming any 'real' table as distinct from the collection."[57] Or, as *Arthur E. Murphy* puts it: "The qualities are not the existent, to be sure, but they are its whole nature, and it has no other."[58]

---

[57]*The Analysis of Mind* (Macmillan, 1921), p. 98.
[58]*Ideas and Nature,* Univ. of California Publications in Philosophy, Vol. 8, 1926, p. 202. See also his article, "Objective Relativism in Dewey and Whitehead," in *The Philosophical Review,* Vol. 36, 1927, pp. 121–144.

That objective relativism admits of no objective distinction between *reality* and *illusions* or *delusions* is clear from the following statement of *A. N. Whitehead:* "Pure presentational immediacy refuses to be divided into delusions and non-delusions. It is either all of it, or none of it, an immediate presentation of an external contemporary world as in its own right spatial."[59] There is no difference between 'delusions and non-delusions'; the former are as objectively real as the latter. What I perceive in nightmare dreams and fever hallucinations is no less real in the objective world than what I perceive in broad daylight when awake and normal.

This is the objective relativism of Whitehead, Dewey, Murphy, and others. It is a peculiar mixture of phenomenalism, subjectivism, objectivism, and neo-realism.

ARISTOTELIAN-SCHOLASTIC REALISM

Along with all these conflicting and confusing theories of knowledge, the age-old doctrine of *immediate perception* maintained its hold on the more conservative philosophers. It teaches that the spontaneous conviction of mankind is in general the correct view, and that we actually perceive the objects of the external world as they are in themselves. The senses do not merely 'represent,' they actually 'present' reality, at least in some form; man, therefore, does *not infer* the existence of objects 'out there' in nature from the existence of some 'representative' image in his consciousness, but *perceives them directly through intuition.* As such, then, this theory subscribes to the doctrine of *natural dualism* and *natural realism,* at least in its main features. Ego and non-Ego, mind and matter, self and world, subject and object, consciousness and nature, psychical and physical, retain their respective individuality, distinct and unconfused, each in its own identity and being; this is natural dualism as opposed to monism and absolutism. The mind perceives the things of the external world directly in some form or other, so that the world is *immediately present* to the mind

[59]*Symbolism* (Macmillan, 1927), p. 24.

in the process of sense-perception without the perpetual inter-
vention of a 'screen of representations,' and what the mind
perceives in its intuition is not its own 'ideas' or subjective states
but the *objects themselves;* this is natural realism as opposed
to idealism and subjectivism.

The bridge between the world and the human mind is the
human body. It is through the body and its senses and nervous
system that external objects are able to contact the mind, and
the mind is able to perceive the external objects. Since, however, the body is itself a part of the external world (as distinct
from the mind), the only way in which the body can become
the 'epistemological bridge' between the mind and the world,
thereby making a direct perception of the world possible, is by
entering into a distinct epistemological union with the mind:
mind and body must be an epistemological unit. They must
act together as the unit of perception. If each were divorced
from the other, as postulated in the radical antithesis of Descartes, there would be no possibility of interaction between
them, and knowledge of the external world could never enter
the mind. This Cartesian antithesis must, therefore, be a false
conception. Mind and body must form *one organic whole.*
Perception is a 'vital' function, but 'extended' in process;
consequently neither the body alone nor the mind alone forms
the adequate basis of perception, but the *animated organism of
mind and body together.*

According to the general aristotelian-scholastic view, the
material objects emit certain active energies (light, sound, heat,
mechanical motion, etc.), and these energies affect the sense-
organs and nervous system, producing therein a *cognitional
image* or likeness of the objects. This image is, of course, not
a 'mirroring' or 'photographing' of the object upon the mind,
but a vital *cognitional determinant* impressed upon sense-consciousness. The sense-consciousness responds in its own way
to this determinant by becoming aware of the presented object.
The mind is thus not conscious of this 'image' itself in the act

of perception, but directly of the 'object'; the 'image' is merely the *means by which* the mind perceives the external reality.

Many modern scholastic philosophers, however, lean strongly in the direction of *representative* perception. They contend that this sensory 'image' becomes directly an object of awareness to the mind, and *in* it and *from* it the mind derives a sense-knowledge of material objects, instinctively referring these 'representations' to the things themselves. This would be *mediate,* not immediate, perception. They adhere to this view, because they are convinced that science has proved that objects are not always in nature as they appear to the senses; they claim that the perceiving subject modifies the physical stimuli in its own characteristic manner (for instance, in color-vision, taste, etc.), so that the result is different from the condition of the objects as they are in nature. In this view *all* qualities of objects exist *formally in the subject* and only *causally in the objects.*

Other neo-scholastics, also influenced by the findings of science, defend the view that the facts prove that some perception (for instance, that of touch) is *immediate,* while other perceptions (for instance, those of color-vision, sound, flavor, taste, etc.) are *mediate* in character. In this view the fundamental sense of touch is the guarantee for the essential truth of the perception of extra-mental reality and serves as a check or control of the other perceptions. This theory is, therefore, partly 'presentative' and partly 'representative,' partly 'immediate' and partly 'mediate.' In any case, however, external reality is revealed to the mind through sense-perception.

Scholasticism combined within its system the best elements of the philosophy of Plato, of Aristotle, of the Neo-platonists, and of St. Augustine. In the main, however, it followed the teachings and principles of Aristotle. Scholasticism reached its highest development in the great minds of *St. Albert the Great* (1193 [or 1206]–1280), *St. Bonaventure* (1221–1274), *St.*

Thomas Aquinas (1225–1274),[60] perhaps the most brilliant genius of synthesis who ever lived, and *John Duns Scotus* (1274 [or 1266]–1308). In the period of transition between medieval and modern scholasticism, the following names are noteworthy: *Thomas de Vio Cajetanus* (1469–1534), *Toletus* (1532–1596), *Fonseca* (1528–1599), *Vasquez* (1551–1604), *Suarez* (1548–1617), and *Sylvester Maurus* (1619–1687).

In general, *scholasticism* advocates a natural dualism of God and creature, mind and matter, thought and thing, as against monism and pantheism; it defends a moderate realism, as against ultra-realism, nominalism, and conceptualism, in the problem of the universals; it is spiritualistic and not materialistic, experimental and not aprioristic, objectivistic and not subjectivistic; in sense-perception it is presentational and not agnostic or representational or idealistic; concerning intellectual knowledge it defends a moderate rationalism, as against sensism, positivism, and innatism; it is common-sense knowledge critically examined and philosophically vindicated.

Neo-scholasticism is the renewal or revival of medieval scholasticism, adapting its fundamental principles and tenets to modern intellectual problems, remaining in close contact with the progress of the natural sciences and employing their legitimate findings as the basis for philosophical research. Neo-scholasticism had its beginnings in the middle of the nineteenth century, and since that time it boasts a long roster of prominent names in various countries.

In *Italy* we may mention *C. Sanseverino* (1811–1865), J. M. Cornoldi (1822–1892), S. Tongiorgi (1820–1865), T. Zigliara (1833–1893), *M. Liberatore* (1810–1892), S. Schiffini (1841–1906), G. Bruni, A. Gemelli, P. Gény, and F. Olgiati. In *Spain, Portugal,* and the Spanish-speaking countries: *James Balmes* (1810–1848), Z. Gonzalez y Díaz-Tuñon (1831–1892), J. M. Orti y Lara, A. Gomez Izquierdo, J. Urráburu, Teixera Guedes,

---

[60]For the views of St. Thomas on the nature of knowledge, see his *Summa Theol.,* Ia, Q. 14.16; Q. 84–88; Ia IIæ, Q. 51.109; *De Veritate; Contra Gent.,* I–IV; *De Anima; De Veritate.*

G. Garcia, E. Valverde Tellez. In *Germany, Austria, Poland, Switzerland:* J. Kleutgen (1811–1883), A. Stöckl (1823–1895), T. *Pesch,* J. Hontheim, *C. Gutberlet,* E. Commer, O. Willmann, J. Jungmann, V. Cathrein, M. Grabmann, A. Lehmen, F. Ehrle, C. Baeumker, J. Fröbes, B. Jansen, J. Geyser, E. Przywara, B. Switalski, P. de Munnynck, P. Mandonnet, J. Donat. In *France* and *Belgium:* Domet de Vorges, P. Vallet, A. Farges, E. Blanc, P. Peillaube, A. Sertillanges, R. Garrigou-Lagrange, J. Maritain, E. Gilson, L. de San, *G. Lahousse, D. Card. Mercier* (1851–1926), M. de Wulf, D. Nys, L. Noel, S. Deploige, R. Kremer, J. Maréchal, A. Michotte. In *Hungary, Bohemia,* and the *Netherlands:* Kiss, Pécsi, and Van de Groot. In *England, Ireland,* and the *United States:* T. Harper, John Rickaby, Jos. Rickaby, R. Clarke, B. Boedder, *M. Maher,* C. Devas, L. Walker, G. Joyce, M. D'Arcy, *P. Coffey,* M. Cronin, W. Poland, J. Driscoll, E. Pace, W. Turner, J. Ryan, F. Sheen, L. Ward, G. Esser, J. Zybura, *T. Moore, H. Gruender, R. Bandas,* J. Barron, J. McWilliams. Many more names could be added.

This brief survey of the systems which have originated in the course of the past three centuries, plainly shows the confusion of thought brought about by Descartes' ill-fated ultra-dualism. It is a veritable *reductio ad absurdum* of his fundamental principles.

SUMMARY OF CHAPTER VIII

From the maze of conflicting theories which followed Kant and Hegel many signalize a return to realism.

1. *Sensism, Positivism, Materialism.* They all agree in this that sense-knowledge is the only true and scientific knowledge.

2. *Natural Realism, Transfigured Realism.* The Scottish School reverted to natural realism. Hamilton, though a follower of Reid, is a relativist and phenomenalist. Spencer restricts all knowledge to phenomena, but admits the existence of an unknown and unknowable ultimate reality; our ideas are 'symbols,' giving us a 'transfigured realism.'

3. *Post-Kantian Realistic Trends*. Among the followers of Kant, who attempted to bridge the gap between noumenon and phenomenon to realism, are Jacobi, Fries, Herbart, Husserl and Meinong.

4. *Neo-Absolutism*. Schopenhauer conceived the Absolute to be the Will; E. von Hartmann, the Unconscious. The Neo-Hegelians, like Bradley, Green, and others, approach the Absolute through experience.

5. *Neo-Psychologism*. It applies the principles of empirical science to consciousness, seeking to harmonize idealism with science. Representative thinkers: Poincaré, Mach, Avenarius, Wundt.

6. *Personalism*. Closely allied to classic idealism, it seeks to avoid the absolutistic implications of idealism by insisting on the element of personality. Typical personalism is dualistic and theistic. Lotze and Bowne are representative.

7. *Pragmatism, Humanism*. It is a protest against idealism and a return to realism: the attitude of looking away from first things, principles, categories, supposed necessities, and of looking toward last things, fruits, consequences, facts. Truth is judged by events and consists in verification; that which 'works' and satisfies human needs, is true. Chief proponents are James, Schiller, Dewey. Dewey stresses instrumentalism; Bergson, intuitionism; Vaihinger, fictionalism; Fawcett, imaginism; Baldwin, pancalism; Blondel, religious pragmatism (modernism).

8. *Neo-Realism*. Neo-realists identify mind and consciousness with objects; objects, when known, are 'ideas' and as such are directly and identically present in consciousness. This is pan-objectivism and epistemological monism.

9. *Critical Realism*. This is a form of epistemological dualism; thought and thing are distinct and independent. The datum of sense-perception is the 'essence' of a thing. Essences are logical entities, the 'what' of a thing divorced from its 'that.'

10. *Emergent Evolution*. Through evolution new and un-

predictable properties originate and thereby form new and higher levels of reality. These emergents have no counterpart in the lower levels. The general trend of evolution is from space-time to matter, life, mind, and deity.

11. *Objective Relativism.* All perceivable objects are relative to the perceiver, so that they owe their nature and existence to the relations in which they stand to the perceiver; and this relativity is such that phenomena are physically objective according to the experience-set of the observer.

12. *Aristotelian-Scholastic Realism.* It is a form of natural realism and natural dualism. Though some neo-scholastics lean toward representative realism, direct perception in some form is maintained. Mind and body are an organic compound and form an epistemological unit of perception.

READINGS

D. C. Macintosh, *The Problem of Knowledge;* D. S. Robinson, *An Anthology of Recent Philosophy, Introduction to Living Philosophy;* L. J. Walker, *Theories of Knowledge;* R. W. Sellars, *The Principles and Problems of Philosophy;* W. Turner, *History of Philosophy;* M. F. McDonald, *The Progress of Philosophy;* J. S. Zybura, *Present-Day Thinkers and the New Scholasticism;* H. G. Townsend, *Philosophical Ideas in the United States;* A. O. Lovejoy, *The Revolt Against Dualism;* M. W. Calkines, *The Persistent Problems of Philosophy;* W. Caldwell, *Pragmatism and Idealism;* W. E. Hocking, *Types of Philosophy;* R. W. Sellars, *Critical Realism.*

Chapter IX

FALLACY OF IDEALISM

The foregoing review of the trends in modern philosophy was necessarily brief. It will suffice, however, to indicate the maze of contradictory theories which have arisen in this relatively short period of time. Almost every thinker has his own particular brand of theory, more or less at variance with that of his fellow-philosophers. There seems to be hardly a single point on which they all agree, when they begin to expound the details of their system. On the surface, there appears to be nothing but intellectual chaos. Viewed from a broader standpoint, however, by far the majority of these theories and systems will be seen to be more or less alike. They reveal a common parentage and show a common kinship. As such, then, they must possess a uniform trait, a fundamental doctrine identical in them all, which underlies all the variants and forms the root-idea from which they derive their origin and then develop into different philosophies. This uniform trait is *idealism,* and the root-idea is the *idealist postulate.*

It would be an impossibility to submit every form and variant of idealism to a critical evaluation. Nor is this necessary. If it can be shown that the fundamental doctrine, the root-idea, of idealism is essentially fallacious, then idealism itself as a system of thought, no matter what its individual shade and shape, will also be shown to be essentially fallacious.

THE COMMON ELEMENT IN IDEALISM

Idealism arose out of the difficulty of understanding and explaining how the human mind can transcend itself and know extra-mental reality. The ordinary man sees no difficulty in this; for him there is no problem. He sees houses; he hears sounds; he smells odors; he tastes flavors; he touches objects: these are plain, everyday facts; what more is there to say? The epistemologist acknowledges these facts, and he finds his problem precisely in these facts. Certainly we see and hear and smell and taste and touch; but *what* do we perceive in these psychical acts and *how* do we perceive these supposedly extra-mental things? The extra-mental objects (if there be such) cannot very well leave their location, travel through the intervening space, pierce the body, and enter the mind in their physical being; the house across the street, for instance, remains across the street, and the red of the rose remains in the rose out there in the garden. And the mind assuredly does not leave the body, flit through space, and envelop the star billions of miles away in its physical being; the mind remains here and the star remains there. How, then, can the mind perceive things at a distance, or how can things get into the mind? It does not seem to solve the difficulty by referring to the stimuli (light-waves, air-waves, etc.), which are supposed to leave the objects and impinge upon the sense-organs; because then we should perceive these stimuli and not the objects from which they come. That, however, is not the case: we perceive apparently objects and certainly not stimuli.

The greatest difficulty lies in the fact of the *dissimilarity* which exists between *mind* and *matter*. The mind is psychical, while the objects are physical; the mind is unextended, while the objects are extended. How can the mind assimilate something so diametrically opposed to its own nature? And how can physical, extended objects impress themselves upon a mind which is altogether devoid of all extension? Can the extended become unextended, or the unextended become extended? Can the physical become psychical, or the psychical become physical? Is this not a contradiction in terms? Since the mind is psychical, it seems perfectly obvious and logical, that nothing but what is psychical can affect the mind and nothing can proceed from the mind but what is psychical. All knowledge, then, since it *proceeds* from the mind and takes place *in the mind,* must be purely mental. Physical objects are, therefore, absolutely excluded from knowledge: *the objects of knowledge are mental objects, ideas.* Consequently, even when we apparently perceive external and extended objects, what we really perceive are 'mental objects,' 'ideas,' 'conscious states,' 'representations,' but not physical, extra-mental things themselves. All we can perceive is our 'ideas' of things; whether anything corresponds 'out there,' extra-mentally, to these 'ideas,' is something we can never actually know. If such extra-mental objects exist, we simply cannot know them, because they are physical entities, and the mind is restricted to the mental, the psychical, the ideal, in all its processes. As far as the mind is concerned, its objects have 'being' only in so far and so long as they are 'perceived': *esse est percipi.* Such 'being' is then not physical, but ideal; and since it proceeds from, and resides in, the mind as its 'subject,' it is subjective. All objects of our knowledge are, therefore, ideal and subjective, because they are mental products. This doctrine, that the mind in its knowing can know only its own 'ideas' or 'percepts,' is *idealism;* and when this doctrine is accepted as an axiom or postulate, it is the *idealist postulate.*

This line of reasoning, formulated in many different ways, though seldom cast into strict logical form, is basic to idealism. It can be worded thus: Objects, so far as the knowing mind is concerned, exist only when perceived; but perception ('being perceived') is a conscious mind-state or 'idea'; hence, objects are only conscious mind-states or 'ideas'; consequently their existence or 'being' (*esse*) is nothing but 'being perceived' (*percipi*): *esse est percipi.* The argument originated with the antithetical dualism existing between body and mind, as postulated by Descartes.

THE FALLACY OF THE IDEALIST POSTULATE

Logic is not the strong point of modern philosophers. They disdain the strictly logical formulation of arguments and prefer the loose language of the essayist. And loose language often hides loose thinking. We can see this clearly in the argument of *Berkeley,* if we cast his thoughts into strict form. A close analysis will reveal the fallacy underlying his argument. Here are his words: "What are the aforementioned objects [houses, mountains, rivers, and, in a word, all sensible objects] but the things we perceive by sense? and what do we perceive besides our own ideas or sensations? and is it not plainly repugnant that any of these [ideas or sensations], or any combination of them, should exist unperceived?"[1] A casual reading of this argument sounds plausible enough; in fact, it almost seems self-evident; and to many this line of reasoning has appeared so transparently and unanswerably obvious, that it has been accepted without question and become the dogma of idealism. It deserves, therefore, to be analyzed more in detail.

It will be evident that the conclusion of the idealist argument will have to be that objects cannot exist *in reality* except when they are *perceived,* because it is the contention of the idealists that the 'being' of objects is their 'being perceived.' So far as we are concerned, they cease to 'be' once they cease to 'be perceived.' Here is the syllogism:

Ideas or sensations cannot exist unperceived;
But sensible objects (houses, etc.) are ideas or sensations;
Ergo, sensible objects (houses, etc.) cannot exist unperceived.

The fallacy lies in the minor premise: "Sensible objects (houses, etc.) are ideas or sensations." The term 'sensible objects' can be taken in two meanings: objects can be called 'sensible' in the meaning of *'actually* sense-perceived' and in the meaning of *'potentially* sense-perceived.' In the first meaning they *are* perceived in the act of perception; and in the second meaning they *can be* perceived. In the first case we have ob-

---

[1] *Treatise Concerning the Principles of Human Knowledge,* p. 259.

jects which are 'within' the act of perception, and in the second case we have objects which are 'outside' the act of perception but are capable of being perceived. In either case such objects would be called 'sensible.' The difference lies in the fact that in the first case these 'sensible' objects are considered as 'perceived,' while in the second case they are merely 'perceivable.' Berkeley confuses the two meanings: he identifies the 'perception of objects' with the 'objects of perception.' His argument merely proves that 'sensible' objects *when perceived,* are 'ideas or sensations'; but it says nothing whatever about such objects *when not perceived.* All that his argument can prove is that 'objects are perceived when we perceive them'; and that, though true, is plainly a redundancy and a juggling of words, but no proof that things 'cannot exist unperceived.'

If he contends that the argument also holds in the second meaning, so that there are no sensible objects outside the act of perception which are unperceived but perceiv*able,* he begs the whole question by presupposing in his premise what is supposed to be the burden of the conclusion. Such a contention is an unwarranted assumption. "Sensible objects are ideas and sensations" when perceived; but that is no proof that they cannot be objects in and for themselves without being perceived. What idealists prove is merely that 'sensible objects *cannot be perceived as existing* without being perceived as ideas or sensations'; but this in no way proves that 'sensible objects *cannot exist* without being perceived as existing.' Because objects, when perceived, have now a 'subjective existence,' it does not follow that such objects have a 'subjective existence *only.*' Things could possibly have an 'objective existence' for themselves and then obtain an added 'subjective existence' in the subject when perceived by the subject. In order to establish their case, idealists would have to disprove this possibility; but this their argument fails to do.

The fallacy of the idealist argument will, perhaps, be more

clear if we cast it into the form of a hypothetical syllogism. It could be made to read in the following manner:

> If something has a purely subjective existence, it has a
>   mental existence;
> But perceived objects have a mental existence;
> Ergo, perceived objects have a purely subjective exist-
>   ence.

The major premise contains a true statement: anything that has a purely subjective existence is mind-dependent, because it is produced by the mind; it has, therefore, a mental existence. The minor premise is also true: when objects are perceived, they are perceived by the mind and as such exist cognitionally in the mind; they have, then, a mental existence. But the conclusion does not follow logically from these premises. It is the *fallacy of false consequent*. The minor premise posits the consequent instead of the antecedent, and that is not logically permissible. If we wish to avoid this inconsistency and make the minor premise posit the antecedent, the syllogism will read:

> If something has a purely subjective existence, it has a
>   mental existence;
> But perceived objects have a purely subjective exist-
>   ence;
> Ergo, perceived objects have a mental existence.

But now the argument does not prove enough. It merely proves that perceived objects have 'a mental existence,' and that is something which the realist admits; the idealist, however, desires to prove that all perceived objects have *nothing but* 'a purely subjective existence,' since it is his contention that the *'esse'* of all perceived objects is their *'percipi.'* The argument does not reach that far. Besides, in the syllogism, as now given, the minor premise states that 'perceived objects have a purely subjective existence.' This statement begs the question in dispute, because here the *'esse est percipi'* is already assumed as true, while the truth of this fact is supposed to be found only in the conclusion.

There is only one more way in which this argument can be formulated so as to be logically correct and consistent. It could be made to read as follows:

> If something has a mental existence, it has a purely
> subjective existence;
> But perceived objects have a mental existence;
> Ergo, perceived objects have a purely subjective ex-
> istence.

This syllogism is consistent, but the conclusion is not true. The major premise, as it stands, is again a begging of the whole question. The fact in question is precisely that which is assumed in the major premise: Is it a fact that, if something has a *mental* existence, it has a *purely subjective* existence? This is the very point which the idealist intends to prove by the argument; hence, to assume its truth in the premises is an illegitimate procedure.

It is thus seen that the fundamental position of the idealist is untenable, because illogical. He cannot prove that the objects we perceive have *only* a subjective existence in the mind; for all he knows, they *may* have a mind-independent, objective existence in nature also. And if objects *can* exist both in nature and in the mind (and no valid reason has been adduced to the contrary), then the fundamental idealist postulate is invalid. *D. C. Macintosh* has summarized the essential fallacy of idealism in these concise words:

"The fallacy may appear as one of equivocation — the common fallacy of 'four terms' — as in the following syllogism: What is subjective (*dependent* on self for existence) is not externally real, but mere idea; all objects of which we are aware

are subjective (*related* to a self which is conscious of them); therefore, all objects of which we are aware are not externally real, but mere ideas. Or, if the equivocation be avoided, the fallacy will remain as that of an 'undistributed middle term,' as in this syllogism: The unreal objectively is subjective (related to a subject); similarly, all of which one is conscious is subjective (related to a subject); therefore, all of which one is conscious is unreal objectively (mere ideas). Or, more simply, psychological idealism may be said to rest upon a fallacious conversion. From the obvious truth that all elements which depend on consciousness for their existence, such as pains, feelings, desires, etc., are in the subjective relation, i.e., are objects for a subject, it is inferred, by the fallacious process of simple conversion, that *all* that is in the subjective relation, all that is object for a subject, is dependent on consciousness and this relation to consciousness for its own existence."[2]

THE EGO-CENTRIC PREDICAMENT

Every form of idealism, whether dualistic or monistic, rests upon the *primacy of consciousness*. Things simply cannot be known, perceived, experienced, except by a conscious mind. Consciousness is thus for them the universal condition of all *knowledge* and also of being. Consciousness *constitutes* its objects; and if this consciousness maintains its own individuality in the human mind, we have dualistic idealism, and if it is merged in a universal Ego, we have monistic idealism. In either case the 'object known' is identified with the 'subject knowing.' We have seen how Berkeley argues for the oneness of the material reality with the perceiving mind. Bradley argues in a similar fashion for the oneness of all reality with sense-experience. Immaterialism, phenomenalism, absolutism, and every shade of idealism, ultimately base their doctrine on the fact that reality is somehow enclosed within the realm of

---

[2] *The Problem of Knowledge* (Macmillan, 1915), p. 95. — Regarding the various kinds of fallacies mentioned in this chapter, see the author's *Science of Correct Thinking* (Bruce Publishing Co.).

consciousness, for the simple reason that we cannot perceive objects as existing apart from conscious perception. This ultimate fact, which is the heart of idealism, thus rests on what has been so aptly styled 'the ego-centric predicament.' Here is *Perry's* exposition of the idealist fallacy as based on the ego-centric predicament:

"No thinker to whom one may appeal is able to mention a thing that is not an idea, for the obvious and simple reason that *in mentioning it he makes it an idea.* No one can report on the nature of things without being on hand himself. It follows that whatever thing he reports does as a matter of fact stand in relation to him, as an idea, object of knowledge, or experience. . . .

"This predicament arises from the attempt to discover whether the cognitive relationship is indispensable to the things which enter into it. In order to discover if possible exactly how a thing is modified by the cognitive relationship, I look for things *out* of this relationship, in order that I may compare them with instances of things *in* this relationship. But I can find no such instances, because 'finding' is a variety of the very relationship that I am trying to eliminate. Hence I cannot make the comparison, nor get an answer to my original question by this means. But I cannot conclude that there are no such instances; indeed, I now know that *I should not be able to discover them if there were.*

"Just in so far as I do actually succeed in eliminating every cognitive relationship, I am unable to observe the result. Thus if I close my eyes, I cannot see what happens to the object; if I stop thinking, I cannot think what happens to it; and so with every mode of knowledge. In thus eliminating all knowledge, I do not experimentally eliminate the thing known, but only *the possibility of knowing whether that thing is eliminated or not.*

"This, then, is 'the ego-centric predicament.' But what does it prove, and how does it serve the purpose of idealism? It should be evident that it proves nothing at all. It is simply a peculiar methodological difficulty. It does, it is true, contain the proposition that *every mentioned thing is an idea.* But this is virtually a redundant proposition to the effect that every mentioned thing is mentioned — to the effect that every idea, object of knowledge, or experience, is an idea, object of knowledge, or experience. And a redundant proposition is no proposition at all. The assertion that an idea is an idea conveys no knowledge even about ideas. But what the idealist requires is a proposition to the effect that *everything is an idea* or that *only ideas exist.* And to derive this proposition directly from the redundancy just formulated, is simply to take advantage of the confusion of mind by which a redundancy is commonly attended.

"It may be argued, however, that the ego-centric predicament is equivalent to an inductive proof of the proposition that all things are ideas. Every observed case of a thing is a case of a thing observed. Neglecting the redundancy, which is sufficient of itself to vitiate the assertion, we remark that the induction proceeds entirely by Mill's 'method of agreement,' which is invalid unless supported by 'the method of difference,' that is, the observation of negative cases. But the ego-centric predicament itself prevents the observation of negative cases. It is impossible to observe cases of unobserved things, even if there be any. In other words, there is a reason *connected with the conditions of observation* why only agreements should be observed. But where this is the case the method of agreement is worthless; and the use of it is a fallacy."[3]

Perry's criticism of the idealist argument from the ego-centric predicament is eminently justified. The argument is essentially fallacious. The only way in which we can become acquainted with things, is to perceive them or have ideas of them; therefore, *if* and *when* and *while* we know them, they *must* be 'percepts' or 'ideas' in our consciousness. The very nature of our knowing demands this. But things could pos-

---

[3]*Present Philosophical Tendencies,* pp. 129–131 (Longmans, Green and Co.).

sibly have existence without being perceived and thus be
mind-independent in their being; all that the ego-centric predicament *can* prove is that things *cannot be perceived without
being perceived,* which truth, of course, amounts to a mere
tautology.

If we now turn to Bradley's idealist argument, it will be
evident that it is nothing but a sample of specious reasoning from the ego-centric predicament. He says: "Find any
piece of existence, take up anything that anyone could
possibly call a fact, or could in any sense assert to have being,
and then judge if it does not consist in sentient experience.
. . . Anything in no sense felt or perceived becomes to me
quite unmeaning."[4] Certainly, things 'in no sense felt or perceived' must be 'unmeaning' *to the perceiver or knower;* for
how could they acquire a meaning for him, if he did not
'feel' or 'perceive' them? That would imply 'knowing' them
without someone knowing them, and 'perceiving' them without someone perceiving them. The very fact of cognition
always involves the perceiver or knower just as necessarily as
the object itself that is to be known; because an object, to be
known, must be known *by someone.* Wherefore, Bradley's
argument only proves that objects cannot exist *for a perceiver
and knower* without sentient experience; but it says nothing
whatever about what objects can or cannot be *for themselves*
outside the knowledge relation, and Bradley's conclusion that
'experience is the same as reality' is thus seen to be entirely
unwarranted. The ultimate nature of reality is still an open
question.

The whole attitude of the idealist, of whatever type he may
be, rests upon a *confusion of ideas.* From the fact that a being,
in order to be known, must be perceived within the consciousness of the perceiver in a mental act, he concludes that the
'reality itself' of the being, and not merely its 'perception,' is

[4] *Appearance and Reality,* pp. 144, 145.

mental. Reality would thus be *immanent* in the knower. The confusion is based on the identification of the 'reality' and the 'perception' of the object known. It is unquestionably true that the 'perception' of an object is mind-dependent and immanent. To assert that an object, *when known,* can remain unperceived, is a contradiction; and it would also be a contradiction to assert that an unperceived object, *when unperceived,* can be known. But it is no contradiction to assume that an object, which has a reality of its own, can remain unperceived by a human mind, either temporarily or forever, either in part or in whole. We would simply not know of its existence until such time when it enters our experience. To deny that such an object can exist as an 'unperceived reality' means to confuse the *reality* of this object with the *perception* of its reality. This is precisely what idealists do, but it is an illogical and dogmatic procedure and therefore fallacious.

The foregoing criticism shows that idealism arises out of the ego-centric predicament and that its arguments involve a faulty logic. This, of course, does not prove that extra-mental reality actually exists; it merely shows that idealism has not disproved the existence of extra-mental objects. The question of the existence of such objects must be solved, not by any *a priori,* but by an *a posteriori* method. Facts alone, together with their proper interpretation, must settle the issue; that is the only scientific and philosophic procedure which can lead us with safety to a definite conclusion.

SUMMARY OF CHAPTER IX

Most modern theories of knowledge are a form of *idealism.* The fundamental position of idealism is fallacious.

1. The *element common* to all forms of idealism is the tenet that *reality lies within the consciousness of the perceiver and the mind cannot transcend its own conscious states.* It arrives at this conclusion through the difficulty of understanding how the mind can perceive objects at a distance and how a psychical mind can conform itself to a physical object. Hence, there has

arisen the *idealist postulate* that the mind in its knowing can
know only its own 'percepts' or 'ideas.' The argument can be
formulated as follows: Objects, so far as the knowing mind is
concerned, exist only when perceived; but perception ('being
perceived') is a conscious mind-state or 'idea'; hence, objects
are only conscious mind-states or 'ideas'; consequently their
existence or 'being' (*esse*) is nothing but 'being perceived'
(*percipi*): *esse est percipi*.

2. The Idealist Postulate of idealism is *fallacious*. Berkeley's
argument that *esse est percipi* is grounded on faulty logic. His
term 'sensible object' is ambiguous, because he does not distinguish between the 'sensible' as perceiv*ed* and as perceiv*able*.
He merely proves that 'sensible objects,' *when perceived,* are
'ideas or sensations,' so that his proof really amounts to the
redundant proposition that 'perceived objects must be perceived.' The fallacy of idealism thus consists in confusing the
statement that 'sensible objects *cannot be perceived as existing*
without being perceived' with the statement that 'sensible
objects *cannot exist* without being perceived as existing.' To
assume that the latter statement is true, is a *petitio principii*.
All arguments which tend to prove that all reality must be
identified with 'ideas' involve either a 'four-term' syllogism,
or an 'undistributed middle,' or a fallacious 'conversion.'

3. The *ego-centric predicament,* or the difficulty to discover
any objects outside the cognitive relationship existing between
object and subject, is responsible for the fallacy of idealism.
Dualistic and monistic idealism rests upon the *primacy of consciousness*. Since consciousness is the universal condition of
knowledge, it is also assumed that consciousness *constitutes the
being* of all objects of knowledge. Due to the ego-centric predicament, every *mentioned* thing is an 'idea,' and from this
idealists conclude that everything *is* an 'idea' and that *only
ideas exist*. But this reasoning is fallacious, because it merely
proves that objects, *if* and *when* and *while* known, must be
'percepts' or 'ideas'; in other words, 'things cannot be perceived
without being perceived,' which is a redundancy and a plati-

tude. The argument, however, does not prove that objects may not exist *in themselves,* as mind-independent things, without being perceived. The whole attitude of the idealists is based on the confusion of identifying the *reality* of an object with the *perception* of this reality; they fail to distinguish between the 'knowledge of objects' and the 'objects of knowledge.'

The foundation of idealism thus rests on faulty logic and on the ego-centric predicament. The existence of extra-mental things is a question which can be settled only by a close analysis of the facts and by the proper interpretation of the facts; not the *a priori,* but the *a posteriori* method can solve the problem.

READINGS

D. C. Macintosh, *The Problem of Knowledge,* Chs. V–IX; D. Card. Mercier, *The Origins of Contemporary Psychology,* Ch. V; R. B. Perry, *Present Philosophic Tendencies,* Chs. VI–IX; J. T. Barron, *op. cit.,* Chs. X, XI; P. Coffey, *op. cit.,* Chs. XIX, XX; William James, *A Pluralistic Universe,* Chs. I–VI; A. J. Balfour, *A Defense of Philosophic Doubt,* Chs. VI, IX; R. W. Sellars, *Critical Realism,* Ch. VI; G. E. Moore, "The Refutation of Idealism," in *Mind,* 1903.

Error in Idealism
Requirements for sense-perception

CHAPTER X

EXTRA-MENTAL AND EXTRA-EGO REALITY

From the welter of conflicting systems and theories of knowledge which have come into vogue during the last three centuries, it is possible to draw but one conclusion: there must be something radically wrong with the starting point and the method used in the attempt to solve the problem of knowledge. When the results are so disastrous, the principle must be faulty. The only logical thing to do, then, is to disregard these systems and begin the solution of the problem from a common-sense standpoint: scrutinize the facts, note their implications, interpret their meaning, and draw the implied conclusions.

Three main factors enter into the problem: the human *mind,* the human *body,* and the external physical *world.* The body, if it exists, is an extra-mental reality, distinct from the mind; but it belongs to the human Ego as an integral part, together with the mind, and as such it would be extra-mental but intra-Ego. The physical world, on the other hand, if it exists, would be extra-mental and also completely external to the perceiving subject; it would be extra-Ego and non-Ego. The best procedure will be, therefore, to see whether we can vindicate the existence and perception of the extended, extra-mental human body, and then proceed to investigate the existence and perception of the extended, external world: because the world cannot come into contact with the mind except through the body. If the existence and perception of the body, as distinct from the mind, cannot be vindicated, then there is no possibility whatever of establishing the existence and perception of the external world at large.

THE DATA CONCERNING EXTRA-MENTAL REALITY

Besides my mind, I perceive within my being a reality which possesses *extensity,* and this reality I call my 'body.' There is a very definite *spatial configuration* to my body. By passing my hand over the body, I obtain a clear impression and touch-perception of its relative size and contour. I know, for instance, that my body occupies a very limited area from head to foot which, measured by a standard rule, will be, perhaps, more than five feet in height and less than six. I know, too, that different members comprise the complex of the body, and that these members occupy separate and distinct *positions,* both in relation to each other and to the body as a whole. Feet and head form the extremities, while the limbs and the torso have intermediate locations.

Touch, especially the experience of double-contact, reveals *voluminousness* in my body. In moving my hands over the body, I obtain an immediate perception of 'up and down,' 'right and left,' 'before and behind.' I thus perceive that my body possesses the three dimensions of length, breadth, and depth. The intra-muscular sense reveals to me the fact that the different parts of my body change position *in space:* I sit, I stand, I lie down, I stretch, I bend backward, I incline forward. I also perceive that the entire body *moves* at times: I walk, I run, I swim, I rise, I climb. *Weight* is revealed to me in the difference experienced in ascending and descending a sharp incline or in being lifted into the air and then dropped to the ground. And *solidity* is manifested to me in the fact that one part of the body cannot penetrate the other.

My experiences also make me aware of various *sense-organs* and their *distribution* and *localization* within the confines of my body. I have eyes to see, ears to hear, a palate to taste, a nose to smell, and touch pervades the entire body. Each organ, I note with intuitive consciousness, has its own *specific type of object for perception:* colors, flavors, sounds, odors, heat and cold, pleasure and pain, hardness and softness, smoothness and roughness, freshness and fatigue. During active sensation I experience, by means of the intra-muscular sense, the precise *place* on and within the body where the sensation is localized; in this manner I experience not only the actual perception as such (for instance, the perception of color, sound, etc.), but also the *organic activity* accompanying this perception, showing me that the perception is mine and belongs to a definite portion of *my body*.

In this manner I have a clear picture of my body in its parts and as a whole. Furthermore, and this is important, in this concrete picture I concretely perceive through immediate awareness that my body is a reality distinct from the thinking mind; it is an *extra-mental reality*. At the same time, however, I am also concretely aware that my body is an integral factor, together with the mind, in the *process of perception*. If I close my eyes, I cannot see; if I open them, I see again. If I touch a burning object, I experience heat; if I withdraw my hand, the sensation ceases. If I push against a wall, I feel resistance; if I step away, the feeling of resistance ends. And since the sensation becomes perception only when the mind adverts to it and becomes aware of it, I notice that both body and mind are necessary for perception, although I clearly realize that both are not the same thing. *But both are felt to belong to my Ego.* It is *my* body and *my* mind; *I* think and am conscious, and *I* weigh so-and-so-much and move about from place to place. Whatever affects my body I am conscious of as affecting *me,* and whatever takes place in my mind I am aware of as taking place in *me*. My Ego is thus perceived to be something that possesses both body and mind, forming a unitary combination of the two which, notwithstanding their distinct differences, makes them act together in perception.

These, then, are in brief the data of consciousness regarding my 'body.' These data cannot be denied; for any person, observing himself in the manner indicated above, will readily verify them through his own experience. The facts must be accepted; it is in the interpretation of them that various theories arise.

THE EXISTENCE OF EXTRA-MENTAL REALITY

In placing an interpretation upon the aforementioned data, it must be borne in mind that no *a priori* presuppositions or theories can be allowed to dictate the explanation. The facts must speak for themselves, and mere difficulties do not constitute impossibilities. The facts must assuredly be accounted for, and that theory alone should be accepted as true which gives the most natural explanation of the data in their entirety. Now, the most natural and most general explanation is the one which claims that my perceptions *reveal my body as an existent reality*.

This view is in agreement with the spontaneous conviction of men in all ages. Even the educated and intelligent, notwithstanding their knowledge of physics and psychology, accept the reality of their own body as an indubitable fact, because this view alone harmonizes with *everyday practical life*. Our entire mode of living is devoid of sense and reason, if the reality of our own body be considered merely as an 'internal state,' 'idea,' 'image,' 'representation,' or 'percept' of the mind. When we give food and drink to the body, when we labor unto fatigue and exhaustion, when we are sick and in suffering, when we break an arm or undergo an operation, when we experience physical comfort and pleasure, when we grow from childhood into maturity and decline into old age — these actualities of life are meaningless except under the supposition that our body is a *physical reality* just as we perceive it to be in consciousness. Idealism, with its reduction of all knowledge to terms of mental 'percepts' or 'ideas,' may do in books and in classrooms, but will serve little purpose in the stark necessities of life which confront man in his bodily being day after day. Idealism puts no bread into the mouth of the starving and eases no pain in the sick. Only an idealist philosopher could be satisfied with the theory that the reality behind his bodily 'appearances' and 'phenomena' is some unknown and unknowable, unperceived and unperceivable *x;* our body is far too real and personal for us to rest content with such vaporous, hypothetical existences. And even the most inveterate idealist is only an idealist *in theory;* when he goes about his daily occupations and supplies the daily needs of his 'phenomenal' body, he acts and behaves like the simplest and most plebeian realist. But a theory that cannot be *lived,* that must be contradicted by every unphilosophical act of daily life, must be essentially wrong.

This view also agrees with *science.* The departments of anatomy, physiology, biology, physics, genetics, medicine, and psycho-physics, when not influenced by the purely theoretical considerations of idealistic thinking, are frankly *realistic:* they accept the human body as given and as perceived, and their treatment of it shows plainly that they are convinced of its reality and existence. Here again, some scientists may be idealists in theory, but in every practical issue they are realists. This, of course, does not prove that realism is necessarily true in itself; it does show, however, that human reason can accept an idealistic interpretation of the human body only by doing great violence to its natural judgment.

After this indirect argument, we must consider the *direct evidence of consciousness.* Consciousness, as was shown before, must be essentially free from error in all matters of which it has immediate intuition. To doubt or deny this is equivalent to the suicide of reason, because then all knowledge must be adjudged illusory. But the evidence of consciousness is transparently clear in testifying to the reality and existence of our body. We can discover no difference between the intuition which consciousness has of mental states and that which it has of the reality and existence of the body. There is indeed a difference in the *object* of awareness, but there is no essential difference in the *nature of the act* of awareness itself. Now, if this act of awareness is perceptive of the reality and existence of internal states, why should it not be equally perceptive of the reality and existence of the human body with which it is so obviously connected? The testimony of consciousness is equally clear and intuitive in both cases. To affirm the validity of its perception in the one case and to deny it in the other, amounts to a practical destruction of its character as a reliable witness in both. We could no longer trust its testimony; certain knowledge would be impossible, and skepticism would inevitably follow. Hence, the testimony of our consciousness concerning the reality and existence of our body as perceived by us must be accepted.

THE PERCEPTION OF EXTRA-MENTAL REALITY

The entire difficulty of the idealists arises from the view, prevalent since Descartes, that mind and body are so antithetical and foreign to each other, that there can be no real communication between the two. The mind is conceived as a purely unextended entity which is the total subject of knowledge. This view of the 'subject of knowledge' is arbitrary and false; it is an unwarranted assumption, contradicted by the very data of consciousness. *My Ego is the real subject of my knowledge:* that is the verdict of my consciousness. The mind is a mere instrument of my Ego, and this is clearly perceived by introspection: *I* think, *I* imagine, *I* remember, *I* judge, *I* reason. It is the Ego, then, and not the mind itself, which is the ultimate subject of intellectual knowledge. And the same is true of sensory knowledge: *I* feel, *I* see, *I* hear, *I* have pain in my hand, *I* have a fever. Thus it is seen that the Ego is the real subject of both intellectual and sensory knowledge, that is, of *all* knowledge. Now, if we analyze our sensory knowledge, we must come to the conclusion that it involves 'extension' in the very *act of perception*. I perceive, for instance, 'colored surface'; but how could I perceive a 'surface' which is extended, if my act of perception were totally unextended? I feel the 'whole length of my arm'; how can I feel or perceive such a thing, if my feeling and perception were wholly mental? I experience a pain 'down my left side'; again, how is such an experience possible, if there be no extension in the act of perception? We could multiply such instances by the thousands. They are evident data of our consciousness. But these facts are unintelligible, if we maintain that sense-perception takes place in an *un*extended subject.

Sense-perception is a vital act, certainly; but it is also an 'extended' act. The *subject* of sense-perception must, therefore, also be a *vital and extended reality*. And since the Ego is the real subject of sense-knowledge, it must be a reality which is both vital (perceptive) and extended. Only a body, however, is extended. Consequently, an extended body must form an integral part of the being of our Ego, in order to account for the *psycho-physical* character of our sense-perception as a vital yet extended act. We are thus forced to conclude that our Ego does not consist solely of our unextended mind, but is a *compound of mind and body,* united in such a way that our Ego is a unified living organism consisting of both. Neither the mind alone nor the body alone can explain sensation and perception; both are required for an adequate explanation. And both must be fused together so intimately in their being, that they form a single principle of perceptive action.

Since our body is an integral part of our Ego and is thus *partly identical* with it, our Ego must be capable of perceiving its body just as well as it is capable of perceiving its own mind with its internal states: both belong as constituents to and in our Ego. There is, then, no intrinsic impossibility for our Ego to perceive its own body; on the contrary, the Ego should be able to perceive that which is a component part of itself as a factor in sense-perception.

The above analysis of the data of our consciousness concerning the reality and perception of our own body shows how arbitrary and fundamentally wrong Descartes was in his treatment of the relation existing between mind and body in the human being. In his eagerness as a mathematician to deduce all knowledge from a single principle he disdained to submit the data of our consciousness to a close scrutiny. Instead, he attempted to give an *a priori* definition of mind and body and built his entire theory of knowledge upon this foundation. The facts of experience certainly do not bear out his antithesis. We are conscious beyond doubt that we are *one single being,* not two, and this presupposes that the mind-body combination in our person is a unitary principle of action. It takes more than a definition and a statement to sever the union between them.

Simply because 'thought' is an *obvious* characteristic of mind, Descartes judged it to be the *exclusive* characteristic of mind and proceeded to define 'mind' as 'thought'; and for the same reason he defined 'matter' (body) as 'extension.' But this is the fallacy of *definition by initial predication,* and on this fallacy the whole system of idealism has been reared.

THE DATA CONCERNING THE NON-EGO WORLD

Unquestionably, much of our knowledge of the external world, which we ordinarily consider directly given in sense-perception, is acquired through a very complicated process of perception, intellectual abstraction, and mental inference. We are not brutes, but intellectual beings; we not only perceive, but think. Consequently, it is not always easy to distinguish what is due to direct sense-perception from that which is the result of our interpreting judgment. Nevertheless, the primary facts are plain and simple. The very data which reveal to us our body as real and intra-Ego, reveal to us *concretely* at the same time and in the same way that bodies exist which are extra-subjective and extra-Ego: they possess the feature of *externality* and *otherness.*

The sense of *touch* is fundamental in this respect. When I move my hand over parts of my body, I perceive that my hand is distinct from these parts. At the same time, however, I also perceive that the parts touched are not foreign to my being but belong to it as well as my hand does: they are all parts and members of the same organic, structural whole. But when my hand touches a book, a desk, an apple, a building, a tree, a human body (other than my own), it is immediately clear to me that these things *do not belong to my being;* they are 'other,' extra-Ego, external, something totally different from my self. All the objects which I contact while moving through space are thus perceived to possess this characteristic of 'otherness.' I can move my own bodily members from place to place, but I observe a definite *resistance* exerted against my body by many things. I cannot walk through them, neither can I surmount them nor push them aside; they are unyielding objects which block my path, so that I am obliged to walk around them. I thus experience objects with triple dimensions, with solidity, with weight, with impenetrability, with permanence and stability.

Besides this passive resistance to my body, I also experience the *active influence* of other bodies upon my own. Fire burns it, water wets it, a stone bruises it, dirt soils it, a heavy object breaks and crushes it. These things are not perceived by me to belong to my organism as a part of my being and self; on the contrary, just because my organism is clearly intuited as consisting of definite members occupying definite limits of space, I *concretely* perceive at the same time that these 'other' objects are external to me, having a real existence for themselves independent of my own.

The sense of *sight* also reveals 'externality' and 'otherness,' when taken in conjunction with the sense of touch and assisted by conscious experience. I soon learn to interpret the visual picture according to the more immediate perceptions of touch. My right hand touches my left arm; and my visual image coincides so completely with my tactual experience, that I thereby discover that the 'thing touching' is my right hand, while the 'thing touched' is my left arm. A number of such experiments helps me to 'identify' visually the various parts of my body with accuracy and security. Once this identification is an established fact, my sight unerringly distinguishes between my own body and objects *external* to my body. A blind man clearly perceives the 'otherness' and 'externality' of objects outside his bodily frame, but a person with sight possesses the added perception of the more far-reaching and more clearly defined visual image. When touch and sight are united in perception, the result provides an overwhelming amount of data which reveal an evidently real and existing material world of 'external' objects. I thus learn that my body occupies a relatively small amount of space, while the world is a tremendously large place filled with innumerable objects, large and small, at rest and in motion, permanent and changing, endowed with characteristics which are partly the same and partly very different from those of my own body.

THE EXISTENCE OF THE NON-EGO WORLD

In establishing the reality and existence of this external, non-Ego world so vividly presented in our perception, the procedure is practically the same as in proving the reality and existence of our extra-mental body. If our own extended body must be admitted as real, there can be hardly less reason to admit the extra-Ego world as real; for, after all, our own body is also *a part of the world at large,* possessing the same general characteristics and features as those possessed by 'external' bodies.

Whatever *theoretical* difficulties idealists may find in the perception of an external world by an unextended mind, it is obvious that their theory does not harmonize with the exigencies of *practical life* as lived by everybody, including these theorists themselves. The things of this workaday world are simply too real to be argued out of existence in this fashion. If our body is real, the world is real. No mother can ever consider her child and her pains to be the same, mere 'felt-experiences.' No soldier in the ghastly turmoil of war, with his leg ripped to shreds by a shell, can be made to believe that the bullets and shells he faced and the men and guns he fought were only 'conscious states.' When the farmer plows his field, and the laborer digs his ditch, and the ironworker rigs his beams, and the engineer runs his train — in short, when man lives his routine life in his daily occupations, he cannot but be a thoroughgoing realist concerning the world of material objects around him. All humanity cannot be wrong, and a few idealist philosophers right, in their view regarding the reality and existence of the external, physical world. If idealist theories cannot agree with this 'realism of the savage,' as demanded by practical living, then so much the worse for these theories: there must be something radically wrong with them.

Plain realism is in accord with the findings of the *sciences*. Astronomy, physics, geology, anthropology, zoology, botany, chemistry, bacteriology, therapeutics — in fact, all the natural sciences have sense and meaning only on the assumption that nature is a real world of existing, extended, material objects. The laws of nature which scientists formulate have application, not to mental states and subjective phenomena, but to the physical objects in a mind-independent existence. Their observations and experiments in no way impugn the realistic conception of the universe; if anything, they confirm it, even when age-old beliefs are proved to be naïve and erroneous.

The reason why our mind is naturally convinced of the reality of the external world as we perceive it to be, lies in the fact that we are intuitively aware that we do not produce our impressions and perceptions of the external objects: we are *passive,* in the sense that our consciousness testifies that the impressions and perceptions are *produced in us from outside*. We cannot produce them at will, nor can we change them at our convenience. But if the objects, as we perceive them, were only internal modifications of our consciousness, without a reality of their own, why this *persistence,* this *regularity,* this *permanent order,* this *compulsion?* Many of our perceptions are painful, unpleasant, nauseous, embarrassing, nerve-racking; though we fain would rid ourselves of them, we cannot. The reason is plain: these impressions are made by objects which are real and over which we have no control. We are *forced* to perceive them, if our senses are within the sphere of their influence.

THE REALITY OF OTHER MINDS

There is one thing in which idealists are egregiously *inconsistent:* they all admit, tacitly or explicitly, the existence of *other minds.* And how could they deny the existence of 'other minds,' when they appeal to them, reason with them, argue with them, quote them, and wrangle with them, all in an effort to convince them of the truth of idealism? But how do they know of the existence and thoughts of these 'other minds'? Our experience is witness to the fact that we have direct and immediate knowledge of no other mind but our own. Our knowledge, then, of 'other minds' can only be indirect and mediate. Then how? Through the medium of *language* and *speech.* Language may be expressed in spoken or written words, or by means of signs; but language in some form is necessary.

Idealists agree that extra-Ego reality either does not exist at all or, if it does, it is an unknown and unknowable quantity, because the mind of man is restricted in its knowledge to its own subjective conscious states. Were this the case, our mind could not know anything about 'other minds,' for the simple reason that they are not only extra-mental but *extra-Ego* with regard to ourselves. The fact of language, however, proves conclusively that 'other minds' are not the unknown and unknowable beings which the idealists would have us believe.

That this 'other mind' is an existent entity distinct from myself is clear from the fact that the *ideas* which I thus receive in the course of this thought-communication from the 'other mind' are often entirely *new* to me and are given to me 'from without.' I am aware beyond the possibility of doubt that these ideas are not my own, are not the product of my own thinking. In many instances these ideas are so foreign to my way of thinking and so antagonistic to my own ideas, that a conflict arises between the two sets of ideas and a controversy or argument ensues between 'my mind' and the 'other mind.' How could this happen, if 'my mind' and the 'other mind' were identical in being? Hence, the fact of language and speech proves conclusively that both 'my mind' and 'other minds' exist and that they are distinct and non-identical.

If my knowledge cannot go beyond my own conscious states, if I cannot transcend the boundary of my own knowing mind, and if all extra-Ego reality is unknown and unknowable to me, so that I cannot refer these 'extraneous' ideas to 'other minds,' then I myself must be the *originator* of all these ideas. Consider the consequences of such a theory. Whenever I read a book or listen to a lecture, the contents of the book or lecture enters my consciousness. And thus all the philosophies of the world, from Thales and Socrates and Plato and Aristotle to St. Thomas Aquinas and Descartes and Kant and Hegel and James, would perforce be the product of my own mind and its thinking! The idealist postulate demands this conclusion. This, however, is ridiculous on the face of it. No one in his sane mind would seriously assert that he alone is the author of all these different, contradictory systems of thought. If they are the result of my own thinking, why the *differences* and *contradictions* between them? And why the *difficulty in understanding* some of these systems, if I am their author? Can anyone seriously doubt that these philosophies originate in 'other minds' and that I merely assimilate their ideas from them?

The whole argumentation can be formulated in the following dilemma. The knowledge which we naturally and spontaneously ascribe to 'other minds' either originates from *them* or from *our* mind. If the former, realism is established, because we possess a true and valid knowledge of extra-mental and extra-Ego reality. If the latter, then we cannot explain why we are not conscious of the process, why so much of this knowledge is foreign to our consciousness, why so many of these ideas and systems are contradictory to our own, and why we are compelled to 'learn' the different languages. In the former case, idealism is refuted and realism proved; in the latter case, there is a contradiction and an illusion in our mental equipment, and universal skepticism must follow. All the evidence points to the former of the two alternatives as being true.

Though our conviction in the reality and existence of the external, physical world is thus established as a fact, we still have to face the question: *How* can our Ego perceive something which is completely non-Ego? What is the *epistemological bridge* between the unextended mind and the extended, external world? The difficulty seems more formidable than it actually is. Once the reality of our own body is proved and admitted, the difficulty vanishes to a great extent. Our body is the 'epistemological bridge' between our mind and the world. Our mind does not contact the physical universe directly, but through and in our body.

It is not necessary to prove that we can perceive *all* reality of the material world. If we can show that physical, external reality can be contacted and perceived *in some phase of its being,* it suffices to prove that external reality exists outside our Ego and can be perceived. Then realism is rationally justified. And this can be shown to be a fact.

Our body is an extended being, occupying space and place in three dimensions. United with the mind into a single organic principle of perceptive action, it forms a sense-conscious being. Our Ego thus feels itself to be a living, sense-conscious, *extended, corporeal substance;* this has been shown previously. As such, then, we should be capable of perceiving extended bodies, whether it be our own body or 'other bodies.' If we can perceive our body as *our own,* then any body, different from our own and in contact with it, should be perceived as *different,* and as 'other.' Such actually is the case.

I walk along the street, and I feel my body moving; my intra-muscular sense tells me that I am taking steps and that each stride covers a certain distance. If I come face to face with a wall or building, my progress is stopped; I find a barrier which effectively hinders me from continuing in motion. No matter how strenuously I push against this barrier, I cannot push it over and proceed on my way. I perceive here the same impenetrability and resistance that I experience in my own body, when I stop the progress of a moving object, like a rolling ball, with my hand or foot. Consequently, just as I know that *my* body is real in resisting the ball, I know that the resisting wall or building is as real as my body; the situation, though reversed, is actually the same in both instances. When I walk alongside a building, holding my hand against it as I walk, I perceive that the building is stationary, while I am moving; but when I stand still beside a train, and feel the train passing along under my outstretched hand, I know that I am stationary and the train is moving. I thus perceive that the building and train are similar to my own body and must be just as real, but are extra-Ego and 'other.' Thus my body becomes a *standard of measurement* with which I can gauge the *size* and *distances* of things in relation to me. The reason 'why' and 'how' I can perceive them lies in their *objective commensurateness* and *corporality,* which is like that of my own body.

It is, then, through *direct contact* with my body and through the sense of touch that I can become immediately and intuitively aware of 'other' bodies in their reality and existence. I perceive my own body as 'identical with self,' while I feel these others as 'non-identical with self.' The perception and the felt-experience is the same in both cases. If my body is perceived to be real, the 'other' bodies must also be real; the former guarantees the latter. In this fashion my body acts as the 'epistemological bridge' between the mind and the world: though an extra-mental thing, my body is organically united with the mind and is related psychically to it; as an extended thing, it is of the same nature as the extended objects in the material world and is related to them. This unique position of the body as an extra-mental, extended being *within the unity of the Ego* enables it to bring the extra-mental, extended objects of the external world into cognitive union with the mind, so that mind and world meet each other in the human body:

there, on this epistemological bridge, is their mutual point of contact. The 'extended' but 'vitalized' body, being a psycho-physical substance, is the natural link between the world of mind and the world of matter, making a perception of the latter within the former both a possibility and a fact.

Considering the facts as manifested in the data of our consciousness, we are compelled to conclude that *realism,* and not idealism, correctly interprets sense-perception with regard to our body and the non-Ego world. The spontaneous conviction and the common-sense view of humanity is seen to be vindicated as substantially valid and true. We have now obtained two truths of tremendous epistemological value: *'The reality and existence of our own body as an extra-mental object and of the external world as an extra-Ego object is a fact; and our body and the universe can be perceived by us as they are in themselves.'* We now have a reflex, philosophical certitude regarding them: idealism cannot explain the fact, while realism does.

SUMMARY OF CHAPTER X

In order to discover whether *extra-mental* and *extra-Ego reality* exists and can be perceived, we must scrutinize and interpret the facts.

1. *Data Concerning Extra-Mental Reality.* Our *body* is such a reality, and it is clearly perceived to possess 'extensity.' It is revealed to us as 'extra-mental,' but an integral factor in the process of sense-perception. Mind and body belong to the Ego and form a unitary principle of action.

2. *Existence of Extra-Mental Reality.* Realism, which accepts the existence of the human body, is in agreement with the facts of everyday life and with the findings of science. Consciousness gives direct evidence of the reality and existence of our body.

3. *Perception of Extra-Mental Reality.* It is possible, because the 'subject of knowledge' is not the unextended mind as such, but the Ego. The perceptive act is vital, but extended, demanding a vital and extended organism as its subject. Such is the

Ego and, since the body is an integral part of this organism, it should be capable of concretely perceiving the body as an extramental reality. Descartes' antithesis is based on the fallacy of 'definition by initial predication.'

4. *Data Concerning the Non-Ego World.* They reveal 'externality' and 'otherness' in objects. Touch shows them as external to our body. The active influence of such objects on our body shows them to be extra-Ego.

5. *Existence of Non-Ego World.* Daily life and science demand that we accept the non-Ego world as real. Our passivity in receiving impressions proves that they are produced in us by 'outside' things; this alone accounts for their persistence, regularity, order, and compulsory perception.

Other minds exist. This is proved by language, which conveys new ideas to my mind; my consciousness testifies to the fact that they do not originate in my own mind. But 'other minds' — whose existence is admitted by idealists — are non-Ego realities.

6. *Perception of the Non-Ego World.* Extra-Ego objects can be perceived because our body, being a psycho-physical reality, is the *epistemological bridge* between the mind and the world. Through touch I perceive my own body as 'identical with self' and other bodies as 'non-identical with self'; this is due to their commensurateness and corporality.

Realism is thus critically established. We have vindicated the spontaneous conviction: *The reality and existence of our body and of the extra-Ego world is a fact; and both are perceived as they are in themselves.*

READINGS

J. G. Vance, *op. cit.,* Chs. VI, VII; P. Coffey, *op. cit.,* Vol. II, Chs. XIV, XV; J. T. Barron, *op. cit.,* Ch. XII; T. Pesch, *op. cit.,* pp. 89–151; J. E. Turner, *A Theory of Direct Realism,* Chs. III–VI; D. Card. Mercier, *Manual, op. cit.,* pp. 393–399; A. K. Rogers, *What is Truth?* pp. 87–92; G. E. Moore, "A Defense of Common Sense," in *Contemporary British Philosophy,* second series, pp. 191–225; John Laird, "How

Our Minds Go Beyond Themselves in Knowing," in *Contemporary British Philosophy,* first series, pp. 216–230; D. Drake, *Mind and Its Place in Nature,* Chs. III, IV; G. F. Stout, *Mind and Matter,* Bk. II, Chs. I, VIII; Bk. IV, Ch. I; C. A. Strong, *Why the Mind Has a Body,* Chs. X, XI, XII.

Chapter XI

REPRESENTATIVE AND PRESENTATIVE REALISM

Realism, which contends that extra-mental and extra-Ego reality exists and can be known by the human mind, must be accepted as the only true and valid theory of human knowledge, because it alone gives an adequate interpretation of the facts and data revealed by our consciousness. By accepting realism, however, as a general theory, the problem of the validity of human sense-knowledge is not completely solved. There are rival theories of realism. Realists are not in accord as to the manner in which the mind receives its knowledge of the external physical world through sense-perception. Due to their divergence of views in explaining the manner in which the mind effects its knowledge, realism appears in two radically different types: *representative* and *presentative* realism. These will now have to be examined and evaluated.

TYPES OF REPRESENTATIVE REALISM

Representative realism (mediate realism, hypothetical realism, cosmothetical realism, inferential realism) is the theory which maintains that the human mind is immediately aware, not of the external objects themselves, but of its own *internal* *representations* only, from which it then *infers* the existence of external, non-Ego reality as their *cause.* Representationists accept, of course, the existence of an external, physical, extra-Ego world, otherwise they would not be realists; but they claim that we are incapable of 'perceiving' it in any way directly and immediately by means of intuitive sense-perception. We have only subjectively produced images or 'representations' in our mind. The mind perceives these images or representations and, since it is aware that it is not their sole cause, *reasons* to the existence of an outside world as their physical cause. The existence of the non-Ego world is thus a matter of inference on the part of our intellect; hence the name 'inferential' realism. And since this gives us no immediate but only a mediate knowledge of the world, we have 'mediate' realism. The world is simply assumed as a necessary hypothesis, in order to give an adequate explanation of the data of sense-perception; therefore the term 'hypothetical' or 'cosmothetical' realism. In any case, we never perceive directly anything but our own internal mental representations, and these are produced partly by the outside objects and partly by the subjective action of the perceiving mind. The question naturally arose: Is there any *resemblance* between these 'representations' and the extra-mental and extra-Ego objects which they represent? The answer led to two main kinds of representative realism: subjective and objective.

According to *subjective* representationism our knowledge of the existence of an extra-mental universe is mediate, indirect, inferential; we know that extra-mental reality *exists*, but that is all we know. What the objects in this universe really are like in nature, is beyond our knowledge, because our 'representations' of these things are merely 'mental images' or 'symbols.' These images or symbols bear no resemblance whatever to the objects they 'represent'; they resemble them no more than the printed words on a page are similar to the things for which they stand. The outside reality itself is absolutely *unknown* and *unknowable*; we can only know that *something exists* which produces this subjective image in us. The 'representations' of our perception are indeed caused by external objects, but they tell us nothing about the reality of the objects which cause them. Such is the view of the hypothetical dualists of modern epistemology. Since, however, this class of representationists admits the existence of some sort of extra-mental and extra-Ego reality, they claim that their theory is a genuine form of realism.

The *objective* representative realists agree with the preceding class of philosophers in contending that what the mind immediately perceives is the mental image or 'representation'; and from this 'representation' they also *infer* the existence of an outside world. But they differ from 'subjective' representationists in claiming that the mental images or 'representations' *resemble* the objects which cause them. They base this resemblance on the Principle of Causality. They argue that an effect must resemble its cause. All operations proceed from the nature or essence of a thing; different natures, then, will produce different kinds of operations. Consequently, the kind of operation will reveal the kind of nature from which it springs. And thus, from the effects of these operations we can logically infer the qualities of the nature operating. Applying this principle to the case of sense-perception, they contend that the 'representations' produced in the mind by external, physical objects enable us to draw a legitimate inference to the qualities and nature of the causes which produce the 'representations' in us. In this manner, these 'representations' are truly 'images' of the things outside and much more than mere 'symbols' of them. The knowledge thus acquired contains genuine information regarding the extra-mental and extra-Ego world, even though we have no immediate perception or intuition of the objects themselves. This view of sense-perception is held by many neo-scholastic philosophers, like *Mercier,*[1] *Jeannière,* and others. Some *critical realists* belong to this class. According to them, the mind perceives the 'essences' of things, not the things themselves; but these 'essences' resemble the nature of the individual realities.

SUBJECTIVE REPRESENTATIVE REALISM

We group in this class all those theories which, while maintaining the fundamental idealist principle that the mind cannot transcend its own conscious states, accept the existence of an

---

[1] *Critériologie Générale,* 1906, n. 140, p. 386: "Mais il nous est impossible *d'affirmer avec certitude l'existence* d'une ou de plusieurs réalités *extramentales* sans employer le principe de causalité."

extended, material reality as the hidden and unknown *cause* of our sense-perception. Such are, for instance, Kant's phenomenalism and Spencer's 'transfigured realism.' There are, of course, many variations of this general theory of representative realism, but they all agree in this that they are a form of *hypothetical* dualism and realism; they *postulate* the existence of extra-mental and extended things, claiming at the same time that the human mind can have no knowledge or perception of them. Such a realism is no realism at all; it is a disguised and veiled idealism. These philosophers intend to be realists, but they could not escape the net of idealism.

The proof of this has already been given in our examination of extra-mental and extra-Ego reality. According to subjective representationism we can know only our own conscious states. All perception of extension and extended objects is merely a conscious state. Therefore, they say, all such perception is nothing but a modification of our mind and reveals nothing of the qualities and nature of the objects themselves.

If this were the case, our knowledge of our body (extra-mental reality) and of the external world (extra-Ego reality), as proved in the preceding chapter, would be purely of an *imaginary* and *subjective* character. And since, according to these thinkers, this knowledge tells us nothing whatever about the things-in-themselves outside the mind, this knowledge is illusory. Our *intellectual* knowledge, however, is based on this sense knowledge, and as such must also be illusory. What value, then, can our knowledge have? It is all a mental construction, a subjective fabrication. That this would destroy the validity of all our knowledge, must be obvious. Skepticism is inevitable.

Practically all subjective representationists, unless they are thoroughgoing idealists, speak of the *brain* and brain-conditions, *nerves* and neural currents, *sense-organs* and sentient experiences. But what meaning have such terms and phrases except that they refer to a *real* body with the side-by-sideness of extended, material parts? If the body is real, we know a great deal about the 'extra-mental' body and its operations, and representationism refutes itself; and if the body is not real, these philosophers are illogical and inconsistent in speaking of such things and building their theory upon them.

The adherents of subjective representative realism admit that *some form* of extra-mental and extra-Ego reality *exists*. Most of them are even willing to concede that this reality consists of a multiplicity of things; they are pluralistic. Some lean toward the notion of a vague 'world stuff,' 'mind-stuff,' or 'neutral stuff,' very much akin to the Absolute of the more pronounced idealists. But whether their conception of extra-mental and extra-Ego reality be pluralistic or dualistic or monistic, they thereby claim to know *more* about this reality than its *mere existence*. This, however, is inconsistent, because their fundamental position is thus relinquished.

Besides, on what grounds do they acknowledge the existence of this reality? On the grounds of causality: these things or this reality is the *cause* of our perceptions. But if the Principle of Causality enables them to infer this existence, why should this same principle not enable them to infer *more* than the mere existence? One can see no logical reason why it should be restricted to this one fact alone. If representationists were consistent with the tenets of their theory, they could not conclude legitimately even to this fact of existence, because in this knowledge they actually *transcend* their own conscious states; they *do* know something which lies *outside* the confines of their mind. Again, if all our knowledge is purely mental, then the Principle of Causality is also nothing but a purely mental product; as such, this principle would demand only a *mental cause* for our perceptions. For them to apply a principle of the mental and ideal order to the real and physical world is, according to their own theory, an illogical and unwarrantable procedure. What, then, is left for them but an unmitigated idealism which must eventually end in solipsism? But that would be intellectual suicide.

Representative realism is the outcome of empiricism, and empiricism is the philosophic offshoot of *science*. Above all things, these philosophers want to be scientists and be in accord with science. We agree with them in the view that science must furnish the groundwork, the raw material, of philosophy. But science is by no means a champion of subjective representative realism. On the contrary, science absolutely demands extra-mental and extra-Ego reality, not only as far as its existence is concerned, but also as regards the *nature, qualities,* and *operations* of the extended, physical *objects* as we know them. Or would anyone seriously assert that the *laws* of science are only 'mental' laws which regulate the relations of 'symbols,' 'ideas,' and 'representations' of the mind? Do they not apply, according to the intentions of scientists, to actually existing objects of a real, material universe? The *scientists themselves* certainly are convinced that they are dealing with extra-mental and extra-Ego realities that have an existence of their own, independent of the mind that conceives and knows them. Subjective representative realism is thus seen to be contrary to all suppositions and conclusions of science. If these things are not real, science loses all meaning and purpose. But a theory that is so subversive of the fundamentals of exact science, must be fallacious.

Subjective representative realism is nothing but a half-hearted idealism and therefore no realism at all. It cannot explain the facts and must be rejected.

OBJECTIVE REPRESENTATIVE REALISM

While *objective* representative realism agrees with subjective representationism in admitting that the mind perceives directly and immediately only 'images' or 'representations,' from which it then *infers* the reality of extra-mental and extra-Ego objects (the human body and the universe), it differs radically from it in contending that these 'images' or 'representations' bear a *resemblance* to these objects and thereby give us a genuine knowledge of their being. They base this contention, as we have seen, on the Principle of Causality.

The question then arises: *Must effects 'resemble' their causes?*

If so, the theory can be considered valid; if not, our knowledge of the external world is no better than that of subjective representationism, which is, as we have just noted, only idealism in disguise. The whole matter, then, resolves itself into this: Does the fact of causality always imply a *similarity* between cause and effect, so that a knowledge of the effect (the 'representations' here) automatically gives us a knowledge of the nature and being of the cause (the extra-mental and extra-Ego objects)?

Experience tells us beyond reasonable doubt that effects do *not* always resemble their causes; in many cases there is no similarity whatever between the two. Our daily contact with causality shows plainly that effects are of two kinds: *univocal* and *equivocal*. 'Univocal' effects are those which are *similar in kind* to the causes which produce them. We see innumerable instances of this in nature. Plants, animals, and men reproduce their own kind, and here the effects are certainly similar to the causes. Horses produce horses, cows produce cows, eagles produce eagles, man produces man, and so on, throughout the entire kingdom of living beings: the offspring (effect) resembles the parent (cause). These are univocal effects similar to their causes.

'Equivocal' effects, on the other hand, are *dissimilar in kind* to their causes. The world is also full of these. The music (effect) of a pipe organ in no way resembles the pipes, the mechanism, the organist, the air (cause). The destruction caused by a shell hitting a building has no similarity to the shell, the exploding powder, the gun, or the gunner. A piece of sculpture representing a horse carries no resemblance to the chisel or the sculptor.

Bearing this in mind, we are now in a position to pass judgment on the validity of the theory of objective representative realism. The main contention, that the 'images' or 'representations' of extended material objects bear a real *resemblance* to these objects, is *groundless* and *gratuitous*. These 'representations' are produced by external objects, but what guarantee can they give us that these 'representations' are *univocal effects?* This is, from what we have seen above, certainly not self-understood; because an effect might be either univocal or equivocal, and there is nothing to show why these 'representations' must be, or will be, univocal rather than equivocal. And if they should happen to be equivocal, their 'resemblance' to the external objects is gone, and then we know nothing about what these external objects are in themselves.

The *only* things the mind can perceive are the 'images,' the 'representations.' They *may* resemble external objects, but they may also, as far as we can tell, be totally unlike the external objects which produce them. Our mind must be forever in doubt on this score. Our knowledge of the external world loses all certainty, and we are again on the threshold of idealism and skepticism.

Objective representative realism thus offers no solution for the problem of the validity of human sense-knowledge. It also is but a veiled and disguised form of idealism and as such is erroneous and fallacious. What, then, is the outcome of our present investigation? Just this: every form of representative realism, whether subjective or objective, restricting the human mind to a knowledge of its own internal conscious states and denying a direct perception of extra-mental and extra-Ego reality, is *no realism at all,* but only a disguised variant of *idealism.*

PRESENTATIVE REALISM

Presentative realism (immediate realism, intuitive realism, natural realism, perceptionism) is the theory which maintains that physical, external objects are 'presented' *directly in some form* to consciousness in sense-perception, so that their reality is perceived *as it exists in itself* 'out there' in nature. In this view the objects are 'present' or 'presented' directly to the mind through the medium of the senses; hence the term 'presentative.' The external object itself is 'immediately' the object which is 'perceived' or 'intuited'; this explains the terms 'immediate' and 'intuitive' realism and 'perceptionism.' And since it is 'natural' for man to think that he actually perceives the objects themselves as they are 'out there in nature,' this theory is also called 'natural' realism. The fundamental thought in presentative realism is that the *objects themselves, in some form or other,* are directly perceived in sense-perception. Because of the active influence of both object and mind upon the sense-process, it is natural that some realists will give a more 'objective' and others a more 'subjective' interpretation of the facts involved. And thus two rival theories have been advanced to account for our experiences: rigid or naïve presentative realism and moderate or critical presentative realism. The difference between these is one of degree, not of principle.

Rigid or *naïve* perceptionism is the realism of the ordinary man and of the philosopher who is convinced that the things he perceives are actually in nature as they *appear to his senses.* If he sees a colored object, the color is really 'outside' in the thing, just as he sees it. Sounds are real tones emitted by the sounding object, just as he hears them with his ear. And all objects are extended, have a definite shape, and are at rest or in motion, just as he experiences them through one or more of his senses. In other words, *all qualities are objectively real as perceived*.

Critical or *moderate* perceptionism claims that *some* qualities of objects are 'objectively' real and as such are perceived immediately and intuitively by the senses; other qualities are not present in the object as such, independent of the sensing subject, but exist only *potentially* or *causally* in the objects. Thus, extension, shape, motion or rest, unity or multiplicity, would be considered 'objective' qualities inherent in the bodies themselves, independent of sense and mind, and as such would be directly perceived. But color and sound, for example, do not exist in the objects themselves as 'color' and 'sound'; these are 'subjective' qualities which exist only in the perceiving senses, with this distinction, however, that they are causally produced in the senses by vibrations coming from the objects 'out there' in nature. In order to understand the problem better, it will be necessary to explain the various kinds of sense-qualities.

It has become customary to divide the sense-qualities of objects into *primary* and *secondary,* or as Aristotle and the scholastics did, into *common* and *proper.* Any object, quality, or feature of reality, which can be perceived by a sense, is called a 'sense-object,' 'sensile,' 'sensible,' or 'sense-quality'; they all mean the same thing. Now, some of the sensibles or sense-qualities can be perceived by a *single* sense *only.* Thus, the organ of sight alone perceives colors; the organ of smell alone perceives odors; the organ of hearing alone perceives sound: such qualities are *proper* or *secondary* sensibles. Other sensibles or sense-qualities can be perceived by *more than one* sense-organ. Extended surface, shape, volume, number (i.e., whether one or many), rest and motion, can be perceived by at least two of the senses, sight and touch: they are *common* or *primary* sensibles.

And this brings us to the very heart of the controversy waged between rigid and critical perceptionism: *Are all sense-qualities 'objective' or are some of them 'subjective'?* Rigid or naïve perceptionism stands for the theory that all sensibles are 'objective'; they are really in the objects as perceived. Moderate or critical perceptionism, on the other hand, claims that the common sensibles are really in the objects as perceived, but the proper sensibles are more or less 'subjective' in character.

THE CASE OF RIGID PRESENTATIVE REALISM

The rigid realist occupies a naturally strong position, for he has practically all humanity to support his view. The man in the street, undisturbed by the findings of science and the psychological difficulties involved in sense-perception, is a naïve realist who is thoroughly convinced that he directly perceives all extra-mental and extra-subjective objects as they *really are in themselves.* The philosopher, who is a rigid perceptionist, is not so unreflecting and unscientific; he knows that he cannot take things for granted and that many objects do not always 'appear' as they 'really are.' Still, while he is fully aware of the many philosophic difficulties inherent in rigid realism, he places himself frankly on the standpoint that all sense-qualities, primary and secondary, are intuitively perceived as they 'really are' in nature, provided the *normal conditions* of sense-perception are present. If conditions are abnormal, errors will be committed; if they are normal, errors can be eliminated. These conditions pertain to the 'sentient subject,' to the 'sensed object,' and to the 'medium' intervening between the object and the subject.

As far as the *sentient subject* is concerned, it is necessary that the sense-organs be free from organic and functional defects. If any of the senses are abnormally constructed or if their proper function is impeded in any important degree, it will be but natural that they cannot register the data properly; distorted perceptions will result, and errors of judgment will be the inevitable consequence. The case would be similar to using defective instruments or tools in highly specialized crafts. Regarding the *sensed objects,* they must be placed at the right distance and in the right setting. Every sense has its own definite field of operation; within this field its efficiency is high, and beyond this field it is low or even nil. A specific relation exists between object and sense, and this relation cannot be appreciably disturbed without incurring the risk of faulty perception. The *medium* intervening between object and sense must also be normal, otherwise perception cannot be normal. A change of the medium will naturally bring about a change in the relation between the object and the subject, with the result that the perception of the object will be distorted. An oar partly submerged in water will appear bent, because a part of the rays of light reaches the eye through the medium of air alone, while the other part reaches it through air and water. In a similar manner, due to the refracting action of the atmosphere at the horizon, the morning sun is seen before it actually rises above the earth's rim, and it appears red and much larger than it really is; variations in the density of the atmospheric medium account for the phenomenon.

It is unquestionable that the *normality of conditions* is an important factor in true sense-perception. Given the presence of normal conditions, the rigid perceptionists claim, our senses must be considered reliable within the sphere of their proper function and enable the intellect to draw proper conclusions from the data presented by the senses. To deny this would mean that our normal senses under normal conditions would give us a false and illusory picture of the world around us; and that would be tantamount to the assertion that *illusion and error* would be the *normal result* of our faculties in their *normal* and *natural operations*. Such an assertion, however, would inevitably lead to general skepticism, because neither our senses in their normal operations nor reason in its legitimate conclusions could be trusted. That, of course, would be the bankruptcy of all knowledge, and science and philosophy would be hopeless and useless occupations. But this is evidently absurd. Consequently, our senses under normal conditions must be reliable sources of information concerning the extra-mental and external world. If errors occur, they are only incidental and accidental and can be avoided by careful and thoughtful attention to the data. *world in all its appearance is just as it is to us.*

This general principle the rigid perceptionists then apply to the perception of *sense-qualities*. And they argue in the following fashion. "There are innumerable instances in which we act with deliberate attention and with a knowledge of the essential normality of our senses. In applying our senses to an object, we are conscious that *all* our sense-perceptions testify with equal force to the existence of certain qualities in the single bodies, namely, motion or rest, volume, shape, and distance. The conjunction of these conditions, however, entitles us to pass a judgment on the sense-qualities of the single bodies, because we thereby find ourselves *forced* to pass this judgment, and we consider any serious doubt to be unreasonable. If our judgment, notwithstanding this compulsion, were false, we would be subject to error out of necessity and would have to despair of all certitude. In special and definite instances, therefore, our reason is capable of judging with certitude on the sense-qualities of bodies.

"With regard to the particular case of the so-called *secondary* sense-qualities, there can be no doubt that our subjective sense-perceptions, if we presuppose the existence of bodies, will find their adequate explanation in nothing but the specific qualities of bodies through which the latter act upon our senses. For even the existence of bodies could not be known to us except by means of those qualities in virtue of which the bodies appear to us as colored in this or that way, as having this or that taste or odor, or as being hard or soft. To deny or doubt the trust-worthiness of our senses in the perception of these qualities would therefore be as much as to question the possibility of a knowledge of the *bodies* themselves."[2]

Immediate intuitive perception of sense-qualities we certainly have. Then why make a distinction between primary and secondary sensibles at all, some of which are supposed to be 'objective,' while others are considered more or less 'subjective'? There seems no reasonable cause *in the qualities themselves* to judge any of them to be more subjective or less objective than the others.

Furthermore, humanity in general has the spontaneous conviction that *all* sense-qualities, primary and secondary, are found in the objects as they appear in perception. This is the verdict of *common sense* and therefore of *natural reason*. Can all humanity be wrong in a matter which is so interwoven with daily experience of the most intimate character? If so, is human reason then not unreliable? And if unreliable, is not every philosophical theory then just sheer waste of time and energy? If we impugn the reliability of reason and our senses, must we not end in the bog of skepticism? We must remember that the constant and universal conviction of mankind gives *presumptive evidence* of tremendous force to this view of the

---

[2] A. Lehmen, *Lehrbuch der Philosophie*, Vol. I, p. 192, 3rd edition (Herder im Breisgau, 1909).

objectivity of *all* sense-qualities without exception. This theory explains the facts so fully and convincingly that it amounts practically to a *scientific and philosophic law of nature.*

ANSWER OF CRITICAL PRESENTATIVE REALISM

As far as the arguments of the rigid realists are concerned, the critical perceptionists subscribe to them, considering their general trend and import. But they deny that the arguments prove that *all sense-qualities* without exception, primary and secondary, must be accepted as *objectively present in the objects* 'out there' in nature just as they 'appear' to the senses. This conclusion exceeds the premises. The argument merely proves that *in general* immediate, intuitive perception of the external, physical qualities of objects is the correct theory of knowledge, but it does not prove that *all* sense-qualities *in particular* are intuited as objectively present in the things themselves. To argue from the 'general' truth of a statement to every 'particular' instance and case which apparently falls under it makes them guilty of the fallacy of passing from an 'absolute' to a 'qualified' statement. Certainly, if the argument were as exclusive as the rigid realists assert, the question would be definitely settled; but that they have not proved. After all, the question is a matter of *facts* properly interpreted. The facts are the same for everybody, and no one denies them; but the interpretation of these facts is a different affair, and *reason* is the arbiter there.

We must always bear in mind, that the *senses* themselves do *not judge:* they merely *report* the presence of certain sense-impressions. It is reason, and reason alone, which judges whether anything 'objective' corresponds outside in nature to the subjective sensations and perceptions thus recorded by the senses. Truth resides in the judgment, and judgment is exclusively the function of the intellect. The senses can do no more than present the data, which reason must then interpret according to its own lights. And if reason, after a careful scrutiny of the data of sense-perception, is forced to judge that certain sense-qualities are not objectively present in nature as perceived by the senses, we must accept the dictates of reason as final. Any other course would be unscientific and unphilosophical and would be bound to lead ultimately into error. General statements will not settle the issue; facts alone can. So let the facts speak for themselves.

Again, rigid idealists assert that the *secondary* qualities of bodies must be objectively present in them; otherwise we would not know even of the *existence* of bodies themselves, and thus the possibility of a knowledge of the *bodies* themselves would be called in question. They are wrong, for they prove too much and therefore nothing. Both rigid and critical presentationists consider the primary qualities as perfectly 'objective,' as really existing *in* the bodies as they are perceived by the sense of touch. It is through these qualities that the existence, extension, shape and voluminousness of bodies are observed in sense-perception. Here we have the essential guarantee of the reality of external bodies, and this guarantee is not invalidated by the assumption that the secondary qualities are not actually present in the bodies as perceived.

Furthermore, rigid perceptionists maintain that there is no foundation *in nature* for making such a radical distinction between primary and secondary qualities. Again they are wrong. Nature itself gives us the ground for making this distinction. The primary qualities are in themselves more *fundamental* in character than the secondary. To have definite shape, volume, weight, and impenetrability, flows necessarily from the extension of bodies. There could be no colors, sounds, odors, flavors, temperature, and resistance, if these primary qualities were not present *before* them, since these secondary qualities need extended surface in order to exist and be what they are. The primary qualities can exist without the secondary, but the secondary cannot subsist without the primary. And then, too, the very nature of the *perceptive act* provides a reason for this distinction. The primary qualities are perceived by *direct contact* between our body and other bodies through the immediate perception of the sense of *touch*. Herein lies the *ultimate* assurance that these bodies and their fundamental qualities are real and objective. Other qualities, like color, sound, etc., are perceived, not through direct contact, but through some 'medium' distinct from the bodies and distinct from the qualities themselves, namely, vibratory motions of ether, air, and so on. Hence, it is false to assert that there is no natural distinction between the two sets of qualities and that bodies could not be known unless the objectivity of secondary qualities were also admitted. It might, then, very well be that the latter are more or less subjective, while the primary qualities alone are objectively present in bodies, without destroying the essential validity of sense-perception.

Finally, rigid perceptionists appeal to the spontaneous conviction and the common-sense judgment of mankind; all men, they say, consider the secondary as well as the primary qualities to reside in the objects as perceived. In answer to this, critical perceptionists maintain that this argument is of very dubious force, because this conviction is *not* at all as *universal* as claimed. In fact, it was the natural philosophy of the ordinary man which coined the phrase that "appearances deceive." This implies the well-grounded judgment that things are not always as they 'appear' to the senses. He corrects many sense-impressions through the *judgment* of his reasoning faculties, so that he is by far not as 'naïve' as many people think. He would never dream, for instance, of accepting the *diminishing perspective* of objects, as seen in his visual picture, as a literal transcription of reality; and that is a very vital point in visual perception. Nor does he believe in the actual *shifting of position* among objects, relative to each other, as he witnesses this phenomenon while traveling in a train or riding in his car, although that is what his eye shows him as clearly as anything else. He is very wary regarding the *real color* of objects, especially when viewed under different kinds of light, even though his eye can make no distinction between the 'objectivity' of the varying color perceptions under changing sources of illumination. He knows that a suit of clothes, which he examines, may appear black under electric light and yet be blue in sunlight. He is aware, too, that there is a considerable element of *subjectivity* in many of his sense-reactions. Sweet wine, for instance, always tastes sour to him after eating sugar, while dry wine appears sweet after lemon juice; he experiences chills of coldness throughout his body, so that his teeth chatter, although the temperature of his body is much higher than usual. Hundreds of similar examples could be adduced which manifest his conviction that things are frequently quite different in reality from what they appear to be according to the testimony of his senses. If he is not fully conscious of the corrective judgment of his interpreting reason in these and similar cases, this is due to the *habitual action* of lifelong experience which enables him to interpret these deceptive appearances correctly without being aware that he is doing so. All of which shows that the spontaneous convictions of the ordinary man do not favor rigid realism as much as is claimed.

Such is the answer of the critical perceptionists to the arguments of the defenders of rigid presentative realism. Their answer so far is *negative* in intent, showing that the opposing arguments lack cogency. More than this, of course, is required in order to prove that critical, and not rigid, presentative realism deserves to be classed as the only theory of sense-perception which explains all the facts. *Facts must prove or disprove a theory.* And critical perceptionists produce a formidable array of facts from science and from everyday life which, according to their view, furnish positive and incontestable proof of the truth of their theory. These facts, at least in their main outline, will now have to be considered.

SUMMARY OF CHAPTER XI

There are two main realist theories: representative and presentative realism. Both claim to be a genuine form of realism, capable of explaining all the facts.

1. *Representative Realism.* It is also called mediate, hypothetical, cosmothetical, or inferential realism. It maintains that the mind is immediately aware, not of the external objects themselves, but of its internal 'representations' only, from which it then infers the existence of external reality as their cause. It is *subjective* representationism, if it contends that these representations are mere 'symbols' of reality, without any resemblance to it. It is *objective* representationism, if it contends that these representations actually resemble the external objects which are their cause, thus giving us a genuine knowledge of these objects.

2. *Subjective Representative Realism.* If this theory were correct, our knowledge of our body and of extra-Ego reality would be imaginary and illusory. For these thinkers to speak of the brain, nerves, and sense-organs is an admission that we can and do know 'extra-mental' reality. They are inconsistent in restricting the Principle of Causality. Their position is contrary to science, because scientists are convinced that their findings refer to a real extra-mental world.

3. *Objective Representative Realism.* Effects may be univocal or equivocal, i.e., similar or dissimilar in kind to the causes. Experience shows that there are many equivocal effects in nature; they do not resemble their causes. Hence, the fact of resemblance must ever remain doubtful. All representative realism is disguised idealism.

4. *Presentative Realism.* It is also called immediate, intuitive, natural realism, perceptionism. It maintains that physical objects are 'presented' *directly in some form* to consciousness in sense-perception. *Rigid* or *naïve* perceptionism contends that all sense-qualities are objectively real as perceived. *Critical* or *moderate* perceptionism contends that some qualities are objectively real as perceived, while others are only potentially or causally in the objects.

5. *The Case of Rigid Perceptionism.* The general proof is as follows. Given the presence of normal conditions, our senses must be considered reliable; otherwise illusion and error would

be the normal result of our faculties in their normal and natural operations. Applying this general argument to secondary qualities, rigid perceptionists claim that we could know nothing of bodies, not even their existence, if these qualities were subjective. Both primary and secondary qualities are equally 'objective' to the senses. It is the verdict of common sense and therefore of natural reason, that all qualities are objective; this amounts practically to a law of nature.

6. *Answer of Critical Perceptionists*. The argument is too general; it merely proves that some qualities must be objective. The reality and existence of external bodies is guaranteed sufficiently by the primary qualities. Primary qualities are more fundamental than secondary; nature itself makes this distinction. The common-sense conviction of mankind is not as universal as claimed; in their daily life men frequently show that they do not consider things to be objectively real as they are subjectively perceived.

READINGS

M. Maher, *Psychology*, Chs. VI, VII; J. Barron, *op. cit.*, Chs. XII, XIII; J. G. Vance, *op. cit.*, Ch. VI; J. Rickaby, *op. cit.*, Part II, Ch. II; P. Coffey, *op. cit.*, Vol. II, Chs. XVI–XX; James McCosh, *First and Fundamental Truths*, 1889; Part II, Bk. I, Chs. I–V; T. Pesch, *op. cit.*, Vol. II, pp. 136–151; A. Lehmen, *Lehrbuch der Philosophie*, 1909, pp. 189–200; A. K. Rogers, *What is Truth?* pp. 100–106; C. D. Broad, *Perception, Physics, and Reality*, Chs. I–III; A. J. Balfour, *A Defense of Philosophic Doubt*, Ch. XI; G. F. Stout, *Mind and Matter*, Bk. IV; R. W. Sellars, *Critical Realism*.

CRITICAL PRESENTATIVE REALISM

In discussing the facts of sense-perception, we deal with ultimate experiences of the human subject, and we must distinguish closely between the facts themselves and the interpretation of these facts. The facts are registered by the senses, but the senses tell us nothing of the 'nature' of these facts: it is the interpreting intellect which gives us an insight into their being. It is the duty of the philosopher to study the facts of everyday life and of science and to draw the conclusions necessarily implied in them. The facts must dictate the theory which attempts to explain them; and any theory which fails to give an adequate account of all the facts of the case must be relinquished in favor of the one which does.

THE PROBLEM OF SECONDARY QUALITIES

Rigid perceptionists and critical perceptionists agree that the *primary* qualities of objects (extension, shape, unity and multiplicity, rest and motion) are objectively real and are perceived as such. The difference between them centers in the problem of the *secondary* qualities (color, sound, odors, flavors, etc.). Rigid perceptionists contend that all primary and secondary qualities are *objective* and *absolute* in the sense that they exist 'out there' in nature, independent of, and antecedent to, the act of perception; they are present and remain present in nature, even if there be no sense-organ in existence to perceive them. Critical perceptionists distinguish between the two classes of qualities and contend that the *secondary* qualities do not exist 'out there' in nature as such, objectively and absolutely, but are *subjective and relative,* in the sense that they exist only in the act of sensation of the perceiver; secondary qualities, therefore, do not exist independent of, and antecedent to, the act of perception. However, these secondary qualities are not 'purely' subjective and relative, because their causes, namely, the bodies and their properties, exist and through their influence produce these sensations of color, sound, etc., in the perceiver. According to critical perceptionists, then, secondary qualities are 'causally' and 'potentially,' but not 'actually' and 'formally,' present in the bodies. When speaking of the 'objectivity' or 'subjectivity' of secondary qualities in the following discussion, the terms must be accepted in the meaning here designated.

The controversy concerning the nature of the secondary qualities has been very keen among philosophers in modern times, especially among the *scholastics*. This is due mainly to the findings of science. Scientists in general favor the subjectivity of these qualities, as will be seen by consulting the standard works of psychology, physics, physiological psychology, and experimental psychology.[1]

The older medieval scholastics considered all qualities as *formally* present in the objects themselves. Redness, for instance, is a physical accident of the rose itself, independent of light; sugar is sweet in itself; ice is cold in itself; a bell really emits a sound. Others distinguished between 'formal' and 'fundamental' qualities. According to them, color and sound as such (and all the other secondary qualities) are not present in the object itself, but in the *medium* which intervenes between the object and the sense-organ; light is colored and air is sound-

---

[1]It is next to impossible to enumerate all the works which deal with this subject. The following may be considered representative. Woodworth, *Psychology;* Troland, *Psychophysiology,* 4 vols.; Spindler, *The Sense of Sight;* Ladd-Franklin, *Color and Color Theories;* Hollingworth and Poffenberger, *The Sense of Taste;* Foster and Tinker, *Experiments in Psychology;* Dashill, *Fundamentals of Objective Psychology;* Myers, *Text Book of Experimental Psychology;* H. Gruender, *Experimental Psychology, De Qualitatibus Sensibilibus;* Titchener, *Text Book of Psychology; Experimental Psychology;* Pillsbury, *Fundamentals of Psychology;* Breese, *Psychology;* Helmholtz, *Physiological Optics;* Hering, *Zur Lehre vom Lichtsinne;* Fechner, *Elemente der Psychophysik;* Wundt, *Principles of Physiological Psychology;* Fröbes, *Lehrbuch der Experimentellen Psychologie;* Millikan-Gale-Pyle, *Elements of Physics.*

ing. This view places color and other qualities *fundamentally* in the objects and *formally* in the medium; but as such they are objective and absolute, independent of, and antecedent to, the perceiver. Among the older prominent scholastics who favored this theory are *St. Albertus Magnus, St. Thomas Aquinas,* and *Suarez.*

Neo-scholastics, generally speaking, seem to lean toward that form of rigid perceptionism which distinguishes between 'formal' and 'fundamental' qualities. Among those who adhere to the *objectivity* of secondary qualities as independent of perception may be mentioned: M. Liberatore, C. Sanseverino, T. Zigliara, Z. Gonzalez, F. Seewis, L. de San, M. Glossner, T. Pesch, E. Commer, B. Loranzelli, A. Farges, G. Lahousse, I. Straub, M. Schneid, van der Aa, S. Schiffini, J. Urráburu, L. Lercher, O. Willmann, C. Willems, C. Boetzkes, P. Gény, A. Michelitsch, de la Vassière, A. Seitz, C. Frick, Lehmen-Beck, J. Maritain, J. Gredt, G. Esser, P. Coffey, and others.

Other neo-scholastics are *critical perceptionists.* They claim that the secondary qualities have only a *subjective* existence in the perceiver, so that their formal being is dependent on the act of perception; as such, then, they exist neither in the objects nor in the intervening medium.

The chemico-physical properties of things, however, are the cause of their production, in as much as the energies of objects influence the sense-organs effectively and through their stimuli produce therein the sensation of color, sound, etc. Among those who defend this view are: D. Card. Mercier, C. Gutberlet, J. Balmes, A. Stöckl, J. Pohle, G. Hagemann, M. Maher, M. Domet de Vorges, J. Linsmeier, P. Fournier, D. Palmieri, S. Tongiorgi, Ch. Lahr, J. Fröbes, P. Balzer, Mattiussi, de Sinéty, H. Gruender, Necchi, P. Siwek, and others.

Critical presentative realists maintain that the facts clearly show the secondary qualities to be subjective in character; i.e., they are not independent of, and antecedent to, the act of sensation, otherwise *contradictory attributes* will have to be predicated of the same object in the same respect. In support of their view, they appeal to experience and science.

TOUCH, TASTE, SMELL, AND HEARING

Touch. 'Heat' and 'cold' are secondary qualities and, to all appearances, are objectively present in the things which come in contact with our body. But *temperature is relative* to the perceiver. If man's body temperature be taken as 'physiological zero,' any object of the same temperature will evoke no thermal experience; but anything below this zero will appear cold and anything above it will appear warm or hot. As the body temperature is heightened or lowered, objects will change from hot to cold and *vice versa,* although nothing was done to change their temperature. Thermal impressions also depend upon humidity. Evaporation from the skin gives the impression of coolness; but if the surrounding air is humid, so that evaporation is impeded, we have the sensation of increased heat, although the temperature is the same. Increased temperature of the air increases its capacity to absorb moisture; hence, even though the temperature of the air be increased, we experience the sensation of greater coolness. Similarly, agitation of the air around the body, for instance, by means of a fan, produces the sensation of coolness, although the temperature of the air has not been changed. If we place the right hand in a vessel of water of $+60°$ and the left hand in a vessel of water of $+100°$ and then place both hands in water of $+80°$, the same water will appear warm to the right hand and cool to the left.

According to science, the sensation of heat is due to electromagnetic radiation. The closer we move to its source, the hotter the object seems to become; and the farther away we move, the less we experience of its heat. If heat were really objective, in the object itself or in the intervening medium, then the space between the sun and the earth should be filled with 'objective heat'; and this heat should be more intense above the earth in the direction of the sun. This, however, is not the case: the temperature decreases as the altitude increases, and interstellar space, according to science, is hundreds of degrees below zero. From this we must conclude that the experience of heat is a subjective reaction of our nervous system.

Taste and Smell. All people are aware that taste is a capricious sense and that 'there is no accounting for tastes.' Taste and smell are physiologically closely related, and many experiences which we attribute to taste are really due to the sense of smell; the confusion is remarkable. The same substance may produce a different taste, depending on what part of the tongue it is placed. Passing from the tip to the base of the tongue, the following changes of quality have been shown by experimentation to take place: sodium chloride changes from salty to slightly bitter; potassium chloride changes from salty to sweet; alum, from sour to sweet; bromo-saccharine, from sweet to bitter. Distilled water, after a solution of hydrochloric or sulphuric acid, tastes sweet. A weak solution of quinine sulphate, after sulphuric acid, tastes sweet at the tip of the tongue and bitter at the base. Objects, however, cannot be objectively sweet and bitter at the same time or change objectively, because of their mere position on the tongue.

It is a common experience that certain substances are delicious to the taste or smell of some persons and nauseating to the taste or smell of others. If flavors and odors were objective qualities, all who can taste or smell should perceive the same objective qualities. The qualities certainly do not change objectively in themselves, simply because different persons perceive them. Men and animals perceive entirely different flavors and odors in the same object. If they taste the same objective flavors and smell the same objective odors, there should be no difference in their reactions. There is, however, a great difference, and this can be adequately explained only on the supposition that flavors and odors are not objective qualities of the objects themselves, but are chemical properties which produce effects according to the subjective character of the perceiving organs.

Hearing. Sound is also supposed to be objective, independent of the organ of hearing. A bell, for instance, emits a sound which corresponds to the note 'c' on the scale. No matter how often we strike the bell, the note will always be the same. Let it be assumed that a bell is clanging at a railway crossing and that its note is 'c.' Here, then, there is nothing to alter the note; the bell continuously emits 'c,' and anyone standing near by hears this identical note as long as the bell rings. However, every person in a rapidly moving train will hear the pitch of the bell rise as they near the bell, and they will hear it sink as they move away; it is only in the immediate vicinity of the bell that they hear the note as 'c.' Everyone in the train, from the engine to the last car, hears a different tone, ranging, for instance, from 'c' to 'e' and from 'c' to 'a' at the same moment of time, although nothing has happened to the bell to change its tone. If the 'objective' tone of the bell is 'c,' it should be physically impossible to hear a different tone, otherwise people would hear tones which are not present and not hear the one 'objective' tone which is present. That, however, is actually what is experienced: each person hears a different supposedly 'objective' tone. Consequently, sound is not objectively present in the bell; to maintain its objective character involves the contradictory property of 'c' and 'not-c' at the same time.

Due to this characteristic of sound, many neo-scholastics place sound, not in the object itself, but in the air or intervening medium. This, however, will not save their position of rigid perceptionism. Persons standing within range of the stationary bell at any point will hear only 'c.' Let us suppose that the middle of the moving train is directly opposite the bell. Then every person standing near the tracks at the head of the train or at the end of the train will hear only 'c,' but every person within the moving train will hear a different tone, as explained above. If, then, the 'objective' tone in the air is 'c,' this tone must be the same wherever the sound happens to travel, and everyone must hear this tone 'c' and no other. That, however, is not the case; the tone is experienced as different by different persons. Consequently, formal sound is neither in the object nor in the air, but in the organ of hearing itself; in nature there are only vibrations of definite length and frequency which are then translated into sound by the individual ears in the act of sensation.

SIGHT: REFRACTION OF LIGHT

Nothing seems more obvious to us than that things are really colored and that color exists in the bodies themselves. This, however, is a matter of judgment, not of sense; the eyes merely report the facts of sight and tell us nothing about the actual reality of what they perceive. If a thorough scientific investigation of the data confirms the theory of objectivity, we must, of course, accept the verdict of science; we must, however, also accept its verdict, if it can show that colors are not objective. This, critical perceptionists claim, science does.

Refraction produces results which are extremely difficult to comprehend and explain, if color is objectively present in objects. The phenomena of the rising and setting *sun* are familiar to everyone. The sun appears much larger than usual; it appears elliptical in shape; it appears as a deep-red or golden ball; it appears to become smaller in size as the morning progresses and larger as it sinks toward the horizon in the evening. We know that none of these things are actually so. The actual sun does not change in size, shape, and color from hour to hour during the day, but remains the same throughout the year. Were the sun 'objectively' red, why do we see it as white during the greater part of the day? Were it white, why do we see it as red in the morning and evening? Were either of the colors objective, we should see nothing but that one color all the time. Since the color changes continually in the unchanging sun, neither can be objective. This becomes even more obvious when we consider that people on different parts of the earth in the east and the west, looking at the sun *at the same instant of time,* receive entirely different impressions regarding its size, shape, and color: it is big and little, red and white, round and flattened, at the selfsame moment. But this is obviously impossible; the *real* sun cannot have such opposite qualities at one and the same moment.

At sunrise the real sun is still actually below the horizon, although we 'see' a red sun in the eastern portion of the sky. The sun, therefore, *is not there at all* where we see it. This phenomenon is due to the refraction of the sun's rays. What we actually see, then, is not the sun as an *object;* it is a consciously apprehended *retinal image,* produced by the radiant energy of the sun in the organ of sight, and that is subjective.

The *stars* in the heavens present a somewhat similar phenomenon. The stars, even those which are called 'fixed,' move at tremendous speeds. We cannot see a star until the light rays emitted by it reach the eye. Light travels at a velocity of over 186,000 miles a second; despite this speed, many stars are so distant that it takes hundreds and thousands of years for their light to reach the earth. Let us assume that a certain star is a thousand light-years away and that it travels in the general direction of west to east at a rate of 1,000,000 miles a year. At the moment, then, when we look at this star, we see it where it was located *one thousand years ago;* this means, that we see it one billion miles to the *west* of where it is *at present.* The star is not there where we see it, and where it actually is we do not see it at all. And this is true of all the so-called fixed stars. We even see the sun only where it was eight minutes ago. It follows, then, that we never see the stars themselves as *real objects* in the heavens, because they are never visible as such where they actually stand. Then what do we perceive? Evidently, a consciously apprehended retinal image.

Rainbows are also phenomena which show that colors are not in the objects, contrary to the seemingly evident testimony of our eyes. The colors of a rainbow seem as objectively real in the mist or in the rain as the colors of flowers or of other objects. Yet the water drops in which the rainbow is seen to exist are colorless. It is all a matter of the refraction and reflection of light rays. That the water drops are in no way actually colored by the light rays, is obvious from the fact that persons not standing at the proper angle will see no rainbow. A dozen persons may view a spray of water, but only a few, those who stand in the right relation to sun and spray, will see the colors; all others will see only a colorless spray. If the colors were objectively present, independent of, and antecedent to, the perceivers, all should be able to see the colored water. The water drops are thus observed to be colored and not colored at the same time, if rigid perceptionism were correct. The same is true of *mirages* and of the *iridescence* seen in oil films, soap bubbles, sea shells, and in the feathers of many birds. Aristotle and many of the older scholastics knew these facts and on their account made the distinction between 'real' and 'apparent' colors.[2]

The phenomena of the rising and setting sun and of the distant stars show that we do not perceive these objects themselves in any form of direct perception; and the rainbows and similar phenomena show that their colors are not in the objects. The images of these things, then, can only be *retinal images;* and they are subjective. Nor can we say that the colors are in the air or ether occupying the space between the object and the eye. Air and ether are colorless in this intervening space. If we stand at right angles to the colored object and gaze straight through the intervening space, we perceive no color traveling from the object to the eye. Where, then, is formal color? Solely in the perceiving organ.

SIGHT: COLOR MIXTURE

There is no 'objective' *white* color in sunlight, although we perceive it frequently. The seven prismatic colors of sunlight, striking the same retinal points of the eye, produce the sensation of white, although there is no 'white' in the spectrum. In fact, all complementary colors do this, as red and green-blue,

---

[2]Aristotle, *De Sensu et Sensibili,* c. 3, n. 9 sqq. St. Albertus Magnus, *Lib. de Sensu et Sensato,* tr. 2, c. 1; *De Anima,* l. 2, tr. 3, c. 7; *Summa de Creaturis,* P. II, q. 21, art. 3, part. 1. Suarez, *De Anima,* l. 3, c. 15, n. 7. Sylvester Maurus, *Quaest. Phil.,* t. III, q. 41.

orange and blue, gold and blue, yellow and indigo-blue, green-yellow and violet. The law of color mixture reads: "For every long wave of the visible spectrum (that is, for every wave not shorter than 563.6 millimicra) a definite short wave can be found so that when the two waves are mixed in appropriate proportions, each component of the mixture will neutralize the chromatic effect of the other and the sensation of *neutral white* will arise; but if the relative strength of the two components is not appropriately adjusted, the neutralization of one component is incomplete and the result of such a mixture is the sensation of an unsaturated color whose tone is determined by that of the stronger component." This law is proved experimentally by means of the *color top* or *color disk* revolving at rapid speed. The disk or top still retains its *original* colors; but as the speed is increased the eye perceives a neutral *gray*. If I take one disk with 170° yellow and 190° indigo and another disk with 300° black and 60° white and revolve them with sufficient speed, both disks will look *exactly alike* in color. The eye sees the same color, though the disks and their colors have not changed. As it is, the eye sees a color which is *not there* and does *not* perceive the colors which *are there*. Snow, steam, foam, and clouds appear as white, but they all consist of colorless water particles. The *mass* of their surfaces simply reflect *all* the colors of sunlight to the eye, and the sensation of 'white' is produced on the retina.

The *contrast box*[3] makes colors appear very different to the eye than they (supposedly) are in reality. A colored background is seen through a compartment, and the latter is illuminated with different intensities of filtered lights. Without changing the background in any way, so that its 'objective' color remains the same, yellow can be made to look like an orange-red or a green; bluish-green, like a slightly greenish black; white, like a purplish red or a bluish green or a blue or a gold or even a black. We have here a case of the *same*

---

[3]For a description of the construction and operation of the contrast box, see H. Gruender, *Experimental Psychology*, pp. 67 ff. (Bruce, Milwaukee, 1932).

color appearing to the eye as a *different* color, and each individual color can, under controlled conditions, be made to look like practically every other color.

If blue and yellow *dry powders* are mixed, the mixture appears as green to the eye, although this gross mixture does not change the original colors in any way. That the powders are still blue and yellow, can be shown by looking at the mixture through a powerful magnifying glass; the blue and yellow particles will be seen to lie in juxtaposition. Where, then, is the green color? Not in the objects, for they remain blue and yellow. Printers make use of this principle in *three-color printing;* red, blue, and yellow, by means of a mere superposition and juxtaposition of colored particles, give the impression of all colors, although there are no intermediate colors present. The light rays, striking the same retinal elements, produce therein a sensation of colors which are blends of the original color particles. *Filtered light* shows the same effect. Take two pieces of glass, one blue and one yellow, and hold them in such a way that they overlap, but with a space between them. You, looking at the overlapped pieces, see them now as green; but others, viewing them from the side, still see them as blue and yellow. The 'objective' color cannot be blue and yellow and also green at the same time. There is no green in the glass, because the glass did not change; still, that is what you observe. Due to the difference of position, the same objects produce the impression of different colors in the eyes of the observers. And so it is with all other colors. If color were 'objective,' independent of, and antecedent to, the act of perception, we are forced to state that this objective color is 'green' and 'not-green,' 'blue and yellow' and 'not-blue and not-yellow' at the same time.

Stereoscopic color vision shows plainly that the blending of colors takes place in the organ of perception. Fasten a piece of bright blue paper over the one picture of a stereoscope and a bright yellow paper over the other; adjust the distance to the eyes in such a manner that only blue light reaches the one eye and yellow light the other eye. Here, then, we have no blending of colors in the object and no blending of light rays between the papers and the eyes. Gazing fixedly and with equal intensity at both pieces of paper (provided both eyes are practically normal in visual strength), the perception of green will gradually appear. This is due to the chiasma, or crossing, of the optic nerve bundles of both eyes to the optic centers in the two hemispheres of the brain. This is an instance of *psychological color mixing,* and it may be considered a crucial experiment: the new color, green, is neither a blend in the object, nor in the intervening medium, nor in the single eyes, but is an effect produced by the light rays in the entire perceptive organ of sight, and it is subjective in character. Since the same principle applies to other colors, color as such cannot be objective.

SIGHT: SCOTOPIC AND PHOTOPIC VISION

There are two kinds of receptors in the retina, *rods and cones,* forming a double apparatus of sight. Physiologists have determined that the cones are the organ of high intensity or *photopic* vision, while the rods are the organ of low intensity or *scotopic* vision. The cones are adapted for brightness and the rods for twilight and darkness. The central portion of the human retina is covered with cones, and here direct vision and color perception take place; the peripheral portion of the retina is covered with rods, and here oblique vision and 'rod-white' perception occur. The cones, therefore, translate the light stimuli into colors, and the rods into 'rod-white' luminosity devoid of color. Nocturnal mammals, like mice, bats, and hedgehogs, possess no cones in their retina; they are color-blind, because color vision would be of little use to them at night. For the same reason nocturnal birds have the cones developed in much smaller quantity than diurnal birds.

Here, then, we have a double apparatus, natural and normal in every respect, designed in a most marvelous manner for functioning in brightness and in relative darkness, one for color vision and the other for neutral luminosity vision. Each operates in its own way, producing its own particular *subjective effect* in the perceiver. A simple experiment will show the double effect of the same light rays. Place three electric lamps (preferably with carbon filaments) in a row, connected together in one circuit and standing about a yard apart. Decrease the current until the filaments barely glow. Stand in such a position that only the center bulb is seen in the line of direct vision, while the two outer bulbs are seen by oblique vision only. In a darkened room the center bulb will now appear with a red glow, while the two outer bulbs will show the 'rod-white' neutral luminosity. No matter how quickly you shift your gaze from one lamp to the other, only the one directly viewed will be red; the other two will immediately change to 'rod-white.' You perceive the lamp as 'red' when its rays fall upon the cones, and as 'rod-white' when its rays enter the eyes obliquely and fall upon the rods. Although the lamps do not change color, the position of your eyes and their rod-and-cone construction produce in your retina a continuous change of color. Color, then, is subjective, dependent on the organ of perception for its existence.[4]

SIGHT: ENTOPTIC PHENOMENA

There are numerous phenomena *within the eye itself* which are impossible to explain according to the theory of objectivity. "Thus, the 'rays' which are such characteristic features of stars, or other bright points in the visual field, are attributable not to the physical luminaries, but to the striated structures of the eye lenses. Halos, surrounding such bright points, are due to the scattering or diffraction of light by cells in the cornea. The 'muscae volitantes,' which may move across a white paper or open sky area, are representations of tissue fragments floating between the vitreous humor and the retina. Darting and sparkling points, seen against bright backgrounds, correspond with

[4]See L. T. Troland, *The Principles of Psychophysiology* (New York: D. Van Nostrand Co., 1930), Vol. II, pp. 70, 71, 117, 118, 179.

the blood corpuscles which pulse through the retinal capillaries. Under violet illumination, the complex branching formation of the retinal blood vessels become clearly visible. These and many other 'entoptic phenomena' demonstrate that changes in ray patterns within the eye can bring about corresponding modifications of consciousness. Such facts strengthen our belief that the consciousness is adequately determined by the retinal images, without references to preceding stages of the response.

"Certain phenomena of binocular vision also contribute to this conviction. If one of the eyes is pressed out of its normal position, the visual pattern in experience is doubled. A similar effect is noticeable in the case of objects upon which the eyes do not properly converge. In these instances, the stimulus conditions external to the eyes are essentially unmodified, but the normal interrelations of the two retinal images are disturbed. . . . In cases of retinal detachment, the visual objects in experience are correspondingly distorted; and may even be doubled or tripled where the receptor layer is folded over upon itself. However, we can go further than this and show that the excitation of the retina, by means other than light, yields corresponding results in the visual-experience field. Thus, pressure produces patches of brilliance, electrical currents yield color patterns, and an alternating magnetic field generates a luminous haze."[5]

When absolutely all light is excluded from the eyes, as in a totally dark room, the resulting sensation is not that of an ideal black, but of a deep gray. This is sometimes called *idio-retinal light,* produced by the self-activity of the retinal elements.[6]

After-images also show the subjectivity of visual perception. If we keep our eyes fixed on a colored object placed on a black ground, we will notice after a time that the color gradually loses something of its luster. Then, if the eye is suddenly shifted to a white surface, we see an image of the same shape and

[5]L. T. Troland, *op. cit.,* Vol. I, pp. 171–173.
[6]L. T. Troland, *op. cit.,* Vol. II, p. 75.

form with the original object, but of a color complementary to the other. An original red object will thus appear as a green image, and *vice versa;* yellow will appear as violet and blue as orange, and *vice versa*. The same effect can be produced, if the eyes, after viewing the object for a time, are closed and a handkerchief or other opaque thing is pressed tight against the eyes, so as to shut out all light. In this *total darkness and within the closed eyes* an after-image of the original object will appear in perfect outline and colored with the complementary color. If, in the above experiment, the eyes are kept closed, but the handkerchief be taken away, so that light can shine through the lids, this image immediately changes into an accidental image of the reverse color. Thus, a bright window in daylight will have dark sashes and light panes, when all light is excluded from the eyes; they will appear as light sashes and dark panes, when light is allowed to enter the eyes through the tissues of the eyelids. This phenomenon brings out a very important fact. The *change of color* here takes place absolutely *within the closed eyes*. Where, then, is this color which is so vividly perceived? Not in any object, but in the eye itself. But if *this* color is subjective, the *original* color must be in the eye as subjective also. Any other explanation would mean playing fast and loose with the facts. The 'cause' of the color is assuredly external and objective; but the 'effect' (the formal color) is internal and subjective.

SIGHT: IMAGE PROJECTION AND PERSPECTIVE

Image projection is another fact which proves that vision is subjective. To say that visual images are projected or 'externalized' seems opposed to all experience; it is apparently evident that we behold distant objects *at a distance*. However, consider the implications of the following experiment. While in a dark room, hold a burning taper about two inches away from one eye, a little in front and at the side, so as to insure oblique vision. Keeping the other eye closed, the field of vision will gradually become red. If the taper is moved slowly up and down, while the eye gazes steadily at the wall opposite, an arborescent figure of a dark color on a red field will appear on the wall. This is the 'choroid figure,' a shadow picture of the retinal arteries and veins upon the seat of vision.

Apparently, this choroid figure is on the wall, and we do not seem to perceive it as present in the eye, although that is the only place where it exists and can be perceived to be. There is no 'objective' red on the wall, nor an arborescent figure; both are 'subjective' perception images within the eye. Is there, then, a process of *real* 'externalization' or projection? Evidently not; the perception takes place within the eye and stays there. Then how can the red field and the shadow figure be perceived as 'external' on the external wall? Because the perception of the wall itself is not external but internal. In fact, all visual perception is but *retinal imaging consciously apprehended as present*.

The same explanation accounts for perception of objects in *perspective*. Parallel tracks seem to converge; highways vanish to a point in the distance; all objects appear proportionately smaller the farther they are away; a near object looks larger than a distant object of the same size. If we accept the view that we perceive a consciously apprehended retinal image, everything is explained, because light must naturally strike the retinal field according to the angles and laws of perspective. This will also explain the apparent shifting of the countryside when we ride in a car or train or airplane, and the apparent position of the stars in a place where they no longer exist. All of which shows that we do not see the objects themselves; visual perception consists in consciously apprehended retinal imaging.

Such, then, is the case of *critical presentative realism*. If these facts force us to the conclusion that the secondary qualities are subjective in character and not objectively present in nature, independent of, and antecedent to, the act of perception, then rigid perceptionism must be abandoned and critical perceptionism accepted. Whether the facts as presented are convincing, is a matter for the individual to decide.

IS CRITICAL PERCEPTIONISM DISGUISED IDEALISM?

Rigid perceptionists claim that this theory destroys the truth-value of all sense-perception; it is a compromise between idealism and realism and as such has the difficulties of both without the merits of either. They are convinced that critical perceptionism must be a wrong theory, because it is against the *natural evidence of the senses;* the senses tell us plainly that secondary qualities are 'objective.' The answer to this objection is simple. The senses tell us nothing about the objectivity or subjectivity of the secondary qualities; they merely *report the presence of these qualities in our perception.* The senses cannot judge about objects and qualities. It is the *intellect alone* which interprets the data furnished by the senses and gives us a reasoned certitude as to whether these things are internal or external, subjective or objective. If rigid realists are convinced of the objectivity of all qualities, they obtain this conviction through *reason,* not through the mere sense presentation of the organs of perception. Hence, if reason comes to the conclusion that the secondary qualities are not objective, it does not go contrary to the testimony of the senses, provided the senses themselves furnish the facts which warrant this conclusion.

Rigid realists claim that critical perceptionism leads to *idealism:* if the secondary qualities are subjective, then the primary qualities must also be considered subjective, because we would never be able to know which particular causes produce the particular secondary qualities as effects. Critical perceptionists answer that the matter is not so desperate as this. The intellect has a very simple way of discovering which bodies are the particular causes of particular effects in our sense-organs. This way: My body is an integral part of my Ego; I am identified with it, and I perceive it is 'mine.' It is an extended reality, possessing triple dimensions; it possesses extended parts and members, and these I also perceive as 'mine.' This is evidenced by my immediate consciousness, and I cannot doubt this testimony. All this was brought out in proving the real existence of extra-mental reality. Independent of all sight-perception, through the *direct contact* of my body with 'other' bodies, it was proved that extended bodies, other than my own, also exist. If my body is real, they are real; if they are not real, mine is not real. I do not need sight or color or sound to prove the real existence and the real extension of extra-Ego bodies. Hence, even if all sight-perceptions be shown to be subjective, I would still have a *reasoned certitude* of extension and extended bodies other than my own, through the *direct* and *immediate contact* of my own body.

From this to the localization of the *causes* of the secondary qualities of color, sound, flavor, odor, and temperature, is an easy step. I see a lamp and touch it; I turn on the light with my hand, and it burns; I extinguish the light, and it is dark. It is clear to me that the lamp is the 'cause' of the sensation of light. I see a colored apple; I place my hand over it, and the color is gone; I remove my hand, and the color appears again. My intellect rightly concludes that this particular object, the apple, produced the sensation of color in me. I put a piece of candy in my mouth, and the taste is sweet; I hold a rose to my nose, and the odor is pleasant. If I remove them, the sensation ceases. I hold a bell in my hand, shake it, and I hear a sound; I stop it, and I no longer hear the tone. All this happens as often as I repeat the procedure. I thus know with certitude just what *particular bodies* are the *particular causes* of the secondary qualities which I perceive. Nothing more is needed for the intellect for its causal knowledge of the bodies and of the secondary sense-qualities. Rigid realists, therefore, are wrong when they assert that the denial of the objectivity of these secondary qualities would destroy our certainty of the existence of the external world. Idealism does not follow from critical perceptionism.

Again, rigid perceptionists claim that man experiences a *natural compulsion* in considering the secondary qualities to be objective; if they are subjective, man must be said to suffer from an *unavoidable illusion*. Critical perceptionists admit that, if there were a *real* mental compulsion here, the question would be settled in favor of the objectivity of the secondary qualities. Such, however, is not the case; it is only an *apparent* mental compulsion. A real mental compulsion exists in analytical judgments like '2 + 2 = 4'; or in a principle which states that 'everything must have a sufficient reason for its existence and being'; also in facts perceived in a direct act of consciousness, like the fact that I am writing at this very moment. We cannot doubt the immediate evidence of our reason or of consciousness; to do so would destroy the essential reliability of our powers of knowledge. But when things are *not self-evident,* one cannot speak of a 'necessary' compulsion of our intellectual judgment.

The rigid realists themselves admit that the intellect can and does commit *errors,* in its judgment concerning the objectivity of some qualities. They lay down certain rules and conditions which the intellect must follow in order to guard itself against rash judgments and errors. But this shows plainly that the objectivity of secondary qualities is *not self-evident;* consequently there can be no necessary compulsion on the part of the intellect to judge these qualities to be objective. At best there may be an *apparent* mental compulsion; in that case, though, even a prolonged misjudgment on the part of unreflecting mankind will not justify the conclusion that a revision of our judgment would imply necessary illusion in normal perception. We see this clearly in the case of the judgment of mankind regarding the apparent movement of the sun around the earth. It is only in the last few hundred years that people have realized that the earth moves and not the sun. This revision of our judgment was due to *science;* our eyes still see no difference between the movement of the sun and the moon. But if science can correct an erroneous judgment prevalent from the dawn of the human race without destroying the validity of sense-perception and of human knowledge in *this* case, there is no reason why it cannot do the same with regard to the objectivity of secondary qualities. Here, too, we have merely an *apparent* mental compulsion of our intellectual judgment. Critical perceptionism, therefore, does not lead to idealism nor does it destroy the essential validity of sense-perception.

This concludes our investigation into the validity of our sense-perception. It has been necessary to wind our way cautiously and laboriously, step by step, through the maze of modern errors back to the common-sense view of *presentative realism*. This we have done. First, it was imperative to expose the fallacy of idealism. Then, we had to establish the existence of extra-mental reality in our own body. Next, the existence of the extra-Ego world of material bodies had to be proved. Further, the pseudo-realism of representationism demanded refutation. Finally, we arrived at the age-old aristotelian-scholastic doctrine of presentative realism; a theory which should never have been abandoned for the excessive dualism of Descartes. It was a very roundabout detour we were forced to make in order to arrive at the solution of this perplexing problem. But the result has vindicated the *spontaneous conviction* of mankind in the reality of the world, and a truth of the greatest epistemological value, namely *the essential validity of sense-perception,* has been critically proved and philosophically justified.

SUMMARY OF CHAPTER XII

In the question of the objectivity or subjectivity of sense-qualities, we must bear in mind that the facts must dictate the theory.

1. *The Problem of Secondary Qualities.* Rigid and critical perceptionists agree that the *primary* qualities are objective. The former claim that the *secondary* qualities are also objective, while the latter claim that they are subjective. By 'objective' rigid perceptionists mean that these qualities are present in nature, independent of, and antecedent to, the act of perception.

By 'subjective' critical perceptionists mean that these qualities are present neither in the objects nor in the intervening medium, independent of, and antecedent to, the act of perception; they are 'causally' and 'potentially' in the objects, but 'formally' and 'actually' in the perceiver.

2. *Touch, Taste, Smell, Hearing.* 'Hot' and 'cold' are relative to the perceiver's body temperature; temperature does not increase with altitude in the direction of the sun. If flavors and odors were objective, all men and animals should taste and smell these qualities in the same way; these qualities change for the same persons. Sound changes with the relative position of the perceiving ears; if sound were objective, all should hear the same tone without change.

3. *Sight. Refraction of Light.* Due to refraction, we perceive the sun before it is above the horizon; the sun also appears to change in size, shape, and color, although the sun does not change. Stars are seen, although they are not present where perceived to be. Rainbows are observed in water drops; but the water is really colorless. The same applies to mirages and iridescence.

Color Mixture. White sunlight is not objective. The colors of a color top remain unchanged, but they change for the eye. The contrast box makes colors appear as different. Pigments and filtered lights show blends of color which are not objective. Stereoscopic color vision reveals psychological color mixing which under no circumstances is objective.

Scotopic and Photopic Vision. The rods and cones are a double apparatus of sight; the cones translate light rays into color vision and the rods into neutral luminosity vision. The effects, of course, are subjective.

Entoptic Phenomena. Many phenomena occur within the eye which are apparently objective. After-images can be seen with closed eyes.

Image Projection and Perspective. The choroid figure appears as if projected and externalized, although it is obviously only an intra-ocular perception. Perspective vision also shows that vision is consciously apprehended retinal imaging.

4. *Disguised Idealism?* Critical perceptionism is not contrary to the natural evidence of the senses: the senses merely report the qualities; it is the intellect which must interpret the data furnished by the senses. It does not endanger the objectivity of the primary qualities, because the extended character of our bodies enables us to know which objects are the causes of our visual perceptions. There is no unavoidable illusion in critical perceptionism due to natural mental compulsion: the facts of perception are the reason why the secondary qualities are considered to be subjective.

The *essential validity* of sense-perception is vindicated and critically established.

READINGS

J. G. Vance, *op. cit.,* Ch. I; H. Gruender, *Experimental Psychology,* Chs. II–VI, *De Qualitatibus Sensibilibus;* A. Lovejoy, *The Revolt Against Dualism,* Ch. II; J. E. Turner, *A Theory of Direct Realism,* Chs. II–VIII; L. T. Troland, *The Principles of Psychophysiology,* Vol. I, Chs. IX–XI; Vol. II, Chs. XIV, XV; A. K. Rogers, *What is Truth?* pp. 55–86; C. D. Broad, *Perception, Physics, and Reality,* Ch. IV; D. Drake, *Mind and Its Place in Nature,* Ch. VI; C. A. Strong, *Why the Mind Has a Body,* Ch. VIII.

CHAPTER XIII

THE PROBLEM OF THE UNIVERSALS

So far we have established the validity of consciousness and of sense-perception as a source of human knowledge. Our consciousness acquaints us with the various mental states which occur within our own self as 'subjective events,' such as thinking, willing, imagining, striving, emotion, sensation. Sense-perception brings our own body and the external world within the field of knowledge, so that we obtain a cognition of them as 'objective events' through the medium of our sense-organs. But we also have an *intellectual knowledge* of things, and this knowledge manifests itself in ideas, judgments, and reasoning. It will now be our task to examine the validity of our intellectual knowledge.

Our reasoning processes consist of judgments, and these processes cannot be valid, if our judgments are not valid. Judgments, on their part, consist of ideas, and hence cannot be valid, if our ideas are not valid. It will, then, be necessary first of all to submit our *ideas* to a critical investigation of their essential validity before we pass on to the validity of our judgments and then to that of our reasoning.

THE PROBLEM OF THE UNIVERSALS

There is a close connection between the intellect and sense, between intellectual knowledge and sense-knowledge. The proper object of our cognition is the *sensible*. Our senses con-

tact the external world by means of a cognitional image
through which the material, external objects are *perceived*.
Thereby the objects become 'present to sense' and also 'present
to consciousness,' and they are thus sensuously 'known.' This
process is the same for men and brutes, because they are sentient beings.

Man, however, is also an *intellectual* being, and as such has
a form of knowledge distinct from sense-perception: man
thinks. In the presence of this 'percept,' the mind forms a
'concept.' Since sense and intellect are both faculties of the one,
identical Ego, the intellect fashions a 'concept' or 'idea' of the
external object perceived by the sense. The intellect now is
aware of the existence of the object, and so the object becomes
'present to sense' and also 'present to intellect' at the same
time. It is really the *Ego* that is the active agent of 'perceiving'
and 'conceiving' and that forms within itself the 'percept' of
sense and the 'concept' of intellect. Our consciousness testifies
to this very plainly: *I* see the thing, *I* have an idea of the
thing. And our experience tells us that our Ego forms the concept of a thing in the intellect after it has had the percept of
it in the sense: we first 'perceive' the thing, and then 'conceive'
it by means of a concept or idea. In other words, our knowledge begins in the senses and ends in the intellect. Intellectual
knowledge presupposes sense-knowledge. The materials for
our ideas are drawn from the percepts of sense, so that we
could have no intellectual knowledge of things, if we did not
have sense-knowledge first. Hence the principle: *'Nihil est in
intellectu quod prius non fuerit in sensu;* nothing is in the intellect which was not beforehand (in some manner) in the
sense.'

Sense and intellect, percept and concept, are thus seen to
exist in close relationship. Nevertheless, there is a great difference between percept and concept, between sense-knowledge
and intellectual knowledge. Both sense and intellect make an
'image,' a 'representation' of the object which is present to
them, but the nature of this image or representation is very

dissimilar. Things in nature are always singular, individual, concrete, and the sense-image of them depicts them in their singularity, individuality, and concreteness, and so this image itself has a content which is *singular, individual,* and *concrete.* When the sense perceives, for instance, a man, it will always be a definite man in all his individual characteristics, such as size, shape, color, age, sex, weight, and mannerisms. Not so the intellect. It apprehends that which pertains to man as man. The *intellectual image* retains only that which all men have in common, that which makes a man to be what he is precisely as a member of the *class* of men, leaving aside all those characteristics which distinguish one man from another, like size, shape, color, age, sex, weight, and mannerisms. Instead of depicting the exterior elements, as the sense-image does, the intellectual image represents the elements which constitute the nature of man: man is conceived as a 'rational, sentient, living, corporeal substance.' This idea now fits every single man and all men as a class; it applies to them individually and collectively. To drop the individualizing properties of a thing in this way and retain the elements common to the class is the process of intellectual 'abstraction.' Intellectual images are, therefore, not singular, individual, and concrete, but *universal, general,* and *abstract.*[1]

In actual sense-perception we have a singular, concrete sense-image which applies only to a single, concrete man; each image is different according to the individual differences existing between the single persons; and each image is restricted according to time and place, depending upon the conditions of time and place prevailing for the individuals perceived. This is not the case with the intellectual image or idea of a man. It is *one* in content, but it applies to *all* men, living and dead, actual and possible; all the individual differences between individual men are eliminated, and the *common element* is represented and expressed; temporal and spatial con-

---

[1]For a more detailed differentiation between sense-image and intellectual image, see the author's *Science of Correct Thinking* (Bruce, Milwaukee), pp. 24 ff.

intellectual idea

ditions are absent in the idea, so that it <u>has value for all times</u> <u>and in all places.</u> The idea of 'man' as a 'rational, sentient, living, corporeal substance,' since it is an abstract and universal image of the elements common to all men, <u>contains those</u> <u>elements of man which are *fixed, unchangeable, necessary:*</u> these elements are such that they <u>cannot be missing</u> without <u>man ceasing to be man,</u> because they constitute that which makes him to be what he is — a 'man,' and these elements must be and will be found in all men at all times and in all places.

What has just been said is true of all concepts or ideas: they are *abstract* and *universal*. We have taken the example of 'man,' because it is fairly obvious; any other object will show these characteristics of the idea just as well. Our idea of a 'plant' as a 'non-sentient, living, corporeal substance' applies to the rose, the pumpkin, the elm, the pine, the chrysanthemum, and to every other plant with equal truth. Our idea of a 'building' fits the home, the business office, the school, the shack, and any other building. Our idea of a 'dog' applies to the mastiff, the bulldog, the greyhound, the poodle, and all other dogs. And so with all other ideas. They apply to every single individual belonging to the class and to the class as a whole. And that is what is meant by a *universal idea:* <u>one that</u> represents some *common nature* or *attribute* <u>which can be</u> applied to a *class as a whole* and to *each individual* of that class.

This brings up the question of the *validity of ideas*. Since ideas are abstract, leaving aside all individualizing factors and retaining an attribute or nature common to one and many, they are *universal*. But therein lies a problem. Ideas are supposed to be representations of things as they are in themselves; then universal ideas must also represent things as they are in themselves. But how can they? A universal idea is one whose thought-content (comprehension) applies to a class as a whole and to each and every member belonging to that class. The idea 'man,' for instance, applies in the same way to 'each man' taken singly and to 'all men' taken together as a class. If this universal idea is a true representation of man as he is in reality, it would seem to imply that 'man,' as found in reality, has a nature which is 'single' in each individual and also 'one' in the whole class. The nature of 'man' would be *one* because it applies to the class as a whole; and it would be *multiple,* because it applies to each individual of the class. How can it be *one and multiple* at the same time? It would seem that, if it is one, it could not be multiple; and if it is multiple, it could not be one. Does this not make our universals essentially invalid? Or how can we reconcile this apparent contradiction in the very nature of the universal ideas? The problem of the universals can be formulated in the question: *How can or do the universals apply validly to things,* so as to give us a genuine knowledge of reality?

IMPORTANCE OF THE PROBLEM

At first sight it might appear that the problem is of trifling significance. But this is not so. If our universal ideas do not give us a true representation of reality, the whole fabric of our *intellectual knowledge is destroyed.* Universal ideas form the warp and woof of this fabric; if they are false representations of reality, our entire intellectual interpretation of reality is false. The judgment is supposed to interpret reality in such a way that the truth of the judgment is a similitude of the truth of the reality expressed in the judgment. If our universal ideas are false, our knowledge of reality is false. Then what becomes of the validity of our intellect and its knowledge? Once we come to the fatal conclusion that our intellect is not a valid source of truth, we have demolished the very foundation of *reason* and of our *reasoning processes;* our reason must be adjudged untrustworthy in its operations and its findings fallacious. Such a conclusion would not only be intellectual suicide for the individual person, but would undermine the very structure of human society in its moral, commercial, economic, political, and international associations. The validity of our intellectual knowledge must be maintained and vindicated, if man is to live as a human being and not be degraded to the sense-level of the brute.

Then, too, if the validity of our intellectual ideas cannot be upheld, *science* is a chimera. It is not the purpose of science to state individual facts and record individual events. It is of no interest to science to know that 'this particular glass of water has a temperature of 56°'; 'this man is white'; 'this plant is ten feet tall'; and so forth. These are individual facts of no importance. What the sciences really attempt to discover are *general truths, permanent facts, necessary relations, universal laws,* which are not only true and valid now and then, here and there, but *always and everywhere,* independent of the individual circumstances and conditions. Such truths, facts, relations, and laws are of incalculable value for mankind in general, since they are the steppingstones of material and intellectual progress. Destroy the validity of these and humanity is poor indeed, because its highest form of knowledge, that of the intellect, is essentially false and unreliable.

Science deals with the *universal.* The basic ideas underlying all scientific thought and investigation are universal. 'Substance, accident, quality, quantity, action, reaction, force, energy, cause, effect, law, principle, condition, experiment, variation, uniformity,' and a host of similiar ideas, are all universal ideas. Take these ideas and their validity out of science and it vanishes into nothing. Such ideas are essential to *all* sciences, and without them the sciences lose all meaning and value. Remove the universal ideas from the pages of scientific books and nothing but the covers would be left.

The same is true of the *scientific laws* formulated by science as the result of its inductive research into the phenomena of nature. These laws can never be expressed in language except with the aid of universal ideas. Consider, for example, Ohm's law: 'The currents furnished by different galvanic cells, or combinations of cells, are always directly proportional to the electromotive forces existing in the circuits in which the currents flow, and inversely proportional to the total resistances of these circuits.' Here again the essential ideas of the law are universals: 'current,' 'cell,' 'combination,' 'force,' 'circuit,' 'resistance.' Or, take the formula of the index of refraction: 'The ratio of the speed of light in air to its speed in any other medium is called the index of refraction of that medium.' 'Ratio,' 'speed,' 'light,' 'air,' 'medium,' 'index,' 'refraction' — these are all universal ideas. We thus see that the laws of science are expressed by means of universals.

Now, the sciences are supposed to be a true representation of *reality*. If they fail in this, they are useless as a source of knowledge. But they cannot be a true representation of reality, unless the universal ideas, which they constantly employ, themselves *represent reality* in a valid manner. The sciences, then, stand and fall with the universals. The problem of the universals, therefore, is not an idle speculation of idle minds, as many scientists and philosophers have asserted, but a vital issue involving the very existence and validity of science itself.

This brings us again to the question: Is there a *reality in nature* which corresponds to our universal idea? If so, how can our universal idea be a correct representation of this reality, considering the fact that it expresses a common nature or attribute which can be applied to a *class as a whole* and to *each individual* of that class? Since the universal has a thought-content which is one-in-many, does this mean that the reality represented by it is also 'one-in-many,' so that all members of a class share in a single nature or attribute common to them all together? And if this is not the case, can the universal be said to interpret reality correctly? How can we harmonize the *individual* things with the *common* essence expressed in the universal idea?

The problem is not simple. On the one hand, we have the apparently obvious fact that the things in the world are *individuals* and possess a single essence of their own. Every individual is a distinct being in itself, having a nature which is not shared by any other being; there are, then, as many distinct natures as there are individuals in existence. There may be two billion men on the globe; but each man is an individual human being in his own right, complete in every respect in his nature, so that we have two billion distinct human natures existing as separate realities, and not merely one single human nature shared by the two billion men in common. This *singularity* of the individual must be upheld. On the other hand, our universal idea is conceived as something which represents a nature or attribute which is *one* in the individual and yet *common to all* as a class. This would seem to be in contradiction to reality as just pointed out. The world consists of 'individuals,' not of 'universal essences.' But if there are not 'universal essences' in the world, common to all the members of a class, the universal idea seems manifestly false. And yet, we must maintain the essential validity of the universal idea, otherwise we will undermine the foundations of our intellectual knowledge and of the sciences. How can we reconcile the seeming antinomy between reality and the universal idea?

HISTORY OF THE PROBLEM

The problem of the universals has vexed the minds of thinkers from the beginning of philosophy in Greece up to the present time. *Plato* (427 or 428 to about 348 B.C.) brought the problem into prominence by his doctrine of the *Ideas*. Socrates (469–399 B.C.) had taught that the 'concept' of a thing is necessary in order to know the reality of a thing. Plato concluded that the 'concept' or Idea is the only reality which is permanent and unchangeable in the continuous flux of concrete phenomena. The Idea is thus the very essence of the reality of 'being' and of the reality of scientific 'knowledge.' The ideas are, therefore, not only *objects of thought,* but also *realities in themselves;* they not only exist as universals in the *mind,* but also as universals in *nature.* Subjectively and objectively they are truly universal. The concepts of our intellect are universal, because they represent the universal Ideas which exist independently of the mind in a world of their own. The

Ideas are real things, beings, essences, which subsist entirely outside the physical world of concrete phenomena which we see around us, in a *transcendental world* of their own, in a heavenly sphere of unchangeable existence, where they have an eternal being.

The physical objects of the material universe are nothing but faint copies of these eternal Ideas, and such objects, since they are singular in essence and in a continual state of change, cannot account for the permanent and universal concepts in our minds; our universal concepts, and the scientific knowledge based on them, can derive their origin only from the eternal and universal Ideas. Man, therefore, must have had a *previous existence* in which he possessed a direct intuition of these Ideas, and his present universal concepts are but the products of a *reminiscence* of his former contemplation of these Ideas in the transcendental realm. There are, then, three distinct worlds for Plato: the world of absolute and eternal Ideas, the world of concrete, ever-changing phenomena (the universe), and the world of universal concepts in our mind. For every single universal concept in our mind there exists a corresponding universal Idea which has its own being in this noumenal world, because our concepts are merely intellectual copies or reproductions of them. These Ideas are *the original* universals, prior in existence to the physical world and to our universal concepts. Our universal concepts are valid, therefore, because they are a faithful representation of reality, namely of the reality of the Ideas which are themselves universal and eternal. By means of this unique theory Plato attempted to show that our universal concepts or ideas have objective value and can give us true scientific knowledge.

Aristotle (384–322 B.C.) realized that Plato's theory was without any basis in fact and that his 'world of Ideas' was pure fiction. The problem would have to be solved without the aid of such a fanciful dreamland of isolated Ideas, because it removed the universals completely from the sense-world to which they are supposed to apply. The reality to which our universal ideas correspond must be present in the things of the sense-world *in some manner*. Plato maintained that our intellect first acquires a knowledge of the Ideas and from them acquires a knowledge of the individual objects in nature; Aristotle reversed the process, claiming that we form our universal ideas from the *sense-impressions* of the external phenomena. Plato considered the Ideas as possessing an existence independent of the sense-world; Aristotle denied such a separate world of Ideas and placed the objective content of our universal concepts in the individual objects existing in nature. Plato attributed a formal universality to the Ideas in their very being; Aristotle taught that there is no universality of being in nature but only individual essences, and the 'universality' of the universal is merely a *logical mode* of our concepts existing *in the mind alone*. In other words, the universal *as a universal* exists only in the mind; the things themselves, of which our concepts are a representation and which the mind universalizes, are individual beings.

Each individual being has its own individual essence, endowed with numerous properties and attributes not found in the others in the same way, so that it is numerically single and separate; but each individual of a certain class or type possesses an essence which is *similar* to that of every other member of that class or type with the similarity of a perfect likeness, so that the intellect grasps this perfectly similar essence, leaving the individualizing characteristics aside, and *universalizes* it in a single idea. The intellect considers this similar essence as being 'one-in-many,' as being a common *class*-nature, although it realizes that in reality itself these essences are all individual and distinct. The foundation for this universality of the universal idea is thus seen to consist in the perfect *similarity* of the essences, after they have been divested of the individualizing differences existing between them. This mental process of 'universalizing' the individual essences is, then, not an arbitrary process of the mind, but is grounded in the similarity of these individual essences themselves; being similar, they are expressed in a universal idea. The *content* of the universal idea is *real* in nature, because it represents the reality of each individual essence; but the *universality* of the universal idea is *mental,* because the individual essence is itself not universal in nature. While Plato advocated an *extreme realism,* Aristotle proposed a *moderate realism,* thereby safeguarding both the validity of the universal idea and the reality of the individual essences.

The problem now rested until the beginning of medieval philosophy. Except for a few sections, the writings of Plato and Aristotle were unknown to Western Europe, having been lost in the disintegration and downfall of the Roman Empire. A passage in the *Isagoge* of *Porphyry* (233–304), the Neo-Platonist, aroused the interest of medieval thinkers concerning the universal ideas and the reality corresponding to them. Porphyry proposed a *triple problem:* Do the generic and specific concepts (universals) exist in the real world, or are they mere products of the intellect? If they are extra-mentally real, are they corporeal or incorporeal things? Are they realized in the concrete individuals of the sense-world or outside and separate from them?[2] It was the first of these questions of Porphyry which the early medieval philosophers tried to answer. Once the question was raised, a controversy ensued which lasted three hundred years before a conclusive answer was found.

From the very outset the tendency of thought was toward *extreme realism,* but it was not always toward the Platonic type. The Ideas of Plato were universal realities which existed in a separate world of their own, entirely distinct from the individual essences or things in nature. *Empiric* ultra-realism placed the universal reality *in the things themselves,* in phys-

[2] "*Mox de generibus et speciebus, illud quidem sive subsistant, sive in solis nudis intellectibus posita sint, sive subsistentia corporalia sint an incorporalia, et utrum separata a sensibilibus an in sensibilibus posita et circa haec consistentia, dicere recusabo: altissimum enim negotium est hujusmodi et majoris egens inquisitionis.*"

ical nature around us. All members of a class possess *one single essence* which is common to them all and in which all share equally, so that they actually have a common class-essence. The individuals no longer possess their own distinct essence, numerically different from that of the other members of the class, but all together possess a single identical essence which is strictly a *universal essence.* The difference between individuals consists merely in *accidentals,* in 'individuating notes' (*notae individuantes*), such as form, figure, place, time, ancestry, country, and name. All men, for instance, form together a single universal essence, humanity; in strict truth, there are no 'men' but only a 'universal man.' Pressed to its logical conclusion, it would lead to the doctrine that all things and persons are a single 'universal being', since 'being' is also a universal idea; and this would be *pantheism.* If medieval empiric ultra-realists refused to take this final step, it was mainly due to their religious beliefs. *John Scotus Eriugena* (born between 800 and 815; died after 877), however, passed the boundary line and taught an undisguised pantheism. *William of Champeaux* (1070–1120), was an empiric ultra-realist, while *Bernard of Chartres* (died about 1130), *Theoderic of Chartres* (died 1155), and *William of Conches* (1080–1154) were ultra-realists of a type which resembled Plato.

Some of the advocates of modern *critical realism* are ultra-realistic in their interpretation of the 'essences' we perceive. These 'essences' are considered as 'universal,' independent of the thinking mind; they bear a close resemblance to Plato's Ideas. Another type of extreme realism is found in *monism.* According to monism, there exists but a single principle of being, constituting all things. Monism, in the strict sense, considers this principle of being as numerically one, uncreated, eternal, and real. It is frequently called the *Absolute;* whether in a pantheistic or naturalistic sense, depends upon the interpretations of the individual philosopher. Others speak of the 'absolute Ego,' 'absolute universal consciousness,' 'cosmic universal idea,' 'universal energy,' 'universal actuality,' 'universal will,' 'the un-

known,' and so forth. The Absolute embraces within itself
everything that exists: the ideal and the real, thought and
thing, mind and matter, spirit and nature, the logical and the
ontological. These things are not really distinct and different
entities; they are but parts, forms, modes, manifestations, or
appearances of the Absolute; they are identified in the Absolute, and the Absolute is self-identical in them all. The Absolute undergoes an eternal and necessary *evolution* by means
of a process of self-determination, which makes it assume these
various forms or modes. Monism is thus opposed to *dualism,*
which affirms the essential distinction between God and world,
mind and matter, living and non-living beings, and to *pluralism,* which asserts that reality consists of numerous individual
substances and not of one sole absolute being. *Spinoza, Fichte,
Schelling, Hegel, Schopenhauer, v. Hartmann, Bradley,* and
many others, were monists. In as much as the Absolute is a
nature which is 'one-in-many,' it is universal; and since this
universality is extra-mental, monism is a form of extreme
realism.

Nominalists deny that the reality corresponding to our universal ideas is in any way universal *in nature* and even deny
that our ideas themselves are universal; only the *names* are
universal. We have collective ideas or images and give them
names, so that we merely designate or 'label' the individuals with the same name; but there are no universal ideas
in the intellect which correspond to these universal names.
This theory, as will be noted, is the very opposite of extreme
realism. Representative medieval nominalists are *Roscelin*
(born about the middle of the eleventh century, and died
about 1100), *Berengar of Tours* (999–1088), *Adelard of Bath*
(beginning of twelfth century), and *Walter of Mortagne*
(died 1174). It is more than doubtful, however, whether these
men should be classed as nominalists in the present meaning
of the term and in the sense as outlined above. Their position
was *negative;* they opposed the extreme realism advocated by

many of their contemporaries without making much of an attempt to give a positive solution of the problem. The phrasing of their thoughts sounded nominalistic, but they scarcely intended more than a refutation of the doctrine of extreme realism. Their views were only a tentative groping for a solution, pointing future philosophers in the right direction; they themselves were content with showing the deficiencies of ultra-realism.

Nominalism proper is the outgrowth of sensism, empiricism, and materialism, in as much as these theories assert that intellectual knowledge is only a refined sense-knowledge. Since the senses can perceive nothing but the individuals in the sense-world, our intellect can fashion ideas only of individual things; hence, our ideas are really singular, not universal. We indeed have *'general images'* of a dog, of a man, of a tree, of a fish, and our so-called universal ideas express such 'general images'; but strictly 'universal' ideas which would represent a common element or attribute as one-in-many, are non-existent in the mind. They maintained a universality in the 'name' and nothing more. This theory was upheld by *Hobbes* (1588–1679), *Locke* (1632–1704), *Berkeley* (1685–1753), *Hume* (1711–1776), *John Stuart Mill* (1806–1873), *Bain* (1818–1903), *Spencer* (1820–1903), *Huxley* (1825–1895), *Sully* (1842–1923), *Herbart* (1776–1841), *Wundt* (1832–1920), *Condillac* (1715–1780), *Comte* (1798–1857), *Taine* (1828–1893), and many others up to our present day. Since many *neo-realists* and *critical realists* are materialists, identifying mind with brain, their theory is more or less nominalistic. While the theories propounded by these thinkers differ on many points, they all agree in considering our intellectual knowledge as nothing more than a mere piecing together of sense-images to which we give a common name or 'label.' The intellect possesses no higher power of 'abstraction,' enabling it to grasp the essences underlying the external phenomena of things and expressing them in universal ideas.

Conceptualism is another theory which developed out of the problem of the universals. It is closer to the correct solution than nominalism, but it falls short of the goal. In opposition to the nominalists, conceptualists defend the universality of ideas in the mind. Like the nominalists they deny the external reality of the universals in nature; but, unlike the nominalists, they maintain that our universal 'names' are expressions of genuinely universal 'ideas,' so that the latter actually represent to the mind an essence which is one-common-to-many. The main point in conceptualism, however, is the contention that the *content* of our universal ideas is *not realized* in any form whatever in the *individual sense-objects:* there is no foundation in the things themselves which would justify the intellect in forming universal ideas. Our universal ideas are thus purely subjective products of the mind without a correlative in nature; in other words, there is nothing in the individuals in nature which is genuinely represented by these universal ideas. This, of course, gives to the universals only a strictly intra-mental significance; as 'universals' they have no objective value. Among the medieval philosophers it is customary to class *Peter Abelard* (1079–1142) and *Gilbert de la Porrée* (1076–1154) as conceptualists. But here again, the defective phrasing of their thoughts and the lack of a complete understanding of the implications contained in their expressions urge historians[3] to class them rather as precursors of moderate realism than defenders of conceptualism proper. The case is different with *William of Ockam* (died about 1347). The problem of the universals had already been solved in his day, and he opposed this solution with a doctrine of his own which was really conceptualistic.

Modern conceptualism is the offspring of idealism. *Kant* (1724–1804) and his followers are the protagonists of this theory. Kant actually tried to prove the validity of our universal

---

[3] See M. de Wulf, *History of Medieval Philosophy,* tr. by P. Coffey, third ed. (Longmans, Green, and Co.), pp. 191–195.

ideas by showing that the categories of the understanding are applicable to the data of sense-intuitions; but his interpretation of the manner in which our universal ideas are formed from these intuitions of sense make them invalid as representations of reality. According to him the data of sense are united with the pure categories of the understanding. These categories, however, are *innate a priori forms* of the understanding and are in no way derived from sense-intuitions. The mind superimposes these categories upon the data of sense, and now we apprehend in these combined products of sense-data and categories relations which are 'universal.' We do not derive our universal ideas by means of abstraction from the sense-data themselves; the universality of the idea is exclusively the product of the intellect, without a foundation in the extramental reality of the things in nature. In fact, the things in nature are noumena which are forever unknown and unknowable to us. Our universal ideas thus have no reality corresponding to them in the outside world and are mere creations of the mind; and that is the theory of conceptualism.

Pragmatists are also to a great extent conceptualists. For many of them the things of the physical world are not 'independent realities,' and we can never know reality as it is in itself; the 'category of transperceptual reality' is after all only 'an intra-experiential affair.' Our abstract concepts are looked upon as 'man-made products' and as 'artificial mental things.' Truth is relative to the individual mind, and all knowledge is valid so far as it satisfies human needs. That there can be *no objective value* to our universal ideas in such a system is obvious. *James, Schiller, Bergson, Dewey,* and their followers all subscribe to this personal 'cash-value' theory of truth and reality. This, however, is the viewpoint of conceptualism, since it robs our universal ideas of an objective foundation in outside reality.

Due to the constant friction of minds in the controversy over universals, a theory of *moderate realism* gradually emerged

toward the end of the twelfth century which satisfied everyone as the correct solution. *John of Salisbury* (died 1180) explained the validity of the universals in its essentials according to the spirit of Aristotle. *Albert the Great* (born 1193
[or 1206, or 1207]; died 1280) formulated a complete solution
along aristotelian lines. It remained, however, for *St. Thomas
Aquinas* (1225-1274) to search into the problem with such
penetration, clarity, and brilliance of thought that this vexing
question was considered to have received its conclusive and
ultimate answer. Against *extreme realism* he maintained that
the universals do not exist as 'realities' outside the mind, neither
in a world of their own nor in the universe of sense-objects.
If extreme realism were correct, we could not explain the
'individuality' of the physical things. Against *nominalism* he
maintained that the universals are more than universal 'names';
our ideas are genuinely universal in the mind. If nominalism
were correct, our intellectual knowledge would not differ from
sense-knowledge. In giving his solution, he maintained that
our universal ideas have more than a 'subjective value' for
the mind; they are really representations of 'extra-mental reality.' He agreed with extreme realism that there must be *some
objective reality* outside the mind which the universals represent; and he agreed with conceptualism that this objective
reality could not consist in *universal essences* outside the mind.

Each of these other systems has an element of truth and an
element of error. *Moderate realism* retains the truth and eliminates the error of all. The separate essence and existence of
every individual being in nature must be upheld inviolably,
because nothing exists in nature but *individuals;* this excludes
all universal essences. But while nature consists of individual
essences, these individuals form *natural classes,* for instance,
fishes, birds, mammals, men, animals, plants, bodies, substances.

The mind apprehends that which the senses cannot perceive,
namely the essence which is *not identical* (as the extreme
realists claim) but *similar with a perfect likeness* in each

individual of a natural class. It is because of this perfect likeness that the intellect recognizes the individuals as belonging
to a class and groups them together in a 'universal' idea. This
similarity of the individual essences constitutes the objective
reason or *foundation* for the universality of the class-idea in the
mind, so that the mind is entitled to 'universalize' the individual essence. St. Thomas summed up his doctrine in the famous
principle: 'Universals are *formally* (i.e., strictly, *as* universals)
in the mind, but *fundamentally* in the things themselves.' As
will be noted, this solution of the problem is in full accord
with the original interpretation of Aristotle, and henceforth
historians have called it the 'aristotelian-thomistic,' or moderate, realism. It is opposed to ultra-realism, nominalism, and
conceptualism.

There are, then, four systems of thought which claim to
give an adequate account of the universals: ultra-realism
(extreme realism), nominalism, conceptualism, and moderate
realism. We must now investigate them.

SUMMARY OF CHAPTER XIII

Our intellectual knowledge consists of ideas, judgments, and
reasoning. In establishing their truth-value, we must begin with
the *validity of ideas*.

1. *The Problem of the Universals*. Our intellect derives its
knowledge originally from the senses: concepts follow percepts.
Concepts or ideas are intellectual representations or images of
things. While the sense-image is singular, individual, and
concrete, the *idea is universal, general, and abstract;* it is not
restricted, like the sense-image, by conditions of time and place,
but is *fixed, unchangeable,* and *necessary* in its content. The
content of the idea is 'one-in-many,' i.e., it represents some
common nature or attribute which can be applied to *a class as
a whole* and to *each individual of that class*.

But therein lies the problem of its *validity*. Since universal
ideas are predicated of individuals and also represent the *class-
essence,* it would seem to follow that class-essences as such

must either exist in nature or that the universals do not faithfully represent reality. Either alternative involves serious difficulties.

2. *Importance of the Problem.* If our universal ideas are not a faithful representation of reality, the foundation of *reason* and of our *reasoning processes* is destroyed. *Science* is concerned with general truths, permanent facts, necessary relations, and universal laws; all this presupposes the validity of universal ideas. The value of science as a true representation of reality thus depends upon the truth-value of the universals. But how can we harmonize the *individual* things of nature with the *necessary* and *common* essence expressed in the universal idea?

3. *History of the Problem.* To safeguard the necessary and universal character of scientific knowledge, *Plato* maintained that for each universal concept of the mind there exists a corresponding universal Idea as a reality in a noumenal world outside the mind and outside the physical universe. *Aristotle* claimed that the mind derives its universal ideas from the individual sense-natures, due to their similarity; he thus advocated a *moderate realism* in opposition to Plato's *extreme realism.*

Medieval *empiric ultra-realism,* in contradistinction to Plato, placed the universal essences *in* the physical world, so that all individuals of a class share in this common nature or essence; this again was ultra-realism. Others disputed this, by disclaiming all universality; they were *nominalists,* since only the 'name' or word was considered universal. *Conceptualists,* on the other hand, asserted that our ideas are truly universal, but there is nothing in the individual things to justify this 'universalization' on the part of the mind. *St. Thomas Aquinas,* following Aristotle, found the justification for the process of universalizing in the *similarity of nature* existing in the individuals and formulated the solution in the principle: 'Universals are formally in the mind, but fundamentally in the things themselves.'

We thus have four theories concerning the universals: ultrarealism, nominalism, conceptualism, and moderate realism.

READINGS

M. De Wulf, *History of Medieval Philosophy,* 1909, Vol. I, pp. 150–198; 321, 322; Will. Turner, *History of Philosophy,* 1903, pp. 264–380; J. Rickaby, *op. cit.,* Part II, Ch. IV; P. Coffey, *op. cit.,* Vol. I, Chs. IX–XII.

Chapter XIV

THE TRUTH-VALUE OF THE UNIVERSALS

The validity of our intellectual knowledge depends on the truth-value of the universals. The problem is based on the apparently evident principle that, when we know an object, we must know the object as it is, or our knowledge is false. If this principle is interpreted rigidly, there must exist an extra-mental universal object corresponding to our universal idea; that would mean *extreme realism*. If we deny not only the extra-mental universal object but also the existence of the universal idea in the intellect, we have *nominalism*. In order to avoid the difficulties of extreme realism and nominalism, we may reject the principle that our knowledge must correspond in every way to the object. If we deny the principle of correspondence altogether and assert that we have universal ideas, but that they are pure fictions of the mind, without any foundation whatever in the extra-mental objects, we subscribe to *conceptualism*. We may, however, accept the principle that an extra-mental object must exist with which our universal idea corresponds, but that it need not exist in the same 'manner' in which the mind knows it; this view, which accepts universal ideas in the mind, with a foundation in the extra-mental individual objects to account for their universality in cognition, is *moderate realism*. We maintain that moderate realism alone correctly solves the problem.

CRITIQUE OF EXTREME REALISM

According to the ultra-realistic view, our universal ideas are representations of objects which are *as such* objectively, extra-mentally, *formally* universal *in themselves*. Universal ideas are supposed to have a content which is 'one-in-many,' because the objects themselves are essences which are 'one-in-many.' This theory rests on the principle that our ideas must correspond in every respect to the objects in order to be true knowledge. For this theory of extreme realism to be correct it would be necessary for the ultra-realists to prove that an *absolute* correspondence between thought and thing is required for the truth of knowledge. This, however, they cannot prove.

As a matter of fact, all knowledge is in the knower according to the nature of the knower. In sense-perception knowledge is obtained according to the character of the individual sense-organ which perceives the object, and each sense reacts in its own way to its respective stimulus. The eye, for instance, reacts to light waves, but not to sounds or flavors or odors or temperature; the ear reacts only to sound waves, but not to other stimuli; and the same is true of the other senses. No single sense conveys a complete picture of the object to the mind; nor do all the senses taken together. Furthermore, in our inquiry into the truth-value of sense-perception we have noticed that the objects do not correspond in absolute fashion to the perceptions of them which take place in our sense-organs. The *manner* in which objects *exist* is somewhat different from the *manner* in which they are *perceived*. This is simply due to the fact that the percept is a 'vital' similitude of the object, and it must conform to the nature of the perceiver. Just as a photograph, while it does not resemble the object in every respect, is a true representation of the thing photographed, so sense-knowledge is a true, though an inadequate and incomplete, representation of the thing perceived. But if sense-knowledge is true, without the necessity of an absolute correspondence between its manner of representation and the object's manner of existence, there is no reason for demanding such an absolute correspondence between the intellectual idea and the object it represents. The intellect could thus group a number of similar individuals under the class-notion of a universal idea, although these objects do not exist *as universals* outside the mind; the manner of representation would be different from the manner of existence, but the *content* of the idea would bear a faithful resemblance to the object itself as it exists in nature. Correspondence between idea and object there must be; but it need not be a complete and absolute correspondence *in every respect*. Hence, the reason which prompted the ultra-realists to postulate the existence of universal objects or essences is seen to be erroneous.

Again, there is *no empirical evidence* whatever for the existence of universal objects or essences outside the mind; it is a pure assumption. The data neither of internal nor of external experience reveal in any way the existence of an object or essence which could be said to be 'one-common-to-many.' Our experience tells us clearly that individual men, trees, animals, stones, metals, and similar objects, exist in nature; but nowhere do we find anything that would correspond to our idea of a universal man, or of a universal tree, or of a universal animal, or of a universal stone, or of a universal metal, and so on. The only actual things we know are single, *individual* objects, not universal natures and essences; and there is nothing in nature to indicate the existence of such universal entities. Not only do the objects in nature appear as individuals; they also *act* as such. Nothing is clearer to us through our experience than the fact that we *are* individual men in our own right; but of universal beings, for instance, of a universal man or humanity, we have no experience at all. Then why accept something for which no objective evidence can be discovered within or outside us?

After this general argument, we must turn our attention to the various types of ultra-realism.

Platonic ultra-realism leads to evident absurdities; hence, it must be false.

We must bear in mind that, according to this theory, the universal essences are *in reality* as our universal ideas are *in the intellect;* in other words, they *really exist* in the same manner as we *conceive* them. Let us see just what this means.

We possess generic universal ideas, like 'animal,' 'organism,' 'body,' 'substance.' By 'animal' we mean 'a sentient organism.' Our idea does not state whether this sentient organism is 'rational' or 'non-rational'; the distinction is omitted, so that the definition applies to both the rational and non-rational animals, to men and brutes, but the idea of 'animal' is *conceived as being neither* rational nor non-rational. And that is precisely the way in which the Platonic Idea or essence of 'animal' *must exist*: it is neither rational nor non-rational, but indifferent. That, however, is impossible. The terms 'rational' and 'non-rational' are contradictory and mutually exclusive. An existent thing must be either one or the other; it cannot be both nor can it be neither. If it is 'rational,' it cannot be 'non-rational,' and if it is 'non-rational,' it cannot be 'rational'; and if it is anything at all, it must be either 'rational' or 'non-rational': otherwise the Principle of Contradiction would be violated. Since, then, the Platonic Idea or essence of 'animal' would be neither a rational nor a non-rational entity, it violates the Principle of Contradiction and is thus an absurdity. And if it is stated that this essence is both rational and non-rational, because our idea of 'animal' applies to rational men and non-rational brutes, it would again violate the Principle of Contradiction, because no entity can be both rational and non-rational at the same time. To state that the universal essence of 'animal' is 'rational' (but not 'non-rational'), would exclude all brutes from this universal essence; and that is inadmissible, because the universal idea of 'animal' in our intellect applies also to the brutes. And it would be equally inadmissible to accept this universal essence as 'non-rational' (but not 'rational'), because then all men would be excluded, although they are included in the universal idea of 'animal' in our intellect. We thus see that the Platonic Ideas or essences either do not correspond to the universal ideas as we have them or they violate the Principle of Contradiction.

Besides, many Platonic essences would exist as realities although they possess *no positive entity*. 'Sickness,' for instance, is a universal idea, applying to all sicknesses as a class and to each particular sickness as an individual case. But 'sickness' is nothing positive; it is a non-entity, a mere privation, because it is the absence of health in someone who should normally be healthy. Although it lacks reality and entity, it would have to exist as a positive essence in the Platonic world of Ideas. But a non-entity cannot exist without being an entity; a non-entity, however, which is an entity, is a contradiction in itself. What has been said here of 'sickness' applies with equal force to all negative and privative ideas, as 'darkness,' 'lameness,' 'insanity,' 'death,' 'absent-mindedness,' 'blindness,' and the like.

Platonic ultra-realism is thus seen to be untenable, because it is self-contradictory. The noumenal world of Ideas is a fiction. Since the 'essence' or 'datum' of *critical realism,* as interpreted by some of its proponents, is extra-mentally 'universal,' outside the conditions of time and space, it is similar to Plato's Idea and as such is also self-contradictory.

Empiric ultra-realism, and any extreme realism which follows its fundamental principle, cannot escape absurd consequences. It maintains that the universal essences exist, not in a Platonic noumenal world, but *in the individuals themselves.* The consequences are fatal to the theory.

According to this view, a numerically single universal nature, corresponding to the universal idea in our intellect, exists in the individual members of a class; this universal nature or essence is thus a being which is really and actually 'one-in-many.' However, this universal nature must be either *really and only one* (universal) in all the individuals, so that they differ in nothing but accidentals, like color, shape, acts, etc.; or this nature must be *individuated* in each member of the class, so that the individuals are different from each other by possessing a complete individual nature distinct from that of the others.

Suppose we accept the first alternative. It would follow, for instance, that there are no 'individual men' in the world, but only a single 'universal man': we would have 'man-in-general,' but no 'individual human natures.' In that case the 'universal man' would indeed be *one* and universal, but it would not be 'one-in-*many*'; as such there would be no correspondence between our idea and this nature, because our idea represents the nature as being present in all and in each. Besides, such a view is contrary to all our *experience*. Our experience testifies beyond any doubt that we possess a distinct human nature of our own. Each of us has his own body, his own mind, his own thoughts and volitions and emotions and perceptions and loves and hates and ailments. We are conscious that we do *not* possess a single universal human nature in common with all other men, so that together we are a numerically single 'universal man.' To assert the contrary is to make our most intimate experience nothing but an illusion.

Then let us accept the second alternative, namely, that this universal nature or essence is *individuated* in each member of the class, giving to each a complete individual nature distinct from that of the others. In that case the *unity* and *universality* of the supposedly 'universal nature' would be destroyed. There would indeed be *many* individual natures, but there would not be '*one*-in-many.' No matter which way the universal nature or essence is viewed and interpreted, it can never be 'one-in-many' as an existing reality: it will either be 'one' and not 'many'; or it will be 'many' and not 'one.' To assert that it could be 'one' and 'many,' universal and individual, at the same time, is a contradiction in terms.

Logically, this form of ultra-realism, like any form of extreme realism, leads to *monism* and *pantheism*. If the specific nature of man is really universal and one in all men, then the generic nature of 'animal' must be one for all men and brutes taken together; men and brutes would no longer be distinct in nature, but form one 'universal animal.' Animals and plants would form one 'universal living being.' All living beings and inorganic substances would form one 'universal material substance.' All material and immaterial substances would form one 'universal substance.' All substances and accidents would form one 'universal being.' There would be *no individuals or classes* at all, but a single reality and being: that is monism. And since God and the world agree in the concept of 'being,' either God must be identical with the world, or the world identical with God: that is pantheism. All individuality of things is destroyed in this way; and thus the fundamental tenet of this form of ultra-realism, namely that the universal essences are found *in the individuals,* is abandoned. The theory has destroyed itself.

Nor is *monistic ultra-realism* capable of avoiding absurdity and contradiction within its theory. Monism, as a theory of being, belongs to ontology and cosmology, separate departments of philosophy; here it will be treated merely as a possible explanation of the validity of our universal ideas.

Monism, whether pantheistic or naturalistic, states that there exists but 'one sole reality,' common to all things; the things in the world are but parts, modes, or manifestations of the Absolute in its process of evolution. This, however, is contrary to *experience.* For one thing, we ourselves are conscious that we are *individuals* and subsisting *substances* in our own right, and not mere parts or modes or appearances or manifestations of one single reality. We are unitary beings, closed off in our entity from other beings, the subjects and causes of our own actions and reactions, and our personal Ego is clearly perceived to be distinct in its consciousness from that of other Egos. Our body, too, manifests itself to our minds as being different in entity from other bodies in the universe; it acts upon them and is acted upon by them, and in no way is it ever perceived to be one in being with them. This is unintelligible and inexplicable in the theory that all things form a single absolute being in which all are identified.

If monism were true, the electron, the stone, the amoeba, the elm, the mosquito, the whale, man, the sun, in fact *all mundane objects,* would consist of one self-identical reality, forming a single being and a single nature. In that case, however, our *consciousness* should reveal this absolute identity of nature between ourselves and the things in the universe, and it should be incapable of making an objective distinction between mind and matter, thought and thing, man and the world, the Ego and the non-Ego. Our empirical knowledge, whether obtained through external or internal experience, testifies that the world consists of a *plurality* of individual beings and not of a universal and absolute reality which is one in them all. *E. G. Spaulding* rightly observes that the empirical method "is a procedure that leads to the conclusion that monism of any kind can be grounded only artificially, and that a pluralism of many entities, of many kinds, in many different *loci,* is the only ontology which stands the test of empirical investigation."[1] Either the Absolute, then, does not exist as monism claims, or our entire knowledge is essentially an illusion. The latter alternative we cannot accept without falling into skepticism. Consequently, the monistic Absolute must be rejected as a mere assumption.

Ultra-realism, in whatever form, is thus seen to be utterly at variance with experience and reason; as such it fails to solve the problem of the universals.

CRITIQUE OF NOMINALISM

Nominalism is the reverse of ultra-realism: it denies the universal altogether. The essences or natures are not extramentally universal, nor are our ideas intra-mentally universal. Our ideas are as individual as the things we perceive with our senses. Modern empiricists consider our intellectual knowledge to be nothing more than a refined sort of sense-knowledge; this being so, it is obvious that our ideas cannot really be 'universal,' representing a content which is strictly 'one-in-many,' but must be as individual in character as the sense-image itself. At best, we can have 'general images' or 'composite images,' a product of several singular sense-images fused together into a vague, indefinite representation, something like the composite photograph resulting from a number of superimposed plates. The

---

[1] *The New Rationalism* (Henry Holt Co., 1918), p. 437.

only thing that is strictly universal is the *name,* or *word,* and that is used merely as a 'label' to designate a number of objects grouped according to some arbitrary pattern. Thus names or words, nominalists say, designate and represent *individuals* or a *collection of individuals,* but never represent anything which is mentally applicable to a class as a whole and to each individual belonging to that class. But in this they are wrong. A little reflection will prove this.

Names and words are *signs* and have a *meaning;* they are signs of *ideas* and they derive their meaning from the *content* of the ideas for which they stand. And since the ideas stand for things, names and words are also used to designate things. Now, if we can show that names and words are used to designate something which is conceived by the intellect as being 'one-common-to-many,' we thereby prove that we really have *universal* ideas. And that is precisely what takes place.

We have names which stand for *singular* objects: 'Peter is a man,' 'Homer was a poet,' 'Plato was a philosopher.' Here the subjects represent a single thing. Other names stand for collective objects: 'The library is large,' 'the army marches on,' 'the herd is scattered,' 'the nation is in revolt,' 'the city is celebrating.' Here the subjects represent a number of individuals taken together *as a group,* but the statements do not apply to the individual members of the group. We have, however, many names and words which apply to a *class* and *to each member* of the class. Take the word 'man.' By 'man' we mean a 'rational animal.' This word represents the class as a class *and* the individual human beings belonging to the class. If we say 'Man is mortal,' just what do we mean? We mean that 'all men' taken together as a class 'are mortal' and 'each individual man' taken separately 'is mortal.' So, too, when science states that 'The living cell has immanent action,' it does not mean that a single cell or a mere collection of cells, but 'all cells' as a class and as individuals 'have immanent action.' Again, zoology tells us that 'the horse is a mammal.' The word 'horse' here does not designate a single animal like Man-o'-War, nor a collection of animals like a herd, but the whole class of equines and each member of that class. Such statements show plainly that these subjects have a content which are conceived as 'one-common-to-many.' And since words and names stand for ideas, our *ideas* have a content which is conceived as 'one-common-to-many.' That, however, is what is meant by a *universal idea*. We have, then, ideas which are not merely singular or collective, but truly universal.

Nominalists admit the universality of our names and words, but deny the universality of the ideas for which they stand. *N. O. Losskü* refutes the contention of the nominalists that the name gives rise to the class. He says: "The contention is that the grouping of things into classes is not in any way determined by the properties of the things themselves, but is due to names. The name gives rise to a class of things, and it is not the class of things that attracts a name to itself. A rejoinder at once suggests itself, which, in spite of its seeming to be almost ironical, is nevertheless very much to the point. If the grouping of things into classes is determined by names — understanding by a name not a universal element but something created afresh in every single act of utterance — how is it that a name is never associated with groups of *heterogeneous* things, such as tiger, coffee pot, candle, and birch tree, but always with groups of *homogeneous* objects — homogeneous not merely in the sense of being connected with one and the same word? The only answer is that we associate with a name not anything which we choose, but only things which *resemble* one another. This, however, means that the name merely assists in the final crystallization of a general idea, and that the essential condition of things being grouped into classes is the *resemblance* between them."[2]

The fact is, that the intellect recognizes this resemblance of objects among themselves, groups the *many* into *one* idea,

---

[2]Nicolai Onufrievich Losskü, *The Intuitive Basis of Knowledge*, tr. by N. A. Duddington (Macmillan, 1919), p. 287. (Italics mine. — Author.)

which is now universal, and uses a word or name to designate the idea. Only because we have universal *ideas,* have we also universal *names.* If nominalism were correct, we should have no universal names, since we have no universal ideas. To have universal names without universal ideas for which they stand, is contradictory. But we have universal names; consequently, we have universal ideas. Nominalism must be rejected, because it maintains that names and words can have a universal significance without deriving this significance from the only source from which it can be derived, namely, from the universal ideas of which they are the signs. The significance of any sign depends on the significance of the thing signified. Hence, the *universal* significance of the *name* depends on the *universal* significance of the *idea.* Ideas are thus universal, and nominalism is false.

CRITIQUE OF CONCEPTUALISM

Extreme realists admit that we have ideas which are universal and claim that the things to which they apply are also universal. Nominalists deny the existence of universal entities and also deny that we have genuinely universal ideas in the mind. *Conceptualists* deny the universality of extra-mental entities as existing in nature, and they admit that the intellect has genuinely universal ideas which are expressed in universal names or words. However, because the objects in the world are singular and not universal, they claim that our universal ideas can have *no objective value.* In other words, since the objects are singular while the ideas are universal, there is nothing in the objects themselves which would correspond in any way to the content of the universal as 'one-common-to-many.' The universality of the idea is a *purely subjective product* of the mind, *without a foundation* in the things themselves which would entitle the mind to group a number of individuals under one (universal) idea. Hence, the universal idea can give us no genuine knowledge of the real nature of the things.

Conceptualists go too far when they assert that there is *no foundation* in things for our universal ideas and consequently that the content of these ideas as 'one-common-to-many' is purely subjective in character. If this were so, then the content of the universal idea would neither be *derived from* the individual things nor *applied to* the individual things. If we can show that they are derived from the individual things through sense-perception and are really applied to individual things as they exist in nature, then we have proved that universals have a *foundation* in these things and possess *objective* value. That indeed is the case.

This is clearly demonstrated by the fact that our intellect can form no universal idea of sense-qualities proper to a certain sense-faculty, if this sense-faculty has always been absent. A person born blind, for instance, cannot form a genuine, universal idea of light or color; and a person born deaf has no idea of what is meant by sound or music. The same is true of any other sense-quality. Whence do we derive our universal ideas of 'man,' 'plant,' 'dog,' 'star,' 'table,' and other objects, except from a previous perception of these things? Our ideas are based ultimately on sense-perception, not on purely intellectual activity; that is why our ideas of *immaterial* things, like the soul, God, spirit, will, and the like, are so inadequate. Hence, conceptualists are wrong when they state that our universal ideas have no foundation in the reality of the objects; we *derive* them from these objects as they exist in nature.

That our universal ideas can be *applied* according to their content as 'one-common-to-many' to objects, is a matter of everyday *experience*. When I state 'Man is an animal,' I most certainly do apply the content 'animal' as a 'sentient organism' to each and every human being and to all human beings who live in this world; and that in a true, genuine sense. The statement has not merely value in my mind, but also in the order of *reality:* men actually *are* 'sentient organisms.' And so with statements like 'The rose is red,' 'the gnat is an insect,' 'the table is round,' and with innumerable other statements which contain universal ideas: they represent facts and objects of the real order. Such statements could never be true, if our universal ideas had no foundation in the reality of the things themselves.

That the *natural sciences* apply the universal ideas incorporated in their *classifications* and *laws* to the physical world, is too obvious for serious dispute. The classifications of animals, plants, and inorganic substances have not only a subjective value for the mind; they really fit, as classes and types, the things of nature. And how could it be otherwise? Science derives its universal ideas of classes and types from its research into the beings which exist in the material world. The only reason why it groups such beings into classes and types is because it finds something 'common-to-many' in them; there is thus a foundation or ground *in the things* for the formation of its universal ideas. So, too, with its *laws*. They represent generalizations based on the behavior of physical bodies. If these bodies did not act uniformly and constantly, science could never formulate such laws, nor would the laws of science apply to them in their respective fields. If scientists can and do predict the actions of physical bodies in nature, this is possible only because these laws have a foundation in the reality of these bodies and actually apply to them independently of the universalizing function of the mind. To deny this is tantamount to denying the validity of all science; and that would be ruinous of all knowledge of the physical world. Skepticism must inevitably follow.

Many conceptualists accept the conclusion that intellectual knowledge is practically an illusion. *Bergson* and *William James* do this in consequence of their anti-intellectualist doctrine of pragmatism.[3] *Kant* and his disciples, although they attempt to establish the validity and necessity of scientific knowledge, are compelled to admit that all scientific classifica-

---

[3]H. Bergson, *L'Évolution créatrice*, Ch. IV. W. James, *A Pluralistic Universe*, Lect. V–VIII.

tions and laws have no objective, but only subjective, value. This follows, of course, with logical consistency from their theory that the reality of things-in-themselves is unknown and unknowable; the only objects we can know are the phenomena. The universality of our ideas is due to certain innate *a priori* forms or categories of the intellect, which are purely subjective in character and are imposed by the mind upon the manifold of sense; as such, then, they can have no objective value.[4] But if the natural sciences are invalid as objective representations of the physical world and are nothing more than subjective constructions of a fictionizing intellect, all knowledge and philosophy is doomed as illusory. That is the logical outcome of a consistent conceptualism; and that we cannot accept, because it means intellectual bankruptcy. Conceptualism must, therefore, be rejected as a false theory.

CRITIQUE OF MODERATE REALISM

A number of conclusions can now be drawn. Extreme realism is correct in asserting the presence of universal ideas in the mind; but it is wrong in assuming that realities exist in the world which are objectively universal as entities. Nominalism is correct in denying the existence of universal entities in the world; but wrong in denying the existence of universal ideas in the mind. Conceptualism is right in denying the universality of entities in the world and in affirming the universality of ideas in the mind; but it is wrong in asserting that there is no foundation for our universal ideas in the objects of the world. The final conclusion, then, must be that we have universal ideas in our mind and that they have a foundation in things themselves. This last is the teaching of *moderate realism,* and the truth of moderate realism is thus established. A more positive proof, however, is required. With experience and reflection as guide, it will be necessary to show how universal

---

[4] For a detailed critique of Kant's conceptualism, see Coffey, *Epistemology,* Vol. I, Ch. XII.

ideas are developed from sense-perception through a process of abstraction.

It is in this process of *abstraction* that we find the solution of the problem of the universals. In order to understand it properly, we must begin with sense-perception. The things in this world are *single* beings, *individual* natures. Universal entities do not exist outside the mind in the material universe or anywhere else; this was proved against extreme realism. These individual beings possess many characteristics peculiar to themselves, so that one differs from the other to such an extent that no two are totally alike in *every* respect; each nature is thus individualized, numerically one, and incommunicable to others. Consider man. Each person has his own individual nature, concretely determined by color, weight, size, shape, etc., so that he is distinguishable from every other person. Our senses perceive these individuals in their concrete determinations, and the phantasm or sense-image represents them with all their concrete similarities and differences.

Once the phantasm or sense-image is made, the *intellect* begins to operate. It gives its attention to this and that trait and attribute and perceives their *whatness,* i.e., that which makes them to be 'what' they are and without which they could not remain 'what' they are; it is the essence of these things. This applies to substances and accidents; in fact, to everything that exists. Take again the example of man. Amid all the characteristics of individual human beings, the intellect is aware that the elements of 'a bodily, living, sentient, rational substance' are present in each individual all the time and *must* be there. A man would cease to be a 'man,' if a single one of them were missing; these elements, therefore, constitute man's essence or 'whatness.' The other characteristics, like weight, color, size, shape, etc., are not necessary; they could be missing in some or all individuals, without a man ceasing to be a 'man'; in other words, these determinations, though present in the individual, are not part of his 'essence' as such.

Here, then, we have the basis for the origin and validity of *universal ideas*. From the sense-image, representing the individuals in all their concrete similarities and differences, the intellect *abstracts* or draws forth an intellectual image of the *essence,* leaving out of consideration the nonessential characteristics which distinguish one individual from the other. This essence, as will be noted, is a *reality,* and it is actually present in the individuals independent of our thinking, though *not in that abstract form* in which it is represented by the intellect. The real individual, as it exists in the physical world, has all the elements of this essence *plus* its concrete, nonessential, differentiating characteristics, while the intellect leaves the latter aside and selects only the essential elements or 'essence.' This essence, as it exists in the intellect, is thus stripped of everything which is not necessary to the 'whatness' of the thing and is now *abstract*. This abstract representation or *idea* in the intellect is, as far as it goes, a true representation of the essence of the thing existing in the objective world, even though it leaves out of consideration the various differentiating characteristics which accompany this individual essence in reality. And since this essence (for instance, man as 'a bodily, living, sentient, rational substance') is recognized by the intellect as being the same with *the sameness of a perfect likeness* in each individual taken singly and in all individuals taken as a class, this comprehension or *content* of the abstract idea is such that it will apply to the class as a whole and to each individual as a member of that class. In other words, the content, though one, is applicable to many: the content is 'one-common-to-many.' And that is what we mean by a *universal idea,* namely, an idea whose content represents an essence which is found to be present in many, so that all, individually and collectively, possess the same (not identical, but *like*) common essence. Such an abstract idea is, therefore, a *true universal*.

There are two kinds of universal ideas: *direct* and *reflex*. A consideration of what has just been said will show the difference between these two types of universals. When the intellect abstracts the 'essence' from the sense-image, it considers at first *nothing but the essential elements* which constitute the thing: this and nothing more is before the intellect through the process of abstraction. At this stage the intellect does not consider whether this essence is 'one' or 'many'; it is interested merely in the 'essential elements' *as such,* without reference to the number of individuals to which they can or cannot be applied. The intellect contemplates the essence in an *absolute* fashion, as it is in itself, simply as the 'whatness' of the thing. Since, however, the essence or 'whatness' represented by the idea is such that it *could be applied* by the intellect to one and many at the very moment the abstraction is made, this idea is already a true universal; but the intellect does not *as yet* reflect on this possibility, nor does it make the actual application. Hence, this idea, considered as the immediate product of abstraction, is called a 'direct,' or 'potential,' or 'metaphysical,' or 'fundamental' universal. This type of universal, therefore, expresses merely the essence or 'whatness' of a thing as it is *in itself,* prescinding for the time being from its singularity or multiplicity.

After having formed the abstract idea of the essence, the intellect *compares* this essence with the essences of *similar* objects; and by means of this act of comparison it becomes aware that this essence is not only found in this one object, but is *predicable of many* similar objects. The content of the idea representing this essence is recognized to be such that it is capable of being realized in any number of individuals: it is 'one-common-to-many.' In this manner the intellect now *formally universalizes* the original idea of the essence abstracted from the sense-image, after having seen that it is applicable to the whole class and to every individual member of the class. This type of universal idea is called a 'logical,' or 'formal,' or 'reflex' universal. It will be noted that the 'direct' universal refers merely to the *comprehension* of the idea, i.e., it expresses an essence which, though in itself 'common-to-many,' is not considered as common to many; while the 'logical' or 'formal' universal refers to the *extension* of the idea, i.e., it expresses an essence which is 'common-to-many' and is considered precisely in so far as it is common to many. In other words, the 'direct' universal possesses a *potential* universality, while the 'logical' universal possesses a *formal* universality in the intellect. The former represents the essence considered *in itself alone* as expressing the 'whatness' of the thing thought about, without regard to whether it is singular or multiple; the latter represents the essence as *formally universal,* as something which is applied or is at least applicable to 'one-and-many.'

It is important to realize this distinction between the direct and reflex universal, because it enables us to understand how universals can be predicated of individuals and still furnish us with a true knowledge of the things in their objective reality. In predicating a universal of the individual things, we apply the *content* expressed in the *direct* universal to the object, because that content represents the essence as such *without the mode of universality* attached to it. In the reflex universal the mode of universality always accompanies the abstract essence, for the reflex universal considers this essence precisely as universal, as 'one-common-to-many.' In other words, we predicate the absolute essence of the individual, and not the 'universalized' essence, so that the *universality* of the idea is not applied to the individual at all. This idea of the essence, considered in itself alone and absolutely, is a true representation of the essence as it exists in the individual and can, therefore, be truly applied to it. Error would enter into our predication, if we applied the content of the abstract essence and *also* its universality to the individual things, because these things are not universal but singular in reality. We thus safeguard both the singularity of the individual and the truth-value of our universal ideas. That we 'universalize' the essence and consider it (in the reflex universal) as 'one-common-to-many,' is merely a *logical mode* of our thought-process and does not change the content in any way: the *content* remains *real,* while the *universality* is a *logical mode* (*ens rationis*) superadded to it.

While the 'universality' of the abstract essence is thus a product of the mind and is not found in the real essence as it exists in nature, the intellect observes a *foundation or reason* in the things themselves which entitles it to universalize the abstract essence in this manner. This universality is founded on the real *similarity* of essence existing between different things, so that the intellect can group them into a *class*. These objects are really alike in their essential elements; all men, for instance, are really 'bodily, living, sentient, rational substances.' After comparing them and seeing the complete likeness of their essences, the intellect groups them into a class and expresses the whole class by means of a *single* (universal) idea; and this idea is now capable of being applied to the whole and to every member of the class — for example, to John, James, Plato, Napoleon, and to all men taken together. Their essences are not identical, but they are really and truly similar; consequently, the objective ground or foundation for the formally universalized idea lies in the similarity of the essences embodied in all the members of the same class. Therefore, the intellect is justified in stating 'John is a man,' applying the universal idea 'man' to the individual 'John,' because it thereby predicates, not the universality, but the *content* of the idea 'man' to 'John,' and this content is perceived to be *actually realized* in him. While, then, the 'universality' of the abstract idea is thus seen to be a product of the mind, there is a real foundation in the things themselves entitling the intellect to universalize this idea and make it 'one-common-to-many.' Both the *things* and the *intellect* contribute their share in the formation of universal ideas: the things contribute the *material* or *content,* namely the 'whatness' or 'essence,' and the intellect contributes the *form* or *mode,* namely the 'universality.' Hence, the universals are real from the standpoint of their material or content, but not according to their form or mode; the form or mode, however, has a foundation in the things themselves. The whole situation can be summed up as follows: In the real order the essence is actually many, but potentially one; in the intellectual order it is actually one, but potentially many.

Reflection and introspection thus prove that the universal as such is a product of the mind with a foundation in the things. Or, as St. Thomas Aquinas expresses it: 'Universals are *formally* (as such, i.e., as universals) in the mind, *fundamentally* in the things themselves.' That is the solution of the problem of the universals as offered by *moderate realism*. If we compare this solution with that offered by the opposing theories of ultra-realism, nominalism, and conceptualism, we will find that it alone explains the obvious singularity of the individual things in nature and the objective value of our intellectual knowledge as applied to these things. Moderate realism is the only correct theory of the universals.[5]

From the above it will be clear that our universal ideas give us a true and genuine (though naturally incomplete and inadequate) insight into reality; they are a valid source of scien-

---

[5]Roy Wood Sellars, in *The Philosophy of Physical Realism* (Macmillan Co., 1932), calls himself a 'logical conceptualist' and an 'ontological nominalist.' It is unfortunate that his use of the terms 'conceptualism' and 'nominalism' is at variance with the standard definitions of these theories as given in history, because as a matter of fact the expression of his own views and of the views of some other critical realists in this matter is identical in substance with the 'moderate realism' of Aristotle and St. Thomas (see pp. 155, 156; 173–175). The following quotation from page 175 shows this plainly: "It will be noted that, while I am an ontological nominalist, I recognize the objective reality of structure and relations. This flows from my physical realism. Similar things have similar properties and structures. And, when we think them, we can think them in terms of the same predicates. The predicate which will disclose one will disclose the other. It has a one-many capacity of disclosure. I am an ontological nominalist because I see no adequate reason to postulate a peculiar entity called a universal to account for these similarities. To me, the ultimate ontological fact is the existence of a multitude of similar substances able to combine in similar patterns and have, in such combinations, similar properties. And this, I take it, is the path science has actually chosen." This is moderate realism. Although Sellars impugns the teaching of Aristotelianism and Thomism, his own theory of knowledge, as given in the *Essays in Critical Realism* (pp. 217 and 218), is closely akin to these systems. (See Edward F. Talbot, *Knowledge and Object*, Catholic University, Washington, D. C.)

tific knowledge, and the truth-value of our intellectual ideas is thus critically and philosophically established.

SUMMARY OF CHAPTER XIV

The validity of our intellectual knowledge depends on the validity of the universals, because our knowledge, to be true, must *conform to reality.* Different theories have been devised to solve the problem: extreme realism (ultra-realism), nominalism, conceptualism, and moderate realism.

1. *Critique of Extreme Realism.* As a *general* refutation of ultra-realism, it may be noted, first, that our knowledge need not correspond with reality in *every respect,* and, second, that there is *no empirical evidence* of any kind to show that universal essences exist.

Against *Platonic* ultra-realism. If generic universals actually existed, we would have 'animals' which are neither rational nor non-rational, 'organisms' which are neither sentient nor non-sentient, etc. There would also be universal realities *without entity,* such as are expressed in *privative* ideas, like sickness, lameness, insanity, etc.

Against *empiric* ultra-realism. If the universal essence is considered to be *really and only one,* it would mean, for instance, that there are no individual men, but only a 'universal man' or 'man-in-general'; that is contrary to our experience, since we are conscious of our own individual nature. If this essence is considered as *individuated* in each member of the class, it would not be universal. Every form of ultra-realism leads logically to *monism* and *pantheism* through the universalization of 'being.'

Against *monistic* ultra-realism. It is contrary to our experience, since we are individual substances with an individual *consciousness.*

2. *Critique of Nominalism. Names* are signs of ideas. But our names are universal, applying to a class and to each member of a class. Consequently, we have universal ideas for

which these names stand. If the name, and not the property of things, determined the grouping of objects into classes, we could not explain why only *homogeneous* things are thus grouped.

3. *Critique of Conceptualism.* Universal ideas must have a *foundation* in the reality of things, because they are *derived* from individual things and *apply* to them. A person born blind has no genuine idea of color or light; this shows that our ideas have a foundation in the things. Experience proves that we really apply these ideas to things, as when we say that 'man is an animal'; we actually mean that the content of the idea 'animal' is found in 'man.' The *classifications* and *laws* of *science* really apply to things, because they are derived from the things in nature.

4. *Critique of Moderate Realism.* From the above it must be clear that universal essences do not exist; but we have universal ideas in the mind and they have a foundation in the individual things: that is moderate realism. Through our senses we obtain a *phantasm* of the individual essence in all its concrete determinations. The intellect now makes a vital similitude of the object, by *abstracting* the essence or 'whatness' of a thing, leaving out of consideration the nonessential characteristics. This 'essence' is actually present in the individuals, but not in this abstract form; individuals are alike through *similarity* of essential elements. The *content* (abstract essence) is expressed in the *direct* universal and is predicated of the individual objects. The *universality* ('one-common-to-many') is expressed in the *reflex* universal and is not predicated of the individual objects. The 'content' is *real,* but the 'universality' is a logical *mode* (*ens rationis*). The similarity of things is the foundation or ground which entitles the intellect to 'universalize' the abstract essence, considering it as 'one-common-to-many.' Hence, the axiom: Universals are formally in the mind, fundamentally in the things.

Universals thus give us a true insight into reality and are a valid source of knowledge.

READINGS

P. Coffey, *op. cit.,* Vol. I, Chs. IX, X, XI, XII; J. Rickaby, *op. cit.,* Part II, Ch. IV; J. Barron, *op. cit.,* Ch. XVII; T. Pesch, *op. cit.,* Vol. II, pp. 168–220; 428–486; R. Clarke, *Logic,* Chs. VIII, IX; J. Donat, *Critica,* cap. IV, art. 1; A. K. Rogers, *What is Truth?* pp. 106–122; 128–158.

CHAPTER XV

THE TRUTH-VALUE OF NECESSARY JUDGMENTS

We have established the objective value of our ideas. They have a 'mode of universality' in the intellect, but they express a 'content of reality'; that which they represent actually exists in the things represented. This naturally leads us to inquire into the validity of our intellectual *judgments*. Judgments consist of ideas. A judgment is a mental act whereby we assert the agreement or disagreement between two ideas. And since our ideas stand for things, what the judgment asserts of ideas it actually means to assert of the things represented by the ideas. When I say, 'This table is square,' I claim that the two ideas 'table' and 'square' are in agreement with each other; but I also claim that the *reality* expressed by the idea 'square' is actually found in the *object* expressed by the idea 'table,' so that the extra-mental 'table' is extra-mentally 'square' in the domain of physical nature. And when I say that 'Gold is not iron,' I not only disunite these two ideas in my intellect, but I also assert that 'gold' and 'iron' are not identical in their physical reality. The truth of such a judgment will depend upon the agreement of the judgment with the *fact* enunciated.

There is no real problem in this. As long as the intellect can acquire a knowledge of the reality of things and represent them by means of its ideas, it can pass a judgment upon the identity or non-identity of things by means of ideas used as subject and predicate. But there is one phase of the judgment which involves a real problem for the philosopher. We derive our ideas from sensible objects. And sensible objects are concrete, individual, changing, temporal, and contingent; they are neither eternal, immutable, nor necessary. However, many of our judgments have the characteristic that they appear to us to be *eternally, immutably, and necessarily true.* Whence do they obtain this character? And how can they be a true representation of reality?

STATEMENT OF THE PROBLEM

We form various kinds of judgments. For example: 'The sun is shining today'; 'three boys are skating on the pond'; 'I took a stroll this afternoon.' These statements express facts known through *experience;* they are true, but they *need not* be true and *could be different.* There is no necessary connection between the subject and predicate of these statements: the sky could be overcast; the boys need not go skating; I did not have to go for a stroll. That we connect these particular predicates with these particular subjects, is simply because the facts happen to be so and not because they must be. The facts are contingent and could easily be otherwise.

Other judgments are such that their truth *must* be so and can absolutely not be different. Take these arithmetical statements: '$2+2=4$'; '$5+4=6+3$'; '$7+3=15-5$'; and the like. Or geometrical axioms, such as: 'Two parallel lines can never meet'; 'the whole is greater than any of its parts'; 'the sum of the angles of a triangle are equal to two right angles'; and so on. And also the philosophical principles: 'A thing cannot be and not be the same thing at the same time' (Principle of Contradiction); 'a thing either is or is not something' (Principle of Excluded Middle); 'a thing must have a sufficient reason for its being and existence' (Principle of Sufficient Reason); 'whatever happens or becomes must have a cause for its happening or becoming' (Principle of Causality). Such principles are adjudged to be true independently of all existential conditions and experience. They are not only true here and there, now and then, for this and that mind; they are *eternally, immutably, necessarily true,* everywhere, always, and for every mind. The connection between these subjects and predicates is adjudged to be *absolute* and *universal,* removed from any possibility of change or error. Our intellect has no choice in the matter; it must give an unequivocal assent to these so-called *first principles,* without being able to prove them by anything like a strict demonstration.

Now, why must the intellect assent to them this way? What is it that influences and *forces* the mind to assent to these judgments? Does the motive which constrains our intellect lie within the *subjective* constitution of the intellect itself, so that it must judge in this fashion simply because its laws of thinking are made that way; or does the motive lie in the *objective* nature of these truths themselves, so that they reveal themselves with evident clarity to our intellect and thus force it to make these judgments? In the first alternative, first principles are true merely for *our* minds and need not be true in themselves; in the second alternative, these principles are true everywhere, always, and for *all* minds without exception, because they are objectively true in themselves independently of our own thinking. In the first alternative, we 'make' them to be true; in the second alternative, we 'discover' them to be true. In the first alternative, their truth-value is restricted to our *intellect* and is purely subjective; in the second alternative, their truth-value applies to *reality* and is objective.

This shows the *importance* of the problem involved in the knowledge of such principles. These principles form the foundation of all scientific and philosophic knowledge, as will be readily observed. Without the objective truth of the Principles of Contradiction, Excluded Middle, Sufficient Reason, and Causality, our entire knowledge of physics, chemistry, astronomy, biology, and all other natural sciences would be without a rational basis in *reality;* they would be subjective constructions of our mind and as such might or might not correspond to the facts of physical nature. Without the objective truth of the axioms of arithmetic and geometry, these sciences would be a mere figment of the mind and might be inapplicable to real things. If these principles were subjective in character, the structure of our intellectual knowledge would lack necessity and universality as a representation of reality; as such they would cease to be real science and real philosophy, because science and philosophy are supposed to give us certain knowledge of ourselves and of the world. It is, therefore, of prime importance for us to know whether the *necessity* which we perceive in the logical connection between the subject and predicate of first principles is objective or subjective, i.e., whether their logical connection and truth is due fundamentally to our *intellect* or to the *reality expressed* in them.

THE THEORY OF ASSOCIATIONISM

The *empiricists,* as we have seen, admit nothing but sense-knowledge of phenomena. For them there is no such thing as a suprasensible intellectual knowledge. Ideas are but refined sense-images; consciousness is a 'bundle' or 'series' or 'stream' of perceptions. The mind is nothing permanent and abiding, and it can never transcend its own internal states. Since the mind itself and all phenomena are but passing, changing, contingent realities, it is obvious that there can be no permanent and necessary knowledge in any form. Their theory of sensism precludes all knowledge which would possess a universal and necessary character. Yet it cannot be denied that we consider these axioms to be necessarily and absolutely true. What is the origin and explanation of this general conviction? It is a fact and must be accounted for.

Hume finds its origin and explanation in the *association* of our ideas. Certain ideas or images are always experienced as going together; certain phenomena always appear in a regular sequence of time or in a definite contiguity in space. Thereupon we uniformly and continuously associate these things together in our mind. This is done in virtue of the *law of association* inherent in the mind itself, because the mind is so constituted; and this is a subjective law with a purely subjective result. Consequently, the 'necessity' which we experience relative to the logical connection between subject and predicate in these principles is not due to anything coming from the reality represented in these judgments, but solely to the *associating force* existing in the mind. It is a subjective and *psychological,* not an objective and *ontological* necessity. The mind does not judge these principles to be true, because it *sees* that they cannot be otherwise; it *cannot see* them to be otherwise, because the mind in its present constitution must judge them to be true. There is nothing *intrinsically* impossible in 2+2 being 5 or 3, or in a circle being square or hexagonal, or in parallel lines meeting in a point, or in a triangle having six right angles, or in an object having contradictory properties, or in a thing coming into existence without a cause. As a matter of fact, according to Hume, Mill, and empiricists generally, the Principle of Causality is nothing but a mental expression of 'invariable sequence': because we observe things following each other invariably in time, we simply judge that the preceding object 'causes' the one following. This, however, is solely due to the fact that they are invariably 'associated' in our sensations as prior and posterior. If we think that an absolute necessity exists in the connection between these subjects and predicates, so that these principles *must* be true for all times and in all places and for all minds, we are harboring an illusion. There is no such objective necessity. For other minds, in other places, at other times, and under other conditions, such principles and axioms may have no truth-value at all; *we,* of course, according to the present constitution of our mind in its laws of association, must consider them as necessarily true and valid. Such is the theory of associationism in its attempt to explain the character of necessity which we perceive to exist in first principles and axioms.

This theory is false and fails to give an adequate account of the logical necessity existing in these judgments. If the theory were correct, we should perforce experience the same psychological necessity of judgment *in every case* where we observe a uniform and constant association of objects or ideas in our consciousness. This, however, is patently wrong. For instance, day follows night in an invariable sequence; but nobody would dream of asserting that the night is the 'cause' of the day. Here we see plainly that constant and uniform association does not in any way force us to the necessary judgment that night 'produces' day. So, too, we perceive that spring invariably follows winter; nevertheless, we do not judge for that reason that winter is the 'cause' of spring. Every time we lift our eyelids during the day, we invariably see; yet we do not think that the lifting of the eyelids 'causes' our actual 'seeing,' since we ascribe it to the power of sight residing in the organ itself. Hence, the necessity inherent in our judgment expressing the Principle of Causality is not derived from the subjective influence of the association of our ideas.

Even when we do assert the necessity of a causal interaction in physical phenomena, this *factual* necessity based on experience is very different from the *absolute* necessity we judge to exist in our first principles and axioms. We always observe, for instance, that water at sea level expands and solidifies at $+32°$ F. and vaporizes to steam at $+212°$ F. We say that water 'necessarily' does this. But we also know that this necessity is not absolute; water *could* act otherwise without destroying the nature of water or the foundations of our knowledge. But compare this judgment with the judgments 'A circle is round,' '$2+2 = 4$,' 'everything must have a sufficient reason,' or with any other first principle, and the difference between the respective 'necessity' of these two types will immediately be apparent: the judgment about water freezing or vaporizing at these temperatures is factually and physically necessary, while the latter judgments are absolutely and metaphysically necessary, because we realize that the latter admit of no exceptions and *must* be true under *all* circumstances. But why the difference for our mind? We certainly never experience any exceptions to water freezing at $+32°$ F. and vaporizing to steam at $+212°$ F. Then, according to the law of the association of ideas, both types of judgments should exhibit the *same* sort of necessity. That, however, is not the case. Consequently, the association of ideas resulting from constant and uniform contiguity or sequence does not account for the necessity we perceive to exist in our judgments expressing first principles and axioms. Associationism thus fails in its attempt to explain the mental facts of our necessary judgments.

Moreover, it takes but a moment's reflection to see that this theory must *destroy all science.* The very foundation of science lies in the Principles of Contradiction, Sufficient Reason, and Causality. If these principles are valid only for our mind and do not apply with inviolable necessity to physical objects in nature, the scientist has no means of knowing whether his conclusions are objectively valid. And if he cannot be sure of this, the knowledge he acquires is nothing but a *purely mental construction* which may or may not agree with extra-mental reality. But science treats of physical systems, not mental constructions. If associationism were a true interpretation of the fact of mental necessity in our judgments about nature, science would be valueless as an explanation of physical phenomena. A theory, however, which destroys science must be intrinsically wrong.

THE THEORY OF FORMALISM

Kant was shocked by Hume's sensism and skepticism, since it destroyed the truth-value of science; it awoke him, as he himself says, from his "dogmatic slumbers." He felt he was called upon to save science. Kant was convinced that science gives us true knowledge, and the judgments resulting from true knowledge are genuinely universal and necessary. Since, however, true science must have an empirical content (i.e., be derived from experience), and since the empirical is only contingent and constantly changing, he naturally put to himself the question: How account for the *universality* and *necessity* so manifestly exhibited in our scientific knowledge? Since the things of experience are only individual and contingent, Kant felt that the 'universality' and 'necessity' of knowledge could not be derived from the things of experience as such. Whatever, then, is 'universal' and 'necessary' in our knowledge cannot come from experience; it can come only from the *mind itself*. Kant considers all knowledge derived from experience as *a posteriori,* and all knowledge supplied by the mind itself as *a priori;* the latter is innate in the mind and independent of all experience. Even scientific induction cannot give us true and strict, but only assumed and relative, universality; a judgment of strict universality, in which no exception is admitted as possible, cannot be derived from experience, but must receive this strict universality from the mind. How, then, does scientific knowledge come about?

As our sensibility gives us objects to perceive, so our understanding gives us ideas or *concepts* of these objects of our sense-intuition. In order to have intellectual knowledge, therefore, our intuitions or phenomena must be brought under certain concepts or *categories* of the understanding; thereby these intuitions become intelligible. In this union of intuitions and concepts knowledge is produced. Just as 'space' and 'time' are the *a priori* mental forms which must be united to the *a posteriori* impressions in order to make intuition possible, so the 'concepts' or 'categories' are the *a priori* forms of the understanding which must be united to the phenomena or sense-representations in order to make judgment and thought possible. These 'concepts' or 'categories,' like 'space' and 'time' with regard to sense-impressions, give *universality* and *necessity* to our thoughts and judgments and must, therefore, be in the mind prior to all experience and independent of all experience. There are twelve such 'categories,' according to Kant, and for each there is a specific type of judgment. They are:

Categories	*Judgments*	*Example*
Quantity:	Quantity:	
(1) Unity	(1) Singular	This S is P.
(2) Plurality	(2) Particular	Some S is P.
(3) Totality	(3) Universal	All S is P.
Quality:	Quality:	
(4) Affirmation	(4) Affirmative	S is P.
(5) Negation	(5) Negative	S is not P.
(6) Limitation	(6) Infinite	S is not-P.
Relation:	Relation:	
(7) Substantiality	(7) Categorical	S is P.
(8) Causality	(8) Hypothetical	If A is B, S is P.
(9) Reciprocity	(9) Disjunctive	S is either P or Q.
Modality:	Modality:	
(10) Possibility	(10) Problematic	S may be P.
(11) Existence	(11) Assertoric	S is P.
(12) Necessity	(12) Apodictic	S must be P.

These categories, of course, do not apply to the extra-mental things-in-themselves; they apply merely to the *phenomena* which are, as we have seen, subjective products of the union between the sense-impressions and the space-and-time forms. These categories are also *a priori* subjective mental *forms,* innate in the mind, and as such their application to the representations contained in the phenomena is the result of a subjective *law* of the mind; they are not derived from experience in any way, but are in the mind prior to all experience. When we, therefore, make the judgment that 'The whole is greater than any of its parts' and consider that this judgment *must* be true in a strictly universal and necessary manner, then this absolute 'universality' and 'necessity' indeed transcends all experience and is valid for all times and places and minds; but this is only true of the 'phenomena' as a subjective mental product existing in the mind and does *not* apply to the extra-mental world of *things-in-themselves*. Our knowledge simply cannot reach to the noumena or things-in-themselves; they remain forever an unknown and unknowable X.

And therein lies the *fallacy of Kant's theory*. He does not succeed in saving science from Hume's skepticism. Science treats of the physical objects of the extra-mental world and not of mental constructions; Kant's world, however, is a world of phenomena, and these phenomena are mental constructions which give us no insight whatever into the nature and reality of things as they are *in themselves*. According to the ultimate findings of Kant's system, we can know nothing whatever about physical nature. He presupposes that physical nature exists in some form or other, because he postulates the existence of 'things-in-themselves' in order to account for our original chaotic sense-impressions; but what this physical world is like is an insoluble mystery. Such, however, is not the view of science. Science is convinced that it reaches *real things* outside the mind; according to Kant, this is impossible. The *laws* which science establishes are considered by scientists to be real laws operating in physical bodies independent of our thinking; according to Kant, these laws merely relate to phenomena within the mind and not to nature at all. That Kant really drew this conclusion, can be seen from his *Critique:* "It sounds no doubt very strange and absurd that nature should have to conform to our subjective ground of apperception, nay, be dependent on it, with respect to her laws. But if we consider that what we call nature is nothing but a whole [*'Inbegriff'*] of phenomena, not a thing by itself, we shall no longer be surprised."[1] That this destroys the validity of science in its very foundations, must be obvious. While treating of the validity

---

[1] *Critique of Pure Reason*, tr. by Max Müller, 2nd ed. (Macmillan, 1900), p. 94.

of sense-perception, we proved that our mind really transcends its own conscious states and perceives the external world; in this we proved that science is correct and Kant is wrong.

Kant distinguishes between 'synthetic,' 'analytic,' and 'synthetic *a priori*' judgments. The *synthetic* judgments are based on experience, such as 'Bodies are heavy,' 'fire burns,' 'this circle is green,' 'the boy runs.' In these the predicate adds a new idea to the subject, and this idea is derived from experience; hence, they are styled 'synthetic *a posteriori*.' Some of these judgments express singular and contingent facts, like the last two examples. Others may express a universal and necessary fact, like the first two, but this is only an empirical, not a strict or absolute, universality and necessity, because exceptions are at least conceivable. The *analytic* judgments are not based on experience, but are always *a priori*. In them the predicate is always found to be contained in the subject, and an analysis of the subject will reveal the presence of the predicate; for instance, 'Bodies have extension,' 'a circle is round.' These predicates do not increase our knowledge of the subject, because they are only 'explicative'; for this reason they are without value for science. In this they differ from 'synthetic' judgments, for the latter add a new idea (contained in the predicate) to the subject with a consequent amplification of knowledge. Not all 'synthetic' judgments, however, are valuable for science, because not all of them possess that *absolutely* 'universal' and 'necessary' character which is required for *scientific* knowledge. Some 'synthetic' judgments are entirely *a posteriori;* for instance, 'This circle is green,' 'the boy is running.' Others, though, express a universality and necessity which is *absolute,* and these admit of no exceptions even in thought; such are judgments like '$7+5=12$,' 'action and reaction are equal,' 'a straight line is the shortest distance between two points,' 'whatever becomes must have a cause,' etc. Whence the absolute character of the universality and necessity of these 'synthetic' judgments? It cannot come from the contingent things, because these things are singular and transitory in nature. Consequently, it must be *a priori* and arise from the *intellect* itself: the intellect communicates this absolute universality and necessity out of itself to these judgments. These are, then, *synthetic a priori* and as such have absolute value for science. Thus Kant.

Many critics[2] have shown that Kant was not justified in designating these judgments as synthetic *a priori:* they are all synthetic (*a posteriori*) or analytic (*a priori*). But that does not concern us. We are here interested in his explanation of the *necessity* we attach to these judgments. Even though the existence of such judgments be admitted, Kant fails to solve the problem of their absolute necessity. Of course, he asserts that this necessity imposed on the judgment by the intellect is absolute and therefore binding at all times, in all places, and on *all minds.* But we must not forget that it is the *individual mind,* according to his explanation, which contributes this necessity to the judgments; and this individual mind is as *contingent, singular,* and *transitory* as any other thing in the world. My mind could thus impose this necessity on my judgments *for me,* so that *I* could not think differently; but that would not mean that these judgments possess an absolute necessity *in themselves* or for *other minds.* According to Kant's own principles, my mind cannot transcend the phenomena of its own making; it is imprisoned within its own subjective world of phenomena. This being the case, it is impossible for me to know even the *existence* of 'other minds,' much less their *nature* and *operations;* they belong to the world of noumena, of things-in-themselves, and are forever excluded from my domain of knowledge. This being the case, I cannot know how these 'other minds' are constituted, nor whether they operate as my own mind does. They may, therefore, for all I can know about them, have an entirely different view of such judgments, because they may be differently constituted.

[2] See, for example, Coffey, *Epistemology,* Ch. VII.

What is the result, then, of Kant's theory? Simply this, that
the absolute necessity of first principles and axioms is the
product of my own individual subjective mind and is without
any value, as far as I can know, for other minds. There would
be indeed a *subjective, psychological* compulsion for my mind
to think in this manner, but I have no way of knowing
whether this necessity applies to *all* other minds. That, however, is the precise character we observe in these judgments:
they are valid for *all* minds. Since my own mind is singular,
it cannot make these judgments absolutely necessary for *all*
other minds. Kant's explanation, like Hume's, makes of this
necessity a purely *relative* and *subjective* thing; and such a
necessity destroys the *objective* character and value of all
science.

Besides, of what value are judgments, and in particular the
most *fundamental* judgments, such as the first principles and
axioms are, unless they rest upon an *intelligent insight* into
their truth? To accept them blindly, is assuredly not certain
knowledge: we 'know' something when we 'see' or 'understand' it, and to 'know' the truth of a judgment means to
grasp intelligently the exact relation between the subject and
the predicate. If one denies that such an insight is required and
asserts that a *blind,* subjective *necessitation* is sufficient to
accept the truth of judgments, then *certitude has no rational
foundation,* and we must despair of all knowledge and truth.
Such is the logical outcome of Kant's theory of judgment. We
do not make these judgments because we perceive the objective relation of subject and predicate, but because a blind,
necessitating law of our mental constitution draws certain
sense-intuitions under certain intellectually empty categories
prior to our judgment, and we do not know *why* these particular categories were imposed by the mind on these sense-
intuitions. Our 'knowledge' is thus as blind as the law that produces it. If this should be *scientific* and *philosophic* knowledge,
it is valueless, because it gives us no intellectual insight into
the nature of the reality our judgments are supposed to repre-

sent. Kant might have saved himself the trouble of writing his *Critique,* for who knows under what subjective, blind, unknown, and unknowable necessity and law of his mind he was laboring when he wrote it.

THE THEORY OF EVOLUTIONISM

Spencer, realizing the weaknesses inherent in the associationism of the older empiricists and in the formalism of Kant and his followers, sought the solution for the obvious necessity of axiomatic truths in *evolution.* This necessity cannot be explained by the ordinary action of mental associations or mental forms, because the individual who makes these judgments under their influence is a singular, contingent being whose span of life is far too brief to acquire associations and mental forms valid for all times and for all minds. Spencer was convinced that long ages were required to mold the human mind in such a way that it accumulated certain *fixed forms of thought* through a process of *innumerable associations* repeated with *incalculable frequency.* In this manner the experiences of the race were crystallized into definite principles and axioms which now express an absolutely necessary relation between certain subjects and predicates in our judgments. Evolution, therefore, can produce what the individual cannot acquire. Heredity, of course, is the source of transmission for these accumulated individual experiences and modifications; for we must remember that, according to Spencer and the vast majority of evolutionists, the mind is only a mode of neural matter and thought a mode of neural action. In the field of knowledge they are empiricists and sensists. It is but natural, then, that they would turn to evolution for an answer to the problem.

This explanation is *inadequate.* At best, we would again have nothing more than a *subjective, psychological* necessity for making such judgments, while we clearly observe that these axiomatic truths are valid not only for the ideal order of the mind but also for the *objective order of reality.* They are thus seen to be based, not on the instinctive, habitual character of hereditary traits of subjective nerve-processes, but on the *rational insight* into the objective relations existing between the *abstract* concepts expressed by the subject and predicate. We have seen in the foregoing chapter that sensism cannot account for the abstractness and universality of our universal ideas; our ideas are more than mere 'generic images' of sense-perception. A higher process is involved in their formation. If sensism were correct, evolution could never do more than fix *concrete, individual sense-images* within the tissues of our neural matter; and such images could never account for the immutable, universal, necessary character of our abstract ideas as used in our judgments; much less could they account for the universality and *absolute* necessity of these principles and axioms under all conditions and circumstances.

Again, as Coffey points out: "The theory proves too much. If it were true that the necessity which characterizes ideal judgments is a product of accumulated ancestral experience, there is no reason why such necessity should not be found to characterize such judgments as 'fire burns,' 'wood floats,' 'sugar is sweet,' 'day follows night,' etc. — in as much as the connections in these judgments must have been the subject matter of a uniform ancestral experience stretching infinitely backward. Yet such judgments are apprehended as *contingent,* not *absolutely necessary.* On the other hand, the theory does not prove enough; for we recognize an absolute necessity in such judgments as '$7+5 = 3+9$,' 'equilateral triangles are equi-angular,' although, as Maher observes, the occasions on which such objects were 'found to be conjoined in experience cannot in the pre-mathematical age have been very frequent.' "[3]

Finally, Spencer teaches that all our knowledge is restricted

[3]Coffey, *Epistemology,* Vol. I, p. 156 (Longmans, Green and Co.).

to our internal conscious states. His theory of knowledge is a *transfigured realism*, and all our ideas are but representations and symbols of the unknown and unknowable reality lying beyond the phenomena of sense. Our knowledge thus gives us no insight whatever into physical nature; it is *subjectivistic* and *relativistic*. As 'science' this knowledge is useless, if we understand by 'science' a demonstrable understanding of real things and real beings. All we would have is a science of 'symbols' and mental constructions engendered in our mind through the countless repetitions of purely subjective sense-processes, which reveal no more of the reality of things than the chemical symbols reveal the physical properties of the elements for which they stand. Such a theory destroys the foundations of science as a rational explanation and interpretation of nature.

THE THEORY OF OBJECTIVE EVIDENCE

Neither the associationism of empiricists, nor the formalism of Kantians, nor the evolutionism of Spencerian scientists can give an adequate account of the universality and necessity inherent in the axiomatic truths or first principles. None of these theories pass beyond a subjective and psychological necessity which compels the individual mind to judge that such first principles are universally and necessarily true. That, however, is not sufficient; because we clearly perceive that these principles are not merely true *for us,* but for *all minds* and, what is far more important, they apply to *all things.* The reason why we judge that the subject and predicate of first principles are logically connected with an *absolute* necessity must lie in something else than an internal, subjective law or form proceeding from the constitution of the mind itself. What, then, forces the intellect to place such an absolute necessity in these judgments? We are here face to face with a *primary fact* and an *ultimate experience* present within our consciousness. Because of this, introspection and reflection alone can answer the question. We must give careful attention to what takes place in making such judgments, in order to discover what prompts and compels the intellect to consider such judgments absolutely necessary in their validity. And in doing this we find that the reason or ground for this necessity is seen to lie in the *cogent objective evidence* of the *logical relation* which exists between the concepts of these judgments, and not in any subjective necessitation arising from the constitution of the mind.

Coffey has given a very lucid and succinct proof in the following words: "When I reflect on my spontaneous assent to such a judgment as that $7+5 = 12$, I observe the following facts: (*a*) that I affirm a *necessary* identity between predicate and subject; (*b*) that I affirm the identity *after having seen it* intellectually through comparison of the concept of '12' with the concept of '$7+5$' (*c*) that I affirm it *because I have seen it.* Moreover, I observe that (*d*) I see the necessary identity because I see that *the concepts necessarily involve such identity;* that (*e*) I do not assert it until I see them involve it and then only because I see them involve it; (*f*) that in order to see them involve it I analyze each concept into its simplest elements: the predicate into a total sum of units ($1+1+1+1+1+1+1+1+1+1+1+1$) and the subject into two lesser sums ($1+1+1+1+1+1+1$) and ($1+1+1+1+1$), whereby I see the former as a whole to be identical with the two latter as its constituent parts. On the one hand I see the parts of a whole; on the other hand I see the whole itself composed of these parts. The identity, therefore, manifests itself to me: I affirm it because it manifests itself to me: it is there objectively revealing itself to my intellect; and this objective manifestation of the *nexus* I call the *objective evidence of the truth of the judgment.* Hence I am conscious that I form such judgments, that I apprehend relations between their constituent concepts, *because I see intuitively* these relations *objectively evident, objectively revealing themselves to me.* Hence I reject as false the assertion that I establish any such relation *without seeing why I do so;* that I synthesize mental terms or concepts *a priori* and *unconsciously* into a complex representation of which I become conscious as a necessary product or unity, without seeing why it is so. I reject such a doctrine as false because introspection convinces me that I *do* see the reason of my mental assertion of the nexus."[4]

We, therefore, perceive the necessity of such judgments on the grounds of *objective evidence* and *intellectual insight.* The same applies to other first principles: they rest on ultimate concepts whose truth is objectively evident. They can all be reduced to the fundamental concept of 'being.' A 'being' is something 'that is or can be.' Hence, 'Whatever is, is'; and that is identical with 'A being is a being.' Reversely, 'Whatever is not, is not'; and that is the same as 'A not-being is a not-being.' This is the expression of the Principle of Identity. And these concepts are so simple and objectively self-evident that the intellect has an immediate *insight* into the truth of their mutual relation, so that it intuitively perceives that these judgments possess an absolute universality and necessity for both the order of thought and the order of reality. In this principle we merely compare 'being' with itself and 'not-being' with itself and perceive the identity of each with itself.

But when we compare 'being' with 'not-being,' we intuitively behold that the one is not the other. We see the evident truth that 'Being is not not-being,' and that these concepts mutually exclude each other with *absolute necessity:* something 'that is' can never, under any and all conditions, be something 'that is not.' Since 'being' and 'not-being' can never be conceived as identical, but must be universally and necessarily in opposition to each other as contradictories, we express this self-evident truth in the Principle of Contradiction: 'A thing cannot be and not be something at the same time.'

Furthermore, a comparison of 'being' and 'not-being' reveals

---

[4]*Epistemology,* Vol. I, pp. 234–235.

the evident fact that there can be *no middle thing* between the two. What could such a thing possibly be? Such a middle thing either 'is' or 'is not': if it 'is,' then it is a 'being'; if it 'is not,' then it is a 'not-being.' Consequently, it will be either a 'being' or a 'not-being,' but not a middle thing *between* the two. It certainly cannot be both a 'being' and a 'not-being' at the same time, because that would be impossible in virtue of the Principle of Contradiction as just explained. Hence, it is evident that 'A thing either is or is not,' and that is called the Principle of Excluded Middle.

From these principles to the Principle of Sufficient Reason is but a step. If a thing is a 'being,' it has its being either from itself (i.e., it is unproduced) or from another (i.e., it is produced by this other): in either case it has a *sufficient reason* for its being. If it is not a 'being,' it is so because it has its being neither from itself nor from another: in both cases it is a 'not-being' because it has *no sufficient reason* for its being. Hence, it must be evident that 'every thing must have a sufficient reason for its being'; if this were not so, then there would be no difference between 'being' and 'not-being.'

This last principle leads necessarily to the Principle of Causality. If a thing is a *contingent being,* i.e., if it has not the sufficient reason for its being in itself, it must have it *in another;* that is to say, this *other* must give being to it. This follows from the Principle of Sufficient Reason. But to 'give being' to another means to 'produce' or 'cause' it. It is, therefore, self-evident that 'every contingent being, i.e., every thing that becomes or happens, must be the effect of a cause.' And so the Principle of Causality is established.

All these principles rest upon the ultimate and absolutely simple concepts of 'being' and 'not-being'; or, to be more exact, upon the one concept of 'being.' Since 'being' is the first and most fundamental concept, these principles based immediately on the concept of 'being' are called in a special sense the *First Principles.* They rest on the fundamental judgment that 'Being is being.' Their universal and necessary truth is thus intuitively perceived to flow from the *objectively* clear and valid concepts of 'being' and 'not-being'; and the intellect does not 'make' their necessary truth, but simply 'perceives' and 'discovers' it. To put their truth into a judgment, then, is nothing more than to express mentally what the intellect perceives to be true objectively. Our conviction as to the absolute necessity and validity of these principles is, therefore, not the result of a blind, instinctive, psychological necessitation due to some hidden law of the mind, but to the objective evidence involved in the concepts and in the logical connection existing between them, so that the intellect is forced by this evidence to assent to their manifest truth in a conscious and intelligent affirmation.

What is the *objective source* of these concepts and principles? The physical world; because our intellect derives its materials from the sensible universe. But how can the individual, contingent things of the world give rise to principles that are universal, absolutely necessary, immutable, and eternal in truth and validity? The answer is the same as the answer for the truth and validity of universal ideas: they are based on the *abstract essences* of things. Through *abstraction* 'being' is divested of all individuality, contingency, actual existence, space-time conditions, and experience-relations. As such, then, the concept of 'being' and the principles based upon it possess a universality and necessity transcending all contingent existence and are valid for all times, for all places, and for all minds.

Our necessary judgments are thus seen to be objectively valid, and their truth-value is now critically and philosophically vindicated.

SUMMARY OF CHAPTER XV

Judgments consist of ideas. Since ideas represent things, judgments must also apply to reality. Some judgments are considered to be *eternally, immutably, and necessarily true*.

This presents a problem, because judgments, like ideas, are derived from the concrete, individual, and contingent world of objects.

1. *The Problem.* Many judgments express experiential facts, and it is clearly perceived that these facts could be different; they 'happen' to be so, but they 'must' not be so. Other judgments are considered to be eternally, immutably, and *necessarily* true, independent of all experience. Such are the *first principles.*

Whence do these first principles derive their absolute necessity? Why is the intellect *forced* to assent to them? Without the objective truth of these principles science would have no rational basis in reality. Does the logical connection between the subject and predicate of these judgments proceed from our *intellect* or from the *reality* expressed in the judgments?

2. *Empiricists,* like Hume and Mill, find the source of this mental compulsion and necessity in the power of mental *association;* there is merely a subjective, *psychological* necessity for making these judgments. This is false. If it were so, we should experience the same compulsion in every case where facts or events are uniformly and constantly associated in the mind; but this is contrary to all experience. Moreover, this theory of associationism *destroys science,* because our knowledge would then be but a purely mental construction which may or may not agree with extra-mental reality.

3. *Kant* considered everything that is universal and necessary in our knowledge to be the result of certain *a priori forms* innate in the mind and antecedent to all experience. Consequently, the absolute necessity of these judgments must come from the *mind alone.* These judgments are the result of a union between the phenomena of sense-intuitions and certain *a priori categories* of the understanding; and these categories are applied to the phenomena according to the workings of an innate, blind law. Our judgments are valid for phenomena, but give us no insight into the reality of the things-in-them-

selves. This view is destructive of *science,* because science is convinced that it reaches *real things* outside the mind.

Besides, this necessitation to judge is due to a blind, subjective law of the mind. Science and philosophy, however, demand an intelligent *insight* into the logical connection between subject and predicate, otherwise our certitude has *no rational foundation;* without this insight we would have no real knowledge.

4. *Spencer* and the evolutionists seek the necessity of our judgments in *evolution.* Innumerable associations repeated with countless frequency through long ages produce certain fixed forms of thought, and this accounts for our necessary judgments. This theory cannot explain our *abstract* ideas; because only concrete, individual sense-images could thus be transmitted, not principles with an *absolute* necessity valid under all conditions and circumstances. Again, all uniform experiences, like 'Fire burns,' etc., should then have the same absolute necessity in our judgments; but that is not the case. Finally, Spencer's 'transfigured realism' destroys the validity of *science,* because reality is considered to be unknown and unknowable.

5. *Objective evidence* alone explains the absolute necessity of these principles. The mind intuitively perceives this necessity of its judgments to proceed from the *objectively evident relation* existing between the subject and predicate of these judgments. The first principles are clearly seen to rest on the concepts of 'being' and 'not-being' and the relation between them. This gives rise to the fundamental Principles of Identity, Contradiction, Excluded Middle, Sufficient Reason, and Causality; and these principles underlie all thought and reality. The mind does not make, but discovers, them.

The *objective source* of these principles lies in the contingent things existing in the physical world. But the mind, through abstraction, divests 'being' of all contingency, actual existence, space-time conditions, and experience-relations; thereby the concept of 'being' and the first principles obtain universality and absolute necessity.

Our necessary judgments are thus seen to be *objectively valid*.

READINGS

P. Coffey, *op. cit.*, Vol. I, Chs. V–VIII; J. Barron, *op. cit.*, pp. 202–206; T. Pesch, *op. cit.*, Vol. II, pp. 220–228; 486–522; J. Donat, *op. cit.*, cap. IV, art. 2; R. W. Sellars, *Critical Realism,* Ch. VI.

How is objective evidence

Sense- knowledge
Mediate & Immediate Reasoning
historical testimony

Chapter XVI

THE CRITERION OF TRUTH

Our investigation so far has shown that we have a knowledge of reality. The senses present reality to the mind through the medium of percepts. The intellect, then, fashions concepts or ideas which are representations of reality in an abstract and universal manner. Mere percepts and concepts do not as yet constitute knowledge; they are the raw materials, rather than the finished product, of knowledge. We have knowledge when we affirm or deny something of something; and that takes place in the *interpretative judgment*. A judgment is always a mental pronouncement about reality in some form or other, and this pronouncement represents the actual condition of reality as it is in itself. Judgments, therefore, possess a *truth-claim*.

Unfortunately, however, our judgments are not always true; quite frequently we discover that they are erroneous. Now what constitutes *truth* and *error?* And how can we *discriminate* between true and erroneous judgments? What is the test or *criterion* of truth? And what is the *ultimate criterion* for distinguishing truth from error? These are important questions that will now have to be answered.

TRUTH AND ERROR

An *idea* is the intellectual representation of a thing. Due to the limited power and capacity of our intellect, we are incapable of grasping the full reality of an object within the content of a single idea. In consequence of this, the intellect turns its attention first to this, then to that property or attribute, and makes a separate concept for each one. In nature, the thing is actually undivided and one, but potentially divisible and many; in the intellect, the concepts of the thing are actually divided and many, but potentially undivided and one. The intellect recognizes this fact. None of these ideas represents the full reality, but each represents an aspect, a phase, a portion of it. The *material* object of the idea is the total object in all its properties and attributes; the *formal* object of the idea is the thing in its single property or attribute, in so far as it is represented by the single idea. In order that the idea be a true representation of the thing, it must agree with its *formal* object. While the idea is thus seen to be a *piecemeal* representation, it is *true as far as it goes:* to be incomplete is not the same as to be incorrect.

Just as the intellect acquires a more or less complete grasp of a thing by means of a *mental division* of its reality into a number of concepts, so it subsequently makes a mental *synthesis* of the object and its attributes in the *judgment*. What was divided in the process of abstraction again becomes united in the act of judgment: the attribute (predicate) is referred back to the thing (subject), as when we say that 'the rose is red,' 'the rose is beautiful,' 'the rose is fragrant,' 'the rose is fresh.' It will be noted that the subject ('rose') stands for the thing in a general way, while the predicate ('red,' 'beautiful,' 'fragrant,' 'fresh') stands for the particular attribute which belongs to the thing and which was recognized as belonging to the thing *in its objective existence*. Thus, what the judgment pronounces of its ideas is *meant* to be pronounced of the reality itself, because ideas are (partial, but true) representations of objective reality. Every judgment implicitly expresses a correspondence between the thing as it is in itself and as it exists ideally in my intellect, although explicitly the judgment merely pronounces an identity between the predicate-concept and the subject-concept. Such is the nature of the *affirmative* judgment.

The *negative* judgment is similar in import. Here I take an attribute *not* found in the thing and *deny* its presence in the thing. Judgmentally, I exclude the predicate-concept from the subject-concept; and in doing this I mean to assert that the reality signified by the predicate is lacking in the thing signified by the subject. Again I express a conformity between the reality as it exists in the real order of nature and as it exists in the ideal order of my mind. When I say that 'The rose is not blue,' 'the rose is not a cabbage,' 'the rose is not dead,' I pronounce the non-identity between subject and predicate as valid in the logical and ontological domain. In the affirmative and negative judgments, therefore, I claim that there exists an agreement between thought and thing.

Therein lies *truth* or *error*. If I judge that an attribute belongs to a thing, and it actually does, then I have truth; so, too, if I judge that an attribute does not belong to a thing, and it actually does not, I have truth. But if I judge that an attribute belongs to it, while it actually does not, or if I judge that an attribute does not belong to it, while it actually does, I have error. For example, I state that 'The rose is red,' 'the rose is not yellow'; if this is so as stated, my judgment is true. If, however, I were to state that 'The rose is yellow,' 'the rose is not red,' while as a matter of fact it is red and not yellow, my judgment would be erroneous.

Truth and error, then, reside formally in the judgment, and not in the ideas taken alone for themselves. *Truth* must, therefore, be defined as the *conformity of judgment to reality;* and *error,* as the *disconformity of judgment to reality.* Common usage and reflective analysis agree in considering truth to be an agreement between mind and thing, and error to be its opposite. Any other definition would be confusing and unwarranted, unless it consist merely in a difference of wording.

CRITERION OF TRUTH, MOTIVE OF CERTITUDE

Since knowledge is useless, if it does not agree with reality, i.e., if it is not true, it is of prime importance to know whether we possess a 'criterion' of truth. By criterion in general we understand a means or rule of discrimination, whereby we can distinguish one thing from another. A *criterion of truth* is a rule, or norm, or standard, or *test by which we distinguish true judgments from those which are false.* The application of this norm or test to a judgment will then enable us to decide whether the judgment is true or false. Since the judgment is a natural mental process, the criterion of truth must be a *natural* norm or test, well within the reach of every individual; and since the judgment is an intellectual process, the criterion of truth must be discoverable by the *intellect*. If there are a number of criteria, there must be one which is final and fundamental and beyond which there is no appeal; because, if every criterion demanded another criterion to establish its worth and validity, we would have an infinite regress and would never be able to come to a definite decision concerning the truth or error of a particular judgment. This final and fundamental criterion, beyond which there is no appeal, is the *ultimate criterion of truth.*

That such a criterion is necessary, must be obvious. Things in nature are at times extremely complicated in their reality. To obtain a more or less complete knowledge of them is a difficult and laborious task, depending on a multitude of conditions relative to the thing itself, to the organs of sense perceiving them, and to the intellect fashioning its concepts and judgments. That error can and does occur in our judgments is too clear to be disputed. Without some criterion of truth we could never detect error and distinguish it from truth; it would then be impossible to correct or change our judgment once it is made. As a result, our knowledge of reality might in many instances be totally at variance with the objective status of things, and we would be completely unaware of the fact; indeed, without such a criterion it would be absolutely impossible for us to become aware of any error in our judgments.

That we actually possess a criterion of truth, must be obvious. This is proved by the very fact that we *change* and *correct* our judgments after having become conscious of error. We could not correct an error, were we not conscious of error; and we could not be conscious of error, if we were not able to distinguish it from truth; and we could not distinguish it from truth, if there were no means or rule or test enabling us to discover both and discriminate them. The *fact of discrimination,* then, proves that we possess a criterion of truth and actually use it. Whoever acknowledges that we have natural certitude in our judgments thereby admits the existence of a natural criterion of truth; and only a universal skeptic will deny that we have certitude.

Certitude is that state of the mind in which the mind gives a *firm assent* to a judgment *without fear of error, due to recognized valid reasons.* The absence of fear is the 'negative' factor in certitude, and all judgments of whose truth we are convinced are alike in this respect. The valid reasons are the 'positive' factor, and according to their convincing strength we distinguish between *moral, physical,* and *metaphysical* certitude (see Chapter II). That we have these different degrees of certitude in our judgments is clear from our internal experience. *Moral certitude* is based on the customary action of human beings, and exceptions to the law are recognized as *physically possible;* as when we are sure that 'Parents love their children.' *Physical certitude* rests on the physical laws of the world, and exceptions here are impossible in the ordinary course of nature, though possible to the Creator; as when we are convinced that 'Iron will sink in water.' *Metaphysical certitude* has its foundation in the metaphysical laws of being, so that an exception is intrinsically impossible, because it would involve an internal contradiction; such is the absolute certainty of ideal principles, as 'The whole is greater than any of its parts.'

Whenever we are 'certain' in such judgments, we are conscious of a motive of certitude. The *motive of certitude* is the *ground which determines us to assent* with firmness to a judgment as true without fear of its contradictory being true. We never assent to a judgment without some *positive reason* which we consider a good or *valid* reason. Valid reasons are the 'motive' of certitude. If we 'doubt' the truth of a judgment, it is because we realize that we either have no reason or motive for its acceptance or because the reasons or motives are about equally balanced for and against its acceptance. If we have a 'probable' judgment, we are conscious that we accept the judgment, but with fear of its contradictory, because the reason or motive for our assent is not of such a nature as to exclude fear of error. Our conscious *experience* is a daily and hourly witness to these different states of mind, and the mere mention of this fact should be sufficient to prove the truth of the statement that certitude is grounded on the motive of valid reasons.

We distinguish between _subjective_ and *objective* certitude. The former consists in the mere *firmness* of our assent, and it does not exclude error in our judgment; it does, however, exclude the *fear* of error, considered solely as a subjective state of the mind itself. Objective certitude consists in the *reasons* contained in the *terms of the judgment,* in virtue of which the judgment is considered to be a true representation of reality. Our judgment being an intellectual act, the grounds or motives, which determine the intellect to give a firm assent to it as true, must possess an 'intellectual' character; that is, they must be such that they appeal to the intellect within the judgment itself. Now, the intellectual element in the judgment which appeals to the intellect is precisely the *truth-value* of the judgment as an interpretation of reality; hence, the same reasons which determine the truth of the judgment also determine the certitude of the intellectual assent. The criterion of truth and the motive of certitude are thus seen to be *conceptually different,* but *objectively identical*. It follows from the very nature of the intellect as a 'cognitive' faculty that the element which constitutes the test or criterion of truth will also be the motive *why* the intellect gives a firm assent to the truth. And just as we must have an ultimate criterion of truth, beyond which there is no appeal, so, too, there must be an *ultimate motive* of certitude which is the foundation for all secondary motives, because at bottom the criterion of truth and the motive of certitude are objectively identical.

The question before us, then, is this: *What is the ultimate criterion of truth?* The answer to that question will also be the answer to the further question as to what constitutes the ultimate motive of certitude, since the 'reasons' of the truth of the judgment are also the 'motive' for our intellectual certitude that the judgment is true. And here again, as in all problems which reach down into the roots of knowledge, a strict demonstration is impossible, because *primary* facts are a matter of ultimate *experience*. The only course open to us is to scrutinize our mental acts closely and carefully and observe just what the intellect uses as its criterion of truth and what is its motive of certitude, when it gives its firm assent to a judgment. Doing this, we will see that this criterion and motive is the *objective evidence of reality*.

NATURE OF OBJECTIVE EVIDENCE

By *objective evidence* we understand that characteristic of *reality* whereby it becomes *objectively manifest to the perceiving faculty*. What the luminosity of a shining body is to the eye, making it clearly visible, that the evidence of reality is for the mind: it makes reality cognitionally clear and intelligibly apparent to the intellect. In virtue of this objective evidence or clear self-revelation of reality in the presence of the intellect, the intellect is capable of forming a judgment which is a correct interpretation of this reality as it exists in its objective being. The intellect sees the reason or ground for its judgment in the reality as it reveals or manifests itself to the mind, and it makes this judgment *precisely because* the reality is thus *seen* to reveal or manifest itself with such clarity. The reason or ground for accepting this judgment as true and the motive for assenting to it with the firmness of certitude have their source, not in the judging subject, but in the evidence of the *object;* in other words, it is the *objective evidence* of reality which determines the judging subject to interpret this reality in the way it does and thereby makes the judgment to be true and certain.

Objective evidence is in relation to the truth and certitude of the judgment what the cause is to its effect.

There are various *kinds of evidence,* according to the manner in which the objective truth of reality becomes apparent to the mind. Objective evidence will be either 'internal' or 'external.'

Internal evidence exists, when the ground for our judgment is clearly perceived to lie *in the reality* affirmed by the judgments. Such, for example, would be the judgments, 'The sun is shining this afternoon,' '2 + 2 = 4,' 'a circle is round.' Internal objective evidence will be *immediate,* when the reality interpreted in the judgment is directly presented either to the intellect or to the senses. That '2 + 2 = 4' and that 'A circle is round' and that 'The whole is greater than any of its parts,' are true judgments based on the evidence of the relations existing between these concepts as immediately perceived by the intellect in contemplating them. And that 'The sun is shining' and that 'This paper is white,' are true judgments based on the immediate evidence of my experience as revealed through my senses. In both cases reality becomes evident to me by being directly presented to my faculty. On the other hand, internal objective evidence will be *mediate,* when the reality manifests itself to my mind, not by means of a direct presentation, but by means of a *process of reasoning* which leads ultimately to reality which is immediately evident. For instance, when I ride over the highway and see the whole countryside drenched with water, I have mediate evidence that 'It rained.' I did not see the rain fall, but it is evident that rain must have fallen; had I seen it fall, I would have immediate evidence of the fact. So, too, the judgment that '15,486 is evenly divisible by 5162' is only mediately evident to most people, until they make the actual division. When a ballistic expert proves that a particular bullet was discharged from a particular gun, it is mediate evidence; had he seen the gun fired, it would be immediate evidence.

External evidence exists, when the ground for our judgment does not lie in the reality itself affirmed by the judgment, but

in some *other reality outside it,* and this external reason is
clearly perceived to be of such a nature as to guarantee the
truth of the judgment and to exclude the fear of error from our
assent. This may be twofold: the evidence of *authority* and the
evidence of the *imprudence of doubt.* The former rests on the
evidence of the motives of *credibility,* in virtue of which the
intellect is convinced that the witness deserves credence because
of his knowledge and veracity. I may not have been present
at the battle of the Argonne; but when I consider the number
and character of the many witnesses who claim to have partic-
ipated in this battle, I have reliable evidence that such an
event actually occurred. Our knowledge of history is thus based
to a great extent on the external evidence of authority. And so
is much of our knowledge of persons, localities, and scientific
discoveries; most of these things we accept on the authority of
others who witnessed them and are trustworthy in their testimony. This is the rational basis of 'belief.' The evidence of
the *imprudence of doubt* is such that it is not sufficient to
compel our assent, but is clearly perceived to be sufficient to
exclude all unreasonable doubt. In this case the absence of
compulsion is frequently due to our lack of insight in consequence of the limited character of our personal faculties. For
me to doubt the truth of some abstruse and complicated mathematical proof, simply because I am not capable of following
the argument, would be unreasonable; provided, of course, that
mathematicians of repute all agree as to its truth and validity.
Similarly, it would be unreasonable to doubt that the one who
claims to be my mother is really my parent, even though I
cannot adduce any positive proof to substantiate the fact. Or,
it would be imprudent on my part to doubt the reality of an
extra-Ego world, merely because some obscurities can be found
in the theory of direct and immediate sense-perception.

Such is the nature of objective evidence. When we say that
the criterion of truth and the motive of certitude is 'objective
evidence,' we mean the objective evidence of reality (internal
and external evidence) revealing itself to the mind. But when

we speak of the 'ultimate' criterion of truth and the 'ultimate' motive of certitude, we claim that both consist in *internal, immediate, objective evidence*. 'External' and 'mediate' evidence are, of course, sufficient to give us certitude, but only because they presuppose internal, immediate evidence to support them. It will be necessary, then, to show, first, that objective evidence in general constitutes our criterion of truth and motive of certitude, and, second, that internal, immediate evidence is our 'ultimate' criterion and 'ultimate' motive, giving validity in the last instance to *all* truths and *all* certitude.

EVIDENCE THE CRITERION OF TRUTH

In proposing this proof, we must bear in mind that a strict demonstration is impossible. Primary facts cannot be demonstrated, but are shown to be true by an appeal to fundamental experience and reflection; what can be shown to be true by a mere exposition of the facts needs no strict demonstration. I cannot demonstrate, for instance, that I actually can see; the fact of seeing is its own proof. Similarly, I cannot 'demonstrate' that evidence is the criterion of truth, because such a demonstration would require the criterion of truth to prove that it is true: that means that I would prove a thing by itself, which would be a begging of the question. Nor can I disprove with a strict demonstration that evidence is not the criterion of truth, because in that case I would have to use evidence to disprove evidence: and that would again amount to a begging of the question. It is only by seeing what actually induces the intellect to accept judgments as true and what actually determines it to give a firm assent to the judgments as true, that I can decide what constitutes this criterion and motive. Now, *experience* and *reflection* clearly show that as a matter of *fact* objective evidence is our criterion of truth and our motive of certitude.

Why do we affirm some predicates of subjects, while we deny other predicates of these same subjects? Because we are convinced that some predicates really *belong* to these subjects and others do *not belong* to them. We certainly do not act arbitrarily in this matter of applying predicates to subjects. Frequently we would prefer to make a judgment one way rather than the other; but we cannot honestly do so, because we know that such a judgment would not be true. This shows plainly that the reason why we consider judgments to be true and assent to them with certitude does not proceed primarily from the *mind* itself. Why is this? Because the intellect needs a *ground or reason outside itself* in order to make a judgment one way rather than the other. If our intellect had the ground or reason for its judgments solely in itself, then our judgments would have no objective value and would not be an interpretation of the objective reality designated by the subject and predicate.

Our judgments, however, are clearly perceived to be an interpretation of extra-mental *things, objects, realities;* in other words, judgments represent a conformity of our intellect to objective reality, and our intellect judges this reality to be so-and-so or not-so-and-so because it is the 'thing' which influences the intellect to judge about it as it does. And *why* and *how* does the thing influence and determine our intellect in judgment? Because the thing *presents itself* with such clarity to the contemplating intellect that the latter plainly sees that the reality of the thing is so-and-so or not-so-and-so and judges accordingly. It is the thing itself which produces in the mind a *clear insight* into its objective reality as being precisely 'this' and 'not that.' But this characteristic of objective reality, whereby it presents itself with unquestionable clarity to the contemplating intellect, is what we understand by 'objective evidence.' In making a judgment, then, which corresponds to this evident reality, the intellect *recognizes* the fact that the judgment is *true* and cannot be otherwise than true; and that is also the ground or reason for its certitude about the truth of the judgment. Consequently, objective evidence is the criterion of truth and the motive of certitude in our judgments.

A consideration of the various *types of truths* confirms this general analysis. In sense-perception the criterion and motive is the clear *presentation* of external objects. In consciousness it is the immediate *union* between consciousness and the presented internal fact or event. In first principles or ideal judgments, as we have seen in the preceding chapter, it is the objective evidence of the *identity* or *non-identity* existing between the subject and predicate manifesting itself in the concepts. In mediate judgments, as we have them in discursive reasoning, it is the obvious *identity* or *non-identity* of two objective concepts with a third, based on the Principles of Contradiction and Identity. In judgments made on the authority of others, it is the clearly perceived *moral impossibility* of error due to the knowledge and veracity of the witnesses relating their immediate experience. In judgments resting on the imprudence of doubt, it is the objective clarity of the *facts* which enables the intellect to see that doubt would be unreasonable under the circumstances.

All these types have this in common that they induce the intellect to adhere to them with an assent of certitude, and the reason for this is that the presented and interpreted *reality* contained in them manifests itself to the intellect with a *clarity* that excludes doubt as to its existence and nature. That, however, is the 'objective evidence' of reality revealing itself to the mind. If this were not so, the only alternative left would be that the *intellect makes* these judgments true; but in that case it would be inconceivable how any judgment could ever be *false*.

We obtain the same result when we compare the attitude of the mind in *certitude, doubt,* and *opinion*. When is the mind in 'doubt'? When it is uncertain whether the predicate really belongs to the subject and should be identified with it. But why is it uncertain? If the reason or ground for identifying the predicate with the subject resided primarily in the mind, there should be no difficulty in identifying or not identifying the predicate with the subject and thereby attaining truth and certitude, because in that case the judgment would *always* correspond with the mind, and there should never be any state of doubt. Doubt, as experience and reflection clearly show, arises out of the inability of the intellect to discover whether the aspect of reality contained in the predicate actually belongs to the *object* represented by the subject. And this is due to the fact that the reality itself is not clearly manifested to the intellect; in other words, it has insufficient 'objective evidence.' When we have an *opinion,* we actually judge that something is 'so-and-so' or 'not-so-and-so'; but we are not free from the fear of error in this judgment. Why? Because we are *not sure* that the thing is *really* as it is judged to be. And why are we not sure? Because the *reality itself is not clear* to the intellect; if it were, there would be neither doubt nor opinion, but certitude, in the mind. It is, therefore, the lack of 'objective evidence' which creates the state of doubt and opinion in the mind; and, reversely, it is the 'objective evidence' of reality which guarantees the truth of the judgment and produces the firm assent of certitude.

Our analysis of truth and certitude thus shows that objective evidence of reality, or reality itself as clearly manifested to the intellect, is the criterion of truth and the motive of our certitude. Without it, the intellect must remain in doubt or, at the very best, can only form a probable opinion, and then the fear of error will always be present.

THE ULTIMATE CRITERION AND MOTIVE

Objective evidence in general is the criterion of truth and the motive of certitude. But not all evidence is equally valuable in establishing the truth of a judgment and in producing the firm assent of certitude. For instance, the external evidence of human authority and of the mere imprudence of doubt is the weakest kind of evidence, because here reality manifests itself to the intellect only indirectly and secondarily. Such evidence always rests on some other evidence which is direct and primary. But it is obvious that we cannot refer one sort of evidence back to another indefinitely, otherwise we would become involved in an 'infinite regress,' and thus nothing would ever be sufficiently evident to give us truth and certitude in our judgments. There must be some criterion of truth and motive of certitude beyond which there is no need of appeal and for which there is no need of further evidence; in other words, there must exist an *ultimate criterion* of truth which is also the *ultimate motive* of certitude. What is it? It is *internal, immediate, objective evidence,* or, in one word, *self-evidence.*

That we cannot give a strict demonstration for this claim, has been pointed out above, when we spoke of evidence in general. We can only make an appeal to intelligence and to primary experience. Now, that evidence will have to be the 'ultimate' criterion of truth and the 'ultimate' motive of certitude which is of such a nature that there can be *no possibility of doubt or error* in the mind as to the conformity of its judgment to the reality it interprets. In order that there be no possibility of *doubt,* the reality must be so clear and luminous before the intellect that there can be no danger of error in its judgment. And in order that there be no possibility of *error,* the reality must again be so clear and luminous that the intellect must see that the reality is actually 'so-and-so' and cannot be otherwise. But this condition is fulfilled only when the reality expressed in our judgments is *self-evident;* that is, when reality manifests itself to the intellect with an evidence which is 'internal' and 'immediate.'

Introspection and experience show this plainly. Let us glance at 'external' evidence. Such evidence may be based either on authority or on the imprudence of doubt. *Authority* cannot be the ultimate criterion of truth and motive of certitude, for the simple reason that it does not exclude the possibility of doubt. The person on whose authority I accept the truth might be mistaken. And if he cannot be mistaken, it is only because *he* has had 'immediate' and 'internal' evidence of the truth. After all, then, I am not relying on my evidence, nor on his word of authority, but on the immediate and internal evidence of the reality manifested to *him;* and that implies that the external evidence of authority must be based ultimately on internal, immediate evidence. The same is true of the evidence of the *imprudence of doubt.* What is evident here to me is that doubt is 'imprudent'; therefore I reject it as unreasonable, and by an effect of the will I induce the intellect to give a firm assent to the judgment. Such an assent does not exclude the possibility of doubt and error; that possibility always remains in judgments of this kind. Consequently, the evidence which merely shows that doubt is imprudent cannot be the 'ultimate' criterion, because the ultimate criterion must exclude the very *possibility* of doubt and error.

And now let us consider *mediate* internal evidence. Such evidence must always have its foundation in 'immediate' evidence. The very fact that it is only 'mediate' shows clearly that it refers to other evidence beyond itself; if it were not so, it would itself be 'immediate.' We have mediate evidence in the various processes of reasoning. But why do we 'reason' to the truth of the conclusion of an argumentation, except for the fact that this conclusion must be *proved* by the evidence contained in the premises from which it is drawn? And if these premises are not self-evident, they must also be proved by other premises which are immediately evident; and if the latter are not self-evident we must continue proving premises until we finally arrive at premises which need no proof, because they are self-evident. Hence, mediate evidence cannot be the 'ultimate' criterion of truth and the 'ultimate' motive of certitude, because it always presupposes immediate, internal evidence to guarantee its own truth.

The only sort of evidence left, then, as the ultimate criterion and ultimate motive, is the immediate, internal, objective evidence, or the *self-evidence,* of reality manifesting itself to the intellect.

Experience shows conclusively that all knowledge is based

ultimately on the self-evidence of reality. The structure of our common, scientific, and philosophic knowledge is a very complex thing, built up gradually and laboriously from previous judgments that have been recognized as true. But if we trace our knowledge back to its origin, we will find that it is based on immediate sense-perception, immediate consciousness, and immediate insight into first principles. And if we examine the truths acquired from these sources, we will observe that they *reveal reality* to us in such a manner that the intellect *clearly perceives* that this reality is so *self-evident* as to exclude the very possibility of doubt and error. And this self-evidence of reality is seen by the intellect to be the final and ultimate ground for its judgments and certitude. We have but to consider that all our knowledge derives its validity from the necessary and universal truth of a few first principles, in order to see for ourselves that self-evidence is the ultimate criterion and motive. Such principles are, as we have seen in the fore-going chapter, the Principles of Identity, Contradiction, Excluded Middle, Sufficient Reason, and Causality. They underlie all science and all knowledge. A little reflection will convince us of this.

There are certain general principles which are the foundation of science and knowledge in all their ramifications. Such are the judgments, 'The whole is greater than any of its parts,' 'two things identical with a third are identical with each other,' 'what is true of a logical whole must be true of the logical parts of that whole,' '2 + 2 = 4,' etc. Once the *meaning* of these concepts is understood, the necessary truth of these judgments becomes self-evident and needs no demonstration. Take, for example, the judgment that 'The whole is greater than any of its parts.' By 'whole' I mean 'a sum of constituent units' and by 'part' I mean 'one of a number of units consti-tuting a sum.' Since the 'whole' is thus seen to be a 'sum,' and a 'part' is seen to be one of the 'units' of this sum, my under-standing of these concepts reveals to me the self-evident truth *beyond the possibility of doubt or error* that 'The whole must be greater than any of its parts.' Because, if this were not so, the 'whole' would not be a 'whole' and the 'part' would not be a 'part'; and that would involve the contradiction that 'being' would not be 'being' but would be identical with 'not-being.' Thus, the truth of this judgment is seen to run through the Principles of Contradiction and Identity down to the fundamental and absolutely simple concepts of 'being' and 'not-being.' If there could be a possibility of doubt and error in this, then truth and certitude is simply impossible of attainment.

And so it is with all principles and all knowledge, whether of the existential or of the ideal order: they rest on the self-evident Principles of Identity, Contradiction, Excluded Middle, Sufficient Reason, and Causality. In other words, the ultimate criterion of all truth and the ultimate motive of all certitude lie in the *self-evidence* (internal, immediate, objective evidence) *of reality* as it manifests itself to the intellect and is recognized by the intellect as such.

But if this is so, how is error possible? It would seem that error should never occur in our judgments. Error, however, is an undeniable fact. What, then, is the cause of error?

THE CAUSES OF ERROR

We have seen above wherein error consists. It is the non-correspondence or disconformity of the intellect with the thing. Just as truth is in the judgment, so is error. It always involves the *affirmation of what is not true* and the *denial of what is true*. Since truth is the result of evidence, error must have its origin in the lack of *real* and in the presence of *apparent* evidence.

Reality as such cannot be false; it reveals itself to the mind *as it is*. Error, therefore, cannot come from reality itself. But if it cannot come from reality, it must have its origin *in the mind*. Now, the mind as such tends toward truth and not toward error; the mind, therefore, is not inherently false. And yet it is evident that the mind does actually assent to judgments which are erroneous. How is this possible? The fact is simply that error is *in* the mind, but does not proceed *from* the mind. It has its cause in the *will*. This needs explanation.

We have seen that in the presence of 'self-evident' reality there is no possibility of doubt or error for the intellect. Unfortunately, however, reality is not always self-evident. Conditions are often such that the reality cannot reveal itself with self-evident clarity to the mind. This clarity is frequently obscured, partly through the *complexity of reality* itself, partly through the *limitations* and *imperfections* inherent in the organs which serve the intellect and furnish it with the materials necessary for knowledge. In consequence of such conditions reality will sometimes appear to the mind other than it really is. In many instances the mind *could* discover what the reality 'really is' by means of a close and exact analysis of all the circumstances, but it is here that the influence of the will enters as a deciding factor and induces the intellect to give its assent to a judgment for which it has *no sufficient evidence*.

But why should the will urge the intellect to assent to a judgment for which there is insufficient evidence? At times the *exigencies of life* and the *need of immediate action* require a definite decision and a definite acceptance of one side of a question. The will then compels the intellect to be satisfied with the limited evidence at hand and to give its firm assent. That error is not only possible, but probable and frequently actual, in such circumstances, is but natural. Again, in many cases, the only evidence available under existing conditions of time, place, educational facilities, etc., is *mediate* or *external*. Rather than refrain from a decision entirely, the will influences the intellect to give its assent. The motives are really *sufficient* for the ordinary purposes of ordinary life; since, however, they do not rest on the 'self-evidence' of reality, they do not exclude all possibility of error, and the intellect may thus pass a judgment which is a faulty interpretation of reality.

In very many instances the will is swayed by *partisanship* and *prejudice*. Likes and dislikes, loves and hates, pleasure and pain strongly influence the will in its decisions and these decisions exert a corresponding influence on the judgments of the intellect. There are even such things as *scientific prejudices.* Since the reality of the universe is so vast and complex, preventing a complete unification and systematization in the limited mind of man, various hypotheses and theories obtain plausibility in the course of time among scientists. All scientists are human, and absolute impartiality in the search for truth is a morally unattainable ideal. Eager to substantiate their own views, they unconsciously favor all partial evidence which seems to prove their hypothesis or theory. They frequently overlook real contrary evidence. Here indeed 'the wish is father to the thought,' and error is the result. That religious prejudices frequently color judgments and lead to errors, needs hardly be mentioned.

Emotional instability and the desire to *shirk protracted labor* are also prolific causes of error. We want short-cuts to results. Our hectic haste of living, our love of ease and indolence, our proneness to distractions of all kinds make us impatient of the drudgery of long and arduous study and research, and that hinders the intellect from bending all its energies to the proper sifting of evidence. All this, added to faulty methods and defective information in our preliminary education, has the tendency to make us slipshod in our search for truth. Many errors could be avoided through greater care and effort in our thinking.

From the above analysis of the causes and occasions of error, we see that error is not an inherent characteristic either of reality or of intellect; it is the result of the determining influence of our will. Error as such is *incidental* and *accidental* to judgments; proper attention to the objective evidence of reality makes it avoidable. And this shows that our judgments are *essentially valid* as true interpretations of reality.

SUMMARY OF CHAPTER XVI

A judgment is always a mental pronouncement about reality; as such, it possesses a truth-claim. What constitutes *truth* and *error*? How can we *discriminate* between them? What is the *criterion* of truth?

1. *Truth and Error.* Judgments refer to reality. Therein lies truth or error. If judgments correctly interpret reality, they are true; if incorrectly, they are false. Truth, therefore, is the *conformity of judgment to reality;* error, the *disconformity of judgment to reality.*

2. *Criterion of Truth; Motive of Certitude.* A criterion of truth is the rule or *test* by which we distinguish true judgments from false; the final criterion, beyond which there is no appeal, is the *ultimate* criterion. Such a criterion is *necessary,* otherwise we could not distinguish truth from error. That we *possess* a criterion, is clear from the fact that we correct erroneous judgments.

Certitude is that state of the mind in which it gives a *firm assent* to a judgment *without fear of error,* due to recognized valid reasons. The *motive* of certitude is the ground or reason which determines us to assent with firmness to a judgment as true; it is the recognized *truth-value* of the judgment. The same reasons which determine the truth of the judgment determine also the certitude of the assent; hence, the criterion of truth and the motive of certitude are objectively identical, though conceptually different. The criterion of truth is *objective evidence.*

3. *Nature of Objective Evidence.* It is that characteristic of reality whereby it becomes *objectively manifest to the perceiving faculty.* There are various kinds of objective evidence.

Internal evidence exists, when the ground for our judgment is clearly perceived to lie *in the reality* affirmed by the judgment. If this interpreted reality is directly presented to the intellect or the senses, this evidence is *immediate;* otherwise it is *mediate. External* evidence exists, when the ground for our judgment lies, not in the reality itself affirmed by the judgment, but in some other reality *outside* it. Such is the evidence of *authority* and of the *imprudence of doubt.* Objective evidence, whether internal or external, is the criterion of truth and the motive of certitude; but the *ultimate* criterion and the *ultimate* motive is internal, immediate evidence, or self-evidence.

4. *Evidence the Criterion of Truth.* Experience and reflection prove this. We do not arbitrarily apply predicates to subjects and consider such judgments true. The intellect needs a *ground* or reason outside itself, because judgments are clearly perceived to be interpretations of extra-mental *reality.* Hence, the clear presentation of reality is the ground for considering judgments to be true and worthy of a firm assent; but that is the 'objective evidence' of reality. All *types* of truths reveal this same fact. The difference between the attitudes of the intellect in *certitude, doubt,* and *opinion* is due to the difference of reality in its self-revelation to the mind.

5. *Ultimate Criterion and Motive.* The ultimate criterion and ultimate motive must be such as to exclude the *possibility of doubt or error.* To do this, reality must be *self-evident;* the 'external' evidence of authority and of the imprudence of doubt does not exclude the possibility of doubt and error, and 'mediate' always rests on 'immediate' evidence. *Experience* proves that all knowledge derives its validity from a few fundamental principles which are self-evident, because they are based on the self-evident concepts of 'being' and 'not-being.'

6. *The Causes of Error.* Error is not caused by reality, because reality reveals itself as it is; nor by the mind directly, because it tends toward truth. Error is the result of the influence of the *will* on the intellect, inducing the latter to assent to a judgment without sufficient objective evidence on the part of reality. The *factors* which move the will in this are manifold: the complexity of reality, imperfections in the organs, necessity of action, partisanship and prejudice, emotional instability and the desire to shirk protracted labor.

Error is thus *incidental* and *accidental*. Our judgments are, therefore, *essentially valid* as true interpretations of reality.

READINGS

P. Coffey, *op. cit.,* Vol. II, Ch. XXIII; J. Barron, *op. cit.,* Chs. XV, XVI, XVIII; J. Rickaby, *op. cit.,* Chs. XIII, XIV; J. G. Vance, *op. cit.,* Ch. X; T. Pesch, *op. cit.,* pp. 281–349; J. Donat, *op. cit.,* Ch. II; A. K. Rogers, *What is Truth?,* pp. 1–44; G. F. Stout, "Error," in *Personal Idealism,* ed. by H. Sturt; R. W. Sellars, *Critical Realism,* Ch. X; J. B. Pratt, *What is Pragmatism?,* Lect. II.

Chapter XVII

FALSE CRITERIA OF TRUTH

In their endeavor to discover a criterion of truth, philosophers advance various theories. Quite naturally, their views are influenced to a very great extent, if not completely, by their general theory of knowledge. Scientists as a rule, when engaged in the practical work of research, submit to the guidance of the objective evidence of reality; they demand that every hypothesis and discovery be tested by 'experiment,' and that is nothing less nor more than an appeal to objective evidence. But even scientists, when they enter the speculative field of philosophy, at times advocate theories at variance with their practical views. Professional philosophers, of course, attempt the solution of the problem of truth and certitude by reasoning from the principles of knowledge in general. As a result, diverse theories have arisen, and these now demand our attention. Some criteria are *intellectual,* and some are *non-intellectual,* in character. By showing their inadequacy, 'objective evidence' as the criterion of truth will be indirectly confirmed.

DESCARTES, MALEBRANCHE, ROSMINI

According to *Descartes* the things of which we have a *clear* and *distinct idea* are true. He accepted his own existence as true, because he had a 'clear' and 'distinct' idea of it. This, then, became for him the criterion of truth.

Now, the 'clearness' and 'distinctness' of our ideas can be taken subjectively and objectively. Taken *subjectively,* it means that the idea as a subjective product of the intellect is clearly and distinctly conceived; it is clear and distinct *to the intellect.* But this does not give us a guarantee that this idea corresponds to reality, and that the reality represented in the idea actually exists. I can have, for instance, a very clear and distinct idea of a centaur or a fairy or a mythological deity; but does that mean that such beings exist? To distinguish between such beings and 'real' beings I need some criterion different from the subjectively clear and distinct ideas of them. Taken *objectively,* it means that the idea is clear and distinct as an interpretative representation of reality; the idea is such, because the *reality itself* is clear and distinct before the mind. In that case, however, we have immediate, objective evidence of reality as the criterion of truth, and not the mere clearness and distinctness of the idea as such. Descartes, however, took this criterion in a subjective sense, because he maintained that the external world cannot be presented to the spiritual mind. As such, his criterion of a 'clear and distinct idea' is inadequate, since it can never show us whether our judgments agree with reality.

Malebranche, accepting Descartes' view that we cannot acquire a direct knowledge of the material world through sense-perception, tried to explain this knowledge by assuming that we have an *intuition* of reality *in the Mind of God:* we see all things in God. The Mind of God, then, is our criterion of truth. This, of course, is contrary to experience. We have absolutely no consciousness of an intuition of God in any form. And if we had, *error* would be utterly *impossible,* otherwise God Himself would have erroneous ideas of things.

Though *Rosmini* (1797–1855) differs from Malebranche in details, fundamentally his view is the same. We have a direct intuition of *Being* in its transcendental ideality, and this innate concept or intuition makes the soul intelligent. Real knowledge, therefore, is derived from this intuition of Ideal Being. The objection against Malebranche's view applies here also: we have no consciousness of such an intuition, and error would be unaccountable, because impossible.

The theories of Malebranche and Rosmini are a form of *ontologism. Gioberti* (1801–1852) maintained a similar doctrine.

THE THEORY OF COHERENCE

Idealistic monism of the Hegelian type does not accept the view that, in order to be true, judgments must correspond with extra-mental reality. There is a simple reason for this: since thought and thing, ideal and real, Ego and non-Ego, are fundamentally identical in the Absolute, there exists no extra-mental reality with which judgments could correspond. The truth of a judgment, then, must be its *coherence,* or consistency, with the whole *system of knowledge* previously recognized as true. When the whole system of accepted judgments is true, any particular judgment in harmony with it will be true; otherwise it will be false. After all, reality is reality for us only in so far as it is known by us; and this knowledge is expressed by us in a systematic body of judgments acknowledged to be a correct interpretation of our experiences.

This criterion of truth, namely the *coherence* of a particular judgment with our general system of knowledge, is *inadequate* and therefore of little value for judging the truth of our mental pronouncements. It is, of course, correct that 'All true judgments are mutually coherent'; but for that reason we cannot simply turn the statement around and say that 'All mutually coherent judgments are true.' Even the tyro in the science of correct thinking knows that a simple conversion of this sort is bad logic; the only permissible conversion must state that '*Some* mutually coherent judgments are true.' But this means that consistency or coherence as such is not necessarily a guarantee of all truth. Idealism, for instance, as a system of thought may have coherence *in itself,* but we have already shown that idealism is based on the initial fallacy of the 'idealist postulate' that we cannot transcend our mental states; of what value, then, is its internal coherence as a 'system'? The Ptolemaic theory of a geocentric planet-system was also coherent, but astronomy has definitely established that it is false and that the Copernican theory of a heliocentric system is correct. Consequently, the mere coherence of a particular judgment with a general system of knowledge is not in itself sufficient to establish its particular truth. Since idealism as a system is false, the criterion of coherence, based on it, is also false.

Furthermore, ordinary *existential judgments* cannot be distinguished as true or false by their coherence with a general system of co-ordinated judgments. Consider judgments like the following: 'It is snowing today'; 'I feel chilly'; 'this paper is white'; 'my pen is out of order.' In what possible way could such mental pronouncements be judged to be true or false by examining their coherence with the systematic body of truths contained in physics, chemistry, biology, astro-physics, or philosophy? Yet they must be true or false. The criterion of coherence, however, will never enable me to decide whether they are true or not. Now, the greatest number of our judgments concern everyday matters like the above; they are inconsequential in themselves, but we must be able to decide whether they agree with reality and as such are true or false. The criterion of coherence is thus seen to be useless.

If driven to its logical conclusion, the theory of coherence will demand that we must have an almost *omniscient knowledge,* otherwise a particular judgment might be in coherence with one system and not in coherence with another. Or shall we say that it must only be consistent with *our own system?* Then the criterion is purely *subjectivistic* and *relativistic,* but that is precisely what a criterion of truth is not supposed to be, because its function should be to tell us whether our judgment is in accordance with the *reality* we are interpreting and not merely with our preconceived and subjective idea of it. Coherence, therefore, is inadequate as the criterion of truth.

FIDEISM AND TRADITIONALISM

Some thinkers, anxious to stem the tide of mental anarchy resulting from the philosophy of Descartes, discredited the power of human reason to reach truth without the aid of some external criterion. They defended the theory that faith or tradition must furnish the ultimate guarantee of the truth of our knowledge.

Pascal (1623–1662), though not a skeptic, maintained that reason was too impotent to arrive at any certitude regarding the great truths which shape the destiny of man, like the existence of God, the immortality of the soul, revelation, and Christianity; we must begin our knowledge with an act of *faith*. *Huet* (1630–1721) demanded the acceptance of Divine Revelation as a basis of certitude; reason can give nothing more than probability in knowledge. That is traditional or historical *fideism*.

This view is extreme. Concerning *supernatural* truths it is indeed correct to say that a revelation is required in order to be certain of them; but it is absurd to think that a divine manifestation is necessary for *natural* truths of the ordinary kind. Why should we need revelation to obtain certitude that 'Wood floats,' 'water freezes,' 'light travels with a speed of over 186,000 miles a second,' 'fire burns,' and a thousand similar facts of the material and natural order? Besides, if we are to believe in a Divine Revelation, we must have *prior certitude* that God really exists and that He has actually revealed certain truths; otherwise our act of faith would be blind and lack a rational foundation. The existence of God, however, cannot be clear to our intellect except through a process of reasoning based on the objective evidence of the Principle of Causality as applied to the world around us. Consequently, objective evidence, not faith, is the ultimate criterion of truth in the order of natural knowledge.

Traditionalism owes its origin to *De Bonald* (1754–1840). According to his view God gave a primitive Revelation to mankind which is handed down as a *tradition* from generation to generation. This belief of mankind reveals itself particularly in *language,* which is not the product of man's rational thinking, but a direct gift from God. Without tradition man can know nothing; all knowledge is derived from it. The ultimate criterion is, therefore, the revelation and authority of God.

De Lamennais (1782–1854) sought the criterion of truth in the *general agreement of mankind* (*le consentement universel*), because that is the voice of God transmitting the primitive Revelation to the individual mind. *Bautain* (1795–1867), *Bonnetty* (1798–1879), *Ventura* (1792–1861), and *Ubaghs* (1800–1875), held similar views. All agree in this that the fundamental act of knowledge consists in *belief*.

Such a belief, however, cannot be the ultimate criterion of truth. The argument against fideism applies here also: we must first have *evidence* that God exists, that He has revealed truths, that these truths have reached us unchanged, and that the instrument of its transmission is tradition or the universal agreement of mankind. Authority, whether it be that of faith in revelation, tradition, or the general verdict of mankind, is an *external* criterion, and its validity must first be proved by *independent reasons* before it can be accepted as trustworthy and true. But this means that 'objective evidence' is the real criterion of truth.

THE TEST OF INCONCEIVABILITY

Spencer, Mill, and their followers, maintained that evolution produced in man's mind certain fixed modes of thought in virtue of which the mind makes necessary judgments, such as '2 + 2 = 4,' 'the whole is greater than any of its parts,' 'every effect must have a cause,' 'a circle is round,' and so forth. In consequence of this fixed grooving of the mind in a definite direction, such judgments are considered to be necessarily true because *their opposites are inconceivable.* '2+2' must be judged to be '4,' not because the terms of this judgment are self-evident *in themselves,* but because we *cannot conceive* that '2 + 2' would be '3' or '5' or any other number. If evolution had developed our minds in a different way, '2 + 2' might be '3' or '5' or any other number; but it so happened that *now* the inconceivability of '2 + 2 = 3' or '2 + 2 = 5' makes the judgment '2 + 2 = 4' to be true. And the same applies to every 'true' judgment: it is true because its opposite is 'inconceivable.'

This *inconceivability of the opposite* is, then, the ultimate criterion of truth.

This theory hardly needs refutation after what has been said before. Evolution, as we have seen, cannot give an adequate explanation of the *absolute* necessity of our axiomatic judgments. We have shown that it is the intellectual *insight* into the self-evident relation existing between the ideas of such judgments *in themselves* which compels our assent to them as necessarily true. Consequently, it is not through their *opposites* that we perceive them to be true. Take the judgment, 'A circle is round.' If and when I know that 'A circle is a plane figure, comprehended by a single curved line, each part of which is equidistant from a common center,' then I know also that it *must* be 'round,' because that is what is meant by the concept 'round.' I do not need to compare the figure of a circle with a triangle, or a square, or a parallelogram, or a hexagon, or a parallelopipedon; all that is required is that I understand the terms contained in the judgment 'A circle is round,' in order to see that it is true. Were Spencer's criterion correct, I would first have to compare the figure of a circle with *every other* geometrical figure and see that it is 'inconceivable' that the circle be this or that or the other figure, before I could know that the circle *itself* is round. The reverse is true: I perceive clearly that the judgment 'A circle is square' is inconceivable, because I see it to be self-evident that 'A circle *must* be round'; it is only *after* I know that 'roundness' is contained in the idea of 'circle' that I realize that any other figure, like a square, triangle, etc., is *not* contained in the idea of 'circle.' In other words, the Principle of Contradiction is based on the Principle of Identity, and not *vice versa*. Hence, the self-evidence of the judgments themselves, and not the inconceivability of their contradictories, is the ultimate criterion of truth.

EPISTEMOLOGICAL MONISM

Neo-realism, in its effort to escape from idealism, went to the opposite extreme: it advocated an epistemological monism which is pan-objectivistic, because it ends by *identifying* the knowing *mind* with the known *object*. "When things are known, they *are* ideas of the mind. . . . Ideas are only things in a certain relation; or, things, in respect of being known, are ideas. . . . The difference between knowledge and things, like that between mind and body, is a relational and functional difference, and not a difference of content. . . . We have become wedded or indeed welded to the phrase — my thought is of an object — when we ought to say and mean — my thought is a portion of the object — or better still — a portion of the object is my thought: — exactly as a portion of the sky is the zenith."[1] Consciousness itself is merely a 'class of things'; consciousness is not *of* things, but things themselves *are* conscious by the mere fact that they are responded to by another entity. In this manner, according to the neo-realists, consciousness is numerically identical with the object of which we are conscious, the Ego with the non-Ego, the mind with nature, the ideas with the things thought of.

This makes the problem of knowledge extremely simple, because it eliminates the mind entirely from the process of knowledge; the only existent realities are the things themselves. Knowledge must always correspond to reality in this theory, because they are both identical. But therein neo-realism *refutes itself*. If we are certain of anything through our consciousness, it is of the fact that we are *not identical* with the objects of which we are conscious. When I am aware of the photograph or paper on my desk, it is futile for me to think that it is not *I* who am conscious *of* the photograph and paper, but that it is the *photograph* itself and the *paper* itself which is conscious. We have proved elsewhere that mind and matter, Ego and non-Ego, the mental and extra-mental, are distinct realities which are not identical in being; to eliminate the mind will never solve the problem of knowledge.

If our consciousness is identical with the objects of which we are conscious, then, of course, our judgments should *always*

---

[1] See Chapter VIII.

correspond to reality and be true. But that is not the whole of the problem of knowledge; we must also explain the possibility and fact of *error*. When, however, we assert that the knowledge of objects and the objects of knowledge are identical in being, there is simply *no possibility of error* in judgments; and that is contrary to *fact* and *experience*. Neo-realists are not always consistent in their teachings. They frequently speak of the mind and the world as really distinct in being. When, however, they explain the nature of the mind and identify it with the objects known (as they do), they deprive both truth and error of all meaning; because under such circumstances any conformity or disconformity between *mind* and *reality* is out of the question. A theory that can give no intelligible explanation of truth and error is false and untenable.

THE CRITERION OF COMMON SENSE

The criteria investigated above are of the intellectual type. Others are *non-intellectual* in character, in as much as they are not founded on the intellectual nature of man.

The Scottish School places the criterion of truth in the *common sense* of man. *Thomas Reid* (1710–1796), the real founder of this school of thought, insisted that our knowledge is based on principles which are evident and are recognized as such by the 'common sense' of man; from these principles man derives a body of primordial 'truths of common sense' which serve as a sort of general fund of knowledge for mankind. So far no objection can be raised against him and his followers, because this view conforms to the doctrine of 'objective evidence' as the criterion of truth. At times, however, the Scottish philosophers seem to teach very plainly that these fundamental principles are accepted through an *instinctive impulse* of human nature, rather than through an *intellectual insight* into the objective truth. In that case, then, the ultimate criterion would consist in some sort of *belief* in the rationality of this impulse, and not in the self-evidence of reality manifesting itself to the mind. Other adherents of the 'common sense' doctrine are *James Oswald* (1727–1793), *James Beattie* (1735–1803), *Dugald Stewart* (1753–1828), and *Thomas Brown* (1778–1820).

If 'common sense' be interpreted as a kind of instinctive belief, it is obviously only a *subjective* criterion of truth and motive of certitude, and as such it is inadequate. Belief necessarily presupposes an *insight* into the *grounds* of this belief, before it can be used as an intelligent guide. We must be sure *beforehand* on indisputable evidence that such an instinct exists in our nature, that it is reliable and not prone to error, and that it can give us intellectual certitude. If these conditions are not present and known to be present, we can have no assurance that our knowledge is true; we would indeed feel the subjective necessity to judge as we do, but we could never verify our judgments and see whether they agree with reality. Now, either we know the grounds of this belief, or we are ignorant of them. If we are *ignorant* of them, our instinctive belief is blind and without rational foundation; and then it is useless as a criterion of truth, because it is contrary to the nature of the mind as an essentially 'cognitive' faculty to be determined in its knowledge by a blind instinct. And if we *know* the grounds of this belief, then the 'objective evidence' of these grounds, and not the belief itself, is the ultimate criterion.

CRITICAL REALISM

Critical realists make a clear distinction between the knowing mind and the objects known: mind and world are diverse realities. The world is known by the mind by means of certain 'characters' or 'essences.' These latter imply "a reference to, and an acceptance of, a real, extra-experiential universe of existents. It is not that we reason to, or infer, such a fact beyond experience. The *belief* is rather an *assumption* which we make by *instinct,* since it is only by *taking for granted* that we are in relation to realities on which the needs of life depend that we are able to maintain ourselves alive at all. . . . An 'object,' therefore, is constituted by a group of characters with which psychological experience makes us familiar, *plus the instinctive sense* that there is something present of which we have to take account, the latter aspect being the outcome of that state of muscular tension which is conditioned by our nature as active beings dependent on an environing world, while the characters are used, also *instinctively,* to give this a specific form."[2] We intuit the 'characters' or 'essences' directly, and these we refer to a physically existing object by means of an *instinctive impulse* of our nature. The ultimate criterion of truth is, therefore, not the 'objective evidence' of reality as such, but a *belief* and an *assumption,* made by *instinct,* that these 'characters' or 'essences' reveal reality as it is.

J. E. Turner very pointedly sums up the situation for critical realism as follows: "All realisms . . . must finally rest, exactly as naïve realism does, upon the process and content of perception — upon this content as more keenly criticized and more rigidly tested; and this analysis must be pursued to a final verdict. If then this content is regarded as not in itself physical, two alternatives arise: either physical reality is never ontologically identical with perceived content, and therefore, since there is no other mode of directly apprehending it, this reality is noumenal; or realism must fall back on an instinctive, but non-philosophic, belief in the known existence of physical reality. This dilemma faces critical realism. If it maintains its universal distinction between physical things themselves beyond our consciousness, and their perceived or apparent sense-characters, then it becomes a noumenalism. But if, on the other hand, it founds its affirmations on instinctive belief, it forfeits all title to be regarded as a philosophic system, whatever other merits it may possess. Or at best it can become a philosophy only of the content of perception as distinct from physical reality itself."[3] In neither alternative can we have a *rational* foundation for our certitude that our judgments cor-

---

[2] A. K. Rogers, *What is Truth?* (Yale University Press, 1923), pp. 65 and 67. (Italics mine. — Author.)

[3] *A Theory of Direct Realism* (Macmillan Co., 1925), pp. 128, 129.

respond to reality; our ultimate criterion of truth would be either *blind instinct* or an unproved and unprovable *assumption*. But such a criterion is *subjectivistic* and useless.

PRAGMATISM AND HUMANISM

Pragmatism, or *Humanism,* is a system of thought which is voluntaristic. The truth of judgments does not arise from their correspondence to reality. The pragmatist criterion of truth consists in the *utility* of a belief in satisfying *human needs* in a *social* way. That is true which 'works,' which has practical value, which leads to beneficial results for human progress, which promotes the best interest of mankind through living experience. Results *make* a belief true or false for the time being. Beliefs *become* true, when they function for the social welfare of humanity; and false, when they cease to function along these lines. Truth is, therefore, nothing static and immutable, but something dynamic and perpetually changing. Consequently, a belief may be true at one stage of development, and the same belief may be false at a different stage; something may be true under one set of conditions and false under another; a theory may be true for one class of people and false for another class, depending on the intellectual and cultural conditions prevailing at a particular time and in a particular locality. Truth, as will be seen, is entirely *subjective* in character.

This interpretation of truth is contrary to the accepted *meaning* attached to the word by all men, whether educated or uneducated, and amounts to a *perversion of language*. To identify 'truth' with 'utility' is nothing less than to reduce the 'true' to the 'good.' The 'good,' however, is the object of the *will,* not of the intellect, while the 'true' has been considered by men at all times to be the proper object of the *intellect*. A lamentable confusion of thought must result from this identification of the 'true' with the 'good.' If both are identical, so that 'truth' is the object of the will, what can possibly be the *object of the intellect*? As a natural faculty of man it must have a natural object, just as well as the will; but if we remove 'truth' from the intellect, the latter is without a proper object with which to exercise its power. The exercise of any power or faculty involves the striving to *realize something,* and that demands an object within its own proper sphere of activity. Every power or faculty of the human organism, internal as well as external, has its proper object; the will, for instance, strives toward the realization of the 'good.' But what could possibly be the object of the intellect except the realization and acquisition of 'truth'? There is no other object assignable or discoverable. Pragmatists may *assert* that the 'true' is identical with the 'good,' but that will never *really* identify such totally disparate things. Their attitude is unjustifiable, because contrary to the fundamental conceptions of men.

Besides, in identifying the 'true' with the 'good,' pragmatists do *not solve the epistemological problem of knowledge.* The problem of 'knowledge' remains just as acute as before; it cannot be solved by transferring the concept of 'truth' from the field of knowledge to the field of action and then denying that a 'problem of knowledge' exists. We must still answer the questions: Is there an objective reality which is extra-mental? Can this reality be known? How is it known? How do our judgments interpret this reality? Do they correspond with it? How can we have certitude about this? These questions constitute the 'problem of knowledge' and the mind of man will not be satisfied, and will continue to exert its powers of reasoning, until these questions are answered or until the mind sinks in despair into skepticism. But ignore this problem the mind cannot. Whether we call the answers to these questions 'truth' or whether we give it another name, makes little difference: it is the problem and its solution that count, and they pertain to the province of the intellect and must be solved by the *intellect* and not by the will. Pragmatism, therefore, does not solve the problem of knowledge by dubbing it 'meta-physics' and then ignoring its existence.

And pragmatists are *inconsistent*. They identify 'truth' with 'utility' and thus transfer it to the province of the will. Nevertheless, they appeal to the *intellect* with a great array of arguments, to prove that 'truth' is to be *judged* according to its beneficial results. Thereby they surreptitiously substitute the intellect for the will as the arbiter of truth and error and unconsciously admit after all that it is the *intellect,* and not the will, which must decide whether their theory or opposite theories give the correct (or 'true') solution of the problem of knowledge and truth. Since they appeal to the reasoning intellect, they must abide by its verdict. Now, it is the verdict of the reasoning intellect, as we have shown, that truth is found in the *judgment interpreting reality* and not in the results which flow from a certain belief. It is not 'utility' which determines the 'truth' of judgments, beliefs, and theories, but the objective evidence of reality. In fact, when pragmatists attempt to prove their own theory, they marshal numerous facts and reasons in order to show that 'utility' and not 'objective evidence' is the criterion of truth and the motive of certitude; and in doing so, they appeal to the *objective evidence* of these facts and reasons to establish their case. Their own attitude and action is their best refutation.

Moreover, pragmatists claim that those beliefs are 'true' which satisfy human needs and produce beneficial results for man in a social way. What *needs,* and what *beneficial results?* We must *know* them, so as to be able to ascertain which beliefs contain 'truth' and which 'error.' In order to know whether needs are real or apparent and whether results are beneficial or harmful, it is necessary for the intellect to discover the *facts* regarding these needs and results and then pass *judgment* on the truth or error of the beliefs. But here again, if any judgment corresponds to the facts at issue, it is 'true'; and if it does not, it is 'false.' Thus it can be seen that truth and error reside in the judgment and their presence is determined by the objective evidence of the facts. The good results may be taken as an index or *sign* of truth, but the ultimate *criterion* of truth lies in the objective evidence before the mind. As long as it is necessary to have a criterion to discriminate between 'real' and 'apparent' needs, between 'beneficial' and 'harmful' results, between beliefs which 'work' and those which 'do not work,' results cannot be considered the ultimate criterion. Results do not appear with labels attached; they can be discerned only by the intellect. Even from a pragmatist standpoint, then, the truth or error of beliefs cannot be decided without the judging power of the intellect. The ultimate criterion for the intellect, however, as has been seen, consists in the clear self-manifestation of reality or *self-evidence*. Hence, pragmatism does not satisfy the 'needs' of the intellect as a theory of truth and knowledge and, judged by its own criterion, is unsatisfactory and therefore false.

Finally, how can I apply the pragmatist criterion to everyday *existential judgments?* I judge that 'My watch is slow,' 'a car is passing,' 'my feet are cold,' and so on. These statements contain truth or error. By what possible results for human progress and welfare am I to decide whether they are true or false? Or will a pragmatist seriously assert that there is no truth or error in these and similar judgments? If he claims there is not, we must dissent; if he agrees that there is, he must admit that his criterion does not apply. A criterion, however, which fails in its essential function, is *worthless,* because it is no criterion at all: it does not 'work.'

RELATIVISM AND TRUTH

There is *relativity in all knowledge.* By the very fact that a thing becomes known, a relation is established between it and the knowing subject. In order that an object be 'known,' it must be cognitionally present *to* the knower and be consciously apprehended *by* the knower; thereby both object and subject obtain a 'reference to,' or 'relation toward,' each other. To say that the mind could know an object without any relation existing between them, would be the same as to say that an object could be known without being 'known' and a subject could know without 'knowing'; but that would be absurd. When we say that the mind can know reality 'as it is in itself independent of the mind,' we do not mean to claim that reality, when known, is independent of the mind in the act of *knowledge,* but that it is independent of the mind in its extramental *existence*.

Maher has given a true and succinct expression of the relativity of knowledge, when he states — "(A) that we can only know as much as our faculties, limited in number and range, can reveal to us; (B) that these faculties can inform us of objects only so far, and according as the latter manifest themselves; (C) that accordingly (*a*) there may remain always an indefinite number of qualities which we do not know, and (*b*) what is known must be set in relation to the mind, and can only be known in such relation."[4] This, however, is not the usual meaning attached to the phrase in modern philosophy. *Relativity of knowledge* there means that character of knowledge in virtue of which it has only *relative value,* i.e., knowledge is not immutably and absolutely true in itself, but is true only according to the mental laws and conditions of the knowing subject. The theory which teaches this doctrine, is called *relativism*. Since knowledge is true only for the individual subject who possesses it and is determined by his peculiar mental constitution, it is also subjective in character. Relativism is thus equivalent to *subjectivism*.

According to relativism, then, knowledge and truth have no absolute and permanent validity: they are valid only for man as he is at present constituted, because they are the immediate product of his cognitional processes, and these processes operate according to the laws which govern his particular organism. Our knowledge of the extra-mental universe, for instance, is valid for *man,* but that does not mean that this knowledge corresponds to *reality as it is*. All forms of idealism and representative realism are thus seen to be relativistic, in as much as these theories subscribe to the doctrine that we

---

[4]*Psychology,* 9th ed. (Longmans, Green and Co., 1930), p. 158.

can know nothing but our internal *subjective states* of the mind. Mentalists deny the existence of extra-mental reality altogether; representational realists, like Kant, Spencer, Mill, Huxley, and the adherents of sensism, positivism, and pragmatism, admit the existence of extra-mental reality, but they maintain that the knowledge of this reality is so transformed and transfigured in perception and intellection as to give *no insight* into what reality *actually is*. Such is the nature of all human knowledge and truth — it is relative and subjective, without objective validity. *Protagoras* (born about 480 B.C.) already defended this doctrine, asserting that "man is the measure of all things."

Relativism attacks the very nature of knowledge and truth in their foundation. It would be next to impossible to convince a confirmed relativist of the erroneousness of his position, because, like the universal skeptic, he admits no fixed and objectively valid laws of reasoning. But for those who still have an open mind it must be clear that *relativism is false*. If there are no truths which are absolutely valid, then even the Principles of Identity, Contradiction, Excluded Middle, and Sufficient Reason possess only relative, temporary, ephemeral value. They are true *now* for *us,* due to the subjective constitution of our mind; but they need not be true *in themselves,* nor need they have been true always in the *past,* nor need they be always true in the *future.* But the consequences of such a doctrine are absurd in the extreme. There could then have been a time, or a time may come, when it would be possible 'to exist' and 'not to exist' at the same moment; to be an 'entity' and also a 'non-entity' at the same moment; in fact, it would be possible to be *neither* an 'entity' *nor* a 'non-entity,' but something *between* 'entity' and 'non-entity,' at the same moment. And it would also be possible for knowledge to be 'true' and 'false' *simultaneously.* These are the inevitable consequences of relativism, if consistently carried to its logical conclusions.

That relativism actually leads to the renunciation of the Principle of Contradiction, at least by implication, can be seen in the most recent of epistemological theories, that of *objective relativism*. According to this theory, knowledge is relative, but this relativity is objective in the datum or character-quality of the thing as perceived. What I am aware of in perceiving a thing is its *quality* or its set of qualities; it is this that I perceive, and not the thing itself. "The qualities are not the existent, to be sure, but they are its whole nature, and it has no other."[5] When perceiving an orange, I perceive the qualities 'yellowness' and 'roundness'; these qualities "are its whole nature, and it has no other"; as such, then, these qualities constitute the objective essence of the orange. The result of this doctrine is that these qualities will be *objectively* that what they *appear* to be, *relative* to each individual from his particular *point of view*. The classic example is that of the penny. You and I look at it from different points of view. From where I stand, it appears as 'circular'; from where you stand, it appears as 'elliptical.' Since our knowledge of these qualities is relatively true to each of us, and since these qualities are objectively the only thing we know of the penny, it follows (according to the theory of objective relativism) that the penny is really and *objectively circular and elliptical at the same time,* since we both look at it at the same time.

The implication of such a relativistic theory is obvious. Things can really have a different size, shape, color, temperature, etc., at one and the same moment; because as things *appear,* they *are,* i.e., to us. As Edward F. Talbot justly observes: "A knowledge of reality becomes an impossibility, since we know things not as they are, but as they appear. Appearances become all; reality vanishes. In becoming all, appearance becomes nothing. There is no common appearance, no unity of perception. Each appearance is proper to a particular point of view and the content present to the different subjects varies not only numerically but qualitatively. Thus we know not reality, and appearance finally fades into the projection of a point of view."[6]

Objective relativism, and every other theory of relativism, thus involves a denial of the most fundamental laws of being and thought — the Principles of Identity, Contradiction, and Excluded Middle. But to destroy their validity means to destroy the very possibility of valid knowledge. The truth of relativism and the truth of the First Principles are *incompatible*. If the First Principles are allowed to stand in their objective validity, realativism is false; but if relativism is accepted, the First Principles must fall as invalid illusions, and all knowledge, *including relativism* as a theory of knowledge, must fall with them. But that would be the suicide of reason and the triumph of universal skepticism. Relativism, therefore, must be rejected, and truth must be taken as something absolute in an objective sense.

So far as the criterion of objective relativism is concerned, it must consist in the *appearance* of the 'character' or 'essence.' This being the only thing we can know about an object, it is plain that our judgments must *always* correspond to it. As such, then, our judgments will always be relatively and subjectively true. But here again the criterion fails as a criterion, because it will never enable the mind to discriminate between 'true' and 'false' appearances. In fact, there can be no such thing as *error* in this system, because every appearance is 'true' for each individual according to his subjective point of view. This, however, contradicts experience; error is a fact, and it must be accounted for. Since the objective difference between truth and error is obliterated in relativism, it is a false system of knowledge.

By exposing the inadequacies and absurdities contained in these various theories regarding the nature of truth and the criterion of truth, we have confirmed the doctrine that the

---

[6] E. F. Talbot, *Knowledge and Object* (Catholic University Press, 1932), p. 53.

ultimate criterion of truth and motive of certitude consist in the internal, immediate objective evidence of reality manifesting itself to the intellect. And thereby another spontaneous conviction of man has been critically examined and philosophically vindicated, namely, that the *judgments* of the intellect are a *true* and *valid* source of knowledge in interpreting reality.

SUMMARY OF CHAPTER XVII

Various philosophers have advanced different criteria of truth, depending on their general theory of knowledge.

1. *Descartes* considered 'clear and distinct ideas' to be the criterion. This would not guarantee the correspondence of the idea with reality. *Malebranche* contended that we know all things through an intuition of them in the Mind of God; *Rosmini* claimed that we know all things through an intuition of Being. This is contrary to our experience.

2. *Idealistic monism* finds the criterion in *coherence* or consistency. But even a false system may be coherent. By this criterion we could not distinguish between true and false 'existential judgments.' To know whether a particular judgment is coherent with a system of knowledge would practically demand omniscience.

3. *Fideism and Traditionalism.* Fideism takes 'faith' and traditionalism takes 'tradition' as the criterion. But before we can accept such an external criterion, we must have *prior certitude* about the validity of the authority demanding this act of faith.

4. *Inconceivability of the Opposite.* Judgments are supposed to be true, because their contradictories are 'inconceivable.' If this were true, a statement would have to be compared with its opposite, before its truth could be ascertained. But First Principles are seen to be absolutely true through a direct comparison of the *concepts* of the judgment, not by a comparison of these principles with their contradictories.

5. *Epistemological Monism (Neo-Realism)*. In this theory the mind is reduced to the object known. This is contrary to all experience. If there is no real mind, distinct from the object known, *error is impossible;* but error is a fact.

6. *Common Sense*. The Scottish School places the criterion in the dictates of 'common sense' which it conceives as based on a blind instinct. *Belief,* then, is the foundation of knowledge. If we are ignorant of the *grounds* of this belief, it is blind and irrational; if we know these grounds, then objective evidence is the criterion, and not belief.

7. *Critical Realism*. We perceive the 'characters' or 'essences' of things and refer them to reality through an *instinctive belief* that these 'characters' are real qualities of things. This means that our knowledge is *not rational*. We could never know whether these 'characters' correspond to reality; we could, then, never distinguish between true and false knowledge.

8. *Pragmatism and Humanism*. 'Utility' is the criterion of truth: beliefs are 'true,' if they produce 'beneficial results.' This is a confusion of the 'true' with the 'good'; and since the 'good' is the object of the will, the intellect would be without an object. This theory evades, but does not solve, the problem of knowledge. Pragmatists are inconsistent, because they appeal to the *intellect* to prove that their theory is 'true.' In order to apply the criterion, we would have to discriminate between 'real' and 'apparent' needs, 'beneficial' and 'harmful' results; but only the intellect can do that through an insight into the *facts* — and then objective evidence is the criterion. Ordinary 'existential judgments' cannot be judged as 'true' or 'false' according to beneficial results for humanity.

9. *Relativism*. Truth and knowledge have only *relative value,* according to the laws and conditions of the individual mind; truth is nothing permanent, absolute, and necessary. In that case the First Principles of Identity, Contradiction, and Excluded Middle have only relative validity. *Objective relativ-*

ism implies the denial of these principles. But that means the destruction of all knowledge and truth and leads to *skepticism*.

READINGS

P. Coffey, *op. cit.,* Vol. II, Chs. XXII–XXV; J. Barron, *op. cit.,* Ch. XVI; J. G. Vance, *op. cit.,* Ch. X; T. Pesch, *op. cit.,* Vol. II, pp. 281–300; J. Rickaby, *op. cit.,* Ch. XII; J. Donat, *op. cit.,* Ch. II, art. 6; A. K. Rogers, *What is Truth?,* pp. 122–127; A. J. Balfour, *A Defense of Philosophic Doubt,* Chs. VIII, X; L. J. Walker, *Theories of Knowledge;* J. B. Pratt, *What is Pragmatism?,* Lects. III, IV.

CHAPTER XVIII

THE TRUTH-VALUE OF REASONING

Percepts lead to concepts, concepts to judgments, and judgments contain truth or error in their interpretative pronouncement about reality. The result of our examination into their validity has vindicated man's spontaneous conviction that human knowledge is essentially trustworthy. Much of our true knowledge is acquired directly by means of immediate sense-perception and by an analysis of fundamental abstract concepts. But reality is often so complex and recondite that it is not self-evident to the mind contemplating it. Many truths cannot be discovered by means of immediate sense-perception as such or by means of a simple comparison of the concepts contained in a judgment. A mediate process of intellection is required in order to disclose the hidden truth. This is the process of *reasoning* or *ratiocination.*

Reasoning is that mental process in which, from truths already known, we *infer* some other truth contained in them and following from them with necessary consequence. The inference draws out and makes explicit a truth which is implicitly present in other truths. This can be done in two ways. We can argue from the logical whole to a logical part of the whole, and then we have a process of *deduction;* or, we can reason from the truth of the logical parts to the truth of the logical whole, and that is the process of *induction.* In the former the inference goes from the more universal to the less universal or particular, and in the latter from the particulars or less universal to the more universal.

Serious objections have been raised against the inferential process involved in deduction and induction. Some philosophers claim that there is an essential flaw in the very nature of these processes. *Critics* If deduction and induction, they say, are as described, they are incapable of leading the mind to a certain knowledge of *new* truths and are, therefore, useless as *inferences*. This attack on the validity of deduction and induction is really an attack on the validity of human reason as a source of knowledge and cannot pass unchallenged.

THE PROBLEM OF DEDUCTION

Francis Bacon (1561–1626) criticized the syllogistic or deductive method as being of no value for the acquisition of real knowledge; instead, he advocated the careful study of nature by means of inductive analysis. Whatever value the syllogism may have is due to the fact that it is based on induction. The *empiricists* and *positivists,* since their theory of knowledge is sensistic, also reject the inferential validity of deductive reasoning as exemplified in the syllogism, because this form of argumentation reasons from the truth of the universals to the truth of the particulars, and sensism will not admit that we have genuinely universal ideas. *John Stuart Mill* launched a vigorous attack on the syllogism as a form of inference. He has this to say:

"It must be granted that in every syllogism, considered as an argument to prove the conclusion, there is a *petitio principii* [a begging of the question]. When we say,

a begging of the question

> All men are mortal,
> Socrates is a man,
> Therefore Socrates is mortal,

it is unanswerably urged by the adversaries of the syllogistic theory, that the proposition, Socrates is mortal, is presupposed in the more general assumption, All men are mortal: that we cannot be assured of the mortality of all men, unless we are already certain of the mortality of every individual man: that if it is still doubtful whether Socrates, or any other individual we choose to name, be mortal or not, the same degree of un-

certainty must hang over the assertion, All men are mortal:
that the general principle, instead of being given as evidence
of the particular case cannot itself be taken for true without
exception, until every shadow of doubt which could affect
any case comprised with it, is dispelled by evidence *aliunde*
[from an outside source]; and then what remains for the syllogism to prove? That, in short, no reasoning from generals
to particulars can, as such, prove anything, since from a general principle we cannot infer any particulars but those which
the principle itself assumes as known."[1]

Mill's line of argument is plain: the conclusion is *already*
contained and known in the major premise; for the major
premise ('All men are mortal') could not be known to be
true, if it were not also *previously known* that the conclusion
is true ('Socrates is mortal'). We must be certain that this conclusion is true before we can assume the truth of the major
premise, because the truth of the major premise could not be
clear without the truth of the conclusion. And yet, by the very
fact that we are attempting to prove the conclusion we admit
that we are *not certain* that the conclusion ('Socrates is
mortal') is true; and that necessarily implies that we are *not*
certain of the truth of the major premise. But to prove something from an uncertain and doubtful premise, is an illogical
process. On the other hand, if we maintain that the major
premise ('All men are mortal') *is* really certain, then it follows
that we must also have *known* before making the syllogism
that the conclusion ('Socrates is mortal') is true and certain;
but in that case, why make the futile attempt of proving something which is already known and certain? In the first instance we have a flagrant begging of the question, and in the
second instance we are not acquiring a new truth. In both instances the syllogism is useless as an inference, because we have
either an *illogical inference* or *no real inference* at all. Such
is the nature of Mill's argument.

[1] *System of Logic* (Longmans, Green and Co., 1930), Bk. II, Ch. I, § 2, p. 120.

The conclusion must be known to be true
before the major premise can be known.

Mill himself explains how we, according to his view, arrive at the general proposition ('All men are mortal') used as the major premise. Changing from 'Socrates' to 'the Duke of Wellington,' he states: "Assuming that the proposition, The Duke of Wellington is mortal, is immediately an inference from the proposition, All men are mortal; whence do we derive our knowledge of that general truth? Of course from observation. Now, all which man can observe are individual cases. From these all general truths must be drawn, and into these they may be again resolved; for *a general truth is but an aggregate of particular truths;* a comprehensive expression, by which an indefinite number of individual facts are affirmed or denied at once. But a general proposition is not merely a compendious form for recording and preserving in the memory of a number of particular facts, all of which have been observed. Generalization is not a process of mere naming, it is also a process of inference. From instances which we have observed, we feel warranted in concluding, that what we found true in those instances, holds in all similar ones, past, present, and future, however numerous they may be. We then, by that valuable contrivance of language which enables us to speak of many as if they were one, record all that we have observed, together with all that we infer from our observation, in one concise expression."[2]

In this interesting passage Mill's sensism and nominalism is apparent. The major premise expresses a general truth; and this "general truth is but an *aggregate* of particular truths." The meaning of Mill is clear: we have *collective* propositions, but none that are truly universal. They give us a "comprehensive expression, by which an indefinite number of individual facts are affirmed or denied at once"; again, this must be understood in the sense of a 'collective,' not a 'universal,' proposition. Mill then shows how the truth of the major premise is the result of an *inductive* process; and he continues: "When,

---

[2]*Loc. cit.,* § 3, p. 122. (Italics mine. — Author.)

therefore, we conclude from the death of John and Thomas, and every other person we ever heard of in whose case the experiment had been fairly tried, that the Duke of Wellington is mortal like the rest, we may, indeed, pass through the generalization, All men are mortal, as an intermediate stage; but it is not in the latter half of the process, the descent from all men to the Duke of Wellington, that the *inference* resides. The inference is finished when we have asserted that all men are mortal."[3]

Mill did not realize it, but in giving this explanation of the genesis of the major premise he ruined the whole value of his initial argument against the validity of the syllogism as a legitimate inference. He himself furnishes the clue which establishes the truth-value of deduction.

THE TRUTH-VALUE OF DEDUCTION

Mill is perfectly correct when he states that we arrive at the truth of the major premise ('All men are mortal') by means of an inductive process of reasoning. But how is this induction made? By a complete enumeration of *all* instances? Not at all. It is impossible for us to observe all the instances which are included in a general statement; we can observe no more than a very limited number. Now — and this is vital — "from instances which we have observed, we feel warranted in concluding, that what we found true in those instances, holds in all similar ones, past, present, and future, however numerous they may be." It is interesting that Mill, the empiricist, includes even the 'future' cases in this generalization. The main point is that Mill admits that we can make a legitimate inference from a *limited* number to a generalization which embraces '*all* similar ones' in the 'past, present, and future'; and that necessarily means that the inference applies also to those *not previously known* and not known *at the time* the generalization is made. But this is a fatal admission.

---

[3] *Ibid.*

In his initial attack on the validity of the syllogism, Mill contended that we could not know that 'All men are mortal,' unless we had a *previous* knowledge that 'Socrates is mortal.' This contention really asserts that we could not know *'All men are mortal'* except through the fact of a *complete* enumeration which, naturally, would then also include 'Socrates' as one of those whom we had perceived to be mortal. Now, Mill admits that 'Socrates' might not have been one of those whose death, like that of 'John' and 'Thomas,' we had actually observed; he could be one of 'the similar ones, past, present, or future,' of whom we have had *no previous* knowledge as to their mortality. Since I felt 'warranted in concluding' that 'All men are mortal,' notwithstanding the fact that I had no previous knowledge of the mortality of 'Socrates,' I can most assuredly *now conclude* that 'Socrates is mortal.' In making this deduction, Mill can no longer assert that the truth of the major premise ('All men are mortal') *depends* on the truth of the conclusion ('Socrates is mortal'), because the truth of this major premise was established *independently* of the truth of the conclusion; it was only from the mortality of 'John' and 'Thomas' and some others that I felt warranted in concluding that 'All men are mortal,' while 'Socrates' and his mortality never entered the inductive process at the time it was made. There will, then, be no begging of the question, when I apply the general truth contained in the major premise to a particular instance, as long as the latter was not involved in the induction which gave me the general truth in the first place. Mill's argument is, therefore, fallacious.

As long as we are 'warranted in concluding' from an *incomplete enumeration* to a universal proposition, so that *not all* the particular instances are *previously* known, we can legitimately infer the truth of those not previously known by drawing them under the extension of the universal proposition. Such an instance, of course, will be contained in the major premise as a matter of fact, but this fact is not actually known to me until I make the deduction; in other words, the conclusion is *virtually* contained and known in the major premise, but not *formally*. And since only that which is 'formally known' is 'actually' known by me, I do really acquire a *new* knowledge when I deduce the truth of the conclusion from the truth of the universal proposition used as the major premise.

Let us take a concrete example. I read in chemistry that 'All substances consisting of carbon are combustible.' Scientists arrived at this generalization through the process of an extensive, though not complete, induction: wherever and whenever the experiment was made, carbon was found to be combustible. Does that also apply to diamonds? Certainly; but *I do not know* as yet that diamonds consist of carbon; I am under the impression that diamonds are a sort of quartz. A year later I read an article on diamonds and discover that they consist of carbon. Do I *now* know that 'diamonds are combustible'? Not yet. While reading about diamonds, I do not think at all about the truth I learned a year before that 'All substances consisting of carbon are combustible.' Then one day it occurs to me *simultaneously* that 'All substances consisting of carbon are combustible' and that 'Diamonds consist of carbon.' And *now* it first dawns on my mind through deduction: 'Well, then, diamonds are *also* combustible,' and I have acquired a *new* knowledge about diamonds. Up to this point I had a knowledge of both facts, 'Carbon is combustible' and 'Diamonds are carbon,' taken separately and without realizing their implication. It was only when both truths are brought *together* before my mind and I realize the *logical connection* existing between them, that I am able to make the deductive syllogism and draw out the necessary conclusion:

All substances consisting of carbon are combustible;
Diamonds consist of carbon;
Ergo, diamonds are combustible.

We find many cases of this kind, where deduction is found

to be a perfectly legitimate *inference*. Science, for example, includes in the class of 'mammals' all animals that breathe through lungs, have hair on the body, and suckle their young. Now, the *whale* lives in water and has the general shape of a fish. Upon closer examination, however the whale was found to breathe through lungs (not gills), to have hair (not scales) on its body, and to suckle its young. What conclusion had to be deduced from these premises? This, that whale is not a fish, but a mammal; and so it happens that *now* the whale is classified as a mammal. Here the argument was made from the universal truth to the particular instance by means of deduction.

In a similar manner, *Pasteur* established by induction that 'Germs derive their origin from parental germs through generation.' At the time practically nothing about germs was known; the number of known existing types was very small. Notwithstanding this meager knowledge, the general principle was proved by induction to be true. Since then many new types of germs have been discovered; we cannot, therefore, say that they were *known* at the time this general principle was formulated. Through a process of syllogistic *deduction*, however, we can now *prove* that every *new* type discovered must have originated through parental generation; and that is a truth of great value for prophylactic medicine.

Einstein maintains that inertia is the same as gravity; consequently all the effects of inertia can also be obtained through gravity. From this he deduced that the rays of light would be bent from a straight course by passing through a gravitational field. Thus, the rays of the stars, passing close to the sun on their way to the earth, should be bent in the direction of the sun. This would follow from his general theory of relativity. Observations of solar eclipses have shown that the light of stars *does* curve toward the sun while passing near by, although the degree of curvature did not seem to agree with the mathematical calculations of Einstein. The point here, however, is that *deduction* can lead to *new* knowledge and truths.

Through deduction *Mme. Irene Joliot-Curie* and her husband *M. Frederic Joliot* came to the conclusion that, since radioactive elements change to lighter elements through disintegration, it must be possible to reverse the process and create the heavier elements artificially by *re-integration*. Thereupon, in 1934, they bombarded common elements, like aluminum, magnesium, and boron, with alpha particles and succeeded in transforming them temporarily into heavier elements. Following their lead, *Ernest O. Lawrence,* of the University of California, shot a stream of positively charged particles from a four-million-volt cathode tube into common table salt, and after a ten-hour bombardment the salt emitted the gamma rays of radium for a period of fifteen hours.

Some of the greatest achievements in astronomy and astrophysics have been made by means of deduction. From a conclusion drawn from the theorems of Conic Sections, *Kepler* established the general principle that certain definite positions are characteristic of an ellipse. Then, by showing that the orbit of Mars presents these definite positions, he concluded that the orbit of Mars is an ellipse. From Kepler's laws of motion the genius of Newton deduced the universal gravitation of matter. His discovery was brought about by one of the most brilliant series of deductive processes ever performed by man.[4] Mathematics has always played a predominant part in the calculations of astronomy, and mathematics is essentially a deductive science. But who would seriously question the validity of the deductions of mathematics?

The characteristic feature of deductive reasoning is this: the conclusion is *virtually* contained in the premises, but not formally. The truth of the conclusion becomes *formally* known through the syllogistic process. As such, then, the formally known truth becomes a *new* truth and extends our knowledge of reality. Consequently, deduction is a *valid inference* and a source of new knowledge. And this is borne out by the many

---

[4] See G. H. Joyce, *Principles of Logic,* 3rd ed. (Longmans, Green, 1929), Ch. XXI.

scientific discoveries made through deductive reasoning, a few of which have been noted above.

Induction, as well as deduction, contains a serious problem concerning its validity as a legitimate inference. In order to appreciate its seriousness it will be necessary to understand clearly wherein induction consists. *Induction* can be defined as *the legitimate inference of universal laws from individual cases,* or, to put it in different words, the logical transition from that which is less universal to that which is more universal.

Induction will be either complete or incomplete. It is *complete,* when it consists of a mere *totalization* of the individual instances expressed in the general statement. If I know, for example, that every single member of a certain Legion Post was an infantryman, I can express this fact in the totalizing general statement that 'All members of this Post were infantrymen.' This is what might be called, in Mill's phrase, an 'aggregate of individual truths.' Such an induction has no value for science, because the statement will not apply to anyone outside this limited aggregation; it does not lead to a universal law applicable to members not included in the original inductive process. Any induction will be *incomplete,* if it is based upon the investigation of a limited number of instances. If these instances are too limited or are non-typical, it will as a rule be insufficient as an inferential process; but if the instances are relatively numerous and typical, it will be a case of scientific induction.

An incomplete *scientific induction* is one which is based on a limited number of instances and from these infers the constant and *necessary relations* existing between things or between the properties of things. The result of this induction is expressed in a *universal* statement which represents a *law of nature,* and as such applies to *all* instances of the past, present, and future, whether known or unknown, whether actual or merely possible. That science makes inductions of this kind and claims that they are valid and legitimate inferential processes of reasoning, leading to new truths and knowledge, need hardly be mentioned.

This, however, involves a serious problem. We know from logic that we cannot legitimately conclude from the truth of the particular to the truth of the universal; what is true of *some* need not be true of *all*. Because 'some' men tell lies, we cannot conclude that 'all' men tell lies; because 'some' soldiers were killed in battle, we cannot conclude that 'all' soldiers were killed; because 'some' animals have wings, we cannot conclude that 'all' animals have wings. The conclusion may not be wider than the premises. But that seems to be the very procedure followed in the process of induction. From 'some' instances observed we argue to 'all' instances, even to those unobserved and unknown. From a *number* of particular cases we formulate a law which is supposed to apply validly to the *entire class* of these and similar cases. Is science, then, not guilty of an *illicit process?* Does this not vitiate the entire inductive inference, making it illogical and therefore valueless for acquiring true knowledge? But if induction is a valid method of reasoning, on what *grounds* is its validity based, so that it is logically justified? Wherein does the *necessity* of the inductive law consist, since it seems to be built upon so insecure a foundation?

Different solutions have been offered, depending to a great extent upon the theory of reality and the theory of knowledge proposed by the various schools of thought. *Empiricists,* who defend a sensistic philosophy and admit no knowledge beyond that of sense-experience, concede only an empirical or experiential validity to the laws formulated by means of induction. Such a law is a mere generalization from observed facts and has no strict value beyond the limits of observation. Within these limits they give us *certitude,* but beyond these limits only *probability.* We, of course, are subjectively convinced that these laws apply in all cases at all times under all circumstances; but this conviction of the 'necessity' of such laws is the result of 'association'; it is a *psychological,* not a logical, necessity. That is why Mill says: "In distant parts of the stellar regions, where the phenomena may be entirely unlike those with which we are acquainted, it would be folly to affirm confidently that this general law [of causation, or causality] prevails, any more than those special ones which we have found to hold universally on our own planet. The uniformity in the succession of events, otherwise called the law of causation, must be received, not as a law of the universe, but of that portion of it only which is within the range of our means of sure observation, with a reasonable degree of extension to adjacent cases. To extend it further is to make a supposition without evidence, and to which, in the absence of any ground from experience for estimating its degree of probability, it would be idle to assign any."[5]

Kant, and with him the *transcendentalists,* maintains that experience and induction can never lead to a knowledge which is strictly universal and necessary. "Experience teaches us, no doubt, that something is so or so, but not that it cannot be different. . . . Experience never imparts to its judgments *true* or *strict,* but only *assumed* or *relative, universality* (by means of induction), so that we ought always to say, so far as we have observed hitherto, there is no exception to this or that rule. If, therefore, a judgment is thought with strict universality, so that no exception is admitted as possible, it is not derived from experience, but valid absolutely *a priori.*"[6] The strict necessity which we ascribe to inductive laws of science is the result of certain *a priori forms* of the mind and is not justifiable on the grounds of experience itself; it is due, therefore, to the peculiar constitution of the human mind which constructs such laws through the subjective force of the mind's own nature. *Reid*

---

[5] *Loc. cit.,* Bk. III, Ch. XXI, § 4, p. 376. See also Bertrand Russell, *The Analysis of Mind,* pp. 93–97.

[6] *Critique of Pure Reason,* pp. 716, 717. (Italics mine. — Author.)

and the Scottish School, on the other hand, find the ultimate reason for the necessity of accepting inductive laws in an instinct of man's nature. The *pragmatists,* due to their theory of dynamic and fluent 'truth,' can see no absolute validity in the laws formulated by the inductive sciences; such laws have only provisional value.[7]

We maintain that induction is a valid process of inference, based on experience and observation. Experience and observation reveal facts which disclose to the intellect the *nature* or *essence* of a thing or property. Since this nature or essence is the *same in kind* for all members of a species or genus, the inductive law governing them will be truly universal and necessary. And if the law is grounded on some essential property or attribute common to all material things, the law will apply throughout the universe, even "in distant parts of the stellar regions," to all things at all times, past, present, and future, whether known or unknown, within and beyond the limits of actual observation.

THE TRUTH-VALUE OF INDUCTION

In order to avoid confusion of thought, it will be necessary to have a clear understanding of the meaning of 'essence' and 'nature' in this connection. The term is used in a threefold meaning. (1) We frequently designate by the term 'essence' anything, attribute, quality, or property, considered in the *abstract,* i.e., divested of all individualizing traits and characteristics. For example, 'humanity,' 'rationality,' 'roundness,' 'redness.' It was used in this sense when discussing the problem of the universals. This is 'essence' in a *wider* sense. (2) It may also mean those attributes, qualities, and properties which are *invariably present* in a being, so that a necessary relation exists between them and the being which possesses them. They are 'essential' in opposition to 'accidental' attributes, qualities, and properties, in as much as the latter may be present or absent

---

[7]See George Mead, in *Creative Intelligence* (Henry Holt and Co., 1917), pp. 176–228.

without affecting a being as to its species or genus. Whatever belongs to the 'essence' in this sense is either a *constitutive* element of the thing's being or *proceeds necessarily* from such a constitutive element. Whatever determines the genus, species, or specific difference of a thing, is a constitutive element of it; for instance, 'rationality,' 'humanity,' 'animality,' 'life,' 'materiality,' and 'substantiality,' in man. But that which flows or proceeds necessarily from such constitutive elements, is an essential property of the thing; such is 'the faculty of speech,' 'the power to laugh,' 'the capability to use tools,' etc., in man. This is 'essence' in a *strict* sense. (3) Finally, it may be taken to designate the *constitutive elements alone,* and not the properties which proceed necessarily from them. In this use of the term 'the faculty of speech,' 'the power to laugh,' etc., do not belong to the 'essence' of man. Here 'essence' is taken in its *strictest* sense. While science endeavors to discover the 'essence' of things in the last meaning of the term, this is usually so difficult of attainment, that it must be satisfied in most cases with 'essence' in the *strict* sense. The *nature* of a thing is its essence considered as the principle of its activities.

We must now inquire into the *validity* of induction as a legitimate logical inference. Induction certainly seems to violate the canons of correct thinking, by passing from the truth of a *few* observed cases to a *universal* law which is supposed to apply to *all* cases of this kind. The conclusion (the universal law) is apparently much wider than the premises (the observed cases) from which it is drawn; and this looks suspiciously like an 'illicit process.' If this charge of an illicit process cannot be shown to be false, induction must be rejected. On what *grounds,* then, are we justified, after investigating a few observed instances, to formulate a universal law? When we examine a case of induction, we will perceive why we are obliged to consider it a valid inferential process.

In combining hydrogen and chlorine, for example, it is noticed that their quantities will not unite in any and all proportions. They combine in no other proportions than 1 to

35.5 by weight, or in other words, 1 to 1 by volume. These proportions are absolutely fixed and stable, no matter how the circumstances are varied. Having discovered this fact by induction, science enunciates the *law* that hydrochloric acid is formed by combining hydrogen and chlorine in the proportions of 1 to 35.5 by weight or 1 to 1 by volume. And this is a *universal law,* valid for all cases, at all times, and under all considerations. Whenever and wherever the experiment is made, the law is verified. And yet, whence comes the *universality* and *necessity* which we perceive to exist in this and other laws?

In the example just given we notice that the discovery of the general law is *not* the result of anything like a *complete enumeration* of all possible quantities of hydrogen and chlorine in all possible combinations and circumstances. Scientists could not and do not attempt the impossible process of a complete enumeration. This universal law is the result of an *abstraction.* We perceive clearly that there must be a *sufficient reason* for this constant and invariable effect; and this reason cannot be anything like chance coincidence, but must be based on a definite, constantly and invariably operating *cause.* Now, there is only one thing that is constantly and invariably present in all these instances and experiments — the *nature* and *essence* of hydrogen and chlorine; the nature and essence of these elements is the cause, and the phenomena observed are the effect. Observations and experiments are made in such number and under such varying conditions until the mind clearly perceives that it is not only the nature of *this* hydrogen and *this* chlorine to form hydrochloric acid in these definite proportions, but that it is the nature and essence of hydrogen *as such* and of chlorine *as such* to produce these constant and invariable effects. We, therefore, prescind from the *particular* natures and essences observed in these few cases and penetrate by abstraction to the *nature and essence in general* of hydrogen and chlorine. Once this stage has been reached, there is no need of further experiments; since the nature and essence of hydrogen and chlorine will always remain the same in all conditions of time and place (for they never can be anything but hydrogen and chlorine), they will produce the same effects always and everywhere. This being certain, this conclusion is expressed in a universal *law;* and the law can now be applied without fail to every instance which may arise in the world or in the laboratory. Science has been increased by a new law, and the mind has been enriched by a new truth.

The relation of the inductive *law* to the individual *phenomena* parallels the relation of the universal *idea* to the individual *things.* Both are the result of the abstractive power of the intellect, leaving aside the individuating differences and grasping the nature or essence common to them all. Thereby the idea and the law become *abstract, necessary,* and *universal,* applicable to the whole class as a class and to every single member of the class, irrespective of time or place. It is precisely this necessary and universal character of the idea and the law which makes them valuable for science and philosophy and constitutes a distinct advance of human knowledge. Scientific laws are expressed in definite categorical statements; and truth, as we know, is only found in categorical judgments which are an actual representation of reality as it is. The laws of science, discovered through induction, are, therefore, not mere figments of the thinking mind, as Kant claims, nor mere empiric generalizations of great probability, as the empiricists assert, nor general statements of provisional value, as pragmatists maintain, but genuinely *universal laws* expressive of reality.

Such is the nature of induction. The instance of the formation of hydrochloric acid is given merely as an illustration of the inductive process as used in every department of science. The details of method will vary, of course, according to the individual problems to be solved, but the fundamental principles of procedure are the same: it is an *abstraction,* passing from the particular to the universal, from the effect to the cause, from the logical part to the logical whole, from the phenomena to the law.

If we now sum up the *underlying principles* of induction, they will be seen to be as follows: (1) Any attribute, quality, or property which, no matter how the external conditions are varied, is found to belong constantly and invariably to a certain thing, must have a *constant* and *intrinsic reason* for itself *in* that thing; and any effect which is constantly and invariably produced by a certain thing, must proceed from a *constant* and *intrinsic cause in* that thing. (2) Whatever is constant and intrinsic in a thing is either its essence and nature or a direct result of its essence and nature, because this nature and essence is the only reality which is constantly and intrinsically in the thing, everything else being accidental and subject to change. (3) Whatever pertains directly to the essence and nature of a thing must be found *in every individual* who possesses such an essence and nature.[8] Since, then, the inferential force of induction does not rest on a complete enumeration of all individual instances, but is grounded on the 'nature' and 'essence' of the beings *as such,* it is evident that induction does not involve an illicit process. On the contrary, the logical grounds are perfectly legitimate and adequate for the formulation of universal laws. Science, therefore, is justified in using induction as an instrument for discovering and establishing physical laws, and these laws reveal new truths and extend human knowledge.

Hence, both deduction and induction are *valid processes of reasoning,* leading to a true interpretation of reality. The objections raised against their validity are seen to be without foundation, and human reason as a source of true and valid knowledge is vindicated. This, of course, has always been a spontaneous conviction of mankind, and the critical examination of our intellectual operations has shown conclusively that this conviction is warranted and correct.

---

[8] See Gény, *Critica,* nn. 404–409; also Joyce, *Principles of Logic* (Longmans: 1908), pp. 216, 217.

SUMMARY OF CHAPTER XVIII

Mediate knowledge is acquired by means of *reasoning,* or ratiocination. When we argue from the truth of the logical whole to that of the logical part, we have *deduction;* when we argue from the truth of the logical parts to that of the logical whole, we have *induction.* Serious objections have been raised against both as a legitimate inference.

1. *The Problem of Deduction.* Empiricists and positivists charge that deduction involves a begging of the question. The major premise is a general statement whose truth *presupposes* the truth of each particular instance comprised within the extension of the general statement; hence, the conclusion is already known before the general statement can be made. So Mill.

2. *The Truth-Value of Deduction.* Mill admits that the major premise is a general statement whose truth is discovered by induction. He also admits that such a general statement is derived from the observation of a *limited* number of instances, yet it is valid for 'all similar instances, past, present, and future.' But this proves that *all* individual instances *need not* have been *previously known* in order to make the general statement a valid major premise in a syllogism; hence, Mill is wrong when he asserts that the conclusion must already be known in the major premise. The conclusion is contained *virtually* in the major premise, but not *formally;* and it is only formal knowledge which is actual knowledge. Consequently, deduction can give us new knowledge by means of a legitimate inference. Besides, many important scientific discoveries have been made through deduction, especially in mathematics and astronomy. *Imprudica*

3. *The Problem of Induction.* Induction is *complete* when it consists of a mere totalization of the individual instances. It is *incomplete* and *scientific,* when it is based on a limited number of instances and from these infers the constant and necessary relations existing between things and between the

Principle of Sufficient Reason

properties of things. It leads to a *universal law*. This, however, seems to involve an illicit process, because the law is apparently an inference from the truth of 'some' to the truth of 'all.' *Empiricists* will not admit certitude for scientific induction beyond the limits of observation. *Kant* and the transcendentalists will not admit a true and strict, but only an assumed and relative, universality for the law. *Pragmatists* consider inductive laws to have only provisional value. We maintain that induction is based on the *nature* and *essence* of the observed things and is, therefore, an inference valid beyond the limits of observation and truly universal.

4. *The Truth-Value of Induction.* What are the *logical grounds* for the universal validity of induction? It is not a complete enumeration of all instances, because such an enumeration is impossible. It is based on *abstraction*. The only sufficient reason for the constancy and invariability of natural effects is observed by the intellect to lie in the *nature* and *essence* of the things observed. From this we conclude that it lies in their nature and essence *as such* to produce these effects. Consequently, wherever and whenever this nature and essence is present, it will produce these effects. This, then, is the sufficient reason for the universality and necessity expressed in the law.

Deduction and induction are, therefore, valid forms of reasoning, and reasoning is critically justified.

READINGS

G. H. Joyce, *Principles of Logic,* Ch. XIV; D. Card. Mercier, *op. cit.,* Vol. I, 391–393; R. F. Clarke, *Logic,* Part III, Chs. V, VI; T. Pesch, *op. cit.,* Vol. II, 522–576; T. Crumley, *Logic,* Chs. XVIII, XXVI; W. B. Pillsbury, *The Psychology of Reasoning,* Chs. VI, VII, VIII; A. J. Balfour, *A Defense of Philosophic Doubt,* Chs. II, III, IV.

Chapter XIX

RECAPITULATION

It is the purpose of epistemology to examine the rational grounds upon which our spontaneous convictions are based, in order to see whether they are philosophically justified. This involves an investigation into the *validity,* or truth-value, of human knowledge; and that in turn involves an investigation into the reliability of the *sources* of our knowledge. These sources are the faculties which furnish the data from which knowledge is derived, and these sources are: consciousness, sense-perception, and intellection. It is characteristic of human knowledge that it claims to be a true representation or interpretation of *reality as it is,* not merely a subjective construction of the mind; and man has the spontaneous conviction that his knowledge actually conforms to extra-mental reality and as such is valid and true.

This, however, is not so simple as it seems. All knowledge is a mental state and therefore subjective; apparently, then, knowledge has only subjective value. Knowledge is fashioned from ideas; what, then, can the mind know but its own ideas? Again, how can extended bodies make an impression on an unextended mind, or how can an unextended mind know extended bodies? There appears to be no common ground between mind and matter.

Ever since the days of Descartes the problem of knowledge has been acute. He inaugurated the modern epistemological problem by introducing *an excessive psycho-physical dualism* between mind and matter, soul and body. These realities are so disparate and antithetical in nature that a contact between them is utterly impossible. It followed with necessity that the mind could not effect a cognitional union between itself and extra-mental reality; the mind could not transcend itself and know the world, and an impassable gulf was placed between them. Either a bridge had to be found to span the intervening distance, or our knowledge of the world is an illusion. In his attempt to explain man's knowledge of his own body and of the world at large, Descartes had recourse to the theory of *innate ideas:* our knowledge is inborn and gradually unfolds itself out of the depths of the mind. Man, then, can know nothing but his own ideas and the internal states within himself; such was the inevitable consequence of his theory of innatism. The capital error of Descartes consisted in his overlooking the fact that man is a unit: body and soul (mind) form a *single psycho-physical organism.*

It was to be expected that subsequent philosophers would not be satisfied with Descartes' theory of innate ideas, and so different systems arose in an endeavor to give a more rational account of our obvious knowledge of the world around us. But practically all accepted the apparently evident principle that the mind can know nothing but its own states. The result was philosophical chaos. Theories succeeded theories in kaleidoscopic confusion. They showed a double trend: if they followed the *mechanistic* body-side of Descartes' views, they developed into empiricism, positivism, materialism, and skepticism; if they followed the *spiritualistic* mind-side of his theory, they branched off into ontologism, transcendentalism, and monistic idealism. And thus the excessive dualism of Descartes was reduced to absurdity.

A reaction toward the *common-sense* view of *realism* was inevitable; all humanity could not be so radically wrong, otherwise true knowledge must be adjudged impossible of attainment. The twentieth century witnessed the return of a saner outlook in the rise of pragmatism, neo-realism, and critical realism. Slowly the pendulum is swinging back to the aristotelianism of the scholastics as the only rational explanation of human knowledge. Philosophers realize at last that the 'idealist postulate,' maintaining that the mind is restricted in its knowledge to its own subjective states, is based on fallacy: the mind of man *can transcend itself* and contact the external world in cognition. The most recent epistemological theories defend some sort of *presentative realism* as the natural explanation of man's knowledge. That they do not succeed completely in their efforts to expound an all-round satisfactory system, is the result of their materialistic and evolutionistic tendencies; and they will never succeed until they come to the scientific and philosophic conclusion that body and mind, though essentially different as physical and psychical entities, are bound together as part-principles of a *psycho-physical organism* in the higher unity of the *Ego*. The *animated body* is the *epistemological bridge* between the mind and the world. Therein lies the solution of the problem of human knowledge.

Strictly speaking, it is not the function of epistemology to explain the 'nature' of the knowing subject; that belongs to the province of psychology. Nevertheless, a careful examination of the data of knowledge points clearly to certain definite conclusions. The data of *consciousness* show that mind and body are constituent parts of the Ego; the Ego is an abiding reality, the ultimate possessor of mental and bodily states. The data of *sense-perception* reveal the indubitable fact that we can and do perceive extra-mental reality in our body and extra-Ego reality in the bodies existing in the external world. This cannot be denied without destroying the foundations of our knowledge. Neither idealism nor representative realism gives an adequate explanation of our knowledge, as manifested in sense-perception; *presentative realism* alone can account for the facts. If we analyze the data, we find that sense-perception is neither a purely mental function nor a purely bodily operation, but an activity which involves the presence of both physical and psychical elements; it is 'extended,' but 'vital,' and as such can proceed only from a psycho-physical base; in other words, an *animated organism* is demanded, if we wish to give a rational account of the process of knowledge as manifested in sense-perception. Any other theory will either necessitate the reduction of the mind to matter (materialism), or the sublimation of matter to mind (idealism), or the complete severance of mind and matter (Cartesian dualism); the first cannot explain our intellectual knowledge, the second cannot explain our sense-knowledge, and the third cannot explain the combination of both. In order to explain the existence and validity of intellectual knowledge and sense-knowledge in man, man must be a unitary being capable of sense-perception and of intellection; and that means that he is an organism, a 'rational animal,' consisting of a vital body and a rational mind.

Our investigation into the data of consciousness, sense-perception, and intellection has shown that our knowledge in these fields is *essentially valid and true*. Errors occur, but they are incidental and accidental. As a general conclusion, then, the spontaneous convictions of man regarding the nature and scope of his knowledge have been critically vindicated. These convictions can no longer be considered unwarranted assumptions; they have now become reflex and philosophical certainties. We have the reasoned and critical assurance that our faculties of knowledge are essentially reliable and give us a truthful interpretation of 'reality as it is'; the information we receive through them is not complete and exhaustive, but it is true and valid as far as they can reach. And that is all that we can expect.

The validity, or truth-value, of human knowledge has been established after a careful scrutiny of the evidence. The 'process' of knowing is still mysterious and obscure; but the 'fact' of its validity should no longer be in doubt. That our solution agrees with the aristotelian-scholastic solution of the problem of knowledge, is simply due to the reason that no other theory will explain the acknowledged data in a satisfactory manner. It alone is capable of giving an intelligible explanation of the cognitional union between reality and the mind.

GLOSSARY OF TERMS

NOTE: In the case of qualified words, always look for the word or noun qualified. For example: in seeking for *Epistemological Monism,* look for *Monism, Epistemological, etc.*

ABSOLUTE. The unconditioned, the ultimate ground of all reality.

ABSOLUTISM, EPISTEMOLOGICAL. *See* Idealism, Absolute.

ACOSMISM. The doctrine which denies or doubts the validity of our experiential knowledge concerning the existence and reality of a material world; immaterialism.

AGNOSTICISM. The doctrine which denies the constitutional ability of the mind to know reality and concludes with the recognition of an intrinsically Unknowable.

ARISTOTELIANISM. The system of thought which in general follows the principles and teachings of Aristotle. Peripateticism.

ASSOCIATIONISM. In the problem of necessary judgments, the doctrine which holds that the necessity of first principles is due to the law of associations as a form of mental compulsion.

CERTITUDE. That mental state in which the mind gives a firm assent to a judgment without fear of the possibility of error, due to recognized valid reasons.

COHERENCE. Coherence, or consistency, with the whole system of knowledge previously recognized as true, is considered by idealistic monism to be the criterion of truth.

CONCEPTUALISM. The doctrine which holds that we have universal ideas in the mind, but there is no objective ground or foundation in extra-mental objects which would entitle the mind to group a number of individuals under one (universal) idea.

CONSCIOUSNESS. The intuitive awareness by which we recognize something as cognitionally present in the mind.

CONVICTIONS, SPONTANEOUS. Common-sense or ordinary convictions which have not been subjected to a critical investigation.

CRITERIOLOGY. The science of the criteria or tests of truth. Frequently used synonymously of epistemology.

CRITERION. The test by which we distinguish true judgments from those which are false.

DEFINITION BY INITIAL PREDICATION. *See* Predication.

DOGMATISM, CRITICAL. The doctrine which, after a critical examination, accepts the three primary truths as essentially necessary for every process of thinking and reasoning prior to the investigation of the various classes of spontaneous convictions.

DOGMATISM, MITIGATED. The form of dogmatism which accepts only two facts as prerequisites for the solution of the problem of certitude, namely, the existence of necessary spontaneous assents (convictions) and the power to examine these by reflection.

DUALISM. The theory that physical objects are independent in their existence and nature from the mental act of perception and knowledge; that there is an essential distinction between 'mental' and 'real' objects and events, so that the latter exist irrespective of whether known or not known by a perceiver.

DUALISM, EPISTEMOLOGICAL. The theory that there exists a duality or non-identity between the content or datum, which is immediately and indubitably presented in the knowledge act at a given moment, and the reality or object known through the content or datum.

EGO. The human person, considered as possessing a body and mind; the subject of all psychical states, such as perception, thought, judgment, affective and volitional states; self.

EGO, ABSOLUTE. The non-individual, pure Ego, neither subject nor object, which posits the world.

EMERGENT EVOLUTION. *See* Evolution, Emergent.

EMPIRICISM. The doctrine which denies or doubts the validity of all intellectual knowledge and admits only the certainty of sense-knowledge.

EPISTEMOLOGY. The science of the validity, or truth-value, of knowledge.

ERROR. Disconformity between mind and thing.

EVIDENCE, OBJECTIVE. That characteristic of reality whereby it becomes objectively manifest to the perceiving faculty.

EVOLUTION, EMERGENT. The doctrine which holds that nature is the product of evolution in such a manner that entirely new and unpredictable properties originate through synthesis and thereby form new and higher levels of reality.

EVOLUTIONISM. In the problem of necessary judgments, it is the doctrine which holds that the necessity of these judgments is due to certain fixed forms of thought which have been engendered in the past history of the human race and have been transmitted by heredity through a process of neural association repeated with countless frequency.

FICTIONALISM. The doctrine which holds that all concepts are fictions of the mind and have fictional value as mental constructions of reality, though they need not be true in themselves.

FIDEISM. The traditional doctrine which holds that all our knowledge must begin with an act of faith in divine revelation, since human reason is impotent to arrive at any certitude regarding the fundamental truths necessary for man to know; also, the doctrine that such truths can be known only by an affective act of faith.

FORMALISM. In the problem of necessary judgments, the theory which holds that the necessity of judgments is due to native *a priori* mental forms.

HUMANISM. *See* Pragmatism.

HYLOPSYCHISM. The doctrine which holds that all matter is instinct with something of the cognitive function; that every objective event has that self-transcending implication of other events which, when it occurs on the scale that it does in our brain processes, we call consciousness.

IDEA. (1) A mental representation of a thing. (2) Platonic Idea: an archetype, or pure immaterial pattern, of which the individual objects in any one natural class are but the imperfect copies, and by participation in which they have their being. (3) Descartes and English philosophers: an immediate object of consciousness.

IDEALISM. In general, the doctrine which holds that the being of things is conditioned by their being known; consciousness is constitutive of its objects; the being of sensible things is simply their being sensed, and their true characters are their sensed characters; the world we know is the world of our perceptual content; the mind cannot transcend its own internal, conscious states.

IDEALISM, ABSOLUTE. The doctrine that the relativity of knowledge implies the subjectivity of the objects of knowledge, so that the universe and everything in it are merely states of the thinker's mind; the real and the ideal, thought and thing, nature and spirit, object and subject, world and mind, are ultimately identified in the infinite and absolute Ego.

IDEALISM, COSMOTHETICAL. The doctrine which holds that the external world exists, but that we have no immediate knowledge of it.

IDEALISM, DIALECTICAL. *See* Idealism, Logical.

IDEALISM, EPISTEMOLOGICAL. The doctrine which holds that the external world has no existence independent of consciousness, but exists as an object of possible experience, as the content of universal experience, or as the content of a knowing mind, as something immanent to consciousness.

IDEALISM, LOGICAL. The doctrine which holds that reality is constituted of logical ideas (logical entities), so that we have direct knowledge of reality in the ideas of logical thought.

IDEALISM, METAPHYSICAL. The doctrine which holds that the real is identical with idea and mind, and the objects are modifications and evolutionary modes of the one, self-existent, absolute consciousness.

IDEALISM, OBJECTIVE. The doctrine which holds that the relation between the subject and the object of thought is one of absolute identity, supposing that all things exist in the absolute reason and that the laws of physics are the same as those of mental representations.

IDEALISM, PSYCHOLOGICAL. The doctrine which holds that the physical object is essentially idea, in the sense of being simply a part of consciousness, a content of conscious life which depends upon consciousness for its existence or at least upon the conscious relation to some subject.

IDEALISM, SUBJECTIVE. The doctrine which holds that the universal subject or Ego (not the Ego of the individual person) is the source of the object, the external world, or non-Ego.

IDEALISM, TRANSCENDENTAL. The doctrine that the mind imposes its own *a priori* forms of synthesis upon the unorganized and unrelated impressions which it receives from an unknown and unknowable thing-in-itself, or noumenon, so that the entire content of perception and thought consists of subjective phenomena.

IDEAL-REALISM. A metaphysical doctrine which combines the principles of idealism and realism.

IMAGINISM. An idealistic doctrine which holds that the world-principle resembles the imagining with which we humans are directly acquainted, and this cosmic imagining is a conscious infinite activity and the creative force of all reality.

IMMATERIALISM. The doctrine which denies or doubts the existence of material reality, admitting nothing but the reality of immaterial or spiritual things; that particular form of skepticism which admits the certitude of intellectual knowledge only, doubting or denying the validity of experiential knowledge; acosmism.

INCONCEIVABILITY. The inconceivability of the contradictory judgment is considered by some philosophers to be the ultimate criterion of truth.

INSTRUMENTALISM. The doctrine which holds that ideas are instruments of action and that their usefulness determines their truth.

MATERIALISM. A naturalistic form of philosophy which finds the ultimate solution of all phenomena, physical and psychical, in the nature and activity of universal matter or force.

MIND. In epistemology, the conscious knowing subject or the conscious knowing part of the subject.

MONADISM. The Leibnitzian doctrine which holds that the ultimate individual beings are monads; they are partly material and partly immaterial, possess innate power of representation, have no means of cognitional intercommunication, and obtain knowledge corresponding to reality through a divinely pre-established harmony.

MONISM. The doctrine which seeks to deduce all the varied phenomena of both the physical and spiritual worlds from a single principle which is in a continuous state of evolution; specifically, the metaphysical doctrine which holds that there is but one substance, either mind (idealism), or matter (materialism), or a neutral substance that is neither mind nor matter but is the substantial ground of both: opposed to dualism and pluralism.

MONISM, EPISTEMOLOGICAL. The doctrine which holds that the content or datum of perception is identical with the reality or object known thereby; that the attributes of the percept as experienced and all its relations, except that of being experienced, are identical with the entities composing the physical world; there is no dualism of things and ideas, but only the class of things.

MOTIVE OF CERTITUDE. The ground or reason which determines us to assent with firmness to a judgment as true without fear of its contradictory being true.

NATURALISM. The doctrine that scientific knowledge of physical objects is the final and only legitimate form of knowledge.

NEO-HEGELIANISM. *See* Neo-Idealism.

NEO-IDEALISM. A more recent form of Absolute Idealism, characterized by an approach to the problem of knowledge through experience rather than by means of aprioristic speculations; neo-hegelianism.

NEO-PSYCHOLOGISM. A more recent form of psychological idealism, characterized by a closer union between empirical science and psychology.

NEO-REALISM. The doctrine which holds that there are existent objects not conditioned by perception or cognition; all the attributes of the percept as experienced and all its relations, except that of being experienced, independently characterize such objects; pan-objectivism.

NEO-SCHOLASTICISM. The system of philosophy which in the main follows the principles and tenets of scholasticism, but adapts it to modern problems.

NOMINALISM. The doctrine which holds that there are neither universal objects outside the mind nor universal ideas in the mind.

NON-EGO. Not-self; the whole world, distinct from man's body and mind and outside his person, as something other-than-self.

NOUMENON. The unknowable reality or thing-in-itself which is postulated as the basis, ground, or cause of the phenomenon.

OBJECT. In epistemology, the thing known.

OBJECTIVISM. The doctrine that things are, when not experienced by us, just what they seem when experienced by us.

OCCASIONALISM. The doctrine which holds that cognition is caused by the sole activity of the mind on the occasion of bodily stimuli; in a special sense, the doctrine which holds that God is the cause of knowledge in the human mind on the occasion of bodily stimuli and also the cause of all actions in bodies.

ONTOLOGISM. The doctrine which holds that man's mind derives all its knowledge through a direct, immediate intuition of God's ideas or of absolute Being.

PANCALISM. A form of esthetic pragmatism.

PAN-EGOISM. The doctrine which attempts to dissolve the antithesis between noumenon and phenomenon, mind and matter, Ego and thing-in-itself, by identifying all reality with the universal consciousness or Ego; a form of absolute idealism, asserting the one-ness of all things in the absolute Ego.

PAN-OBJECTIVISM. *See* Neo-realism.

PAN-PHENOMENALISM. The doctrine which holds that the human mind can know nothing but the phenomena or appearances of things.

PAN-PSYCHISM. The doctrine which interprets the qualitative essence of material force and energy as a sort of psychical activity and appetency, so that all material reality, in its ultimate analysis, is endowed with psychical powers.

PANTHEISM. The doctrine which holds that the universe is identical with God; the reduction of God to the universe, or of the universe to God.

PARALLELISM, PSYCHO-PHYSICAL. The doctrine which holds that mind and matter are not substances, that the psychical and physical are but a manifold of interrelated occurrences; subject and object are concepts which are due to the reflection resulting from the interrelations of the various components of the absolutely unitary contents of our immediate experience.

PERCEPTIONISM. *See* Realism, Presentative.

PERIPATETICISM. *See* Aristotelianism.

PERSONALISM. That form of idealism which gives equal recognition to both the pluralistic and monistic aspects of experience and which finds in the conscious unity, identity, and free activity of personality the key to the nature of reality and the solution of the ultimate problems of philosophy.

PHENOMENALISM. The doctrine that the appearances of things are their reality; there are no things in themselves, but only things in relation to our experience.

PHENOMENON. In epistemology, the appearance that is produced by the action of a thing upon a percipient.

PLURALISM. The doctrine which holds that reality cannot be reduced to either one ultimate form of being (monism of either mind or matter) or two ultimate forms of being (dualism of mind and matter), but to many mutually irreducible ultimate forms of being.

POSITIVISM. A form of naturalism which denies the legitimacy of philosophical problems and methods and claims that science is the only knowledge which is exact and ultimate.

POSTULATE, IDEALIST. The postulate, or axiom, considered by idealists as self-evident, that all objects of knowledge are mental objects, ideas, conscious states.

PRAGMATISM. The doctrine, or rather attitude, which places all knowledge and truth in a direct relation to life and action; it judges the value of ideas, judgments, hypotheses, theories, and systems, according to their capacity to satisfy human needs and interests in a social way.

PREDICAMENT, EGO-CENTRIC. The predicament involved in every act of knowledge that no thinker is able to mention a thing that is not an idea, for the obvious and simple reason that in mentioning it he makes it an idea; it is, therefore, impossible to discover whether the cognitive relationship is indispensable to things which enter into it.

PREDICATION, DEFINITION BY INITIAL. The fallacy which consists in considering an 'obvious' characteristic of a thing as the 'exclusive' characteristic of that thing, and then defines the thing as consisting solely and exclusively of this particular characteristic.

RATIONALISM. The method of proving propositions by appealing to abstract and universal principles. *deductive reg*

REALISM. In general, the doctrine which holds that objects have an existence independent of their being known so that their relation to the subject in knowledge is only an external, not an internal or immanent, relation.

REALISM, ARISTOTELIAN-THOMISTIC. The doctrine which holds that man does not infer the existence of external objects from representative images or 'ideas' in consciousness, but perceives them directly in some form through a presentation of the objects themselves in sense-perception.

REALISM, COSMOTHETICAL. *See* Realism, Representative.

REALISM, CRITICAL. The doctrine which holds that we know physical objects by means of, and in terms of, logical ideas, but that it is the external object which we know and to which this complex act of cognition is directed; what we perceive is existentially identical with the independent reality, but it has, when being perceived, certain qualities — notably the sense qualities — which it does not possess when not perceived.

REALISM, CRITICAL PRESENTATIVE. That form of presentative realism which holds that some qualities of objects are real and as such are perceived immediately, while others are not actually and formally, but only potentially and causally, present in the objects; these latter have no formal existence independent of the perceiving subject. Also called moderate presentative realism.

REALISM, EPISTEMOLOGICAL. The theory that the real object has an existence independent of the experient's perception and thought.

REALISM, HYPOTHETICAL. *See* Realism, Representative.

REALISM, IMMEDIATE. *See* Realism, Presentative.

REALISM, INFERENTIAL. *See* Realism, Representative.

REALISM, INTUITIVE. *See* Realism, Presentative.

REALISM, MEDIATE. *See* Realism, Representative.

REALISM, MODERATE. In the problem of the universals, it is the doctrine which holds that there are no universal realities outside the mind, but we have universal ideas in the mind, and there is a foundation in the things themselves for these universal ideas; universals are formally in the mind, but fundamentally in the things.

REALISM, MODERATE PRESENTATIVE. *See* Realism, Critical Presentative.

REALISM, NAÏVE PRESENTATIVE. *See* Realism, Rigid Presentative.

REALISM, NATURAL. *See* Realism, Presentative.

REALISM, NEW. *See* Neo-Realism.

REALISM, OBJECTIVE REPRESENTATIVE. That form of representative realism which holds that our 'representations' or 'ideas' resemble the external objects.

REALISM, PRESENTATIVE. The doctrine which holds that physical, external objects are presented directly in some form to consciousness in sense-perception, so that their reality is perceived as it exists 'out there' in nature. Also called immediate, intuitive, natural realism or perceptionism.

REALISM, REPRESENTATIVE. The doctrine which holds that the human mind is immediately aware, not of the external objects themselves, but of its own internal 'representations' or 'ideas' only, from which it then infers the external, non-Ego reality as their cause. Also called mediate, hypothetical, cosmothetical, inferential realism.

REALISM, RIGID PRESENTATIVE. That form of presentative realism which holds that the things perceived are actually so in nature as they appear to the senses. Also called naïve presentative realism.

REALISM, SUBJECTIVE REPRESENTATIVE. That form of representative realism which holds that our 'representations' or 'ideas' do not resemble the external objects.

REALISM, TRANSFIGURED. The doctrine which holds that the reality underlying appearances is totally and forever inconceivable to us; we know only appearances (phenomena) of reality and in them reality is transfigured or altered to such an extent that there is no resemblance between reality and the perceptual knowledge we have of it; Spencer's subjective representative realism.

RELATIVISM. The doctrine that every known object is relative (in relation) to the knowing subject and as such is dependent in its being upon the knowing subject and incapable of existing apart from consciousness; the doctrine of the immanence of relations as constitutive of their being.

RELATIVISM, OBJECTIVE. The doctrine that the existence and character of experienced data depend upon the occurrence of percipient events and therefore upon the nature and situation of the experiencing organism as their essential and proximately determining factor; that the object known possesses the character exhibited by the datum only 'in relation to' this given organism; and that the perceptual content is 'objectively' present in nature precisely as experienced in perception and cognition, according to the relative standpoint of the individual perceiver.

REPRESENTATIONALISM. *See* Realism, Representative.

SCHOLASTICISM. The system of philosophy, prevalent in the middle ages, which follows the general lines of Aristotle's principles. It advocates a natural dualism of God and creature, mind and matter, thought and thing, as against monism and pantheism; it defends a moderate realism, as against ultra-realism, nominalism and conceptualism; it is spiritualistic and not materialistic, experimental and not aprioristic, objectivistic and not subjectivistic; in sense-perception it is presentational and not agnostic or representational or idealistic; concerning intellectual knowledge it defends a moderate rationalism, as against sensism, positivism, and innatism; it is common-sense knowledge critically examined and philosophically vindicated.

SELF-CONSCIOUSNESS. Reflex consciousness, by means of which the Ego apprehends itself concretely in its own mental acts and states; self-awareness.

SENSATIONALISM. The doctrine which holds that sensation is the sole origin of knowledge.

SENSISM. *See* Sensationalism.

SKEPTICISM. The reasoning of one who doubts the possibility of knowledge of reality; the systematic doubt which characterizes a philosophic skeptic.

SKEPTICISM, ABSOLUTE. The absence of any leaning toward either side of any question, when maintained as a philosophic principle.

SKEPTICISM, PYRRHONIC. *See* Skepticism, Absolute.

SOLIPSISM. The skeptical attitude, in which the thinker is certain only of his own personal internal states of mind.

SPINOZISM. The doctrine of Baruch Spinoza which holds that there exists but a single substance, infinite and uncreated, of which nature (matter) and thought (mind) are the attributes; it is a pantheistic, absolute, metaphysical monism.

SUBJECT. In epistemology, that which possesses knowledge, perception, thought, consciousness; the mind, in so far as it possesses internal states of knowledge; the knower.

SUBJECTIVISM. The doctrine which holds that we can immediately know only what is present in consciousness.

TRADITIONALISM. The doctrine which holds that God gave a primitive revelation to mankind which is handed down as a tradition from generation to generation, and this tradition is the ultimate foundation of knowledge and criterion of truth.

TRANSCENDENCE. The characteristic of human knowledge enabling the mind to pass beyond the limits of its own internal state and to know extra-mental reality.

TRUTH. Conformity between mind and thing.

TRUTHS, PRIMARY. The First Fact: my own existence — 'I exist.' The First Principle: the Principle of Contradiction — 'It is impossible for a thing to be and not to be at the same time.' The First Condition: the essential trustworthiness of reason — 'Reason is capable of knowing truth.'

ULTRA-MECHANISM. The doctrine which excludes the human body as an essential participant in the vital functions of man, so that the body is considered to be actuated solely by mechanical forces.

ULTRA-REALISM. The doctrine which holds that we have not only universal ideas in the mind, but that there exist extra-mental universal realities corresponding to them.

ULTRA-SPIRITUALISM. The doctrine which postulates an excessive dualism between mind (soul) and body in the human Ego, destroying the conception of man as an organism, so that a cognitional communication between them is impossible.

UNIVERSAL. An idea, the content of which is predicable of a class as a class and of each individual member of a class.

BIBLIOGRAPHY

ADAMS, GEORGE P., *Idealism and the Modern Age* (Yale University Press, 1919).
—— *Ideas in Knowing and Willing*, Univ. of California Publ. in Philosophy, Vol. 8 (1926).

ALEXANDER, S., *Space, Time and Deity*, 2 vol. (Macmillan, 1927).

American Philosophy Today and Tomorrow, ed. by H. M. Kallen and Sidney Hook (Lee Furman, Inc., New York, 1935). Essays by M. J. Aronson, C. E. Ayres, E. S. Bates, B. H. Bode, F. S. Cohen, H. T. Costello, W. Durant, I. Edman, R. T. Flewelling, E. B. Holt, S. Hook, J. A. Irving, H. M. Kallen, K. Koffka, A. Locke, A. E. Morgan, A. E. Murphy, E. Nagel, H. A. Overstreet, J. H. Randall, H. W. Schneider, W. H. Sheldon, T. V. Smith, P. Weiss, M. Williams.

ARISTOTLE, *Aristotle's Psychology* (*De Anima* and *Parva Naturalia*), tr. by William A. Hammond (Macmillan, 1902).

ARONSON, M. J., "The Humanization of Philosophy," in *American Philosophy Today and Tomorrow*, ed. by H. M. Kallen and S. Hook (Lee Furman, Inc., New York, 1935).

AVELING, FRANCIS, *Personality and Will* (Appleton Co., 1931).

AYRES, C. E., "The Gospel of Technology," in *American Philosophy Today and Tomorrow*, ed. by H. M. Kallen and S. Hook (Lee Furman, Inc., New York, 1935).

BAILLIE, J. B., "The Individual and His World," in *Contemporary British Philosophy*, 1st series, ed. by J. H. Muirhead (Macmillan, 1924).

BALFOUR, A. J., *A Defense of Philosophic Doubt*, 2nd ed. (Hodder and Stoughton, London, 1920).

BALMES, JAMES, *Fundamental Philosophy*, tr. by H. F. Brownson (Sadlier Co., 1875).

BANDAS, RUDOLPH G., *Contemporary Philosophy and Thomistic Principles* (Bruce, Milwaukee, 1932).

BARRON, JOSEPH T., *Elements of Epistemology* (Macmillan, 1935).

BAX, E. B., "The Analysis of Reality," in *Contemporary British Philosophy*, 2nd series, ed. by J. H. Muirhead (Macmillan, no date).

BERGSON, HENRI, *Creative Evolution*, tr. by Arthur Mitchell (Holt Co., New York, 1926).

——— *Matter and Memory*, tr. by N. M. Paul and W. S. Palmer, 5th ed. (Macmillan, 1911).

——— *The Introduction to a New Philosophy* (*Introduction á la Métaphysique*), tr. by S. Littman (Luce and Co., Boston, 1912).

BERKELEY, GEORGE, *Principles of Human Knowledge*, ed. by A. C. Fraser (Oxford, 1901).

BOAS, GEORGE, *The Datum as Essence in Contemporary Philosophy* (Niort, Priv. Print., 1927).

BODE, BOYD H., "Consciousness and Psychology," in *Creative Intelligence* (Holt Co., New York, 1917).

BOODIN, J. E., *Truth and Reality* (Macmillan, 1911).

BOSANQUET, BERNARD, "Life and Philosophy," in *Contemporary British Philosophy*, 1st series, ed. by J. H. Muirhead (Macmillan, 1924).

——— *The Meeting of Extremes in Contemporary Philosophy* (Macmillan Co., 1921).

BRADLEY, F. H., *Appearance and Reality* (Macmillan, 1893).

——— *Essays on Truth and Reality* (The Clarendon Press, 1914).

BRIGHTMAN, EDGAR S., *A Philosophy of Ideals* (Holt and Co., 1928).

BROAD, C. D., "Critical and Speculative Philosophy," in *Contemporary British Philosophy*, 1st series, ed. by J. H. Muirhead (Macmillan, 1924).

——— *Perception, Physics, and Reality* (Cambridge University Press, 1914).

BROWN, HAROLD C., "Intelligence and Mathematics," in *Creative Intelligence* (Holt Co., New York, 1917).

CALDWELL, WILLIAM, *Pragmatism and Idealism* (Black, London, 1913).

CALKINS, MARY WHITON, *The Persistent Problems of Philosophy*, 5th ed. (Macmillan, 1925).

CARR, H. W., "Idealism as a Principle in Science and Philosophy," in *Contemporary British Philosophy*, 1st series, ed. by J. H. Muirhead (Macmillan, 1924).

——— *The Philosophy of Change* (Macmillan, 1914).

——— *The Problem of Truth* (Dodge Publ. Co., New York, 1913).

COFFEY, P., *Epistemology*, 2 vol. (Longmans, Green, and Co., 1917).

Contemporary British Philosophy, 1st series, ed. by J. H. Muirhead (Macmillan, 1924). Essays by J. B. Baillie, B. Bosanquet, C. D. Broad, H. W. Carr, R. B. Haldane, L. T. Hobhouse, Dean Inge, John Laird, J. S. Mackenzie, J. E. McTaggart, C. L. Morgan, J. H. Muirhead, C. Read, B. Russell, F. C. S. Schiller, W. Temple.

——— 2nd series, ed. by J. H. Muirhead (Macmillan, no date).

Essays by James Ward, E. Belfort Bax, D. Fawcett, G. D. Hicks, R. F. A. Hoernlé, C. E. M. Joad, G. E. Moore, J. A. Smith, W. R. Sorley, A. E. Taylor, J. A. Thomson, and C. C. J. Webb.

COSTELLO, HARRY TODD, "A Philosopher Among the Metaphysicians," in *American Philosophy Today and Tomorrow*, ed. by H. M. Kallen and S. Hook (Lee Furman, Inc., New York, 1935).

Creative Intelligence, by John Dewey, Addison W. Moore, Harold C. Brown, George H. Mead, Boyd H. Bode, Henry W. Stuart, James H. Tufts, Horace M. Kallen (Holt Co., New York, 1917).

DESCARTES, RENÉ, *Discours de la Méthode*.

―――― *Méditations Touchant la Philosophie Première*.

―――― *Principia Philosophiae*, tr. by John Veich, 13 edit. (Will. Blackwood and Sons, Edinburgh and London, 1902).

DEWEY, JOHN, *Essays in Experimental Logic* (Univ. of Chicago Press, 1916).

―――― *Experience and Nature* (Open Court Publ. Co., 1925).

―――― *How We Think* (Heath Co., Boston, 1909).

―――― *The Quest for Certainty* (Minton, Balch, and Co., 1929).

―――― *Reconstruction in Philosophy* (Holt, 1920).

―――― *The Significance of the Problem of Knowledge* (University of Chicago Press, 1897).

―――― *Studies in Logical Theory* (Univ. of Chicago Press, 1903).

―――― "The Need for a Recovery of Philosophy," in *Creative Intelligence* (Holt, 1917).

DE WULF, MAURICE, *History of Medieval Philosophy*, 3rd ed., 2 vol. (Longmans, Green, and Co., 1925).

―――― *Scholasticism Old and New*, tr. by P. Coffey (Benziger Bros., New York, 1907).

DONAT, JOS., *Critica*, ed. 6 (Felician Rauch, Innsbruck, 1928).

DRAKE, DURANT, *Mind and Its Place in Nature* (Macmillan Co., 1925).

―――― "That Elusive Doctrine of Essence," in *The Philosophical Review*, Vol. XXXVII (1928).

―――― "The Approach to Critical Realism," in *Essays in Critical Realism* (Macmillan, 1920).

EDMAN, IRWIN, "The Naturalistic Temper," in *American Philosophy Today and Tomorrow*, ed. by H. M. Kallen and S. Hook (Lee Furman, Inc., New York, 1935).

ELLIOT, HUGH S. R., *Modern Science and the Illusions of Professor Bergson* (Longmans, Green, 1912).

Essays in Critical Realism, by Durant Drake, A. O. Lovejoy, James B.

Pratt, A. K. Rogers, George Santayana, Roy W. Sellars, C. A. Strong (Macmillan, 1920).

ESSER, GERARD, *Epistemologia* (Soc. of the Div. Word, Techny, Ill., 1934).

FAWCETT, DOUGLAS, "Imaginism," in *Contemporary British Philosophy*, 2nd series, ed. by J. H. Muirhead (Macmillan, no date).

FERNKORN, CARL M., *Denken und Erkennen* (Greifwald, L. Bamberg, 1930).

FICHTE, J. G., *Werke*, 6 vol., ed. by Fritz Medicus (Felix Meiner, Leipzig, 1911).

FLEWELLING, RALPH T., "The New Task of Philosophy," in *American Philosophy Today and Tomorrow*, ed. by H. M. Kallen and S. Hook (Lee Furman, Inc., New York, 1935).

FOSTER, W. S., AND TINKER, M. A., *Experiments in Psychology* (Holt, 1929).

FRÖBES, JOSEPH, *Lehrbuch der Experimentellen Psychologie*, 2 vol. (B. Herder, Fribourg, 1915).

———— *Psychologia Speculativa*, 2 vol. (B. Herder, Fribourg, 1927).

GAETANI, F. M., *Psychologia* (Rome, 1930).

GÉNY, PAUL, *Critica*, ed. 9 (Rome, 1927).

GILSON, ETIENNE, *The Philosophy of St. Thomas Aquinas*, tr. by Edw. Bullough, 2nd ed. (Herder, St. Louis, 1929).

GLENN, PAUL J., *Criteriology* (Herder, St. Louis, 1933).

GREDT, Jos., *Elementa Philosophiae*, 5th ed. (Herder, Fribourg, 1929).

GREEN, T. H., *Prolegomena to Ethics*, 2nd edit. (Clarendon Press, Oxford, 1884).

GRUENDER, HUBERT, *De Qualitatibus Sensibilibus* (B. Herder, Fribourg, 1910).

———— *Experimental Psychology* (Bruce, Milwaukee, 1932).

HALDANE, VISCOUNT R. B., "The Function of Metaphysics in Scientific Method," in *Contemporary British Philosophy*, 1st series, ed. by J. H. Muirhead (Macmillan, 1924).

———— *The Pathway to Reality*, 2 vols. (Murray, London, 1903).

———— *The Philosophy of Humanism* (Yale Univ. Press, 1922).

HAMILTON, SIR WILLIAM, *Lectures on Metaphysics*, ed. by H. Mansel and J. Veitch (1859).

HARTMANN, E. VON, *Philosophy of the Unconscious*, tr. by W. C. Coupland (Macmillan, 1884).

HEGEL, GEORG, *The Logic of Hegel*, tr. by Will. Wallace (Clarendon Press, Oxford, 1892).

———— *The Phenomenology of Mind*, tr. by J. E. Baillie, 2 vol. (Macmillan, 1910).

HICKS, G. D., "From Idealism to Realism," in *Contemporary British Philosophy*, 2nd series, ed. by J. H. Muirhead (Macmillan, no date).

HOBHOUSE, L. T., "The Philosophy of Development," in *Contemporary British Philosophy*, 1st series, ed. by J. H. Muirhead (Macmillan, 1924).

———— *The Theory of Knowledge*, 2 edit. (Methuen, London).

HOCKING, W. E., *Types of Philosophy* (Chas. Scribner's Sons, 1929).

HOERNLÉ, R. F. A., "Idealism and Evolutionary Naturalism," in *Philosophy Today*, ed. by E. L. Schaub (Open Court Publ. Co., 1928).

———— *Idealism as a Philosophy* (G. H. Doran, 1927).

———— "On the Way to a Synoptic Philosophy," in *Contemporary British Philosophy*, 2nd series, ed. by J. H. Muirhead (Macmillan, no date).

HOLLINGWORTH, H. L. AND POFFENBERGER, A. T., *The Sense of Taste* (Moffat, Yard, and Co., 1917).

HOLT, E. B., *The Concept of Consciousness* (Macmillan, London, 1914).

———— "The Place of Illusory Experience in a Realistic World," in *The New Realism* (Macmillan, 1912).

HOOK, SIDNEY, "Experimental Naturalism," in *American Philosophy Today and Tomorrow*, ed. by H. M. Kallen and S. Hook (Lee Furman, Inc., 1935).

HUME, DAVID, *Treatise on Human Nature*.

INGE, W. R., "Philosophy and Religion," in *Contemporary British Philosophy*, 1st series, ed. by J. H. Muirhead (Macmillan, 1924).

JAMES, WILLIAM, *A Pluralistic Universe* (Longmans, Green, 1909).

———— *Essays in Radical Empiricism* (Longmans, Green, 1912).

———— *Meaning of Truth* (Longmans, Green, 1909).

———— *Pragmatism* (Longmans, Green, 1907).

———— *Principles of Psychology* (Holt Co.. New York, 1918).

JOAD, C. E. M., "A Realist Philosophy of Life," in *Contemporary British Philosophy*, 2nd series, ed. by J. H. Muirhead (Macmillan, no date).

KALLEN, HORACE MEYER, "Philosophy Today and Tomorrow," in *American Philosophy Today and Tomorrow*, ed. by H. M. Kallen and S. Hook (Lee Furman, Inc., New York, 1935).

———— "Value and Existence in Philosophy, Art, and Religion," in *Creative Intelligence* (Holt Co., New York, 1917).

KANT, EMMANUEL, *Critique of Pure Reason*, tr. by Max Müller, 2 edit. (Macmillan, 1927).

———— *Sämmtliche Werke*, 8 vol., ed. by G. Hartenstein (Leopold Voss, Leipzig, 1867).

KNUDSON, A. C., *The Philosophy of Personalism* (Abingdon Press, New York, 1927).

LADD, GEORGE T., *Knowledge, Life, and Reality* (Dodd, Mead, and Co., 1909).

LADD-FRANKLIN, C., *Color and Color Theories* (Harcourt, Brace, 1929).

LAIRD, JOHN, "How Our Minds Go Beyond Themselves in Their Knowing," in *Contemporary British Philosophy*, 1st series, ed. by J. H. Muirhead (Macmillan, 1924).

LEHMEN, A., *Lehrbuch der Philosophie*, 3rd edit., 4 vol. (Herder, Fribourg, 1909).

LEIBNITZ, GOTTFRIED W., *New Essays Concerning Human Understanding*, tr. by A. G. Langley (Macmillan, 1896).

———— *The Monadology*, 2 ed., tr. by Robert Latta (Oxford Univ. Press, 1925).

LEIGHTON, JOSEPH A., *Man and the Cosmos* (Appleton Co., New York, 1922).

LENZEN, V. F., *Scientific Ideas and Experience*, University of California Publ. in Philosophy, Vol. 8 (1926).

LOCKE, JOHN, *An Essay Concerning Human Understanding*, ed. by A. C. Fraser (Oxford, 1894).

LOEWENBERG, J., *The Metaphysical Status of Things and Ideas*, Univ. of California Pub. in Philosophy, Vol. 8 (1926).

LOSSKÜ, NICOLAI O., *The Intuitive Basis of Knowledge*, tr. by Nathalie A. Duddington (Macmillan, 1919).

LOTZE, HERMANN, *Microcosmus*, tr. by E. Hamilton and E. E. C. Jones, 2 vols. (Scribner and Welford, New York, 1885).

LOVEJOY, A. O., "Pragmatism versus the Pragmatist," in *Essays in Critical Realism* (Macmillan, 1920).

———— *The Revolt Against Dualism* (Norton and Co., 1930).

MACINTOSH, DOUGLAS C., *The Problem of Knowledge* (Macmillan Co., 1915).

MACKENZIE, J. S., "Constructive Philosophy," in *Contemporary British Philosophy*, 1st series, ed. by J. H. Muirhead (Macmillan, 1924).

MAHER, MICHAEL, *Psychology*, 9th edit. (Longmans, Green, and Co., 1930).

MAJOR, DAVID R., *An Introduction to Philosophy* (Doubleday, Doran, 1933).

MARITAIN, JACQUES, *An Introduction to Philosophy*, tr. by E. I. Watkin (Longmans, Green, 1930).

MARVIN, WALTER T., "The Emancipation of Metaphysics from Epistemology," in *The New Realism* (Macmillan, 1912).

McCOSH, JAMES, *First and Fundamental Truths* (Chas. Scribner's Sons, 1889).

McDONALD, MILO F., *The Progress of Philosophy* (Standard Text Press, 1930).

McDOUGALL, WILLIAM, *Modern Materialism and Emergent Evolution* Van Nostrand, New York, 1929).

McTAGGART, J. ELLIS, "An Ontological Idealism," in *Contemporary British Philosophy*, 1st series, ed. by J. H. Muirhead (Macmillan, 1924).

MEAD, GEORGE H., "Scientific Method and Individual Thinker," in *Creative Intelligence* (Holt Co., New York, 1917).

———— *The Philosophy of the Present* (Open Court Publ. Co., 1932).

MERCIER, D. CARD., *A Manual of Modern Scholastic Philosophy*, 2 vol. (Herder, St. Louis, 1916).

———— *Critériologie Générale* (Alcan, Paris, 1906).

———— *The Origins of Contemporary Psychology* (P. J. Kenedy, New York, 1918).

MERCIER, LOUIS J. A., *The Challenge of Humanism* (Oxford University Press, 1933).

MILL, JOHN STUART, *An Examination of Sir William Hamilton's Philosophy*, 2 vol. (Spencer, Boston, 1865).

———— *System of Logic* (Longmans, Green, 1930).

MONTAGUE, WILLIAM P., "A Realistic Theory of Truth and Error," in *The New Realism* (Macmillan Co., 1912).

———— *The Ways of Knowing* (Macmillan, 1925).

MONTAIGNE, MICHAEL DE, *Essays*, tr. by Ch. Cotton, ed. by W. C. Hazlitt, 5 vols. (London, 1923).

MOORE, ADDISON W., *Pragmatism and Its Critics* (Univ. of Chicago Press, 1910).

———— "Reformation of Logic," in *Creative Intelligence* (Holt Co., New York, 1917).

MOORE, G. E., "A Defense of Common Sense," in *Contemporary British Philosophy*, 2nd series, ed. by J. H. Muirhead (Macmillan, no date).

———— "The Refutation of Idealism," in *Mind*, Vol. XII (1903), pp. 433–453.

MORGAN, C. LLOYD, "A Philosophy of Evolution," in *Contemporary British Philosophy*, 1st series, edit. by J. H. Muirhead (Macmillan, 1924).

———— *Emergent Evolution* (Williams and Norgate, 1923).

Münsterberg, Hugo, *Science and Idealism* (Houghton, Mifflin and Co., 1906).

Muirhead, J. H., "Past and Present in Contemporary Philosophy," in *Contemporary British Philosophy,* 1st series, ed. by J. H. Muirhead (Macmillan, 1924).

—— *The Real and the Ideal,* Univ. of California Publ. in Philosophy, Vol. 8 (1926).

Murphy, A. E., "A Program for a Philosophy," in *American Philosophy Today and Tomorrow,* ed. by H. M. Kallen and S. Hook (Lee Furman, Inc., New York, 1935).

—— *Ideas and Nature,* Univ. of California Publ. in Philosophy, Vol. 8 (1926).

—— "Objective Relativism in Dewey and Whitehead," in *The Philosophical Review,* Vol. XXXVI (1927).

Murray, D. L., *Pragmatism* (Constable, London, 1912).

Otto, M. C., "Instrumentalism," in *Philosophy Today,* ed. by E. L. Schaub (Open Court Publ. Co., 1928).

Overstreet, Harry Allen, "The Plight of Philosophy," in *American Philosophy Today and Tomorrow,* ed. by H. M. Kallen and S. Hook (Lee Furman, Inc., New York, 1935).

Paton, H. J., *The Idea of Self,* Univ. of California Publ. in Philosophy, Vol. 8 (1926).

Pepper, Stephen C., *Transcendence,* Univ. of California Publ. in Philosophy, Vol. 8 (1926).

Perrier, Jos. L., *The Revival of Scholastic Philosophy* (Columbia Univ. Press, New York, 1909).

Perry, Ralph B., *An Approach to Philosophy* (Chas. Scribner's Sons, 1905).

—— "A Realistic Theory of Independence," in *The New Realism* (Macmillan, 1912).

—— *Present Philosophical Tendencies* (Longmans, Green, 1912).

—— *The Present Conflict of Ideals* (Longmans, Green, 1918).

Personal Idealism, ed. by Henry Sturt. Essays by G. F. Stout, F. C. S. Schiller, W. R. Boyce Gibson, G. E. Underhill, R. R. Marett, Henry Sturt, F. W. Russell, H. Rashdall (Macmillan, 1902).

Pesch, Tilmann, *Institutiones Logicales,* 3 vols. (Herder, Fribourg, 1889).

Philosophy Today, ed. by E. L. Schaub (Open Court Publ. Co., 1928).

Pillsbury, W. B., *The Psychology of Reasoning* (Appleton Co., 1910).

Pitkin, Walter B., "Some Realistic Implications of Biology," in *The New Realism* (Macmillan, 1912).

PRATT, JAMES B., "Critical Realism and the Possibility of Knowledge," in *Essays in Critical Realism* (Macmillan, 1920).
—— *Matter and Spirit* (Macmillan, 1922).
—— *What is Pragmatism?* (Macmillan, 1909).

RANDALL, JOHN H., JR., "Historical Naturalism," in *American Philosophy Today and Tomorrow*, ed. by H. M. Kallen and S. Hook (Lee Furman, Inc., New York, 1935).
RASHDALL, HASTINGS, "Personality, Human and Divine," in *Personal Idealism*, ed. by H. Sturt (Macmillan, 1902).
READ, CARVETH, "Philosophy of Nature," in *Contemporary British Philosophy*, 1st series, ed. by J. H. Muirhead (Macmillan, 1924).
RICKABY, JOHN, *The First Principles of Knowledge*, 2nd edit. (Longmans, Green, and Co., 1926).
ROBINSON, DANIEL S., *An Anthology of Modern Philosophy* (Crowell, New York, 1931).
—— *An Anthology of Recent Philosophy* (Crowell, New York, 1929).
—— *Introduction to Living Philosophy* (Crowell Co., 1932).
ROGERS, ARTHUR K., "The Problem of Error," in *Essays in Realism* (Macmillan, 1920).
—— *What is Truth?* (Yale Univ. Press, 1923).
ROYCE, JOSIAH, *Lectures on Modern Idealism* (Yale Univ. Press, 1919).
—— *The Problem of Christianity* (Macmillan, 1913).
RUSSELL, BERTRAND, "Logical Atomism," in *Contemporary British Philosophy*, 1st series, ed. by J. H. Muirhead (Macmillan, 1924).
—— *Our Knowledge of the External World* (Norton and Co., New York, 1929).
—— *The Analysis of Mind* (Macmillan Co., 1921).

SAMSON, LEON, *The New Humanism* (Ives Washburn, New York, 1930).
SANTAYANA, GEORGE, *Scepticism and Animal Faith* (Chas. Scribner's Sons, 1929).
—— *The Realm of Essence* (Chas. Scribner's Sons, 1927).
—— "Three Proofs of Realism," in *Essays in Critical Realism* (Macmillan, 1920).
SCHILLER, F. C. S., "Axioms as Postulates," in *Personal Idealism*, ed. by H. Sturt (Macmillan, 1902).
—— *Problems of Belief* (G. H. Doran Co., 1924).
—— *Studies in Humanism* (Macmillan, 1907).
—— "Why Humanism?" in *Contemporary British Philosophy*, 1st series, ed. by J. H. Muirhead (Macmillan, 1924).

SCHINZ, ALBERT, *Anti-Pragmatism* (Small, Maynard and Co., Boston, 1909).

SCHOPENHAUER, ARTHUR, *The World as Will and Idea,* tr. by R. B. Haldane and J. Kemp (Kegan Paul, Trench, Truebner and Co.).

SELLARS, ROY W., "A Re-Examination of Critical Realism," in *The Philosophical Review,* Vol. XXXVIII (1929).

——— *Critical Realism* (Rand, McNally and Co., 1916).

——— "Current Realism," in *Philosophy Today,* ed. by E. L. Schaub (Open Court Publ. Co., 1928).

——— "Knowledge and Its Categories," in *Essays in Critical Realism* (Macmillan, 1920).

——— *The Principles and Problems of Philosophy* (Macmillan, 1926).

——— *The Philosophy of Physical Realism* (Macmillan, 1932).

SHELDON, WILMON H., "The Task of Present-Day Metaphysics," in *American Philosophy Today and Tomorrow,* ed. by H. M. Kallen and S. Hook (Lee Furman, Inc., New York, 1935).

SINCLAIR, MAY, *The New Idealism* (Macmillan, 1922).

SMART, H. R., "*Logical Theory,*" in *Philosophy Today,* ed. by E. L. Schaub (Open Court Publ. Co., 1928).

SMITH, J. A., "Philosophy as the Development of the Notion and Reality of Self-Consciousness," in *Contemporary British Philosophy,* 2nd series, ed. by J. H. Muirhead (Macmillan, no date).

SMITH, NORMAN K., *Prolegomena to an Idealist Theory of Knowledge* (Macmillan, 1924).

SMITH, T. V., "Truth Beyond Imagination," in *American Philosophy Today and Tomorrow,* ed. by H. M. Kallen and S. Hook (Lee Furman, Inc., New York, 1935).

SMITH, WALTER, *Methods of Knowledge* (Macmillan, 1899).

SPAULDING, EDWARD G., "A Defense of Analysis," in *The New Realism* (Macmillan, 1912).

——— *The New Rationalism* (Holt Co., New York, 1918).

SORLEY, W. R., "Value and Reality," in *Contemporary British Philosophy,* 2nd series, ed. by J. H. Muirhead (Macmillan, no date).

SPENCER, HERBERT, *First Principles* (Appleton Co., New York, 1883).

SPINDLER, F. N., *The Sense of Sight* (Moffat, Yard, and Co., 1917).

STÖCKL, ALBERT, *Lehrbuch der Philosophie,* 2nd edit. (1869).

STOUT, G. F., "Error," in *Personal Idealism,* ed. by H. Sturt (Macmillan, 1902).

——— *Mind and Matter* (Macmillan, 1931).

STRONG, C. A., *Why the Mind Has a Body* (Macmillan, 1903).

——— "On the Nature of the Datum," in *Essays in Critical Realism* (Macmillan, 1920).

———— *The Origin of Consciousness* (Macmillan, 1918).

STUART, HENRY W., "The Phases of the Economic Interest," in *Creative Intelligence* (Holt Co., New York, 1917).

TALBOT, EDW. F., *Knowledge and Object* (Catholic Univ., Washington, 1932).

TAYLOR, A. E., "The Freedom of Man," in *Contemporary British Philosophy*, 2nd series, ed. by J. H. Muirhead (Macmillan, no date).

TEMPLE, WILLIAM, "Some Implications of Theism," in *Contemporary British Philosophy*, 1st series, ed. by J. H. Muirhead (Macmillan, 1924).

The New Realism, by Edwin B. Holt, Walter T. Marvin, William P. Montague, Ralph B. Perry, Walter B. Pitkin, Edward G. Spaulding (Macmillan, 1912).

THOMAS AQUINAS, ST., *Summa Theologica. De Veritate; De Anima; Contra Gentiles*.

THOMSON, J. A., "A Biologist's Philosophy," in *Contemporary British Philosophy*, 2nd series, ed. by J. H. Muirhead (Macmillan, no date).

TOWNSEND, H. G., *Philosophical Ideas in the United States* (American Book Co., 1934).

TROLAND, LEONARD T., *The Principles of Psychophysiology*, 4 vols. (Van Nostrand Co., 1929).

TUFTS, JAMES H., "The Moral Life and the Construction of Values and Standards," in *Creative Intelligence* (Holt and Co., New York, 1917).

TURNER, J. E., *A Theory of Direct Realism* (Macmillan, 1925).

TURNER, WILLIAM, *History of Philosophy* (Ginn and Co., 1903).

UNDERHILL, G. E., "The Limits of Evolution," in *Personal Idealism*, ed. by H. Sturt (Macmillan, 1902).

URBAN, W. M., "Value Theory and Æsthetics," in *Philosophy Today*, ed. by E. L. Schaub (Open Court Publ. Co., 1928).

VAIHINGER, HANS, *The Philosophy of As If*, tr. by C. K. Ogden (Harcourt, Brace, 1924).

VANCE, JOHN G., *Reality and Truth* (Longmans, Green and Co., 1917).

VERDA, SISTER MARY, *New Realism in the Light of Scholasticism* (Macmillan, 1926).

WALKER, LESLIE J., *Theories of Knowledge*, 2nd edit. (Longmans, Green and Co., 1924).

WALLACE, WILLIAM, *The Logic of Hegel, Prolegomena* (Clarendon Press, Oxford, 1894).

WARD, JAMES, "A Theistic Monadism," in *Contemporary British Philos-*

ophy, 2nd series, ed. by J. H. Muirhead (Macmillan, no date).

———— *The Realm of Ends* (Putnam's Sons, 1911).

WEBB, C. C. J., "Outline of a Philosophy of Religion," in *Contemporary British Philosophy*, 2nd series, ed. by J. H. Muirhead (Macmillan, no date).

WEISS, PAUL, "A Memorandum for a System of Philosophy," in *American Philosophy Today and Tomorrow*, ed. by H. M. Kallen and S. Hook (Lee Furman, Inc., New York, 1935).

WICKHAM, HARVEY, *The Unrealists* (The Dial Press, New York, 1930).

WHITEHEAD, ALFRED N., *Process and Reality* (Macmillan Co., 1929).

———— *Symbolism* (Macmillan Co., 1927).

WILLMANN, OTTO, *Geschichte des Idealismus*, 3 vols. (Vieweg, Braunschweig, 1894).

WOODWORTH, R. S., *Psychology* (Holt, 1931).

WUNDT, WILHELM, *Outlines of Psychology*, tr. by C. H. Judd (Engelman, Leipzig, 1897).

ZYBURA, J. S., *Present-Day Thinkers and the New Scholasticism* (Herder, St. Louis, 1926).

INDEX